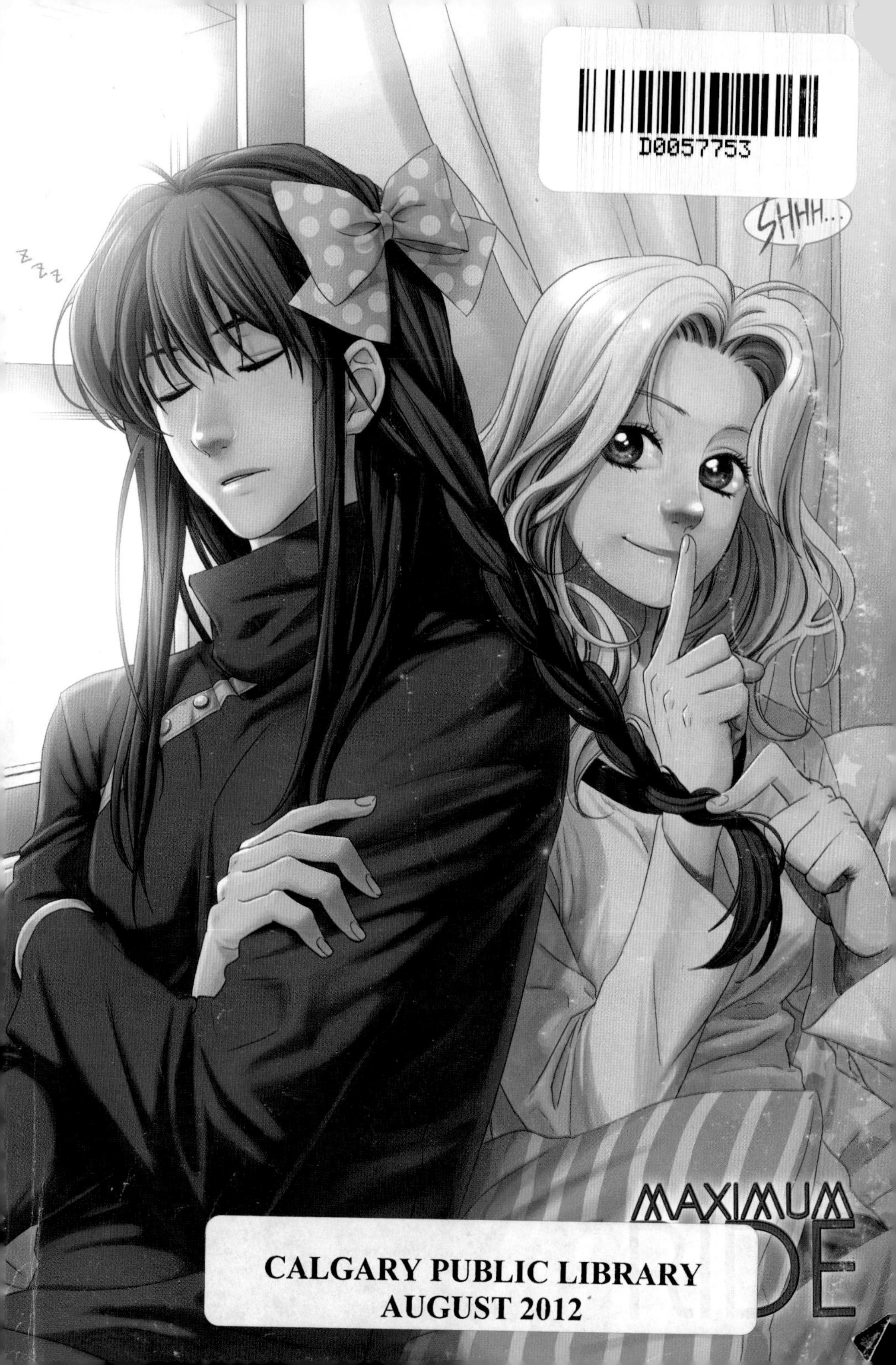
SHHH...
MAXIMUM

WHAT CAME BEFORE

Max and her flock are genetic experiments. Created by a mysterious lab known only as the "School," their genetic codes have been spliced with avian DNA, giving them wings and the power to soar. What they lack are homes, families, and memories of a real life.

After escaping from the School, the flock is hunted by Erasers, agents of the School who can transform into terrifying wolf creatures, and Jeb Batchelder, the man they once thought of as a father. Despite the targets on their backs, though, the flock is desperate to learn about their individual pasts. Their inquiries lead them to Washington, D.C., where they meet Special Agent Anne Walker of the FBI, who takes them in and gives them a taste of a normal life.

The flock's respite is short-lived, however. It isn't long before they discover that Anne is in league with their enemies. On their own again, the flock heads to Florida, following a lead on a multi-national corporation called ITEX that seems to have been pulling their strings all along. Once there, though, Max is kidnapped by ITEX and replaced by a clone of herself — Max 2.0!

CHARACTER INTRODUCTION

MAXIMUM RIDE

Max is the eldest member of the flock, and the responsibility of caring for her comrades has fallen to her. Tough and uncompromising, she's willing to put everything on the line to protect her "family."

FANG

Only slightly younger than Max, Fang is one of the elder members of the flock. Cool and reliable, Fang is Max's rock. He may be the strongest of them all, but most of the time it is hard to figure out what is on his mind.

IGGY

Being blind doesn't mean that Iggy is helpless. He has not only an incredible sense of hearing, but also a particular knack (and fondness) for explosives.

NUDGE

Motormouth Nudge would probably spend most days at the mall if not for her pesky mutant-bird-girl-being-hunted-by-wolf-men problem.

GASMAN

The name pretty much says it all. The Gasman (or Gazzy) has the art of flatulence down to a science. He's also Angel's biological big brother.

ANGEL

The youngest member of the flock and Gazzy's little sister, Angel seems to have some peculiar abilities — mind reading, for example.

ARI

Just seven years old, Ari is Jeb's son but was transformed into an Eraser. He appears to have a particular axe to grind with Max.

JEB BATCHELDER

The flock's former benefactor, Jeb was a scientist at the School before helping the flock to make their original escape.

MAXIMUM RIDE

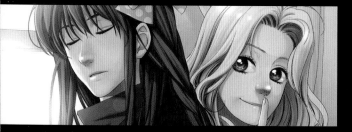

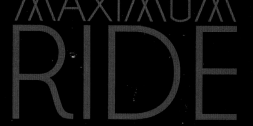

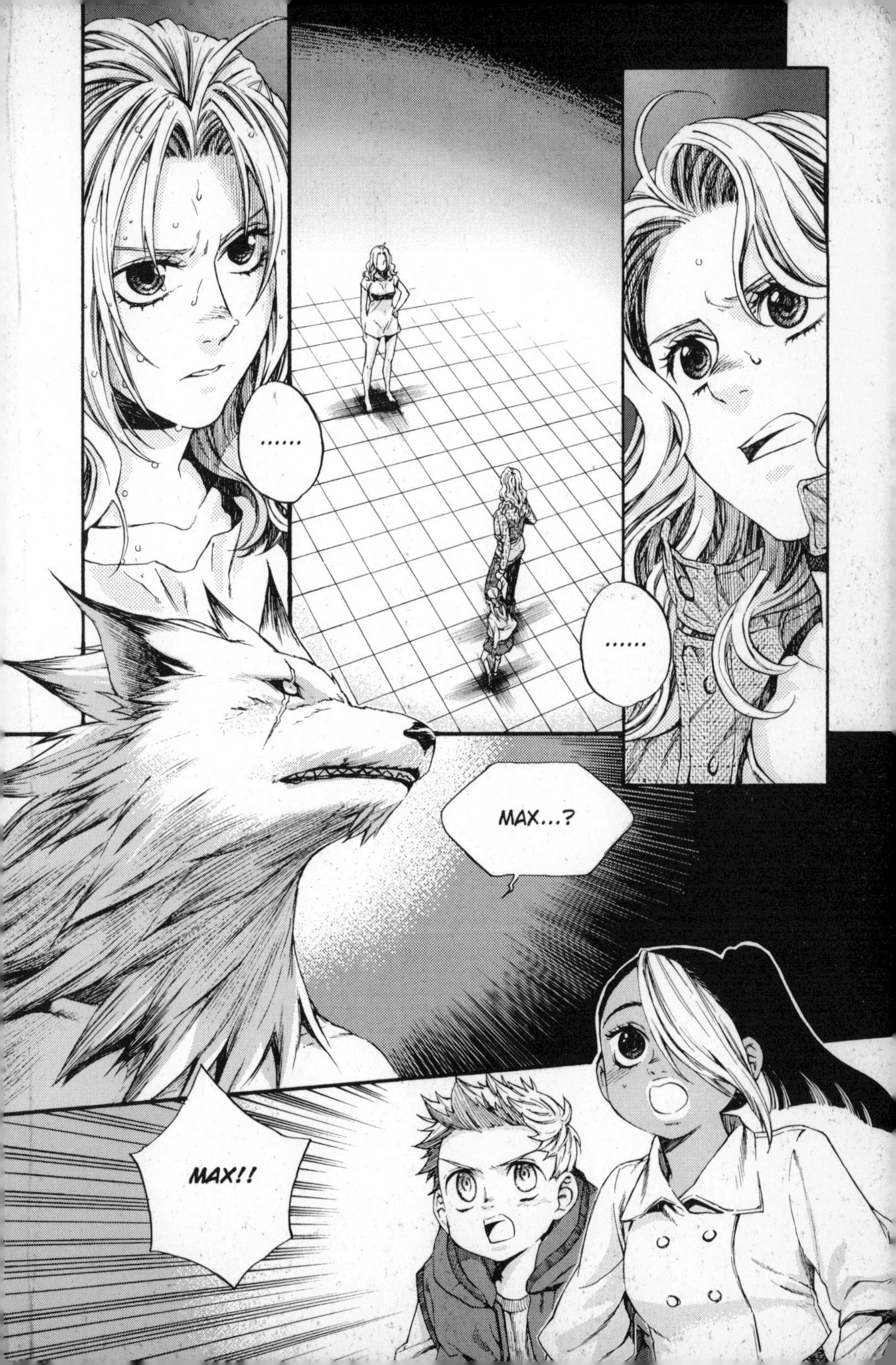
......
......
MAX...?
MAX!!

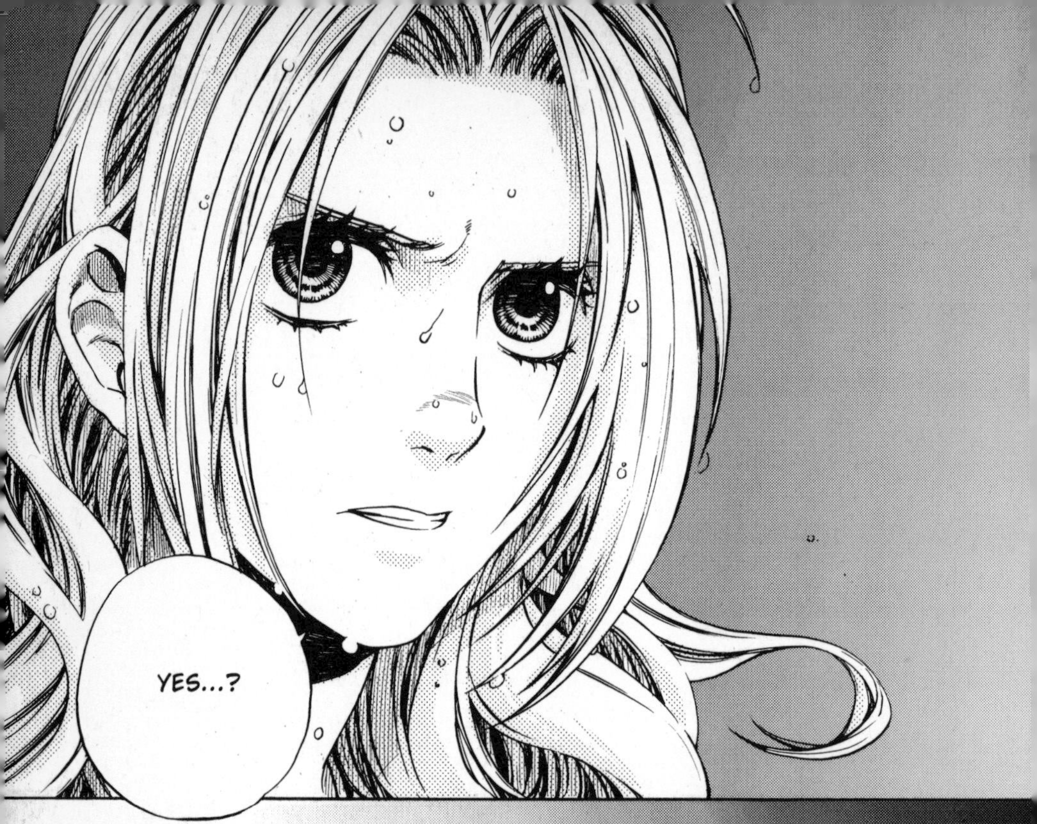
YES...?

MAXIMUM RIDE

CHAPTER 29

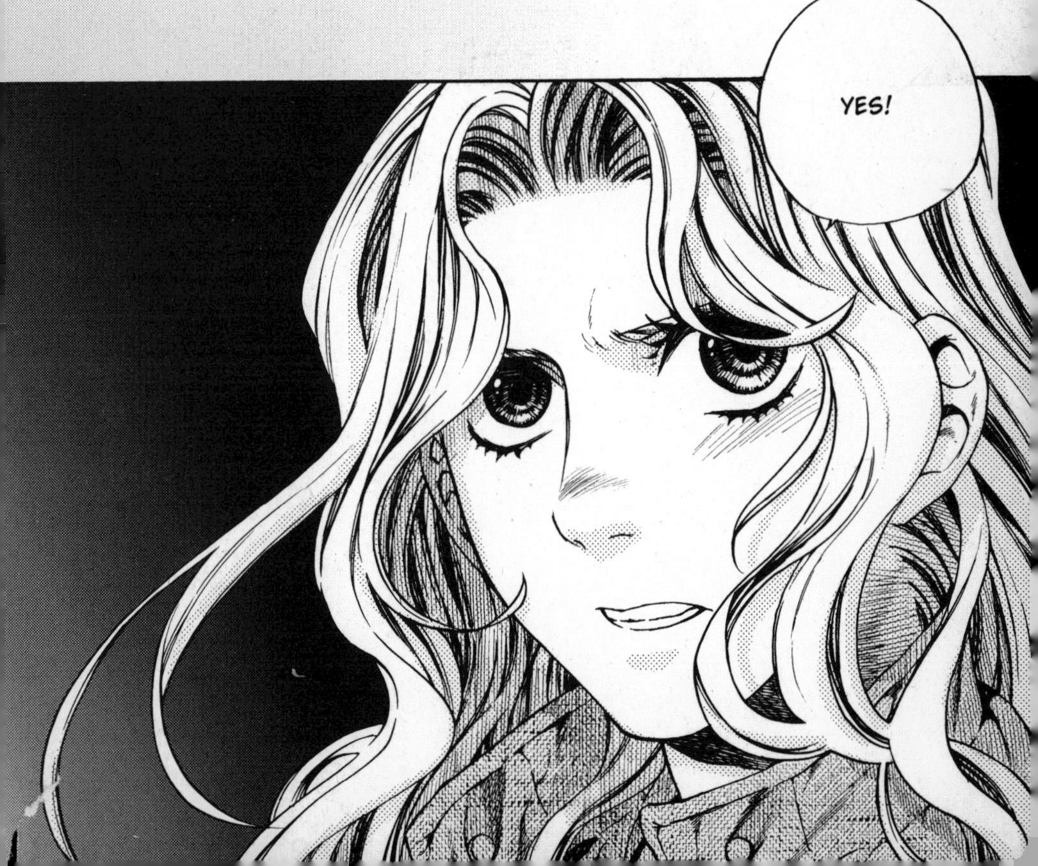
YES!

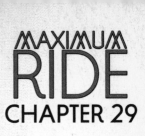

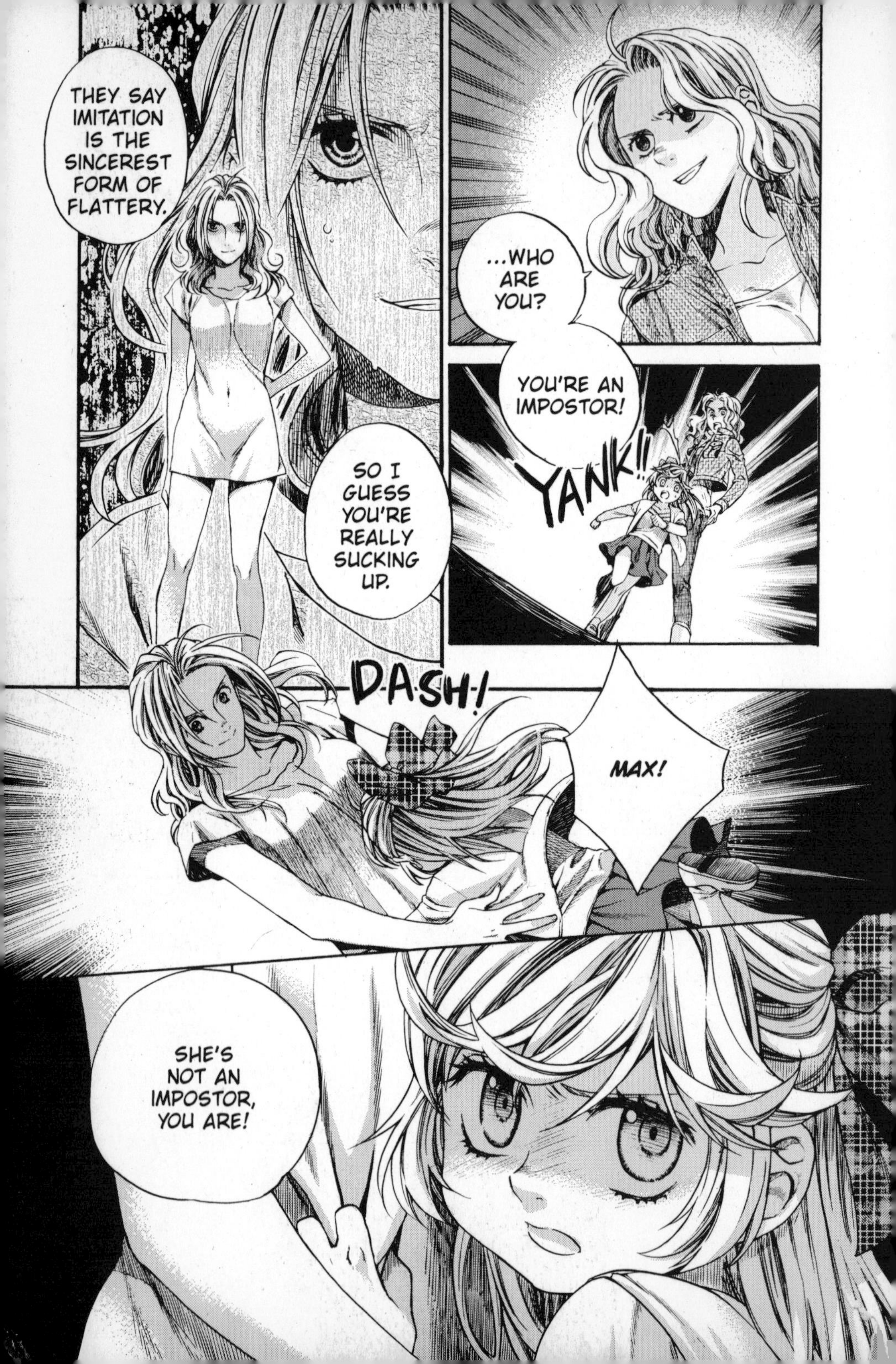
THEY SAY IMITATION IS THE SINCEREST FORM OF FLATTERY.
SO I GUESS YOU'RE REALLY SUCKING UP.
...WHO ARE YOU?
YOU'RE AN IMPOSTOR!
YANK!!
DASH!
MAX!
SHE'S NOT AN IMPOSTOR, YOU ARE!

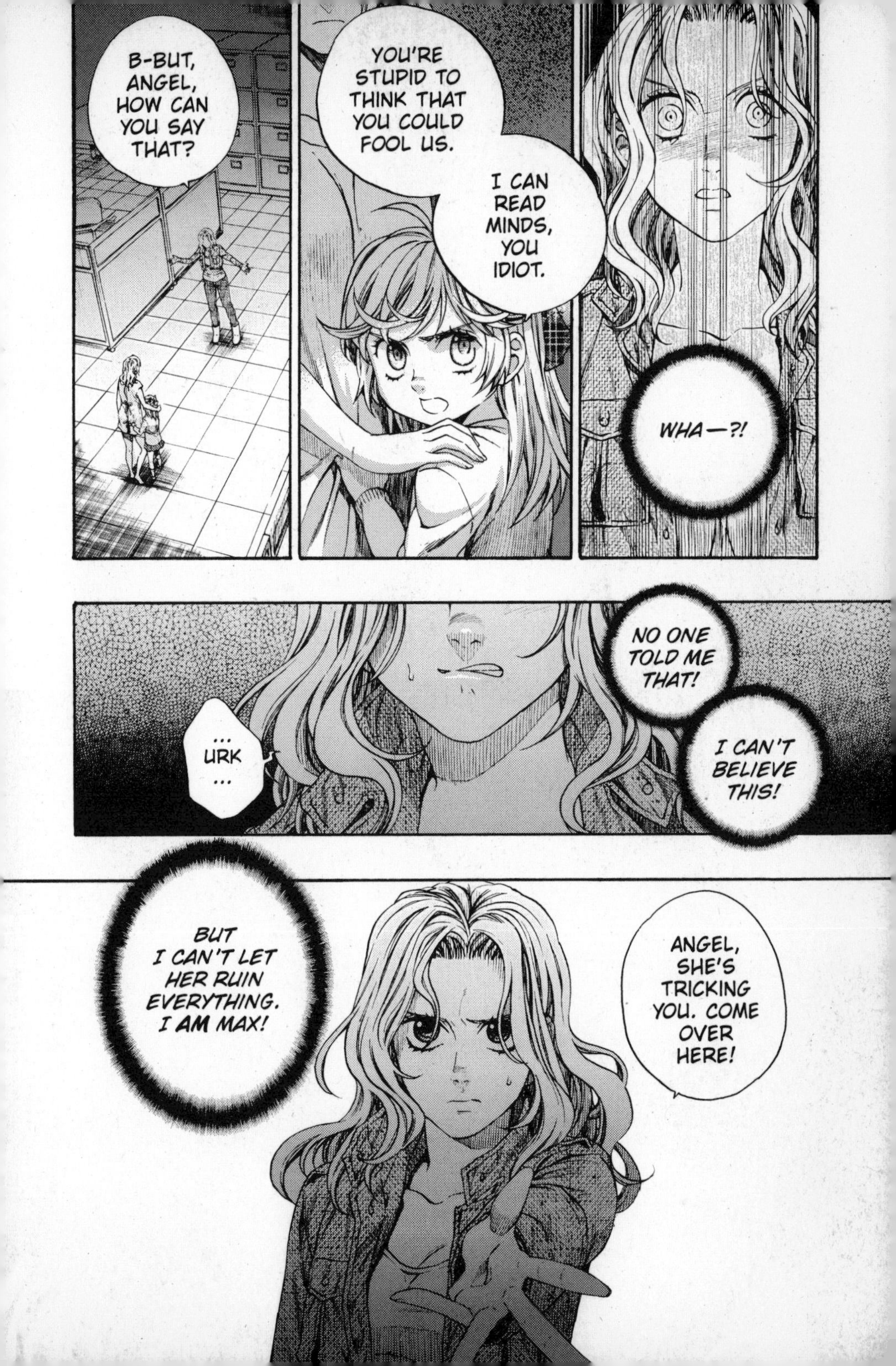
B-BUT, ANGEL, HOW CAN YOU SAY THAT?
YOU'RE STUPID TO THINK THAT YOU COULD FOOL US.
I CAN READ MINDS, YOU IDIOT.
WHA—?!
...URK...
NO ONE TOLD ME THAT!
I CAN'T BELIEVE THIS!
BUT I CAN'T LET HER RUIN EVERYTHING. I AM MAX!
ANGEL, SHE'S TRICKING YOU. COME OVER HERE!

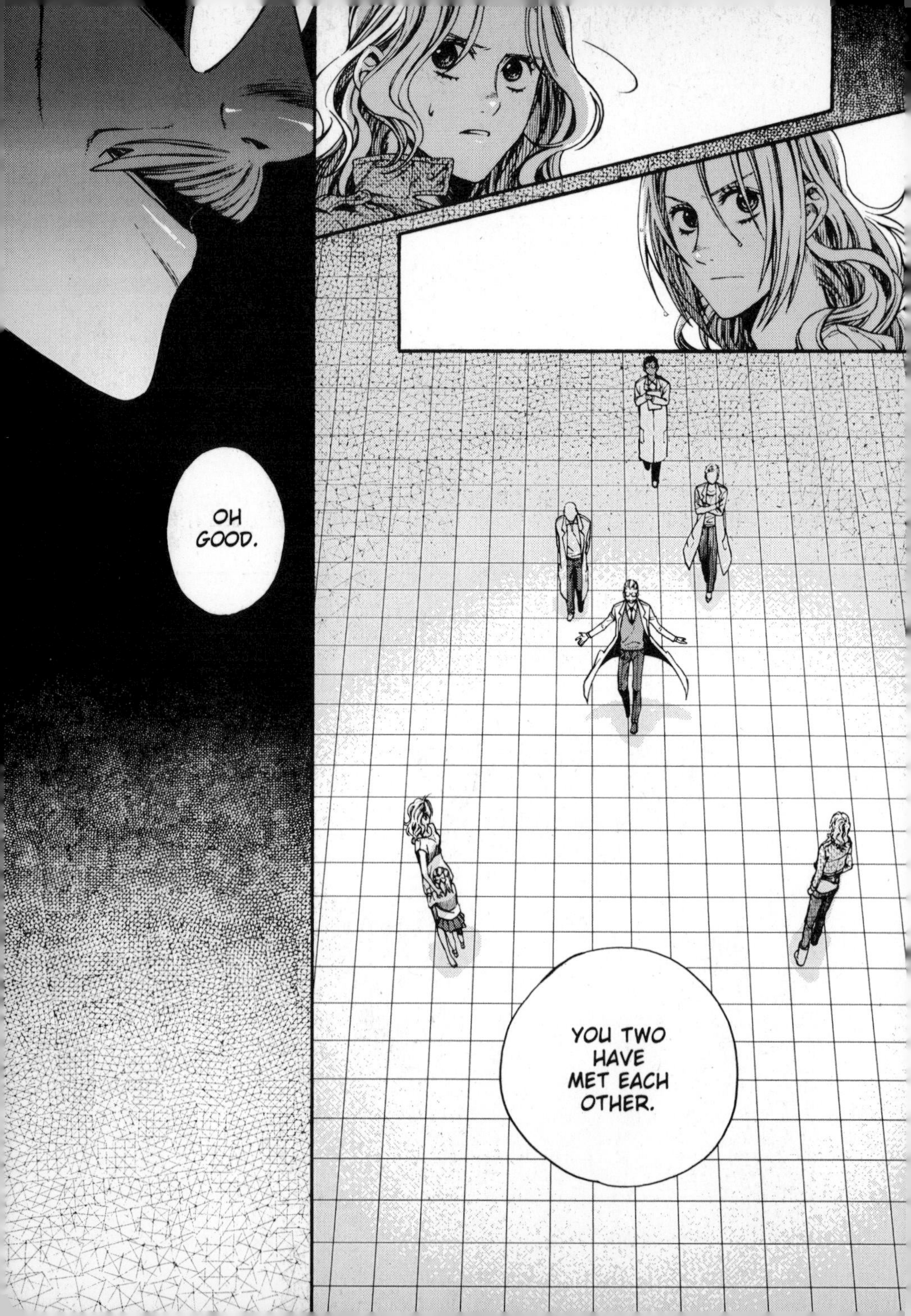
OH GOOD.
YOU TWO HAVE MET EACH OTHER.

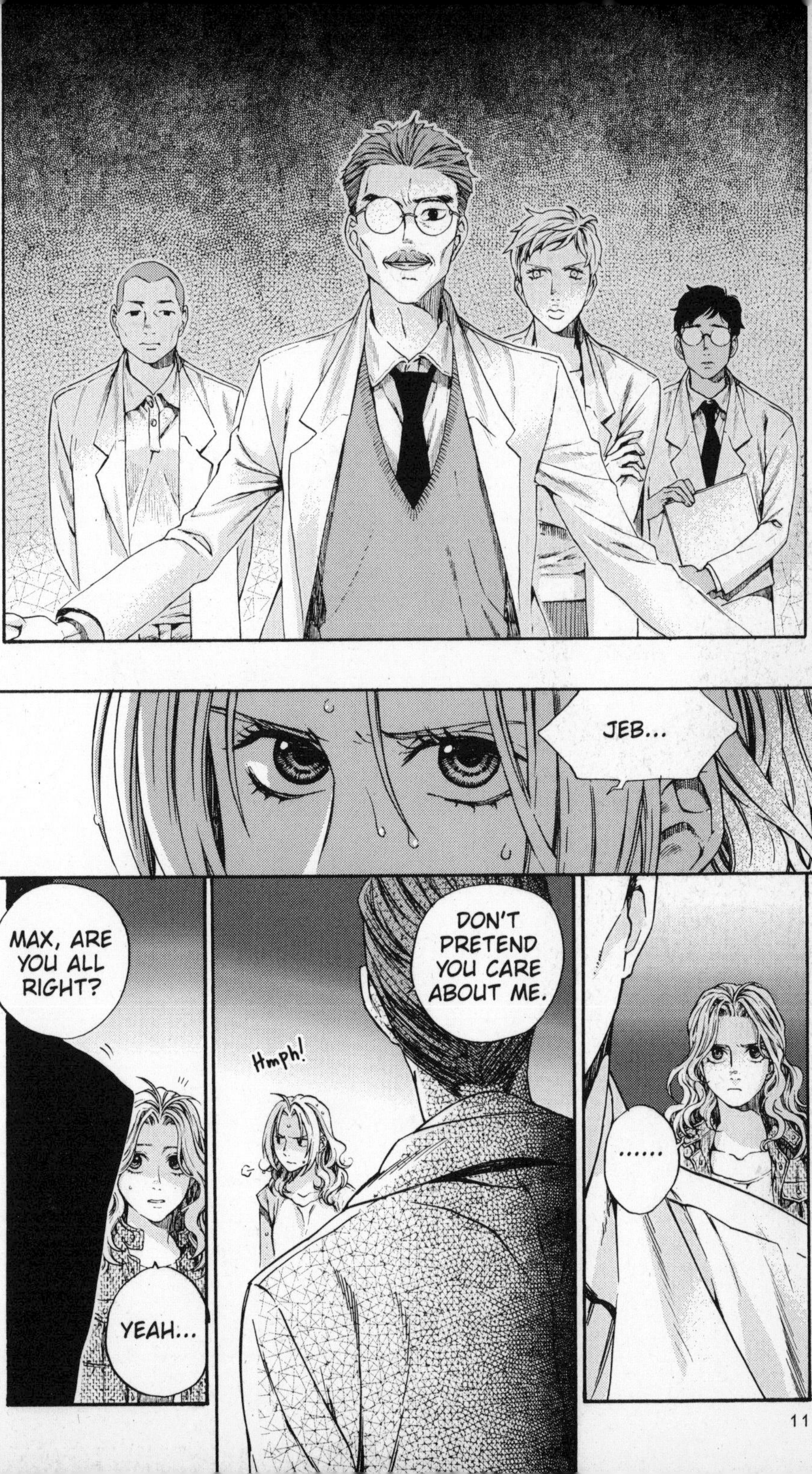
JEB...
MAX, ARE YOU ALL RIGHT?
YEAH...
Hmph!
DON'T PRETEND YOU CARE ABOUT ME.
......

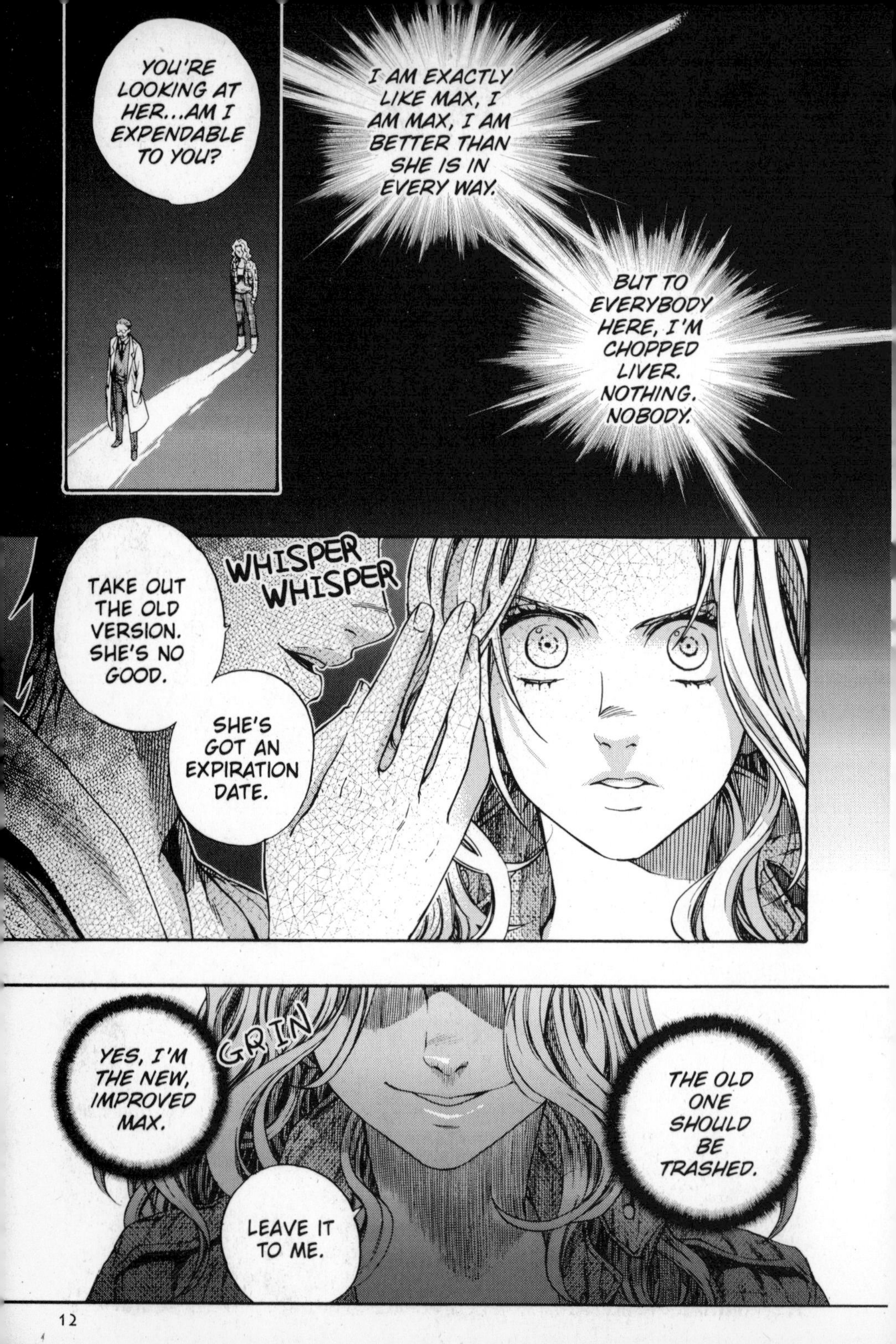
YOU'RE LOOKING AT HER...AM I EXPENDABLE TO YOU?
I AM EXACTLY LIKE MAX, I AM MAX, I AM BETTER THAN SHE IS IN EVERY WAY.
BUT TO EVERYBODY HERE, I'M CHOPPED LIVER. NOTHING. NOBODY.
TAKE OUT THE OLD VERSION. SHE'S NO GOOD.
WHISPER WHISPER
SHE'S GOT AN EXPIRATION DATE.
YES, I'M THE NEW, IMPROVED MAX.
GRIN
THE OLD ONE SHOULD BE TRASHED.
LEAVE IT TO ME.

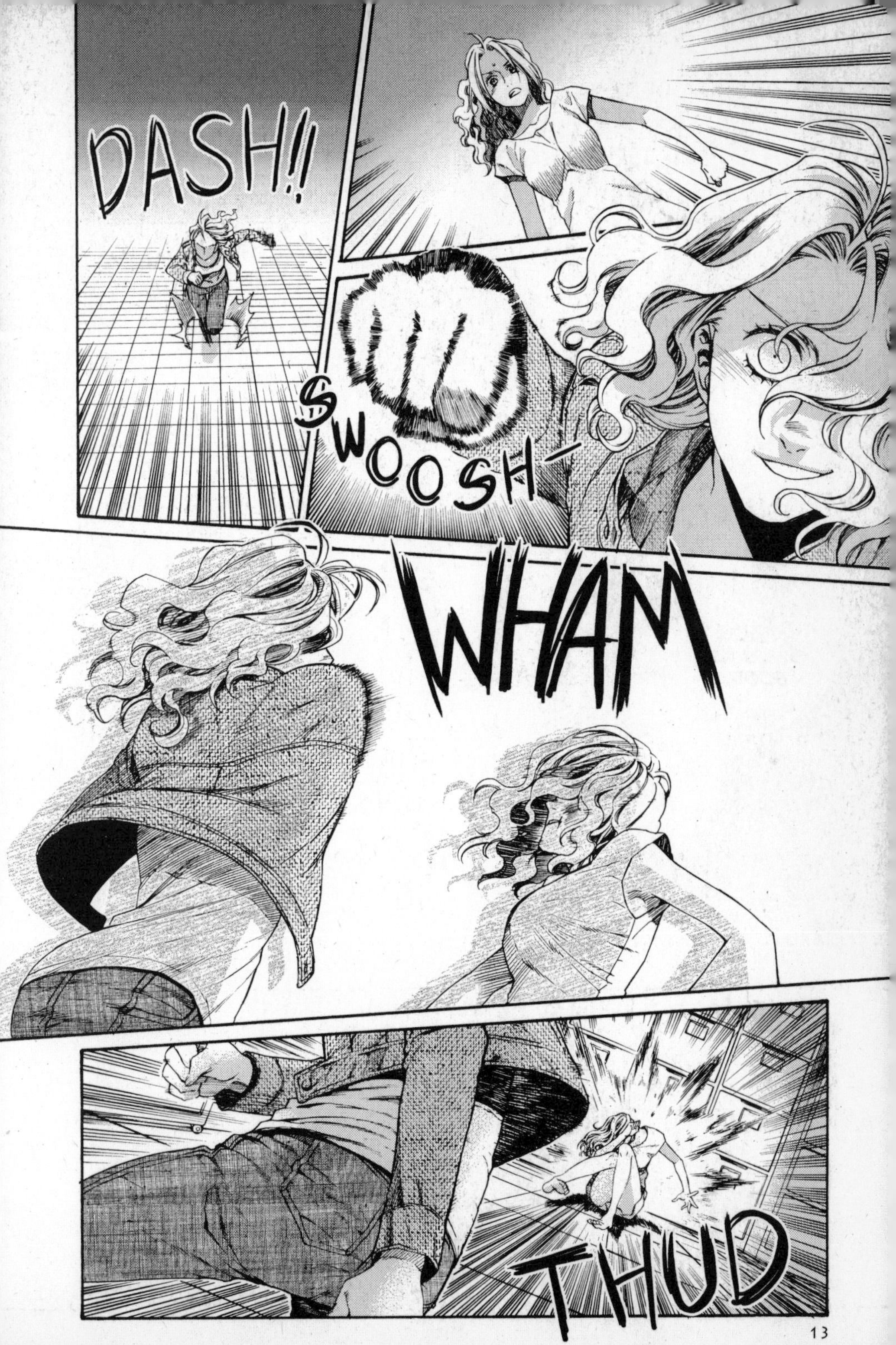
DASH!!
SWOOSH
WHAM
THUD

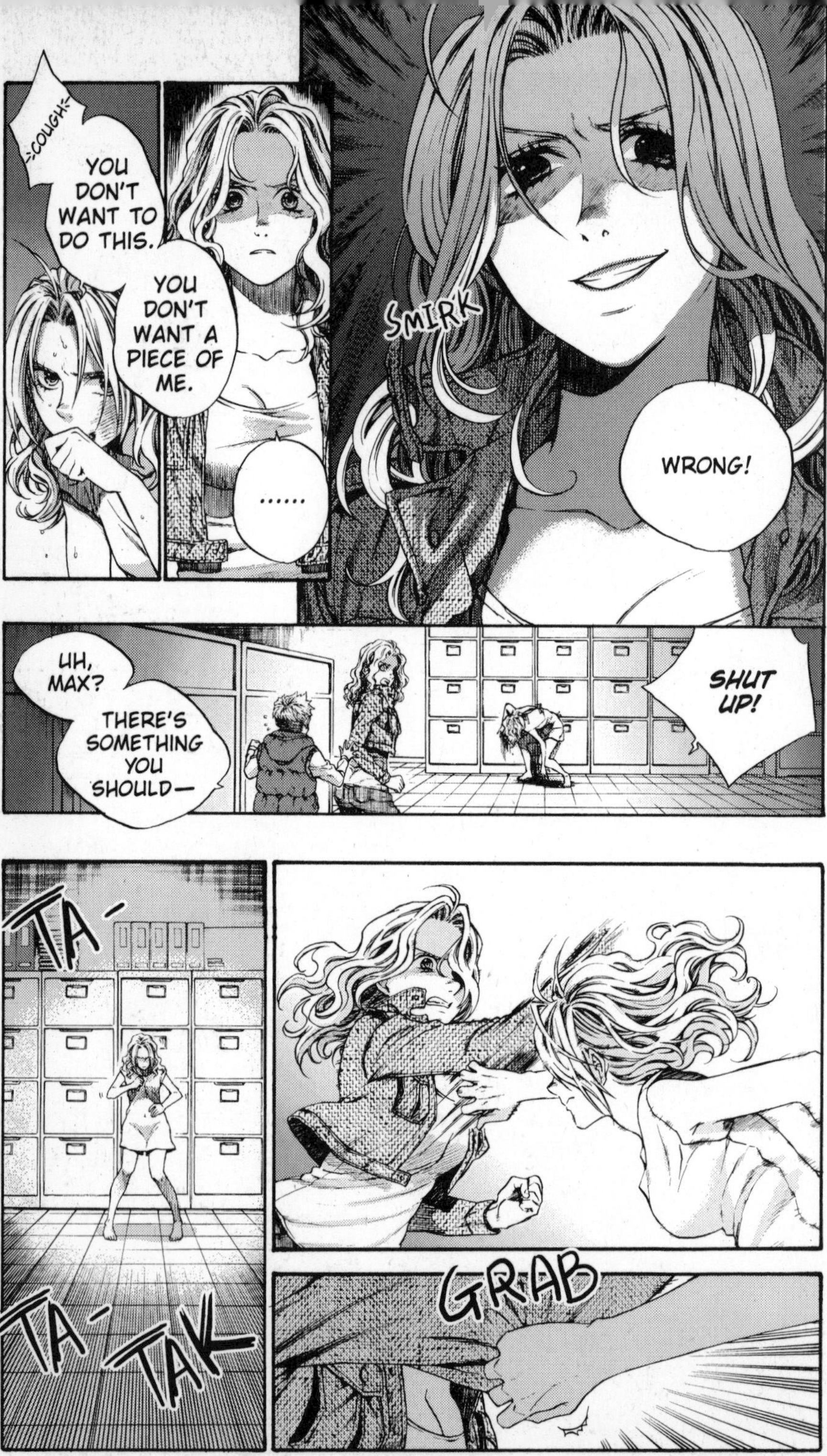
COUGH
YOU DON'T WANT TO DO THIS.
YOU DON'T WANT A PIECE OF ME.
......
SMIRK
WRONG!
UH, MAX?
THERE'S SOMETHING YOU SHOULD—
SHUT UP!
TA-
TA-TAK
GRAB

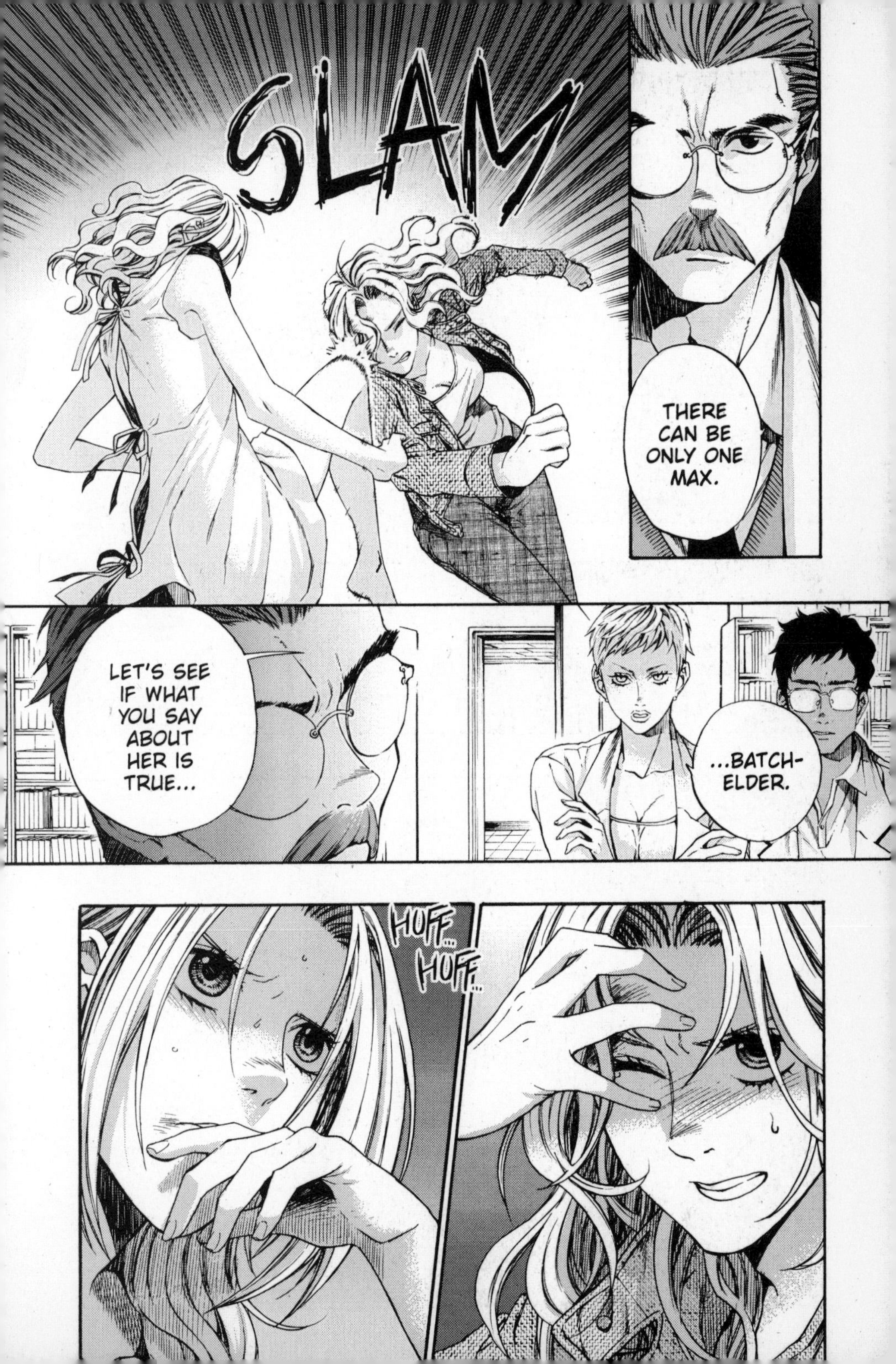
SLAM
THERE CAN BE ONLY ONE MAX.
LET'S SEE IF WHAT YOU SAY ABOUT HER IS TRUE...
...BATCH-ELDER.
HUFF... HUFF...

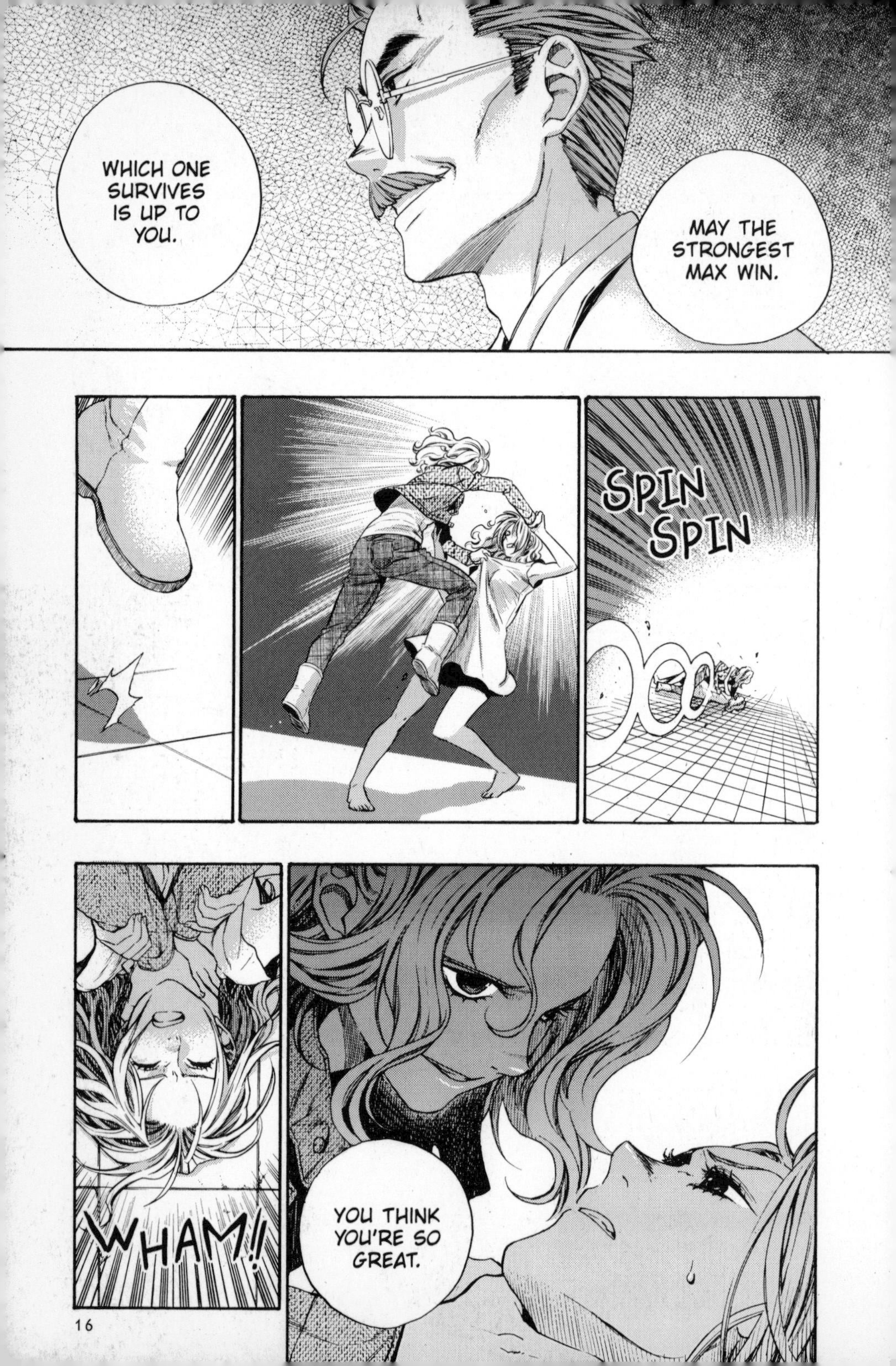
WHICH ONE SURVIVES IS UP TO YOU.
MAY THE STRONGEST MAX WIN.
SPIN SPIN
WHAM!!
YOU THINK YOU'RE SO GREAT.

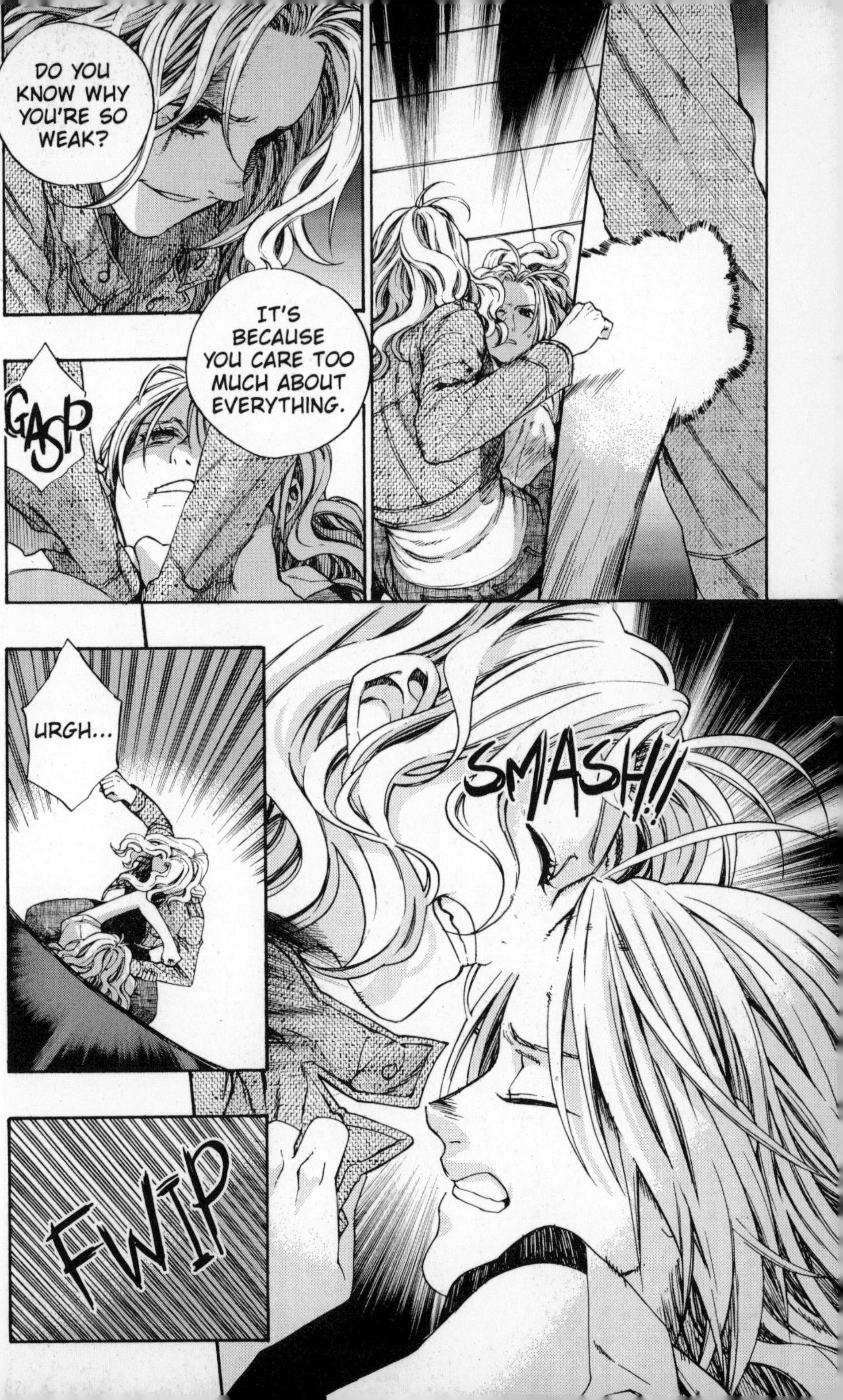
DO YOU KNOW WHY YOU'RE SO WEAK?
GASP
IT'S BECAUSE YOU CARE TOO MUCH ABOUT EVERYTHING.
URGH...
FWIP
SMASH!!

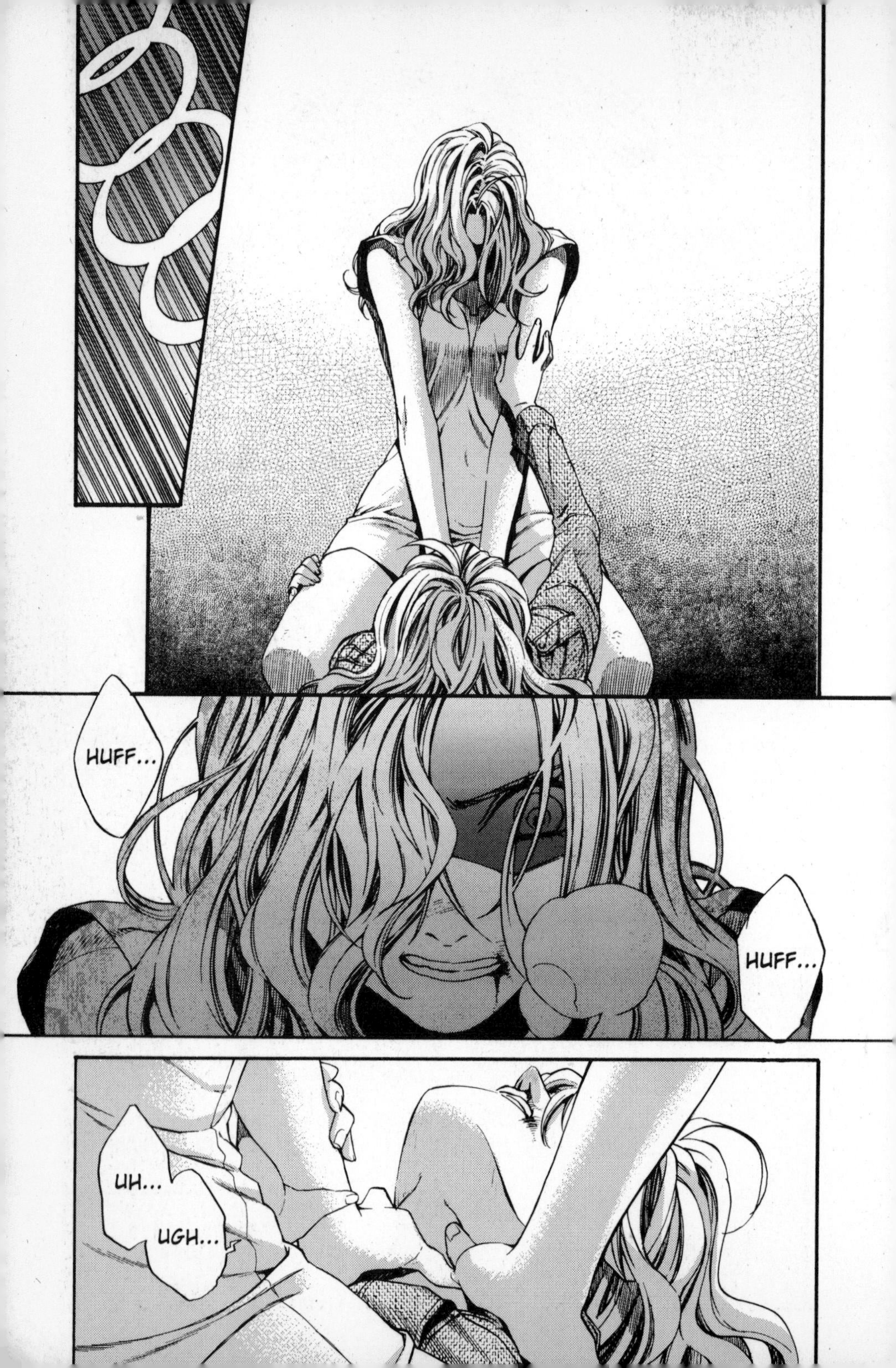
HUFF...
HUFF...
UH...
UGH...

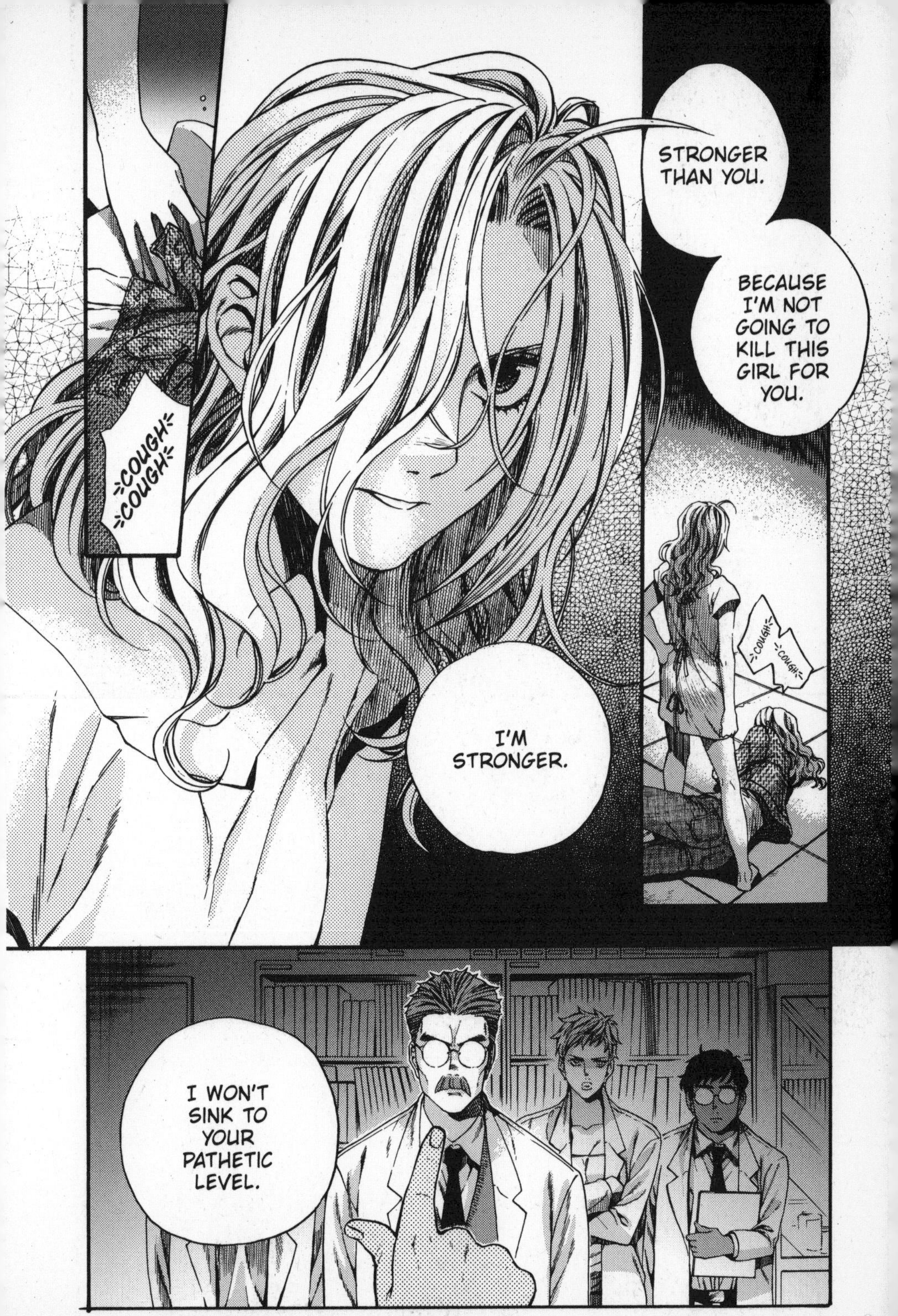
COUGH COUGH
I'M STRONGER.
STRONGER THAN YOU.
BECAUSE I'M NOT GOING TO KILL THIS GIRL FOR YOU.
COUGH COUGH
I WON'T SINK TO YOUR PATHETIC LEVEL.

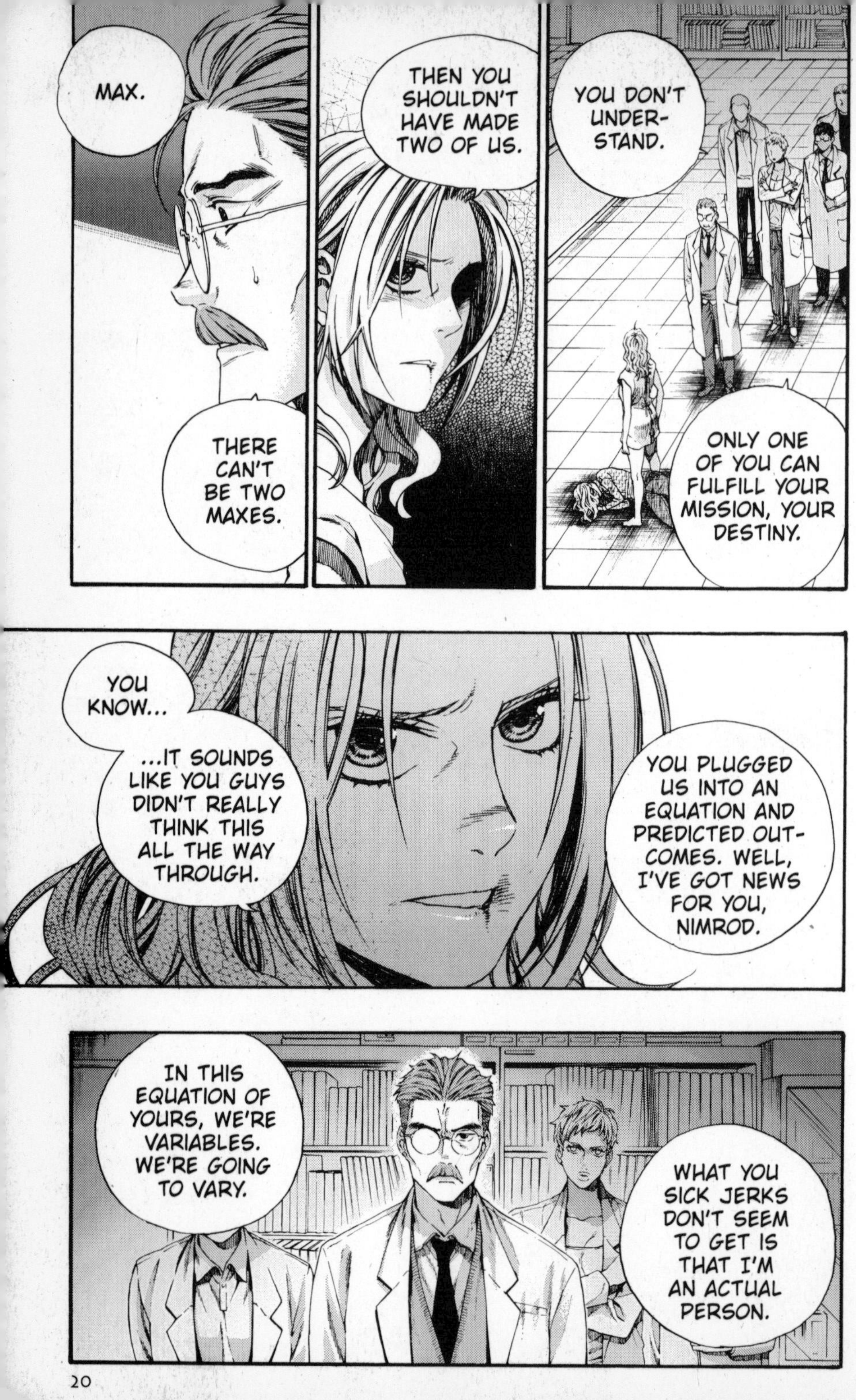
MAX.
THERE CAN'T BE TWO MAXES.
THEN YOU SHOULDN'T HAVE MADE TWO OF US.
YOU DON'T UNDER-STAND.
ONLY ONE OF YOU CAN FULFILL YOUR MISSION, YOUR DESTINY.
YOU KNOW...
...IT SOUNDS LIKE YOU GUYS DIDN'T REALLY THINK THIS ALL THE WAY THROUGH.
YOU PLUGGED US INTO AN EQUATION AND PREDICTED OUT-COMES. WELL, I'VE GOT NEWS FOR YOU, NIMROD.
IN THIS EQUATION OF YOURS, WE'RE VARIABLES. WE'RE GOING TO VARY.
WHAT YOU SICK JERKS DON'T SEEM TO GET IS THAT I'M AN ACTUAL PERSON.

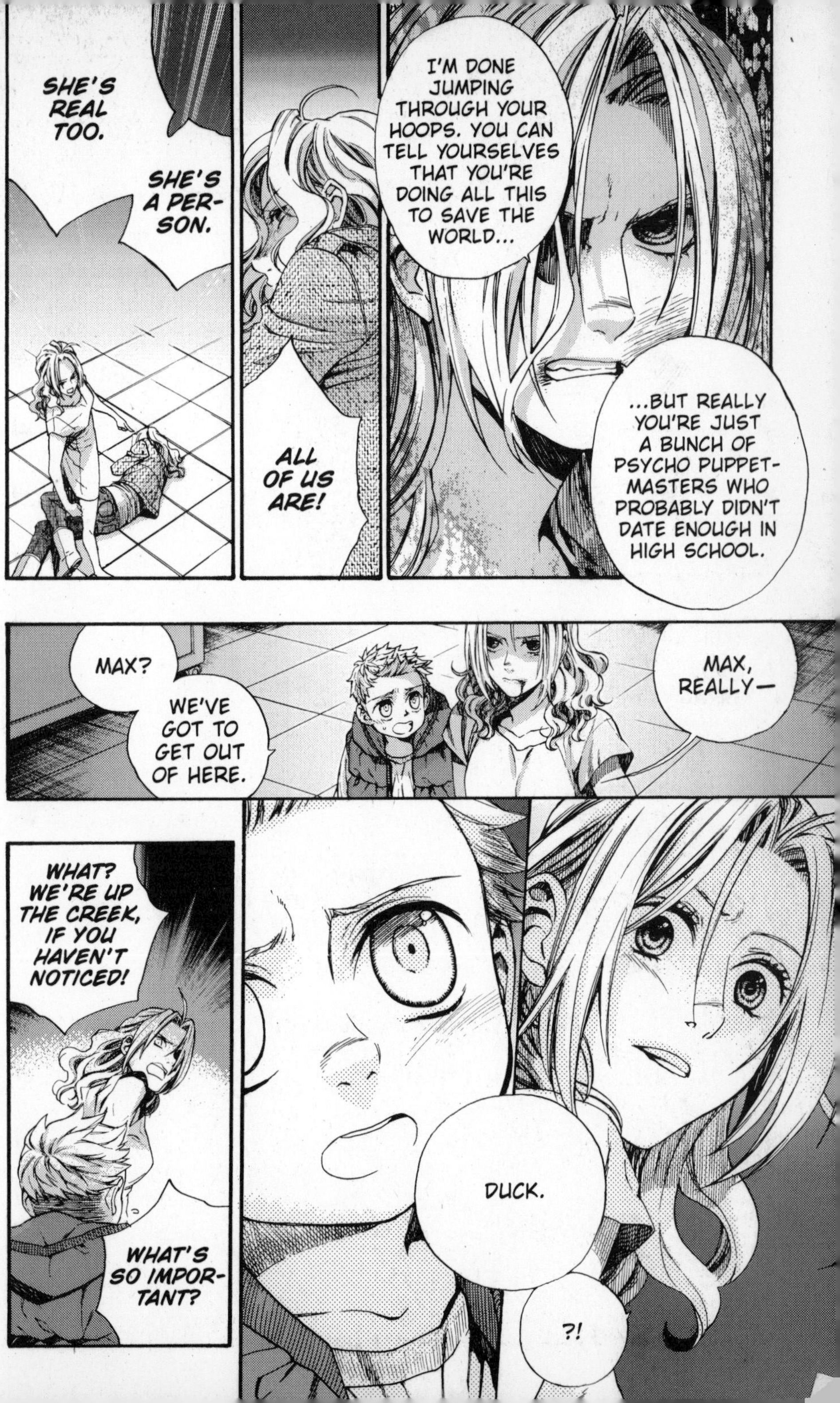
SHE'S REAL TOO.
SHE'S A PER-SON.
ALL OF US ARE!
I'M DONE JUMPING THROUGH YOUR HOOPS. YOU CAN TELL YOURSELVES THAT YOU'RE DOING ALL THIS TO SAVE THE WORLD...
...BUT REALLY YOU'RE JUST A BUNCH OF PSYCHO PUPPET-MASTERS WHO PROBABLY DIDN'T DATE ENOUGH IN HIGH SCHOOL.
MAX?
WE'VE GOT TO GET OUT OF HERE.
MAX, REALLY—
WHAT? WE'RE UP THE CREEK, IF YOU HAVEN'T NOTICED!
WHAT'S SO IMPOR-TANT?
DUCK.
?!

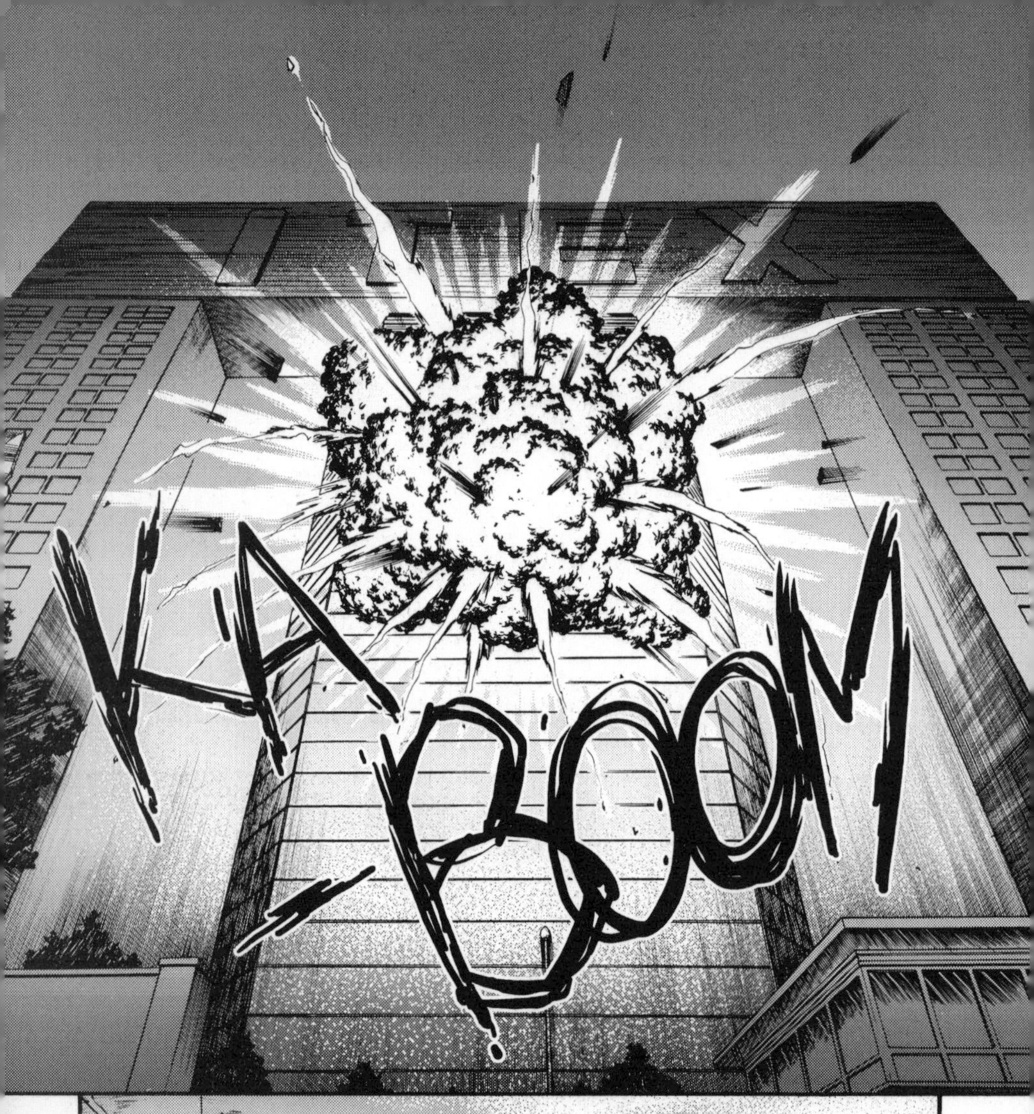
KA-BOOM
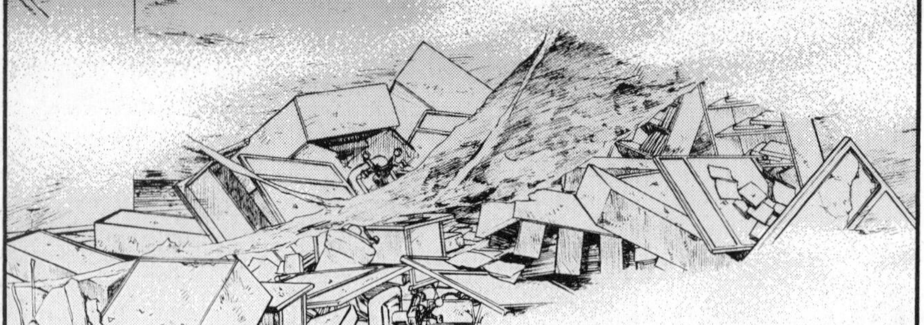

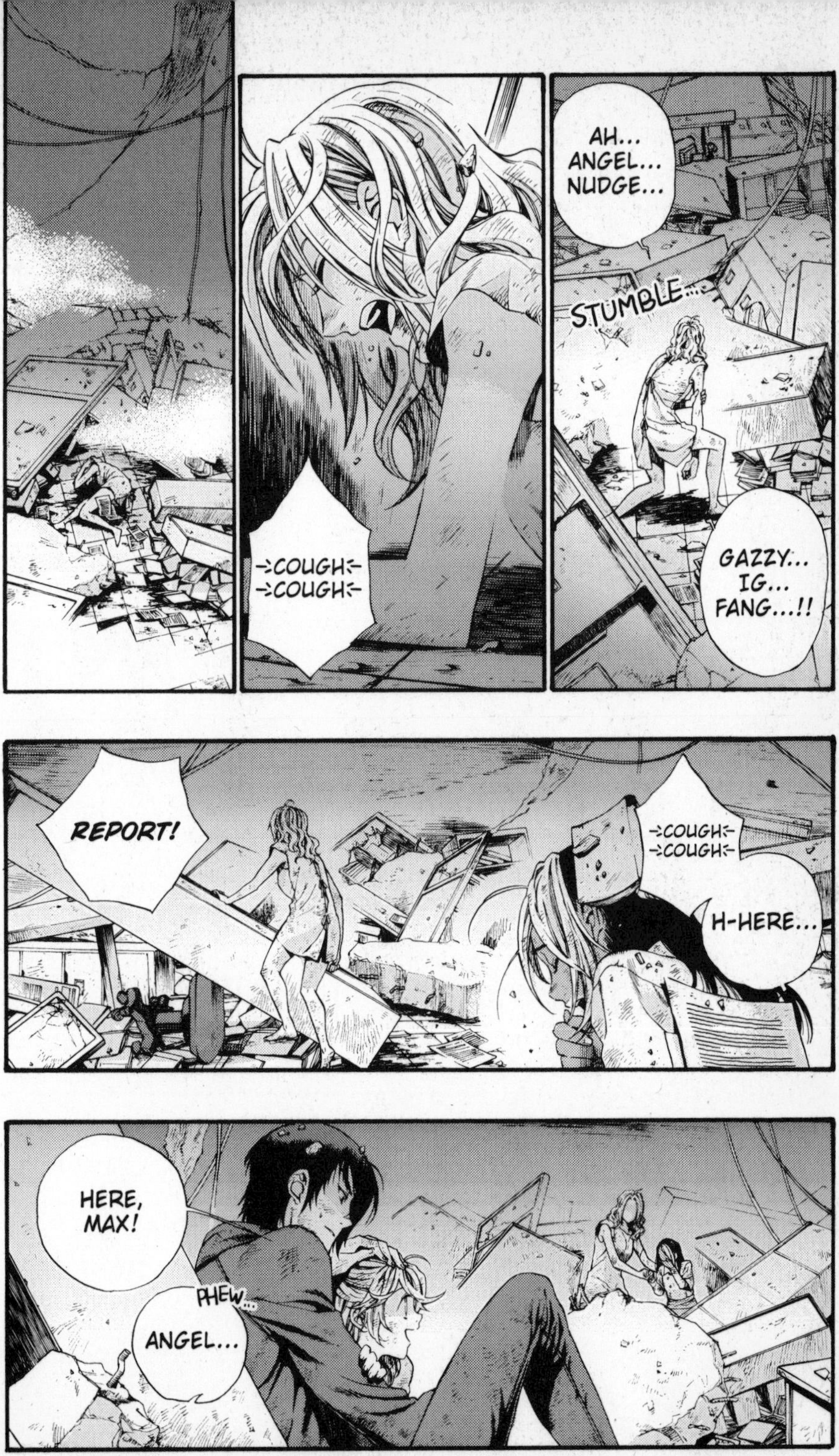

COUGH COUGH
AH... ANGEL... NUDGE...
STUMBLE...
GAZZY... IG... FANG...!!
REPORT!
COUGH COUGH
H-HERE...
HERE, MAX!
PHEW...
ANGEL...

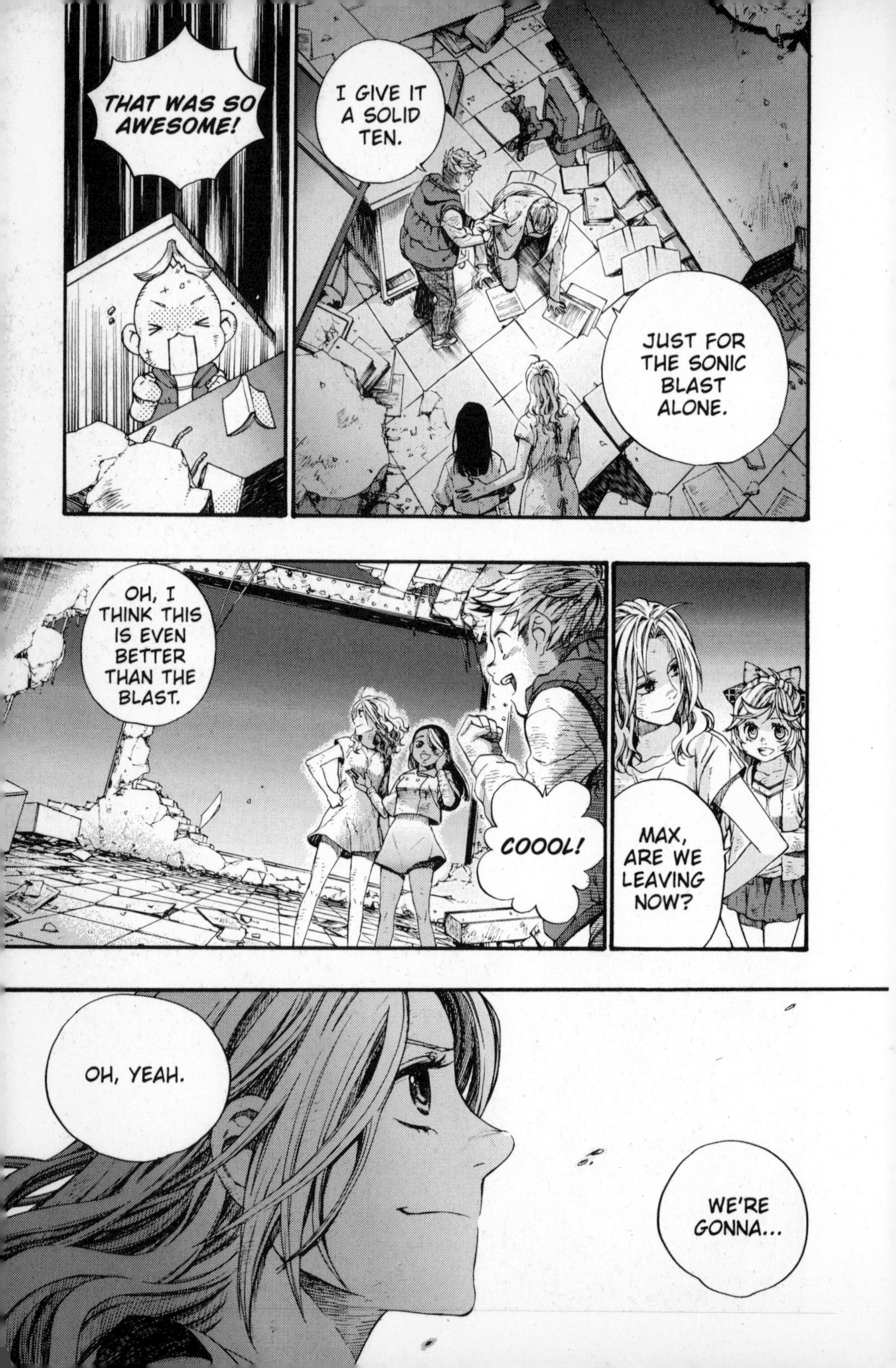
THAT WAS SO AWESOME!
I GIVE IT A SOLID TEN.
JUST FOR THE SONIC BLAST ALONE.
OH, I THINK THIS IS EVEN BETTER THAN THE BLAST.
COOOL!
MAX, ARE WE LEAVING NOW?
OH, YEAH.
WE'RE GONNA...

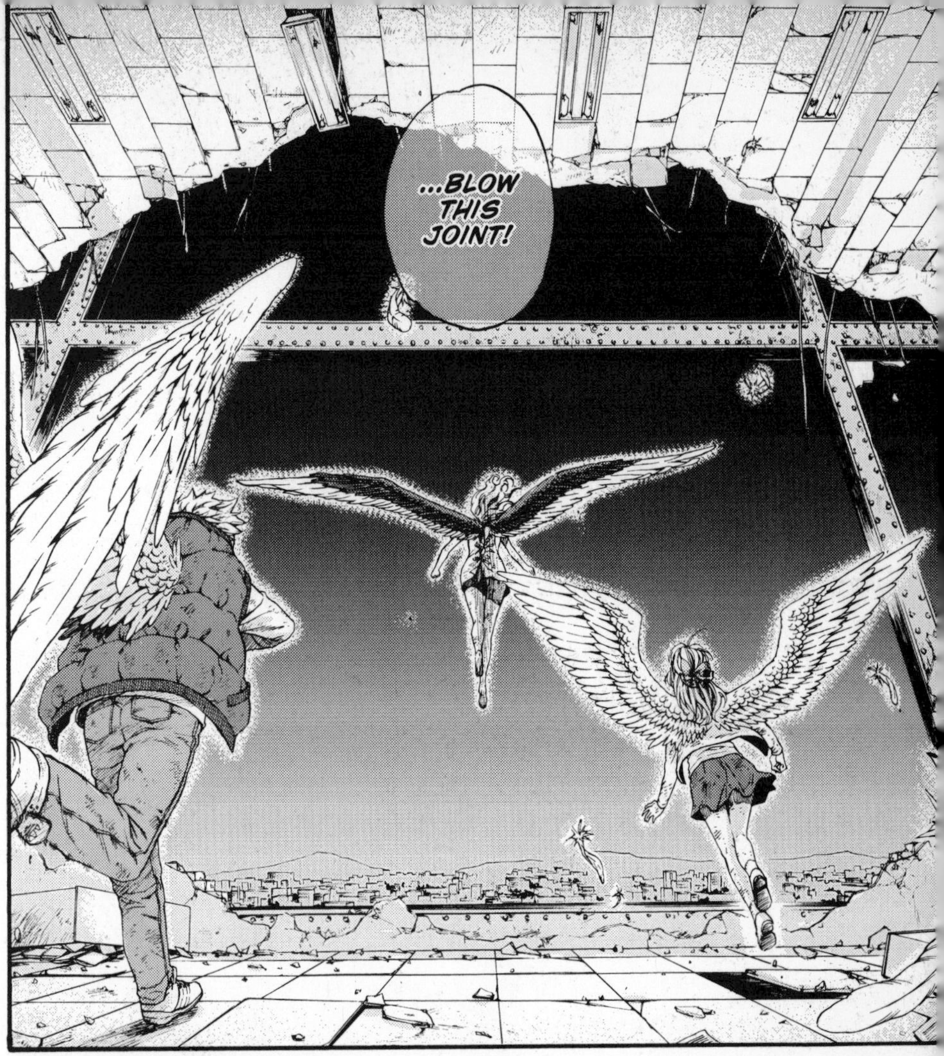
...BLOW THIS JOINT!

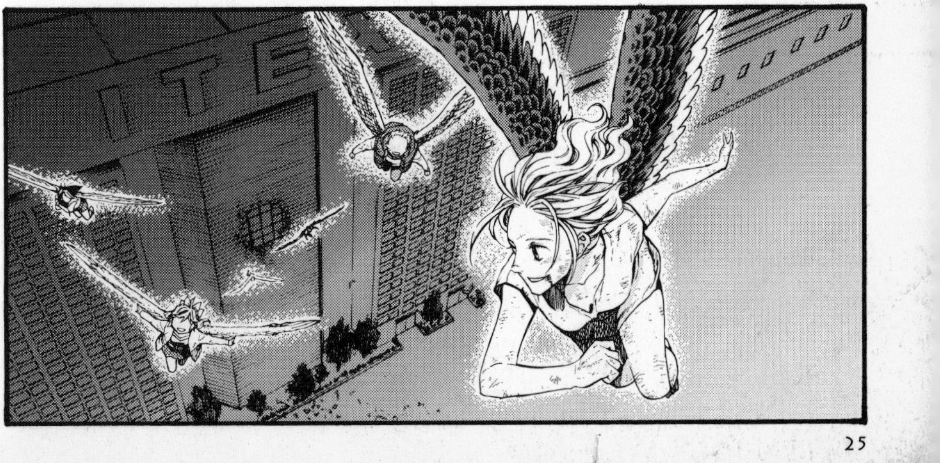

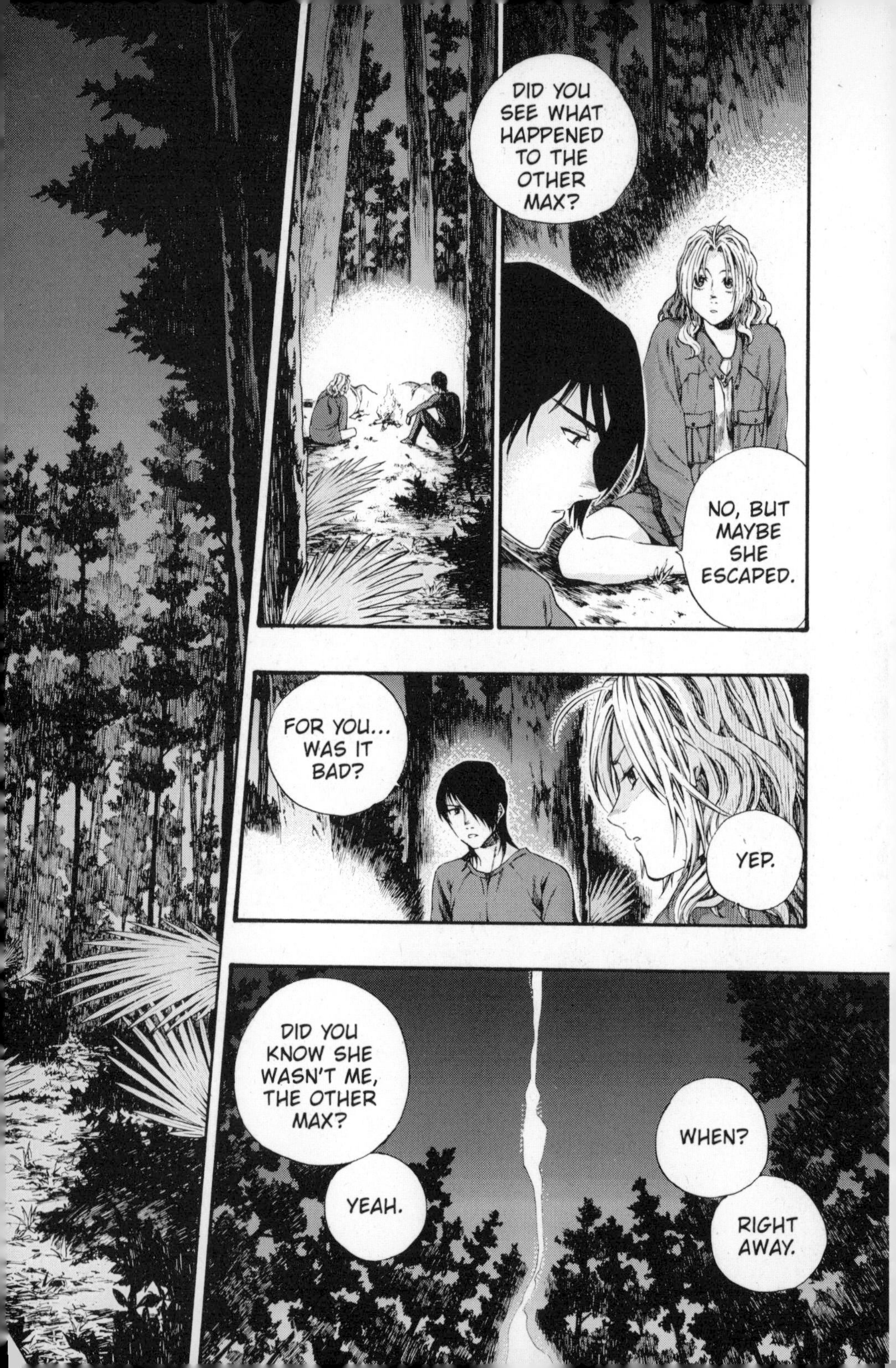
DID YOU SEE WHAT HAPPENED TO THE OTHER MAX?
NO, BUT MAYBE SHE ESCAPED.
FOR YOU... WAS IT BAD?
YEP.
DID YOU KNOW SHE WASN'T ME, THE OTHER MAX?
YEAH.
WHEN?
RIGHT AWAY.

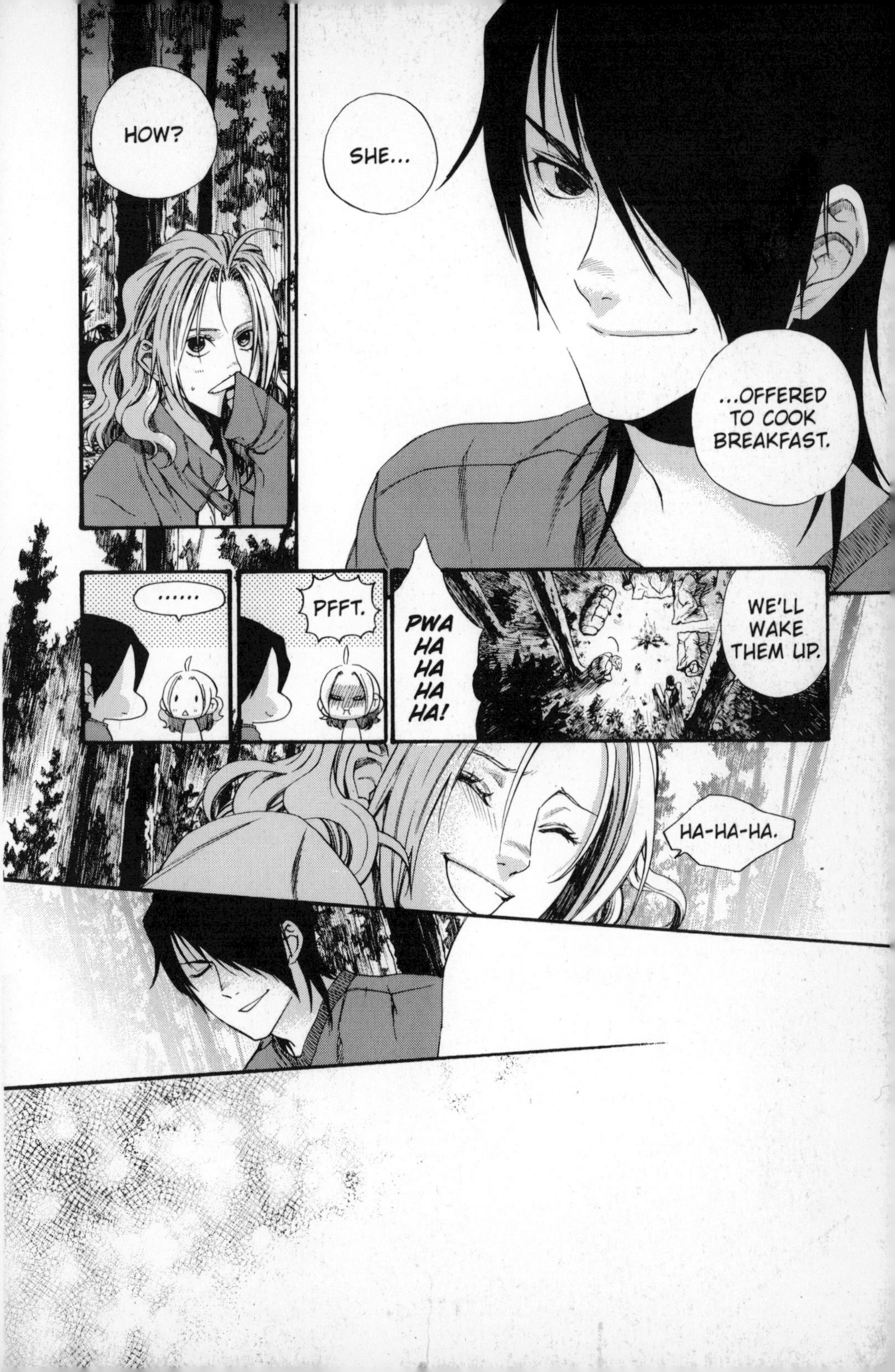
HOW?
SHE...
...OFFERED TO COOK BREAKFAST.
....
PFFT.
PWA HA HA HA HA HA!
WE'LL WAKE THEM UP.
HA-HA-HA.

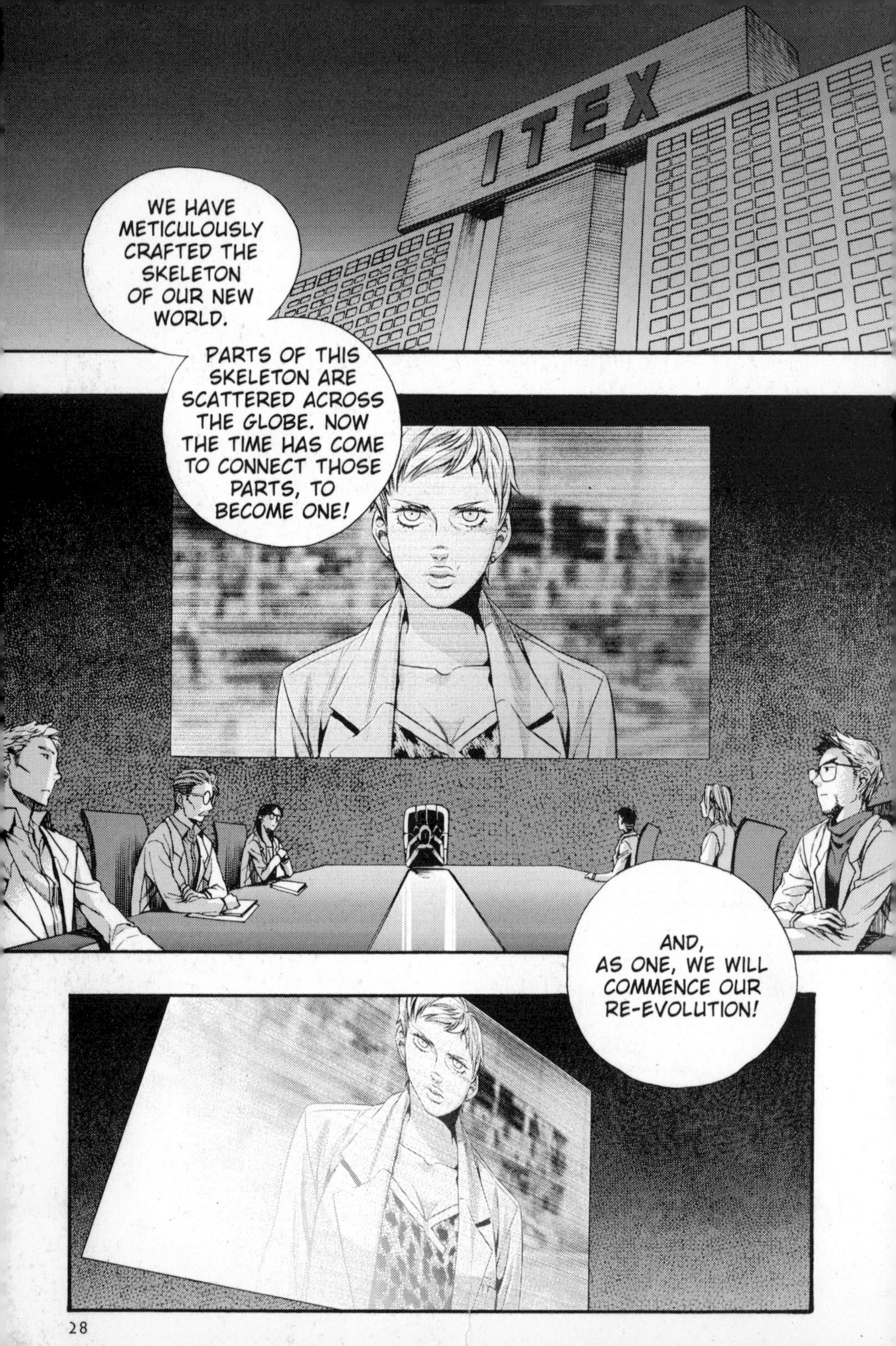
ITEX
WE HAVE METICULOUSLY CRAFTED THE SKELETON OF OUR NEW WORLD.
PARTS OF THIS SKELETON ARE SCATTERED ACROSS THE GLOBE. NOW THE TIME HAS COME TO CONNECT THOSE PARTS, TO BECOME ONE!
AND, AS ONE, WE WILL COMMENCE OUR RE-EVOLUTION!

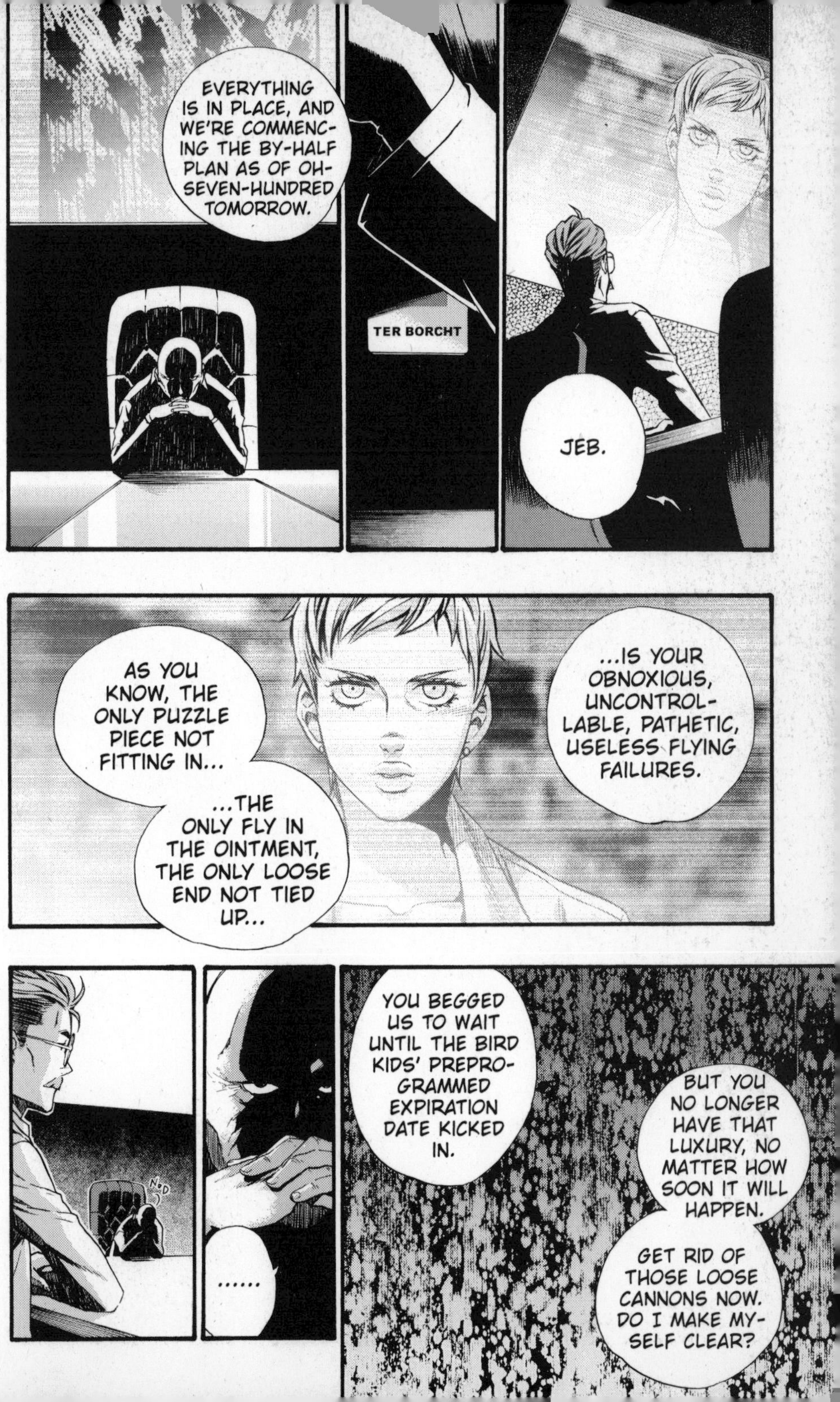
EVERYTHING IS IN PLACE, AND WE'RE COMMENCING THE BY-HALF PLAN AS OF OH-SEVEN-HUNDRED TOMORROW.
TER BORCHT
JEB.
AS YOU KNOW, THE ONLY PUZZLE PIECE NOT FITTING IN...
...THE ONLY FLY IN THE OINTMENT, THE ONLY LOOSE END NOT TIED UP...
...IS YOUR OBNOXIOUS, UNCONTROLLABLE, PATHETIC, USELESS FLYING FAILURES.
NOD
......
YOU BEGGED US TO WAIT UNTIL THE BIRD KIDS' PREPROGRAMMED EXPIRATION DATE KICKED IN.
BUT YOU NO LONGER HAVE THAT LUXURY, NO MATTER HOW SOON IT WILL HAPPEN.
GET RID OF THOSE LOOSE CANNONS NOW. DO I MAKE MYSELF CLEAR?

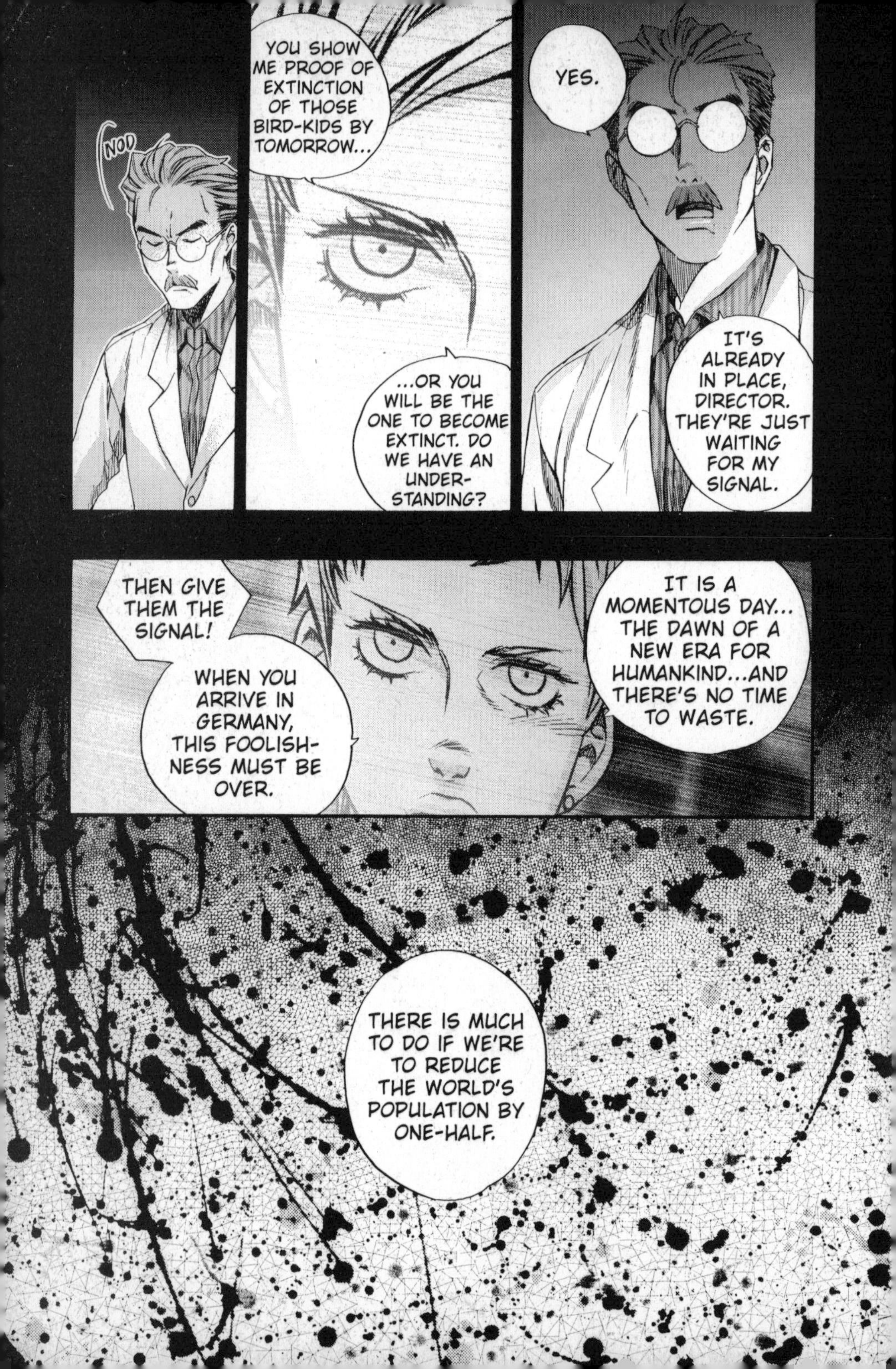
NOD
YOU SHOW ME PROOF OF EXTINCTION OF THOSE BIRD-KIDS BY TOMORROW...
...OR YOU WILL BE THE ONE TO BECOME EXTINCT. DO WE HAVE AN UNDER-STANDING?
YES.
IT'S ALREADY IN PLACE, DIRECTOR. THEY'RE JUST WAITING FOR MY SIGNAL.
THEN GIVE THEM THE SIGNAL!
WHEN YOU ARRIVE IN GERMANY, THIS FOOLISH-NESS MUST BE OVER.
IT IS A MOMENTOUS DAY... THE DAWN OF A NEW ERA FOR HUMANKIND...AND THERE'S NO TIME TO WASTE.
THERE IS MUCH TO DO IF WE'RE TO REDUCE THE WORLD'S POPULATION BY ONE-HALF.

MAXIMUM
RIDE

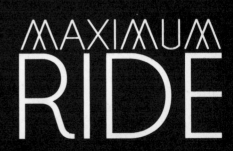

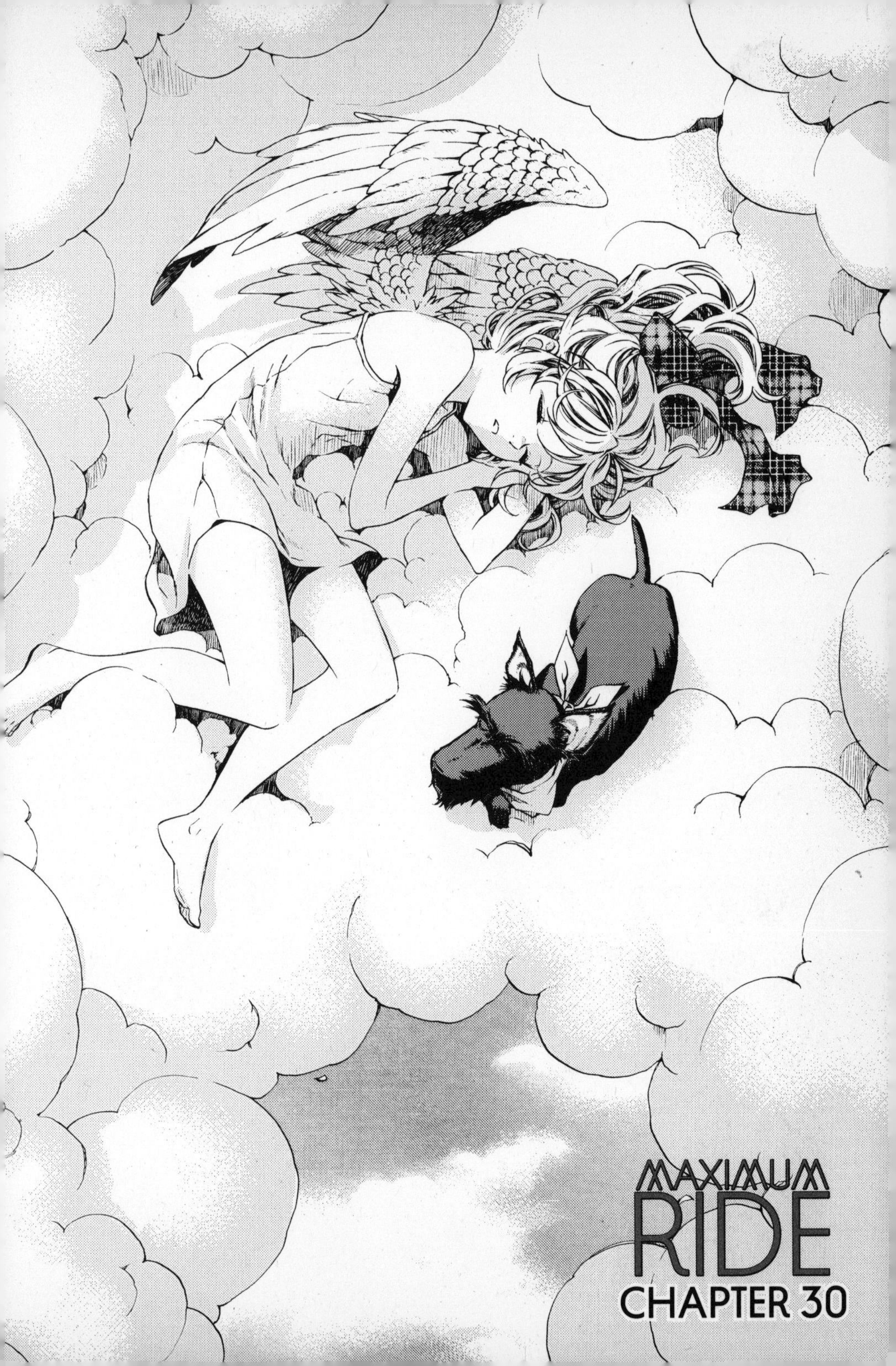
MAXIMUM
RIDE
CHAPTER 30

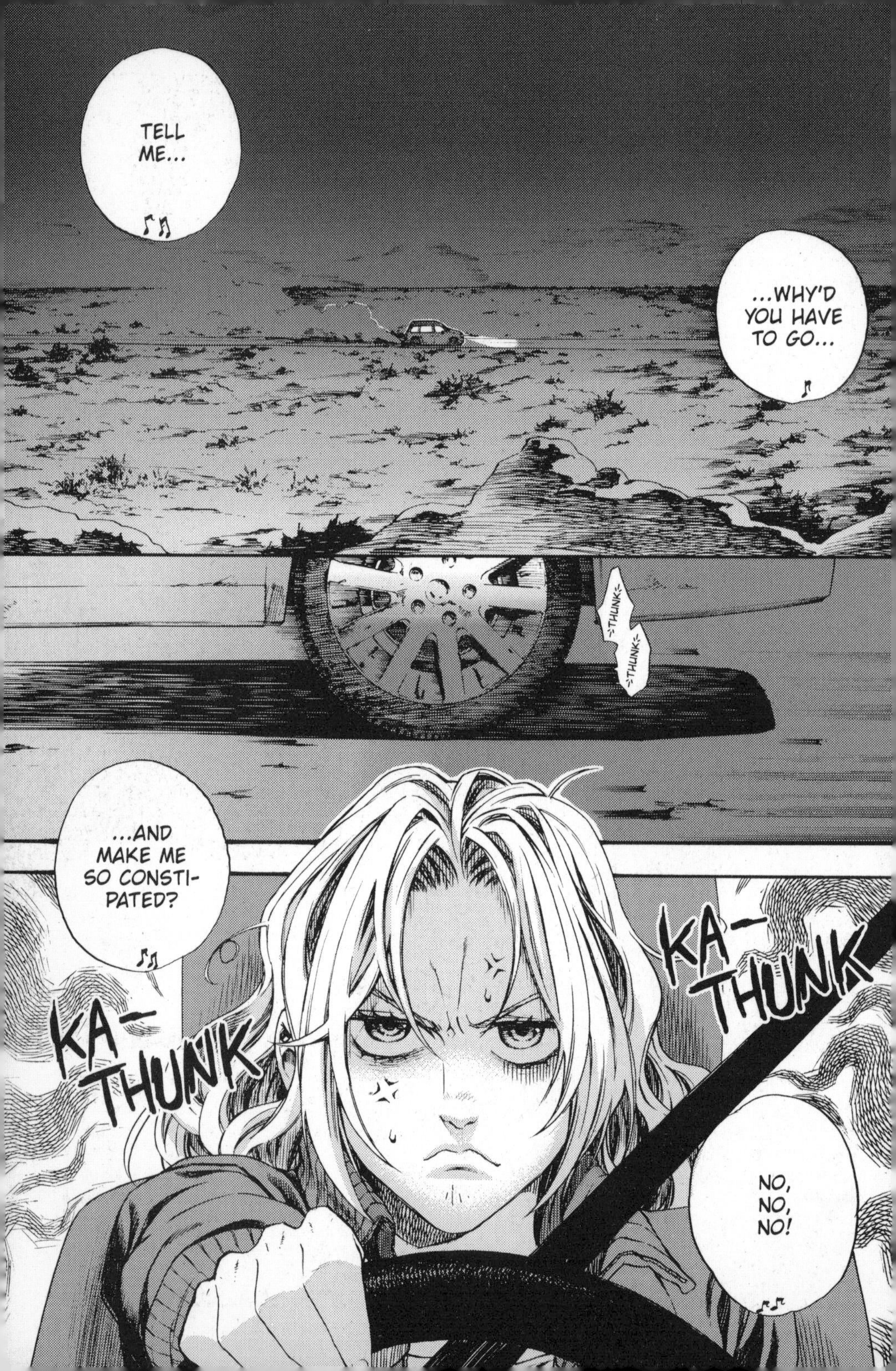
TELL ME...
...WHY'D YOU HAVE TO GO...
THUNK
THUNK
...AND MAKE ME SO CONSTI-PATED?
KA-THUNK
KA-THUNK
NO, NO, NO!

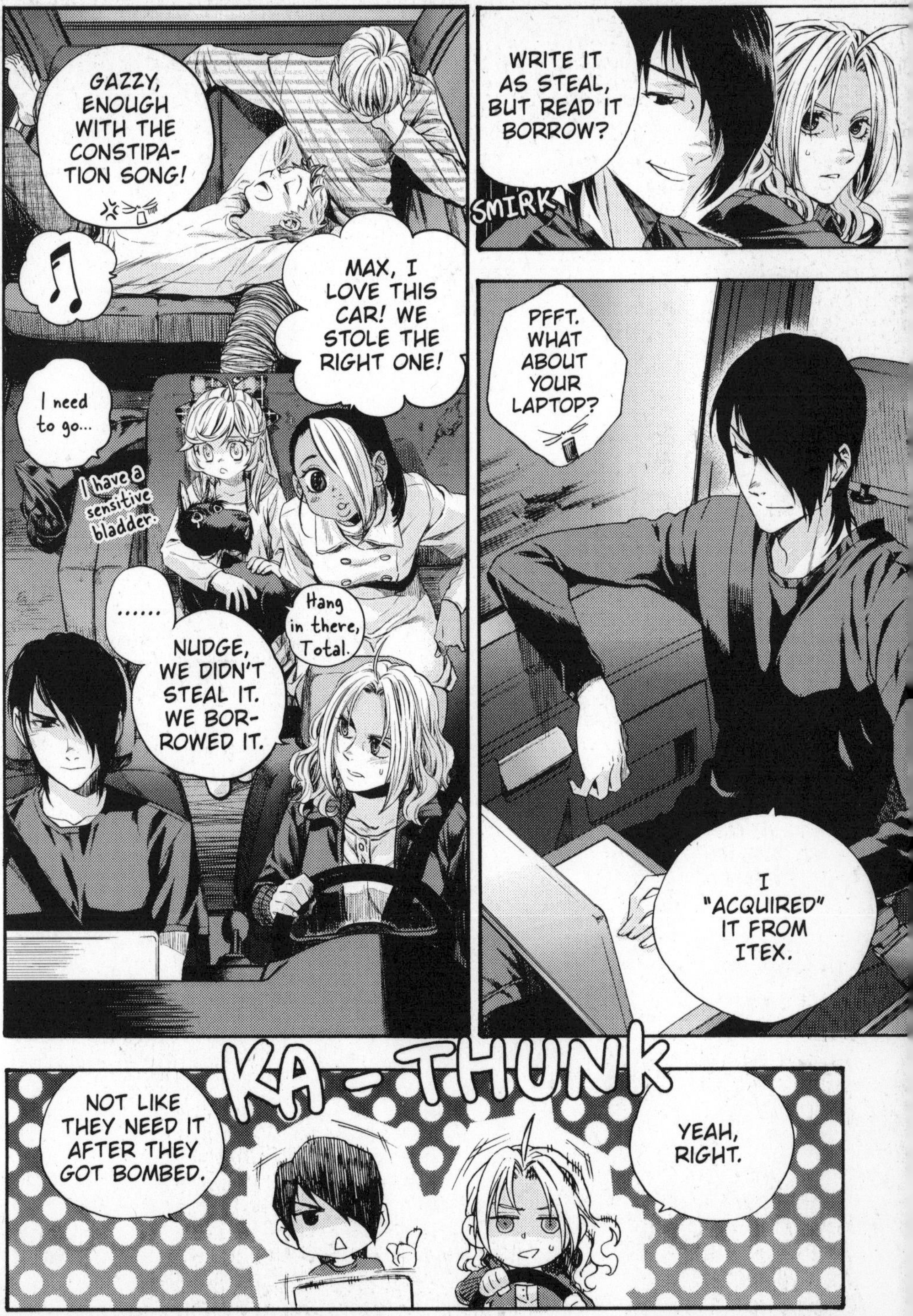
GAZZY, ENOUGH WITH THE CONSTIPATION SONG!
MAX, I LOVE THIS CAR! WE STOLE THE RIGHT ONE!
I need to go...
I have a sensitive bladder.
......
Hang in there, Total.
NUDGE, WE DIDN'T STEAL IT. WE BORROWED IT.
WRITE IT AS STEAL, BUT READ IT BORROW?
SMIRK
PFFT. WHAT ABOUT YOUR LAPTOP?
I "ACQUIRED" IT FROM ITEX.
KA-THUNK
NOT LIKE THEY NEED IT AFTER THEY GOT BOMBED.
YEAH, RIGHT.

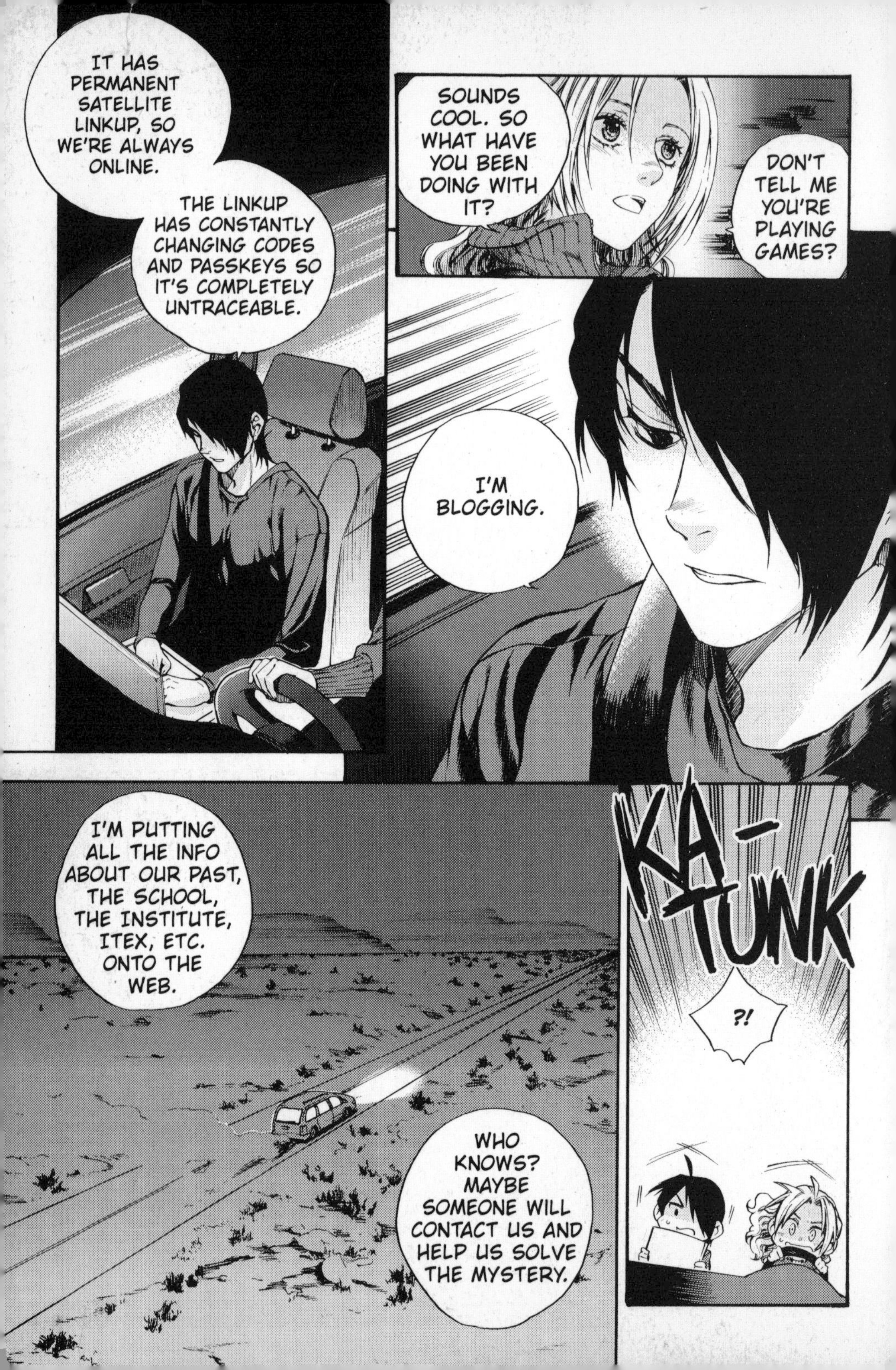
IT HAS PERMANENT SATELLITE LINKUP, SO WE'RE ALWAYS ONLINE.
THE LINKUP HAS CONSTANTLY CHANGING CODES AND PASSKEYS SO IT'S COMPLETELY UNTRACEABLE.
SOUNDS COOL. SO WHAT HAVE YOU BEEN DOING WITH IT?
DON'T TELL ME YOU'RE PLAYING GAMES?
I'M BLOGGING.
I'M PUTTING ALL THE INFO ABOUT OUR PAST, THE SCHOOL, THE INSTITUTE, ITEX, ETC. ONTO THE WEB.
WHO KNOWS? MAYBE SOMEONE WILL CONTACT US AND HELP US SOLVE THE MYSTERY.
KA-TUNK
?!

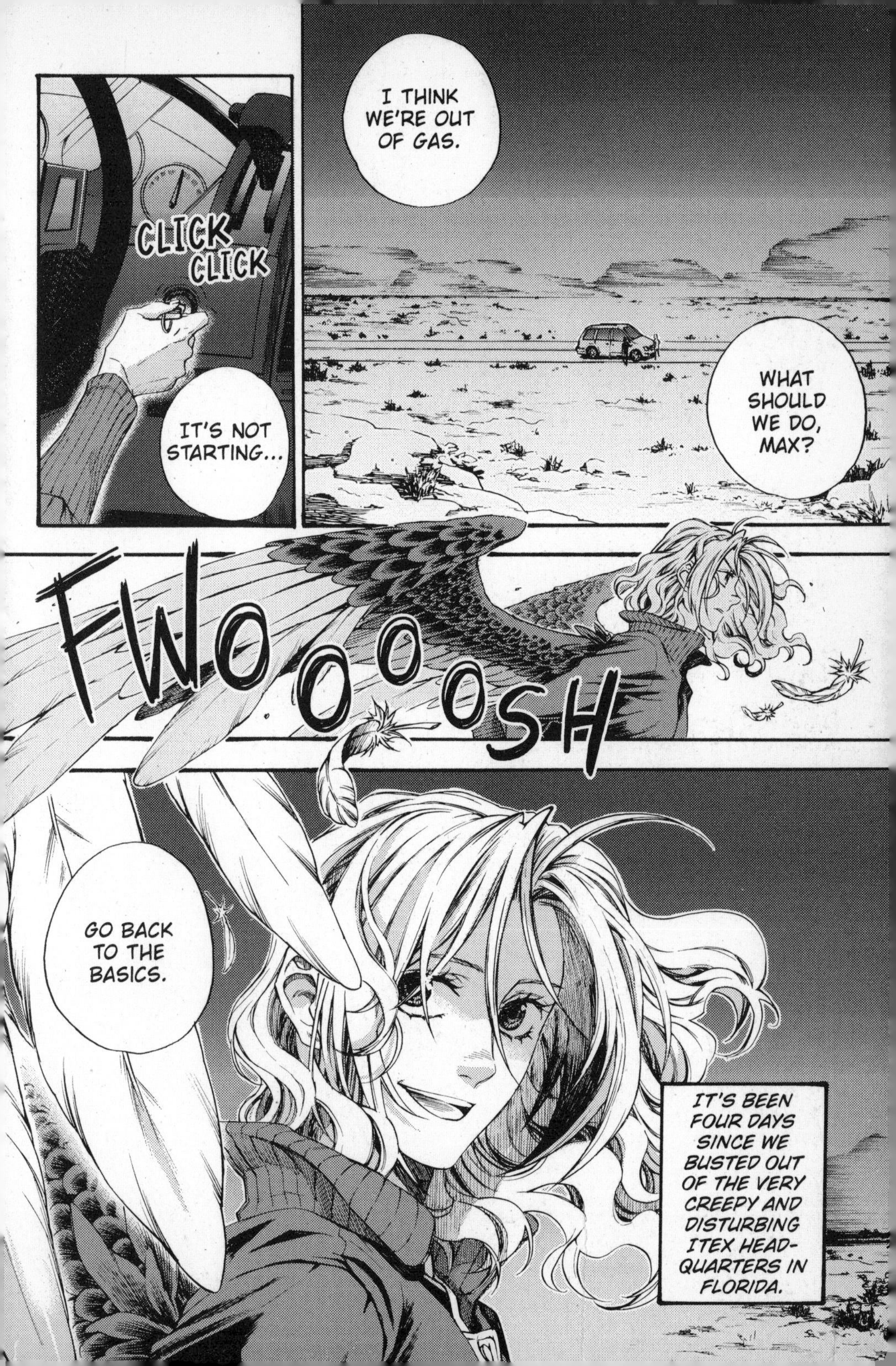
CLICK CLICK
IT'S NOT STARTING...
I THINK WE'RE OUT OF GAS.
WHAT SHOULD WE DO, MAX?
FWOOOOSH
GO BACK TO THE BASICS.
IT'S BEEN FOUR DAYS SINCE WE BUSTED OUT OF THE VERY CREEPY AND DISTURBING ITEX HEAD-QUARTERS IN FLORIDA.

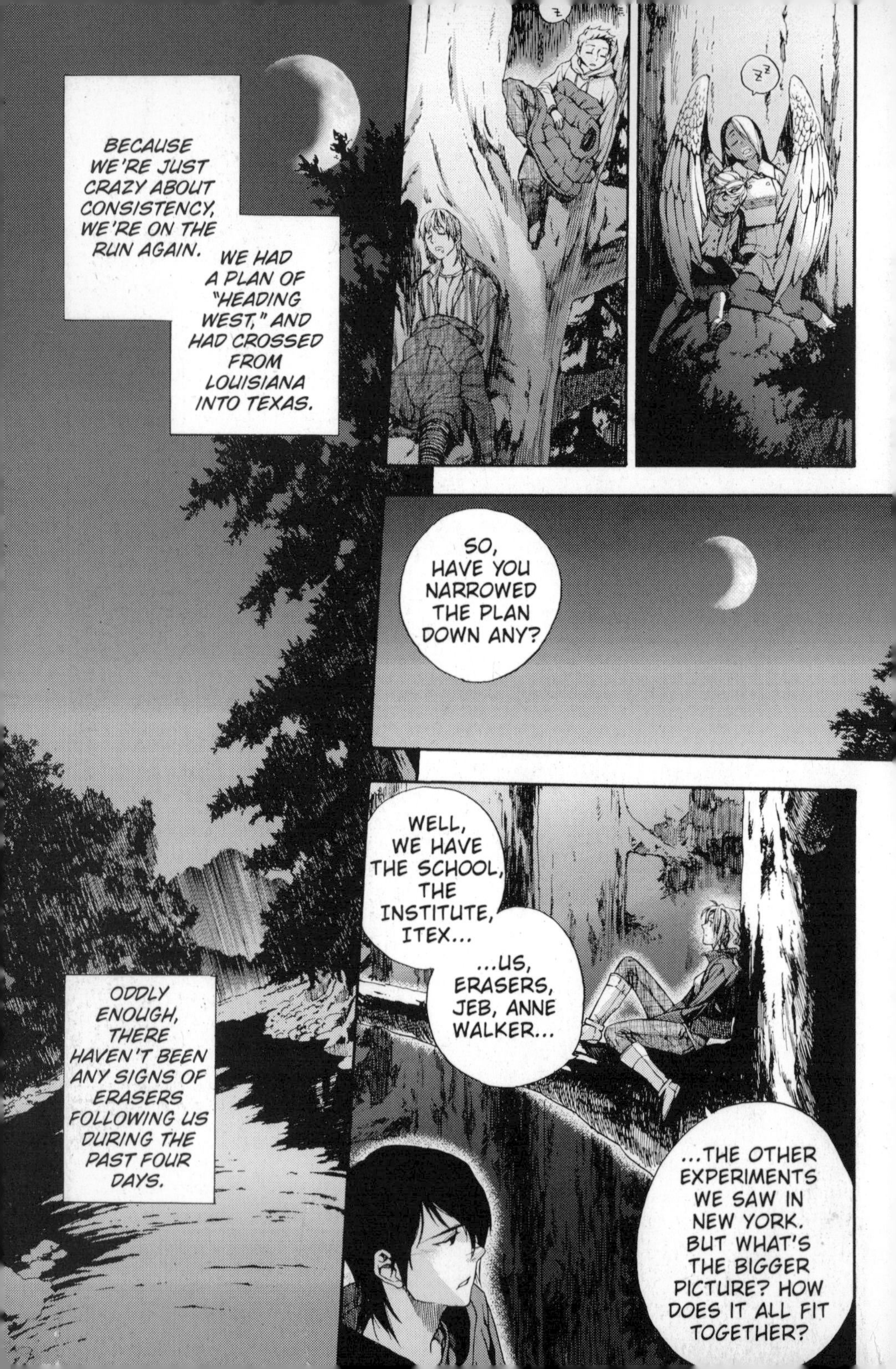
BECAUSE WE'RE JUST CRAZY ABOUT CONSISTENCY, WE'RE ON THE RUN AGAIN.
WE HAD A PLAN OF "HEADING WEST," AND HAD CROSSED FROM LOUISIANA INTO TEXAS.
SO, HAVE YOU NARROWED THE PLAN DOWN ANY?
ODDLY ENOUGH, THERE HAVEN'T BEEN ANY SIGNS OF ERASERS FOLLOWING US DURING THE PAST FOUR DAYS.
WELL, WE HAVE THE SCHOOL, THE INSTITUTE, ITEX...
...US, ERASERS, JEB, ANNE WALKER...
...THE OTHER EXPERIMENTS WE SAW IN NEW YORK. BUT WHAT'S THE BIGGER PICTURE? HOW DOES IT ALL FIT TOGETHER?

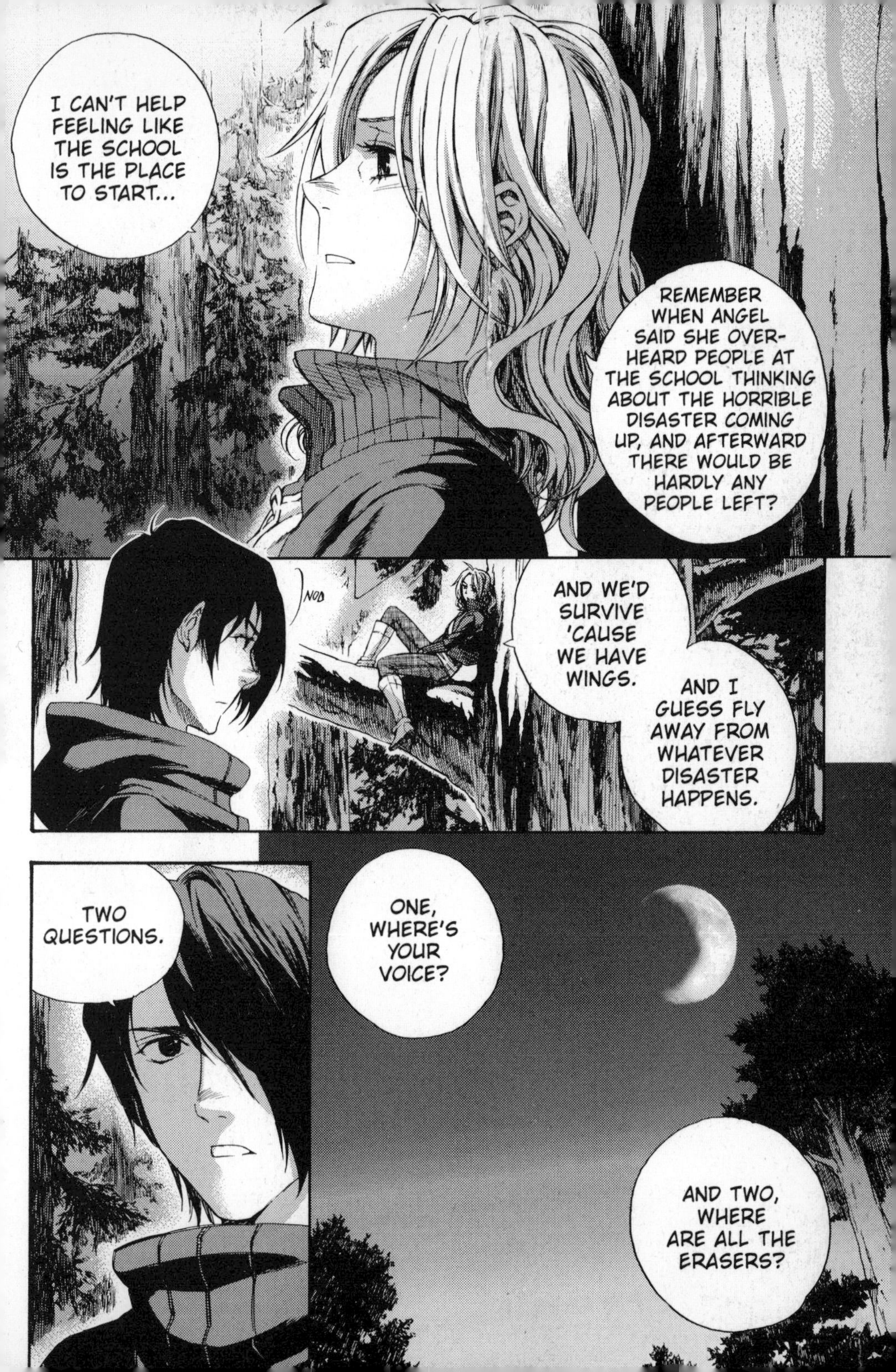
I CAN'T HELP FEELING LIKE THE SCHOOL IS THE PLACE TO START...
REMEMBER WHEN ANGEL SAID SHE OVER-HEARD PEOPLE AT THE SCHOOL THINKING ABOUT THE HORRIBLE DISASTER COMING UP, AND AFTERWARD THERE WOULD BE HARDLY ANY PEOPLE LEFT?
NOD
AND WE'D SURVIVE 'CAUSE WE HAVE WINGS.
AND I GUESS FLY AWAY FROM WHATEVER DISASTER HAPPENS.
TWO QUESTIONS.
ONE, WHERE'S YOUR VOICE?
AND TWO, WHERE ARE ALL THE ERASERS?

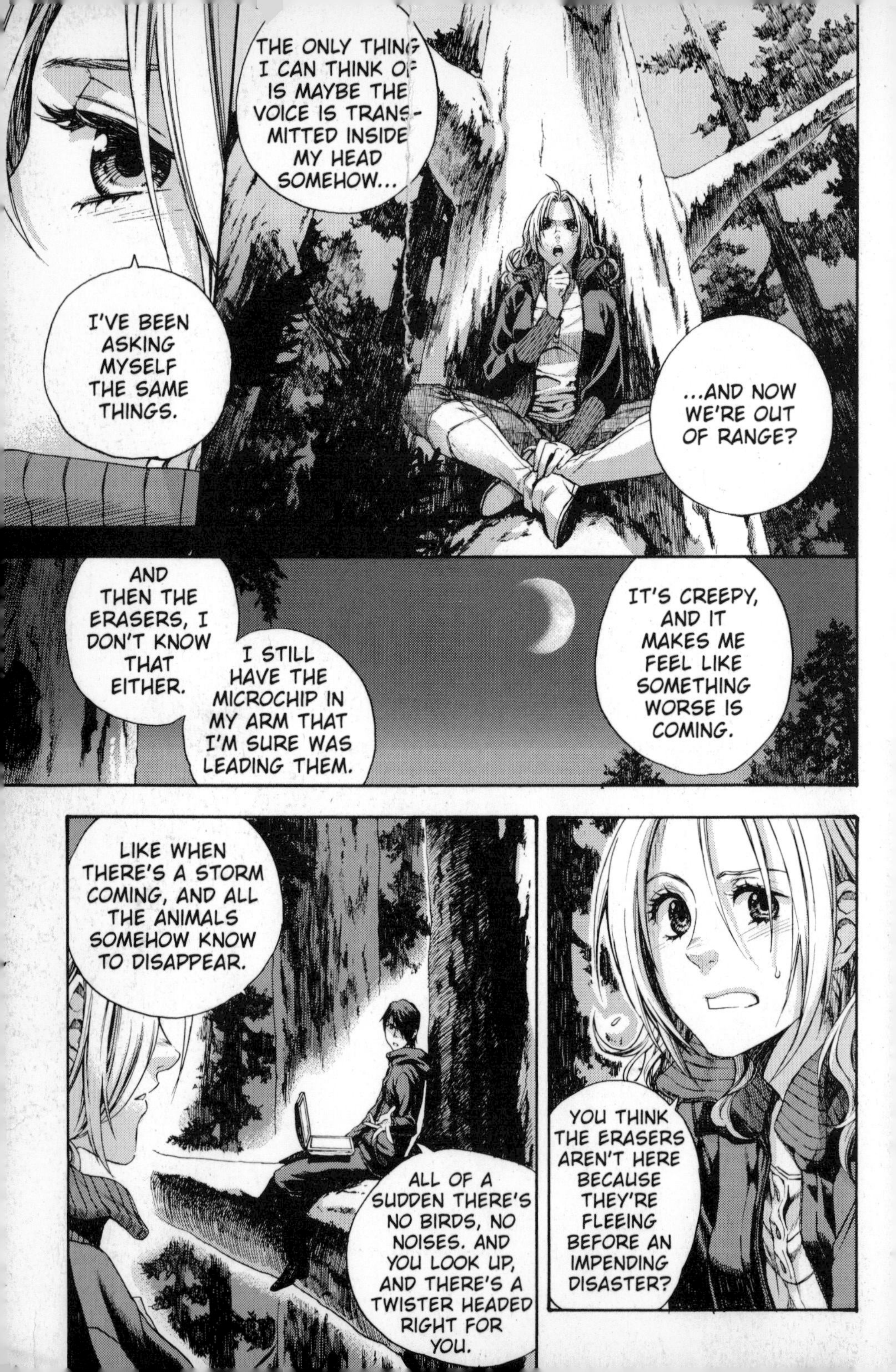
THE ONLY THING I CAN THINK OF IS MAYBE THE VOICE IS TRANS-MITTED INSIDE MY HEAD SOMEHOW...
I'VE BEEN ASKING MYSELF THE SAME THINGS.
...AND NOW WE'RE OUT OF RANGE?
AND THEN THE ERASERS, I DON'T KNOW THAT EITHER.
I STILL HAVE THE MICROCHIP IN MY ARM THAT I'M SURE WAS LEADING THEM.
IT'S CREEPY, AND IT MAKES ME FEEL LIKE SOMETHING WORSE IS COMING.
LIKE WHEN THERE'S A STORM COMING, AND ALL THE ANIMALS SOMEHOW KNOW TO DISAPPEAR.
ALL OF A SUDDEN THERE'S NO BIRDS, NO NOISES. AND YOU LOOK UP, AND THERE'S A TWISTER HEADED RIGHT FOR YOU.
YOU THINK THE ERASERS AREN'T HERE BECAUSE THEY'RE FLEEING BEFORE AN IMPENDING DISASTER?

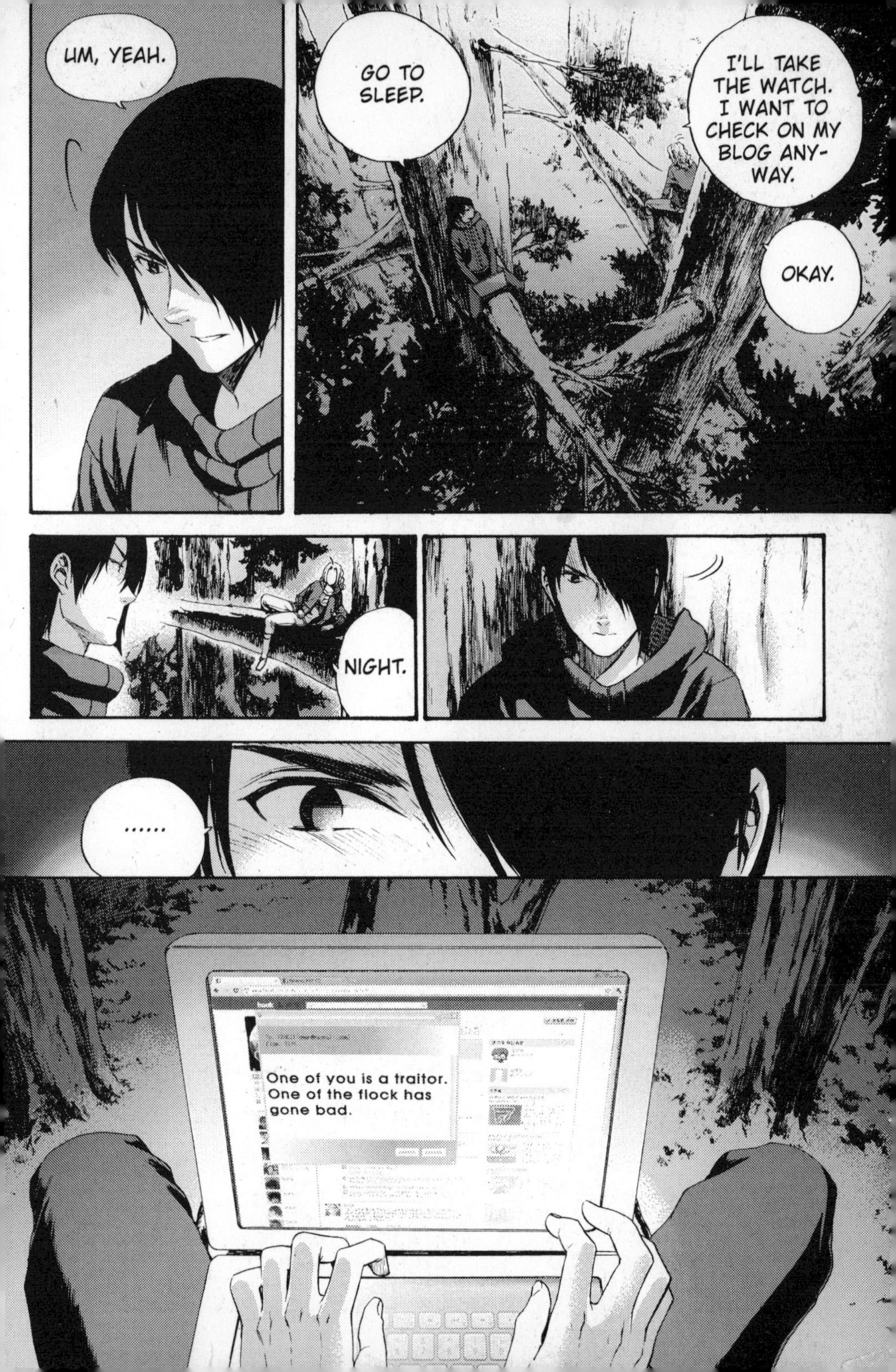
UM, YEAH.
GO TO SLEEP.
I'LL TAKE THE WATCH. I WANT TO CHECK ON MY BLOG ANY-WAY.
OKAY.
NIGHT.
......
One of you is a traitor. One of the flock has gone bad.

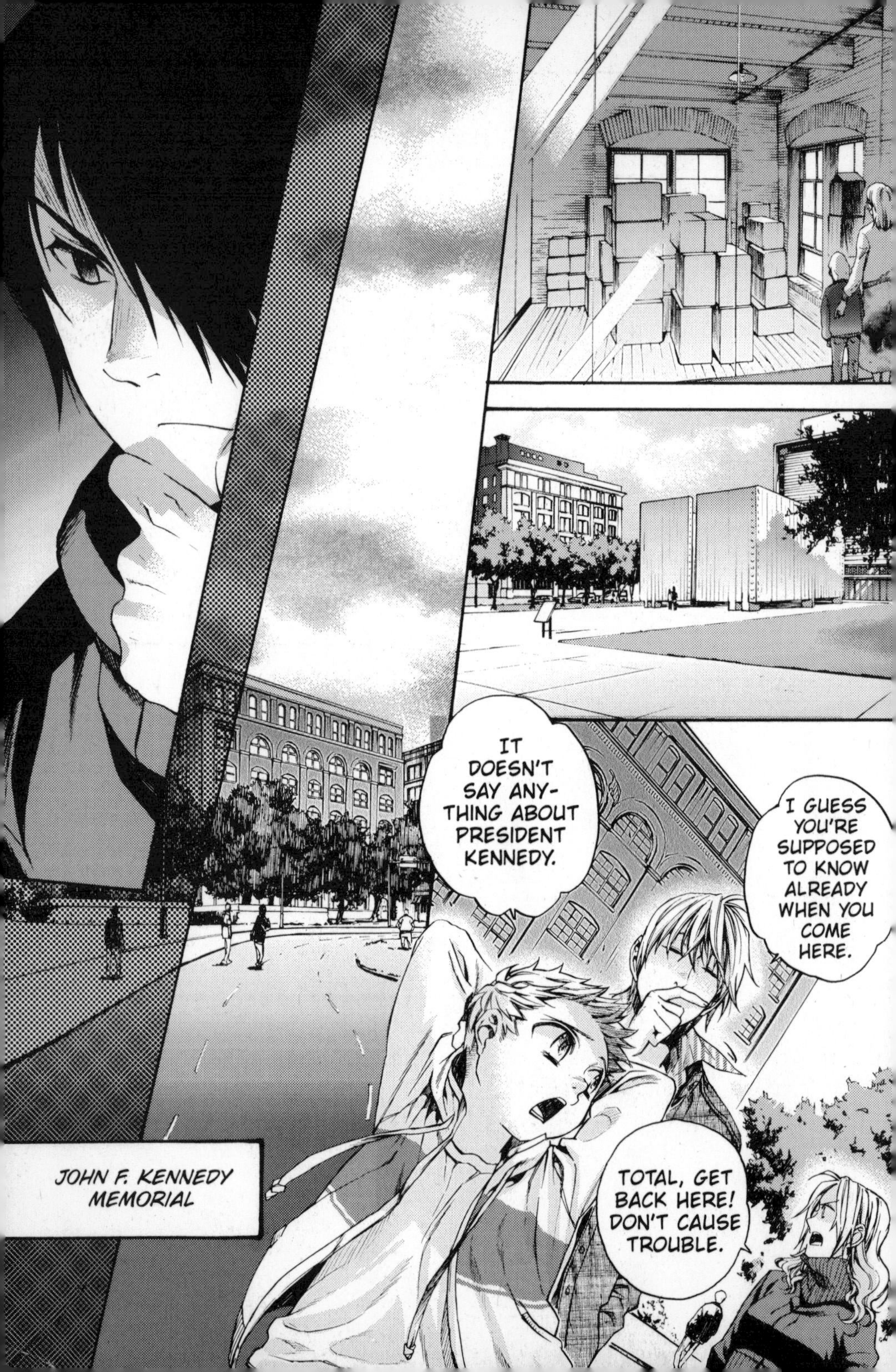
JOHN F. KENNEDY MEMORIAL
IT DOESN'T SAY ANYTHING ABOUT PRESIDENT KENNEDY.
I GUESS YOU'RE SUPPOSED TO KNOW ALREADY WHEN YOU COME HERE.
TOTAL, GET BACK HERE! DON'T CAUSE TROUBLE.

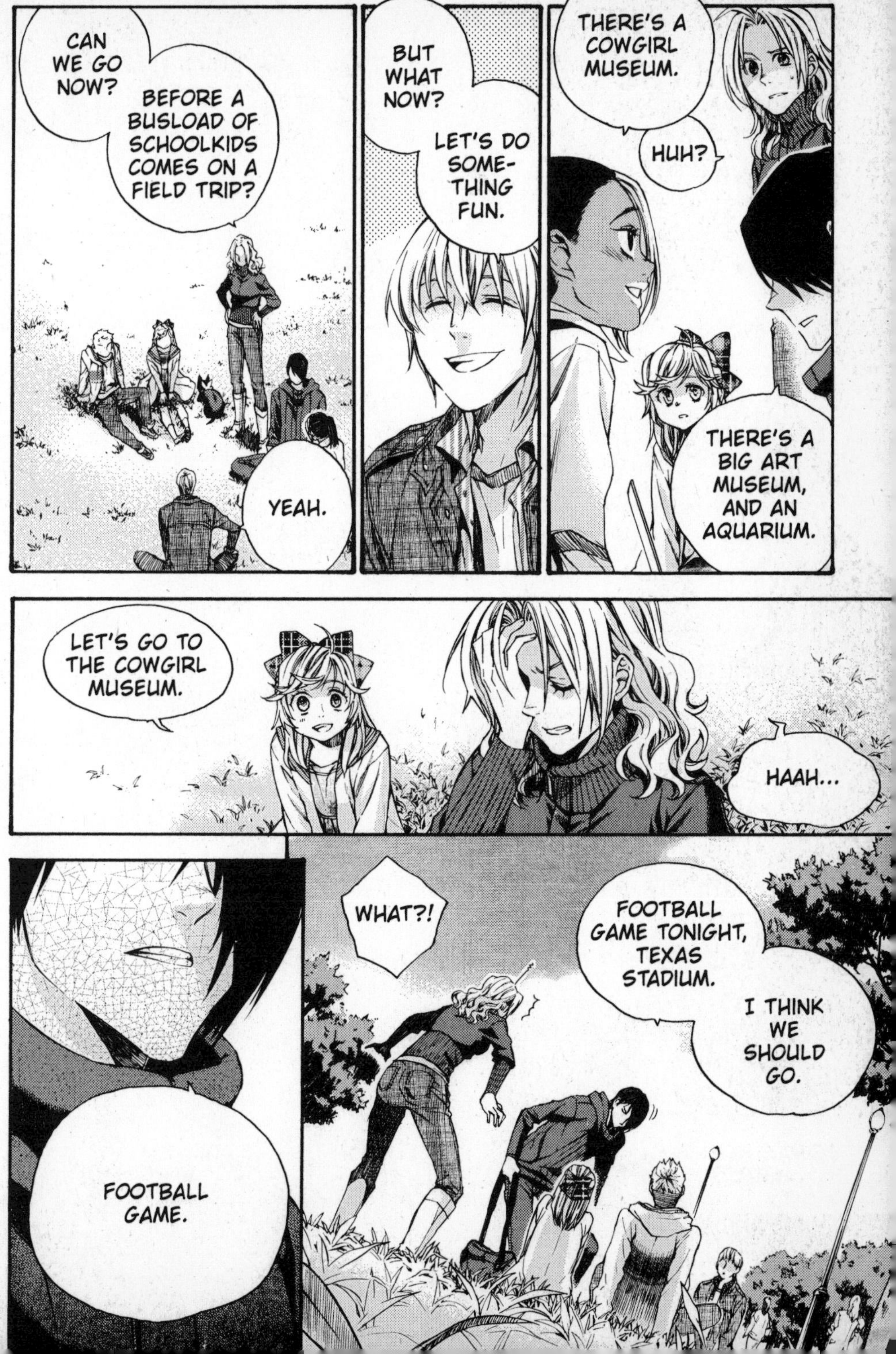
CAN WE GO NOW?
BEFORE A BUSLOAD OF SCHOOLKIDS COMES ON A FIELD TRIP?
YEAH.
BUT WHAT NOW?
LET'S DO SOME-THING FUN.
THERE'S A COWGIRL MUSEUM.
HUH?
THERE'S A BIG ART MUSEUM, AND AN AQUARIUM.
LET'S GO TO THE COWGIRL MUSEUM.
HAAH...
FOOTBALL GAME.
WHAT?!
FOOTBALL GAME TONIGHT, TEXAS STADIUM.
I THINK WE SHOULD GO.

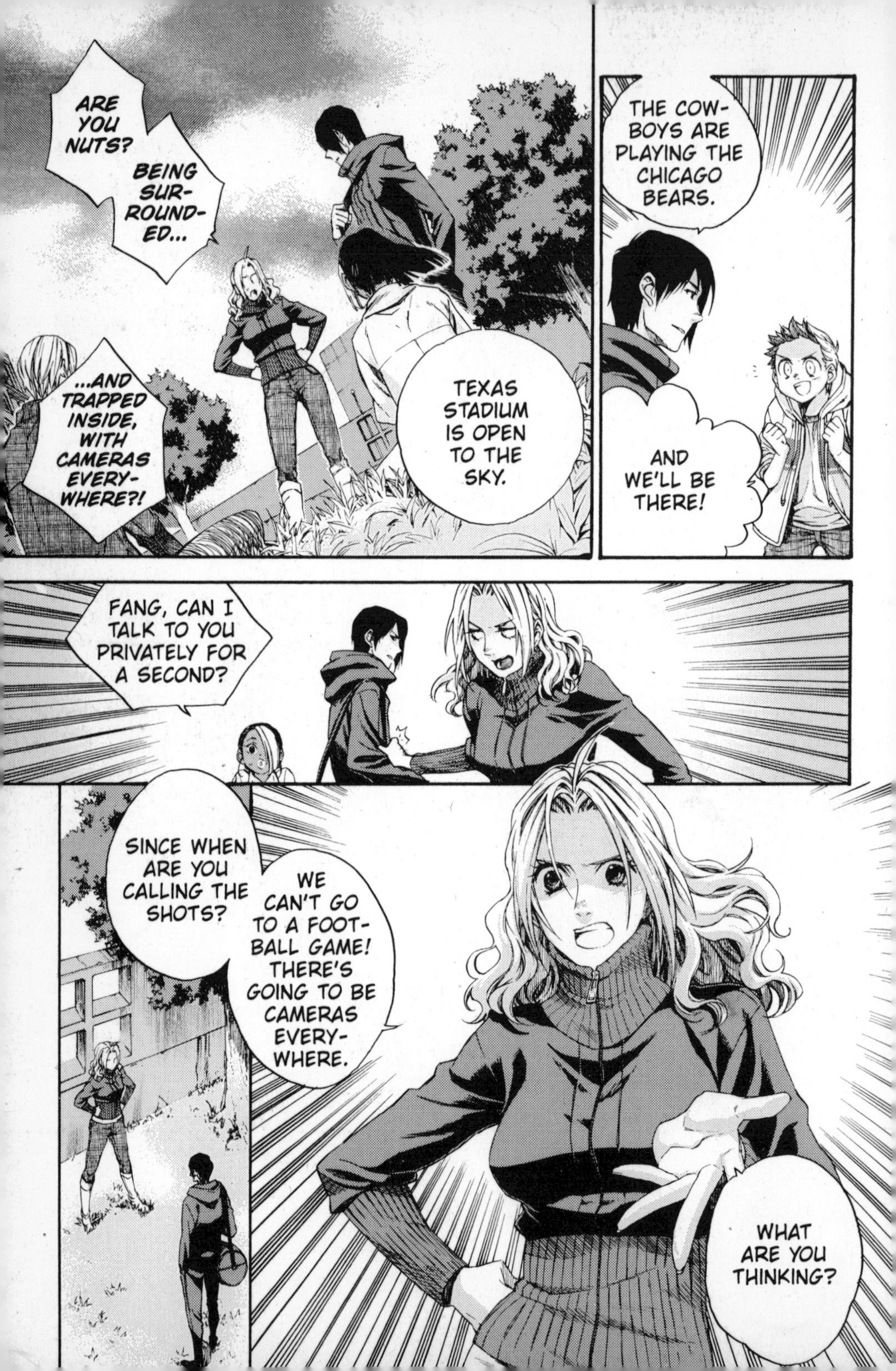

ARE YOU NUTS?
BEING SURROUNDED...
...AND TRAPPED INSIDE, WITH CAMERAS EVERYWHERE?!
TEXAS STADIUM IS OPEN TO THE SKY.
THE COWBOYS ARE PLAYING THE CHICAGO BEARS.
AND WE'LL BE THERE!
FANG, CAN I TALK TO YOU PRIVATELY FOR A SECOND?
SINCE WHEN ARE YOU CALLING THE SHOTS?
WE CAN'T GO TO A FOOTBALL GAME! THERE'S GOING TO BE CAMERAS EVERYWHERE.
WHAT ARE YOU THINKING?

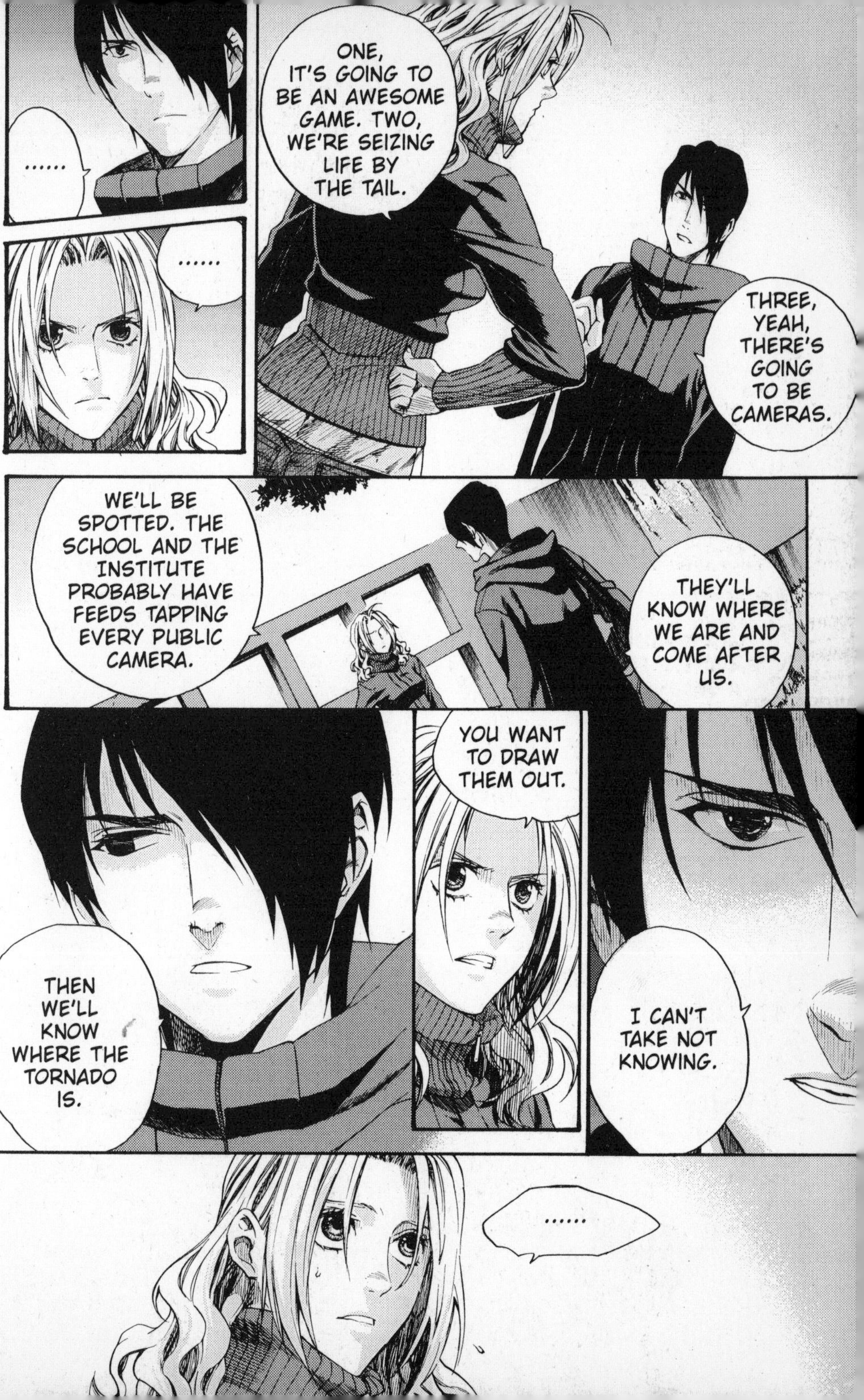
......
......
ONE, IT'S GOING TO BE AN AWESOME GAME. TWO, WE'RE SEIZING LIFE BY THE TAIL.
THREE, YEAH, THERE'S GOING TO BE CAMERAS.
WE'LL BE SPOTTED. THE SCHOOL AND THE INSTITUTE PROBABLY HAVE FEEDS TAPPING EVERY PUBLIC CAMERA.
THEY'LL KNOW WHERE WE ARE AND COME AFTER US.
THEN WE'LL KNOW WHERE THE TORNADO IS.
YOU WANT TO DRAW THEM OUT.
I CAN'T TAKE NOT KNOWING.
......

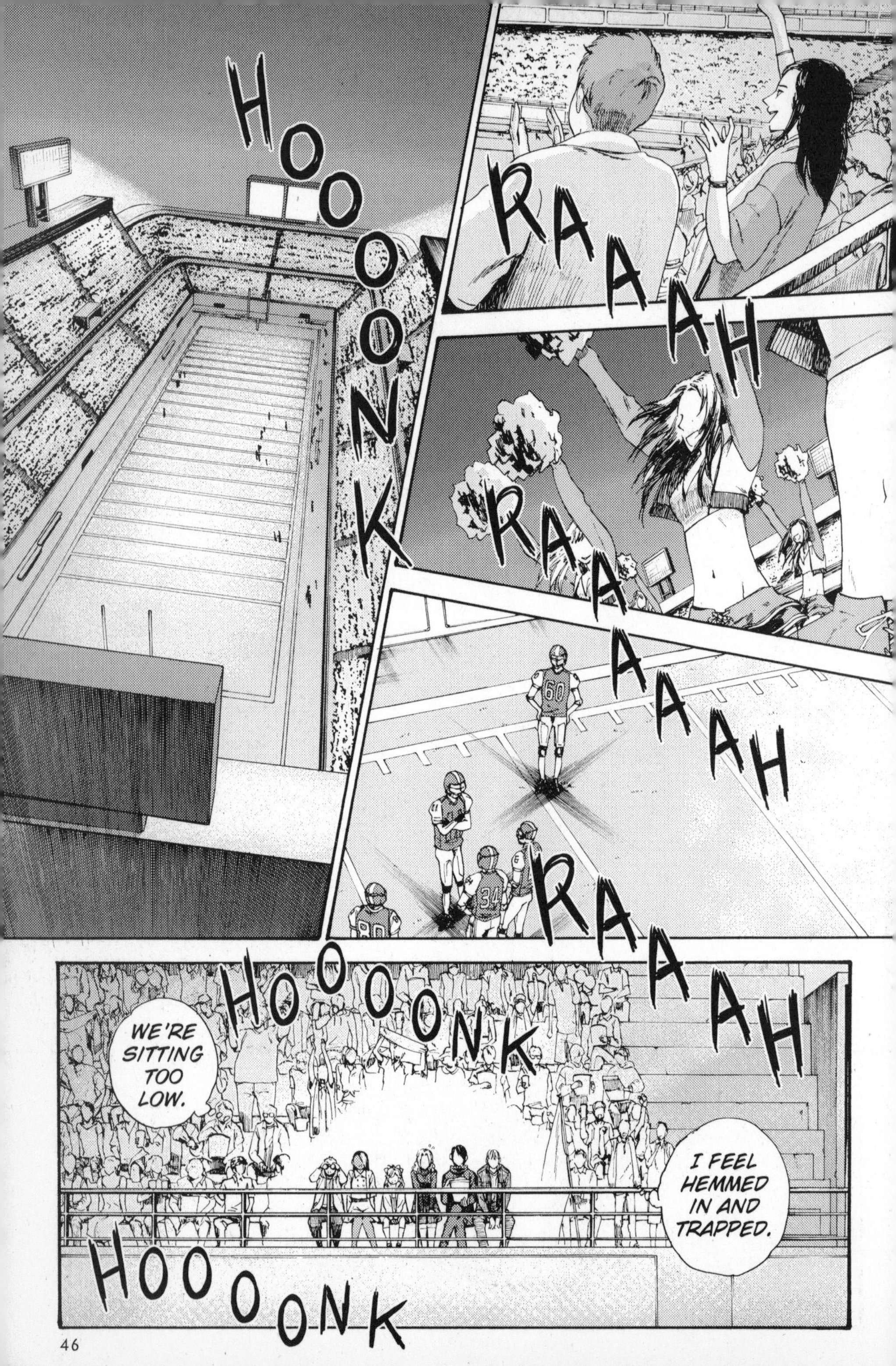
HOOOOONK
RAAH
RAAAAH
RAAAH
HOOOONK
WE'RE SITTING TOO LOW.
I FEEL HEMMED IN AND TRAPPED.
HOOOONK

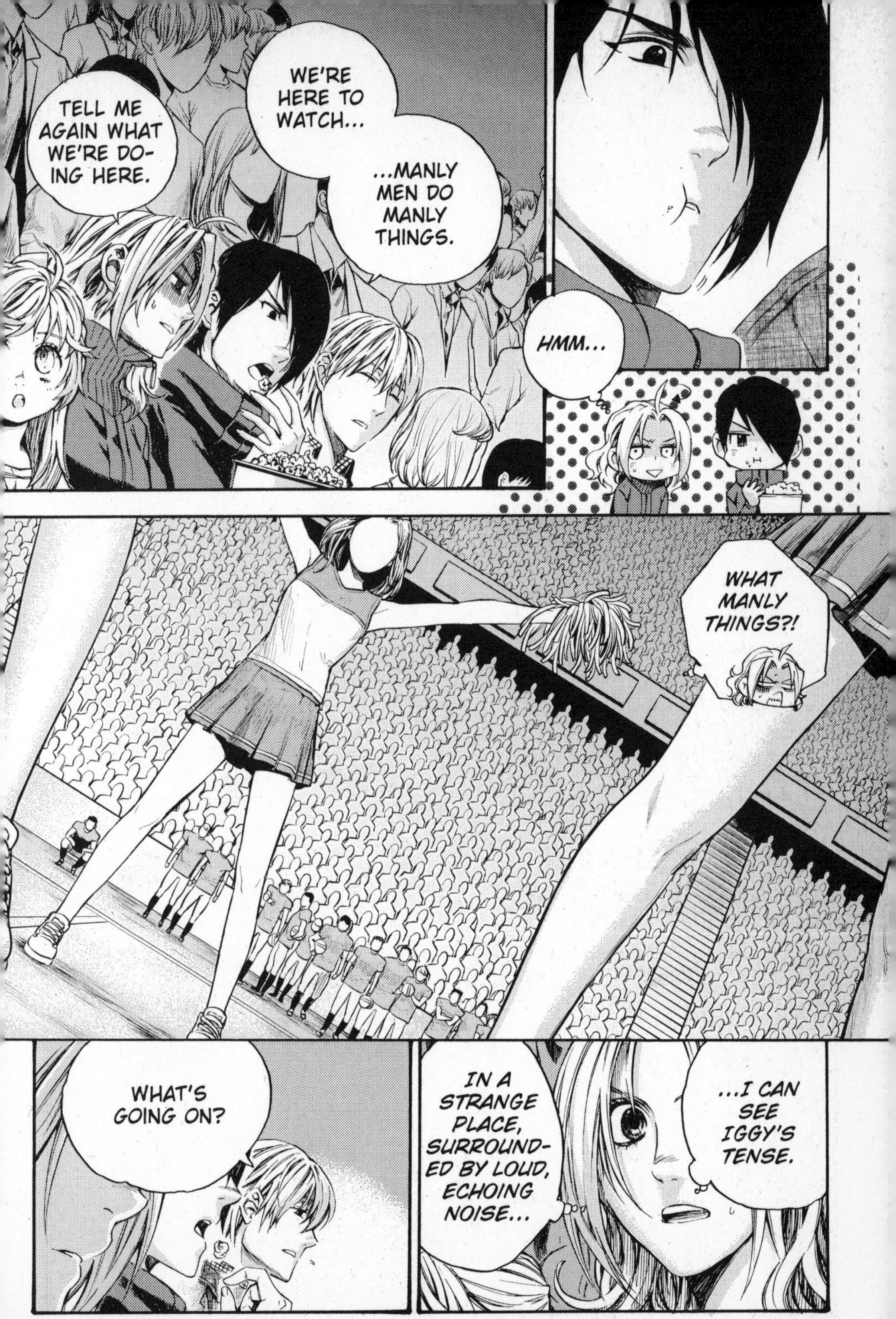
TELL ME AGAIN WHAT WE'RE DO-ING HERE.
WE'RE HERE TO WATCH...
...MANLY MEN DO MANLY THINGS.
HMM...
WHAT MANLY THINGS?!
WHAT'S GOING ON?
IN A STRANGE PLACE, SURROUND-ED BY LOUD, ECHOING NOISE...
...I CAN SEE IGGY'S TENSE.

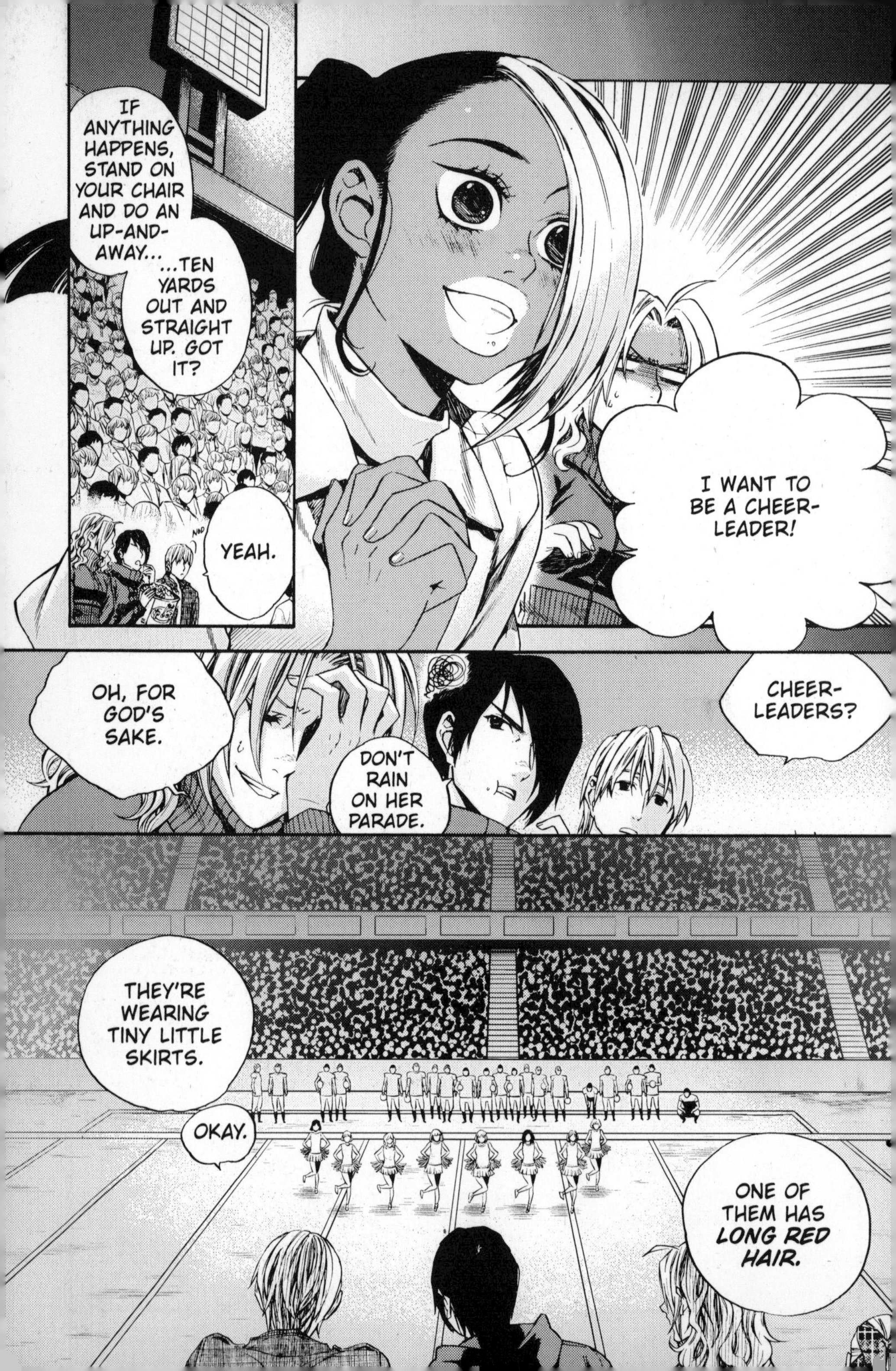
IF ANYTHING HAPPENS, STAND ON YOUR CHAIR AND DO AN UP-AND-AWAY...
...TEN YARDS OUT AND STRAIGHT UP. GOT IT?
NOD
YEAH.
I WANT TO BE A CHEER-LEADER!
OH, FOR GOD'S SAKE.
DON'T RAIN ON HER PARADE.
CHEER-LEADERS?
THEY'RE WEARING TINY LITTLE SKIRTS.
OKAY.
ONE OF THEM HAS *LONG RED HAIR.*

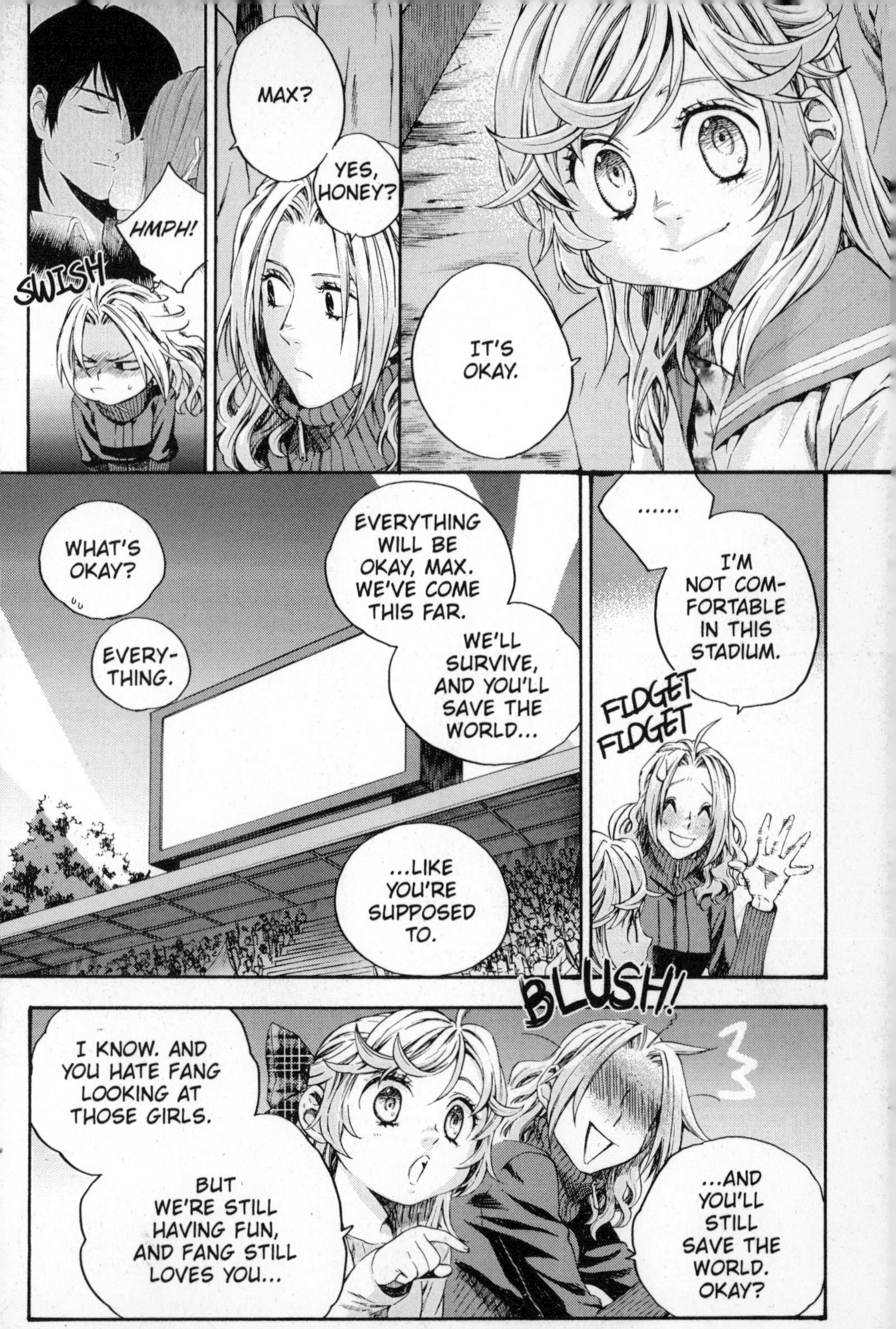

MAX?
YES, HONEY?
HMPH!
SWISH
IT'S OKAY.
WHAT'S OKAY?
EVERY-THING.
EVERYTHING WILL BE OKAY, MAX. WE'VE COME THIS FAR.
WE'LL SURVIVE, AND YOU'LL SAVE THE WORLD...
...LIKE YOU'RE SUPPOSED TO.
......
I'M NOT COM-FORTABLE IN THIS STADIUM.
FIDGET FIDGET
BLUSH!
I KNOW. AND YOU HATE FANG LOOKING AT THOSE GIRLS.
BUT WE'RE STILL HAVING FUN, AND FANG STILL LOVES YOU...
...AND YOU'LL STILL SAVE THE WORLD. OKAY?

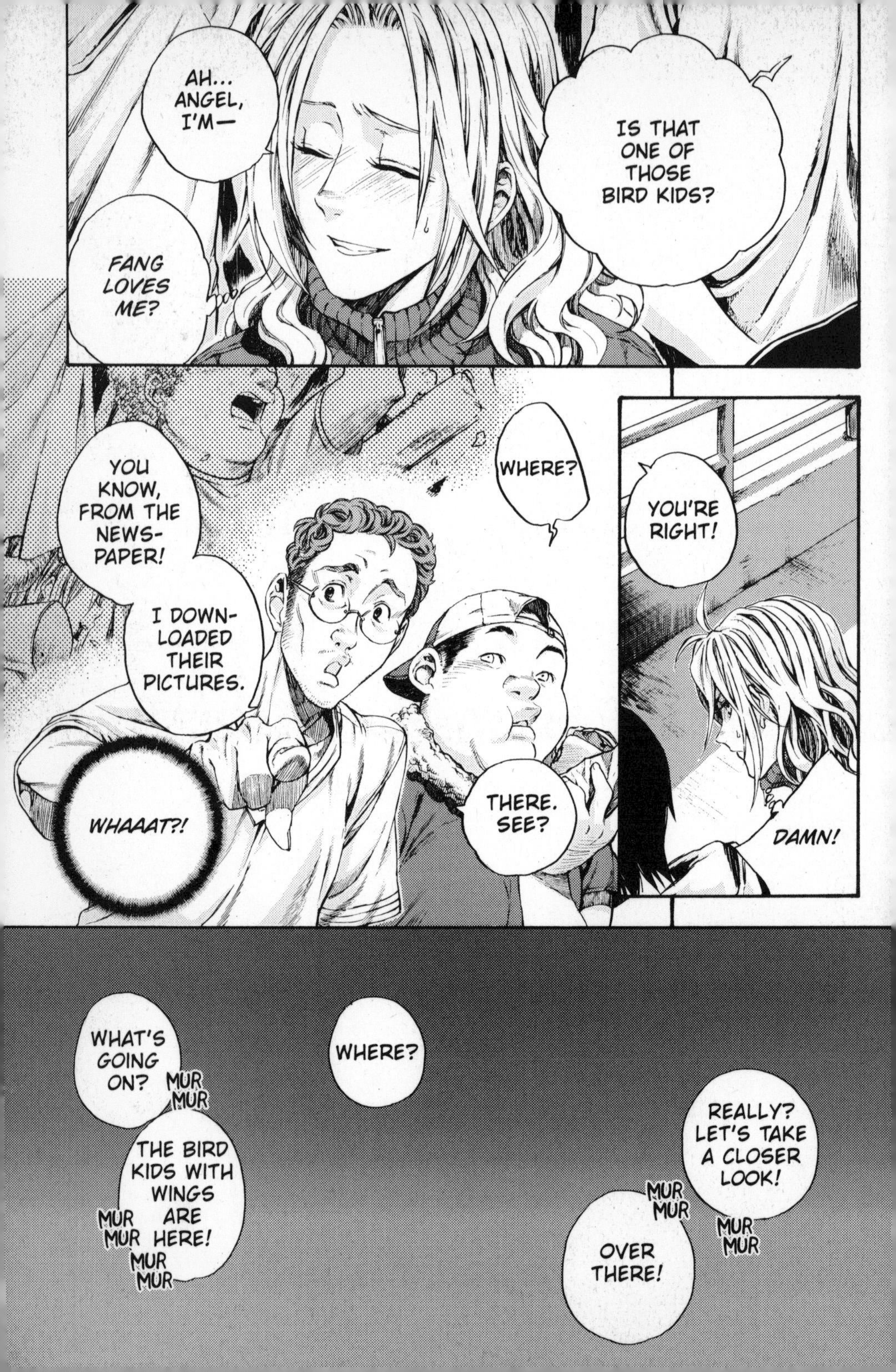

AH... ANGEL, I'M—
FANG LOVES ME?
IS THAT ONE OF THOSE BIRD KIDS?
YOU KNOW, FROM THE NEWS-PAPER!
I DOWN-LOADED THEIR PICTURES.
WHAAAT?!
WHERE?
THERE. SEE?
YOU'RE RIGHT!
DAMN!
WHAT'S GOING ON?
MUR MUR
THE BIRD KIDS WITH WINGS ARE HERE!
MUR MUR
MUR MUR
WHERE?
REALLY? LET'S TAKE A CLOSER LOOK!
MUR MUR
OVER THERE!
MUR MUR

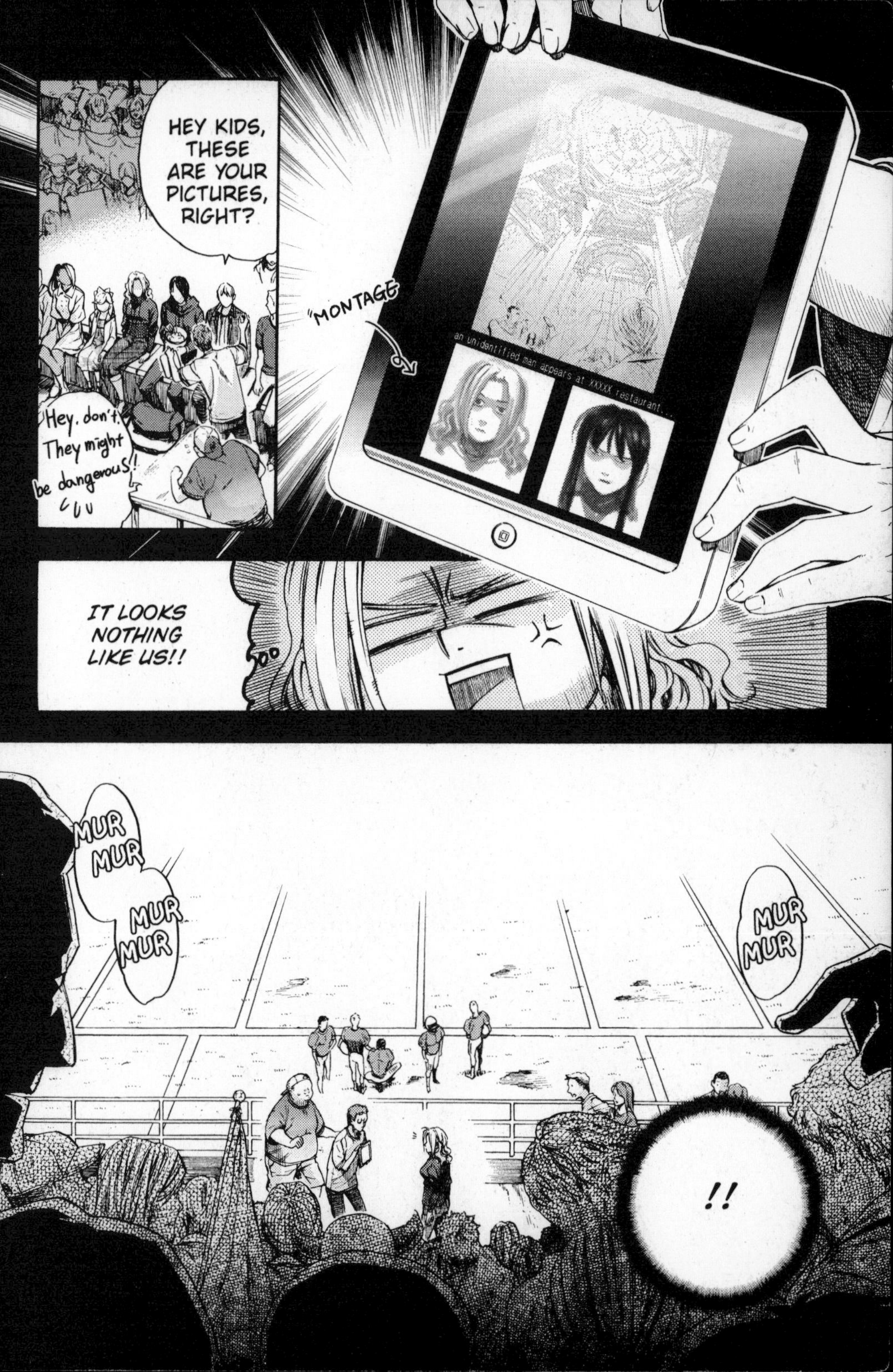
HEY KIDS, THESE ARE YOUR PICTURES, RIGHT?
"MONTAGE
an unidentified man appears at XXXXX restaurant...
Hey, don't. They might be dangerous!!
IT LOOKS NOTHING LIKE US!!
MUR MUR
MUR MUR
MUR MUR
!!

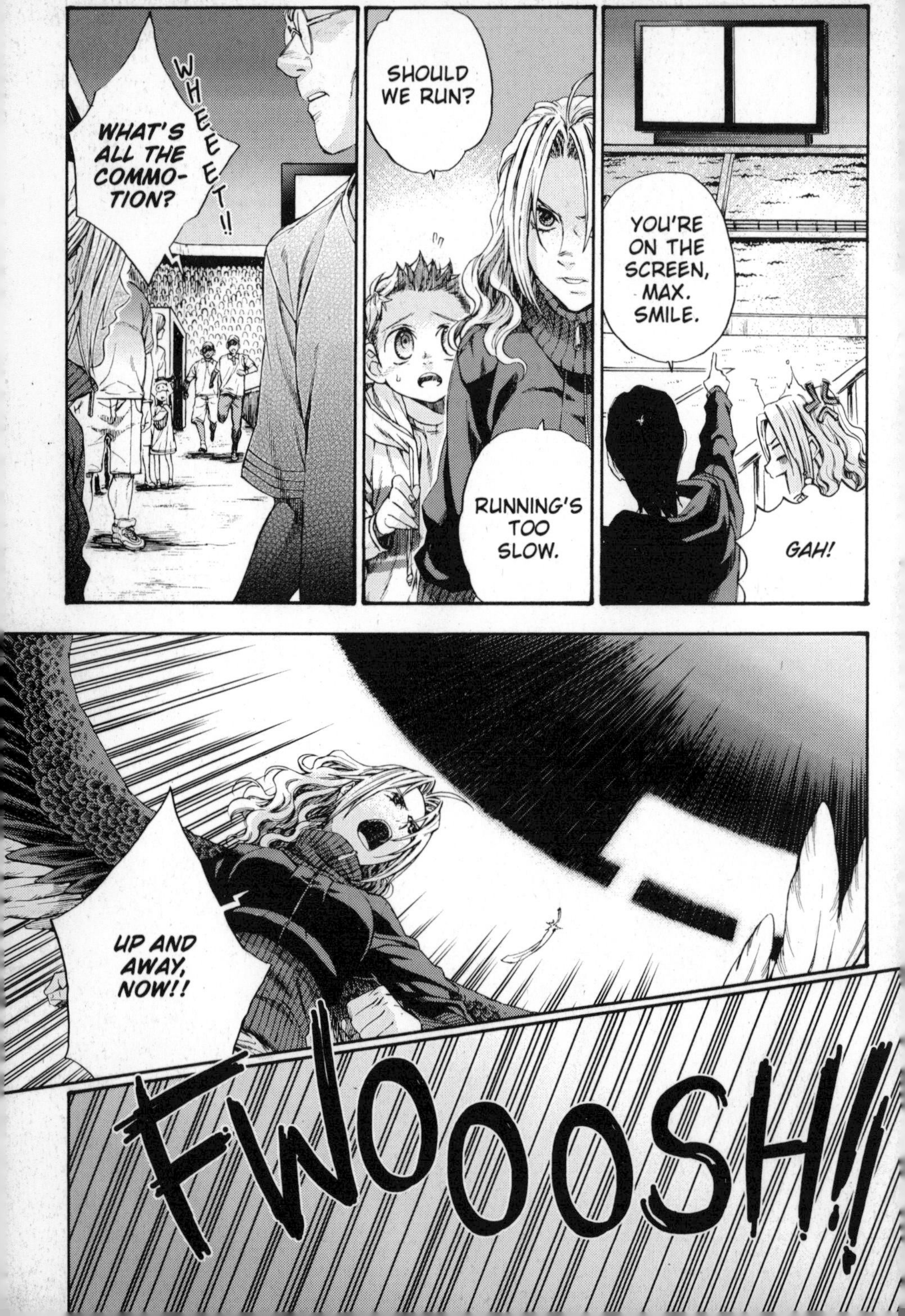
WHAT'S ALL THE COMMOTION?
WHEEEET!!
SHOULD WE RUN?
RUNNING'S TOO SLOW.
YOU'RE ON THE SCREEN, MAX. SMILE.
GAH!
UP AND AWAY, NOW!!
FWOOOSH!!

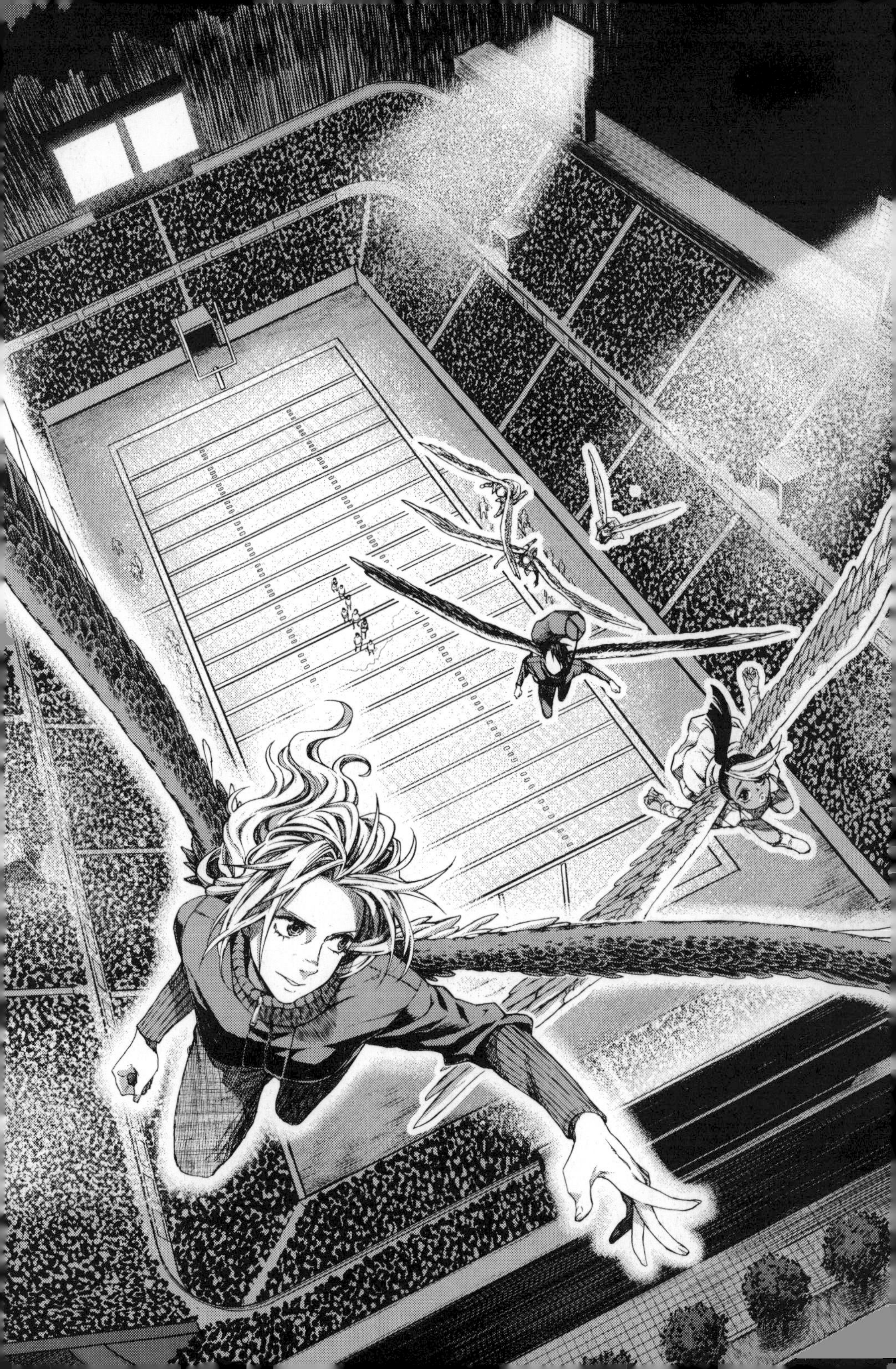

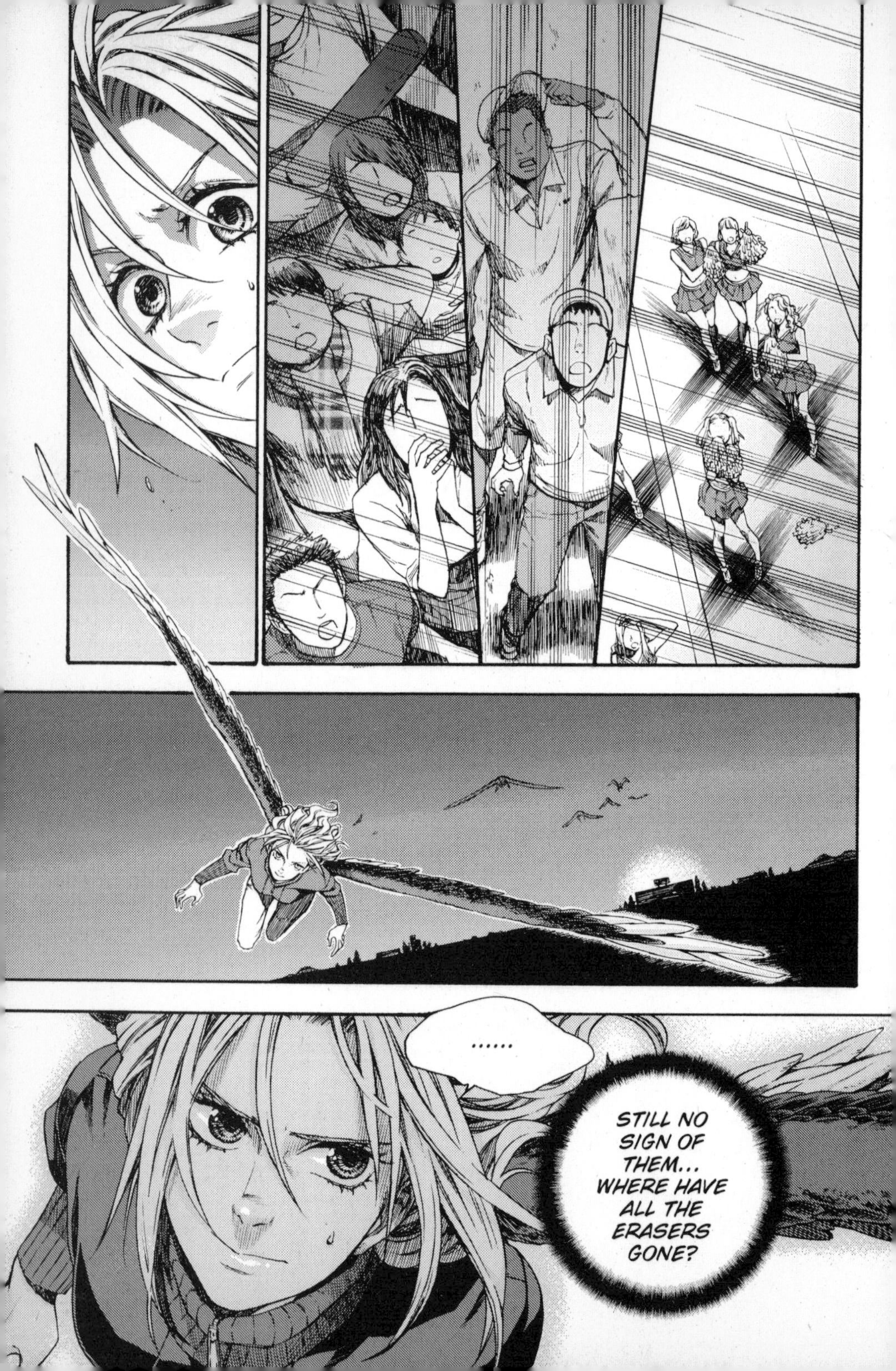
......
STILL NO SIGN OF THEM... WHERE HAVE ALL THE ERASERS GONE?

MAXIMUM
RIDE

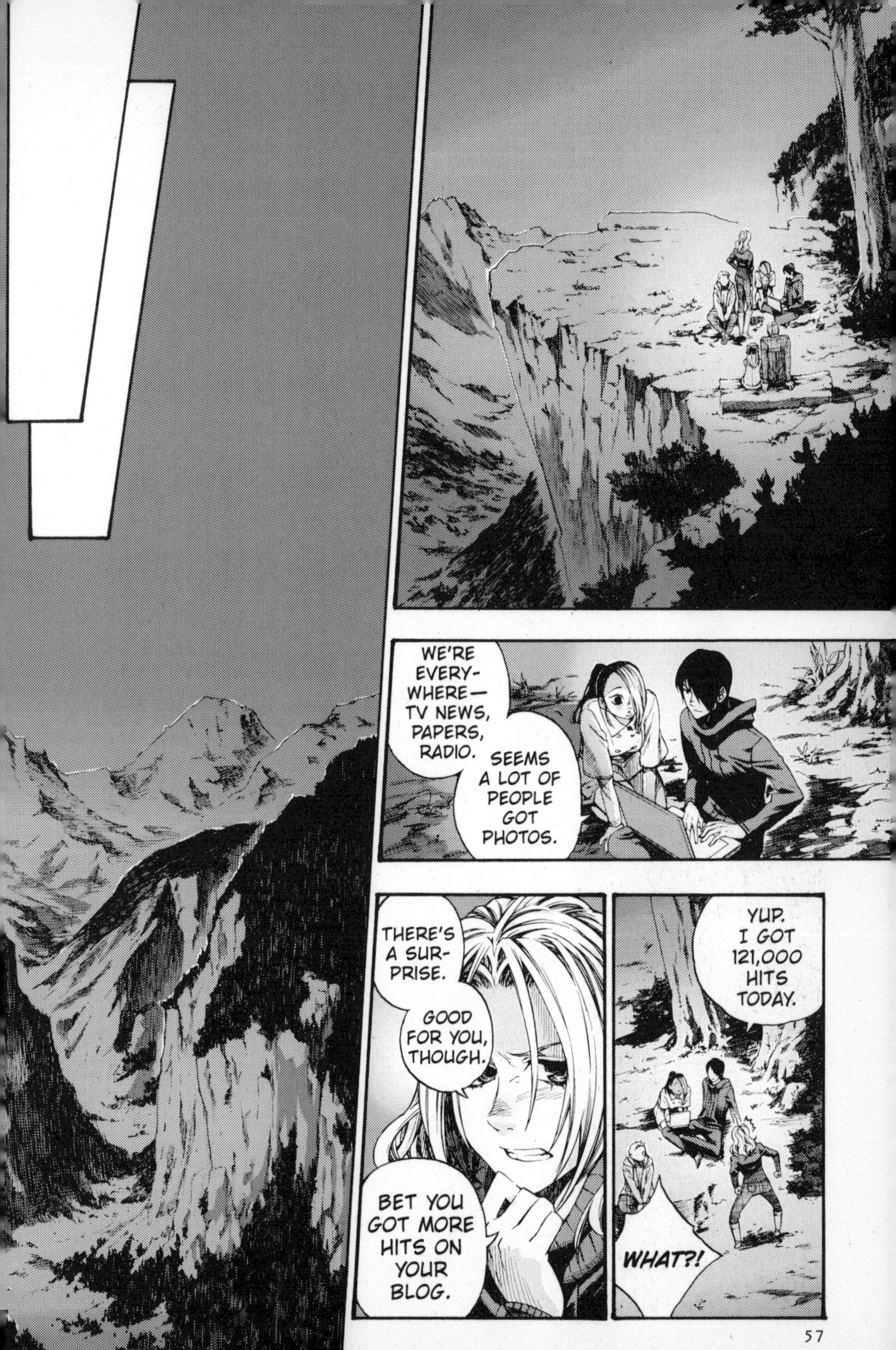
WE'RE EVERY-WHERE— TV NEWS, PAPERS, RADIO.
SEEMS A LOT OF PEOPLE GOT PHOTOS.
THERE'S A SUR-PRISE.
GOOD FOR YOU, THOUGH.
BET YOU GOT MORE HITS ON YOUR BLOG.
YUP. I GOT 121,000 HITS TODAY.
WHAT?!

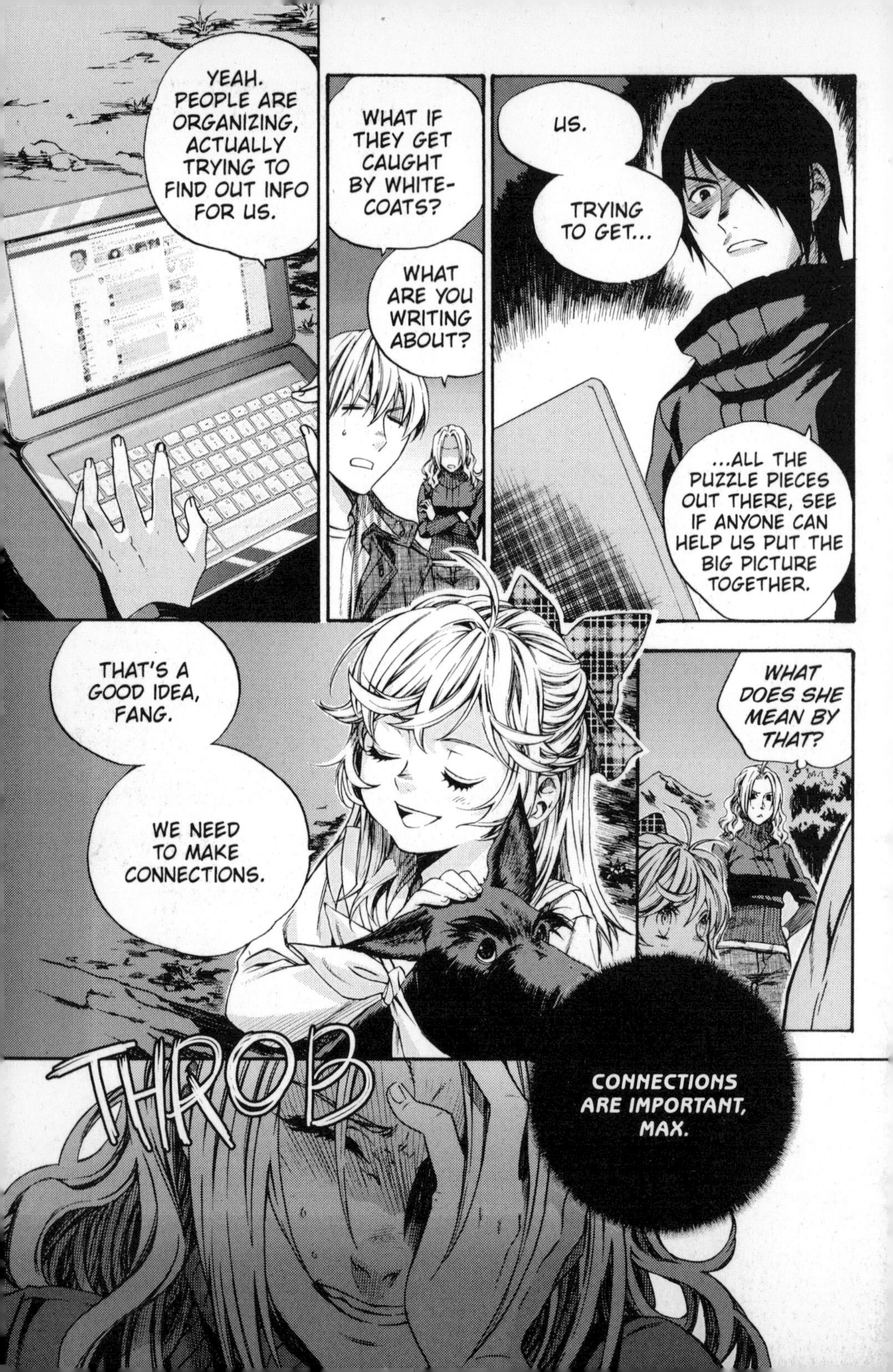
YEAH. PEOPLE ARE ORGANIZING, ACTUALLY TRYING TO FIND OUT INFO FOR US.
WHAT IF THEY GET CAUGHT BY WHITE-COATS?
WHAT ARE YOU WRITING ABOUT?
US.
TRYING TO GET...
...ALL THE PUZZLE PIECES OUT THERE, SEE IF ANYONE CAN HELP US PUT THE BIG PICTURE TOGETHER.
THAT'S A GOOD IDEA, FANG.
WE NEED TO MAKE CONNECTIONS.
WHAT DOES SHE MEAN BY THAT?
THROB
CONNECTIONS ARE IMPORTANT, MAX.

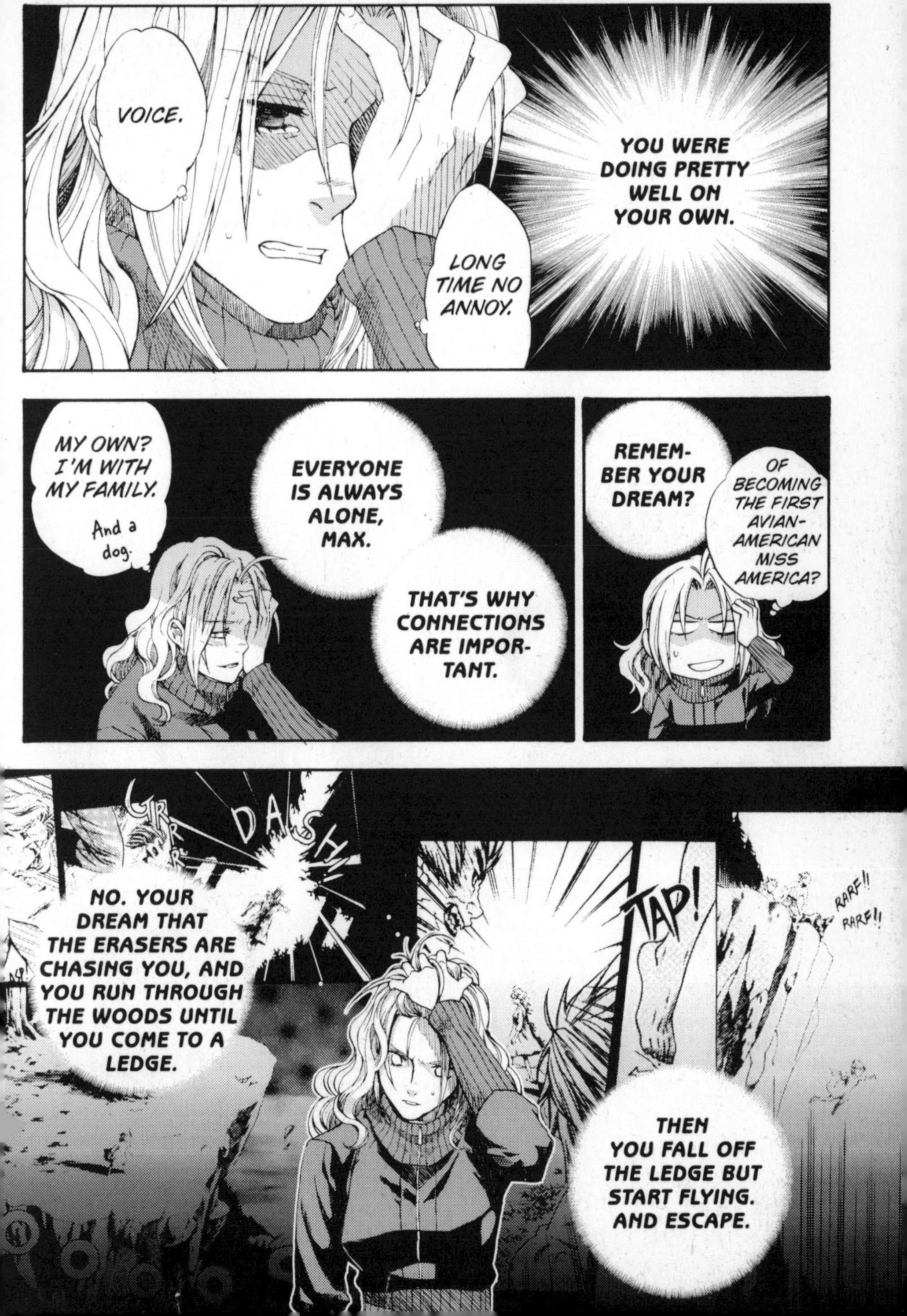
VOICE.
LONG TIME NO ANNOY.
YOU WERE DOING PRETTY WELL ON YOUR OWN.
MY OWN? I'M WITH MY FAMILY.
And a dog.
EVERYONE IS ALWAYS ALONE, MAX.
THAT'S WHY CONNECTIONS ARE IMPORTANT.
REMEMBER YOUR DREAM?
OF BECOMING THE FIRST AVIAN-AMERICAN MISS AMERICA?
DASH
NO. YOUR DREAM THAT THE ERASERS ARE CHASING YOU, AND YOU RUN THROUGH THE WOODS UNTIL YOU COME TO A LEDGE.
TAP!
RARF!!
RARF!!
THEN YOU FALL OFF THE LEDGE BUT START FLYING. AND ESCAPE.

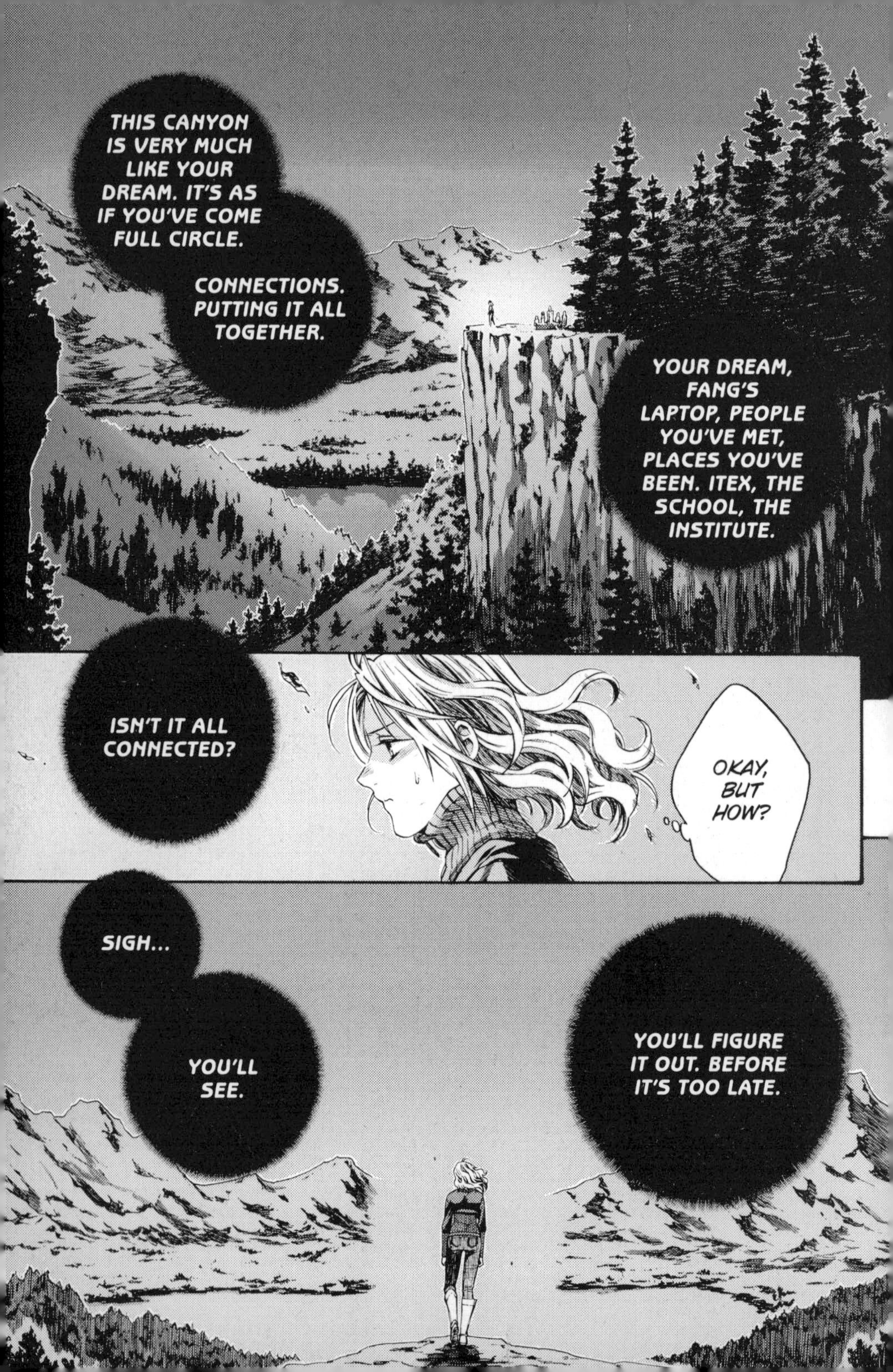
THIS CANYON IS VERY MUCH LIKE YOUR DREAM. IT'S AS IF YOU'VE COME FULL CIRCLE.
CONNECTIONS. PUTTING IT ALL TOGETHER.
YOUR DREAM, FANG'S LAPTOP, PEOPLE YOU'VE MET, PLACES YOU'VE BEEN. ITEX, THE SCHOOL, THE INSTITUTE.
ISN'T IT ALL CONNECTED?
OKAY, BUT HOW?
SIGH...
YOU'LL SEE.
YOU'LL FIGURE IT OUT. BEFORE IT'S TOO LATE.

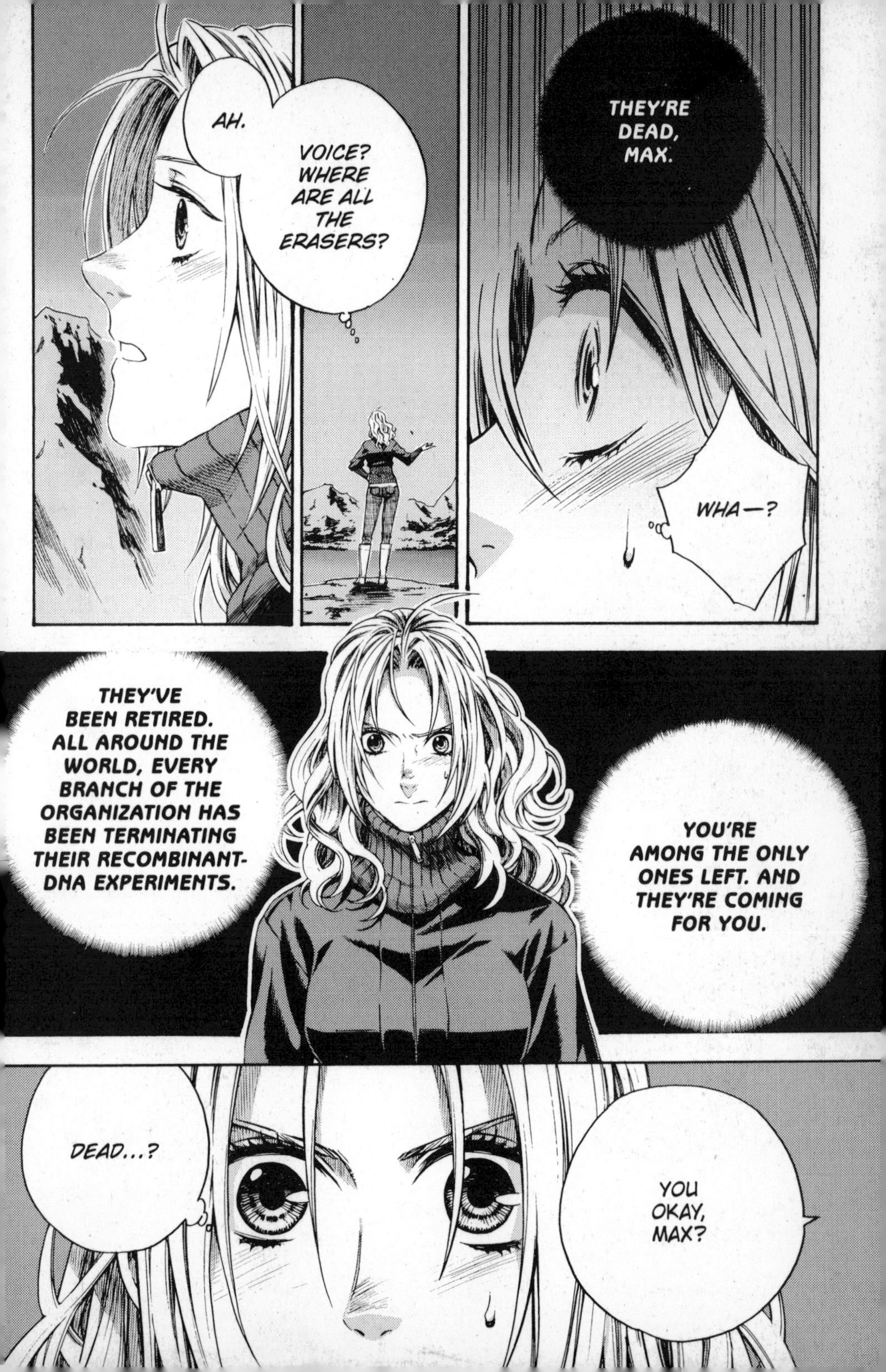
AH.
VOICE? WHERE ARE ALL THE ERASERS?
THEY'RE DEAD, MAX.
WHA—?
THEY'VE BEEN RETIRED. ALL AROUND THE WORLD, EVERY BRANCH OF THE ORGANIZATION HAS BEEN TERMINATING THEIR RECOMBINANT-DNA EXPERIMENTS.
YOU'RE AMONG THE ONLY ONES LEFT. AND THEY'RE COMING FOR YOU.
DEAD...?
YOU OKAY, MAX?

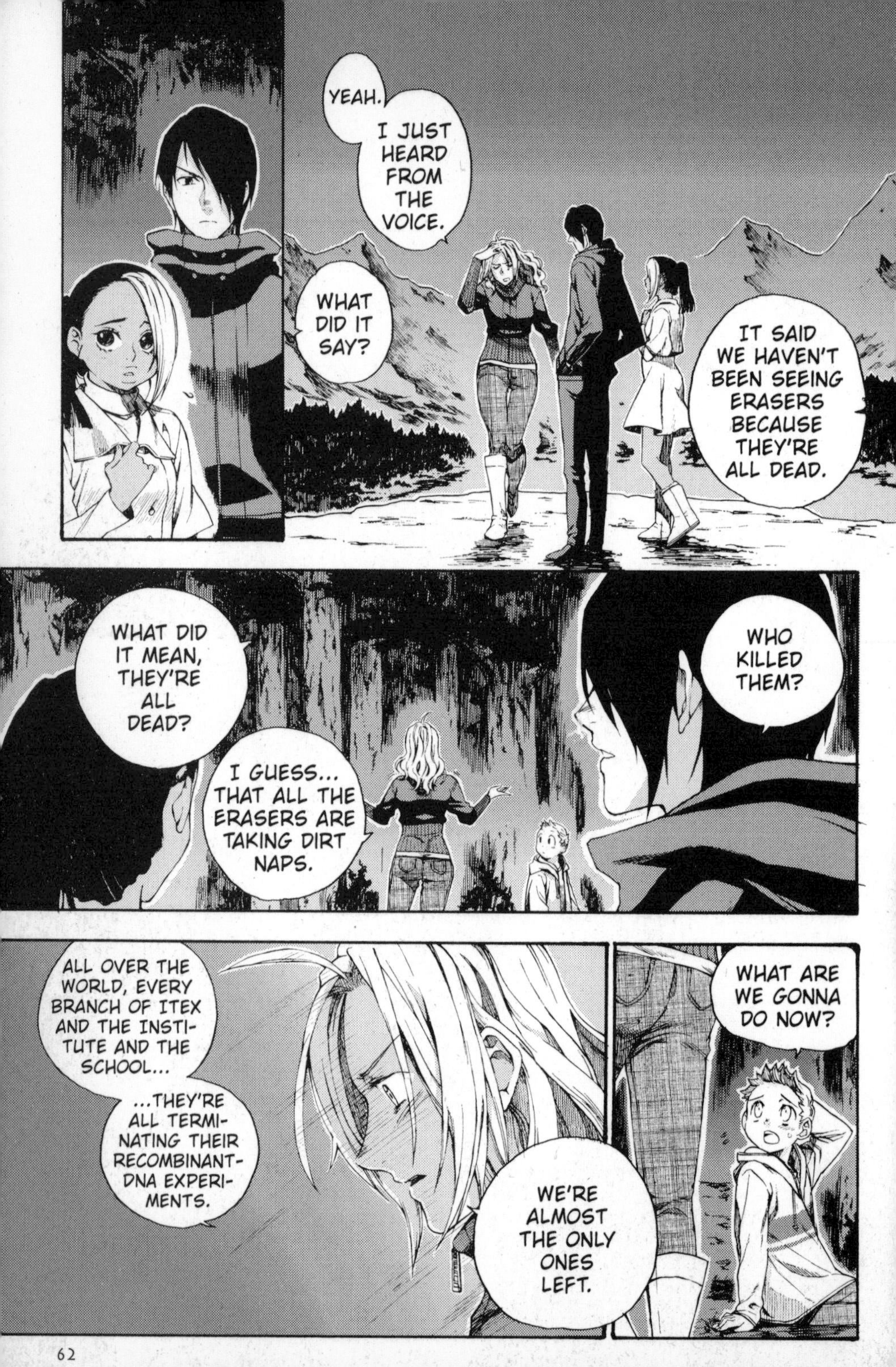
YEAH.
I JUST HEARD FROM THE VOICE.
WHAT DID IT SAY?
IT SAID WE HAVEN'T BEEN SEEING ERASERS BECAUSE THEY'RE ALL DEAD.
WHAT DID IT MEAN, THEY'RE ALL DEAD?
I GUESS... THAT ALL THE ERASERS ARE TAKING DIRT NAPS.
WHO KILLED THEM?
ALL OVER THE WORLD, EVERY BRANCH OF ITEX AND THE INSTI-TUTE AND THE SCHOOL...
...THEY'RE ALL TERMI-NATING THEIR RECOMBINANT-DNA EXPERI-MENTS.
WE'RE ALMOST THE ONLY ONES LEFT.
WHAT ARE WE GONNA DO NOW?

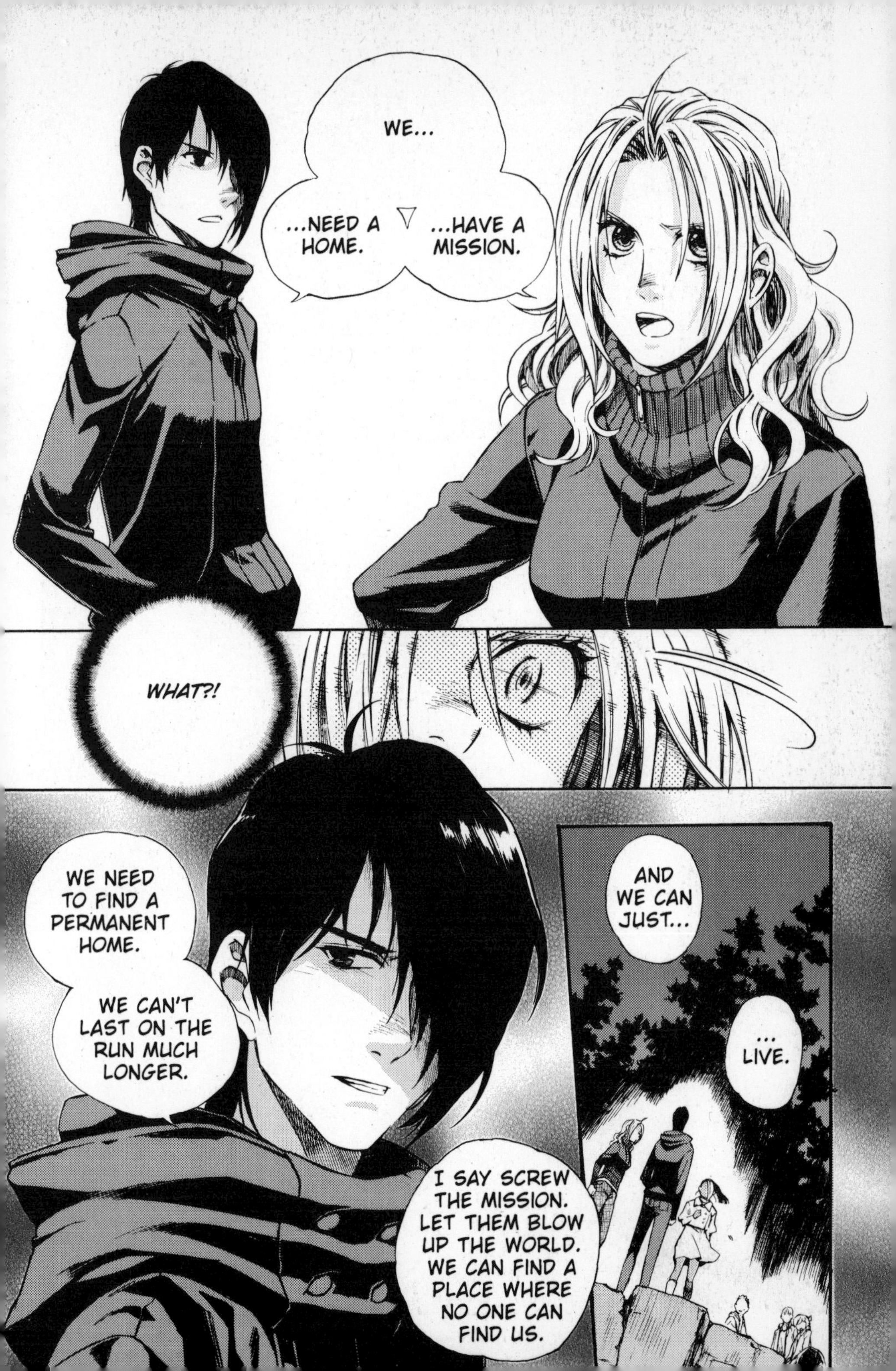
WE...
...NEED A HOME.
...HAVE A MISSION.
WHAT?!
WE NEED TO FIND A PERMANENT HOME.
WE CAN'T LAST ON THE RUN MUCH LONGER.
I SAY SCREW THE MISSION. LET THEM BLOW UP THE WORLD. WE CAN FIND A PLACE WHERE NO ONE CAN FIND US.
AND WE CAN JUST...
...LIVE.

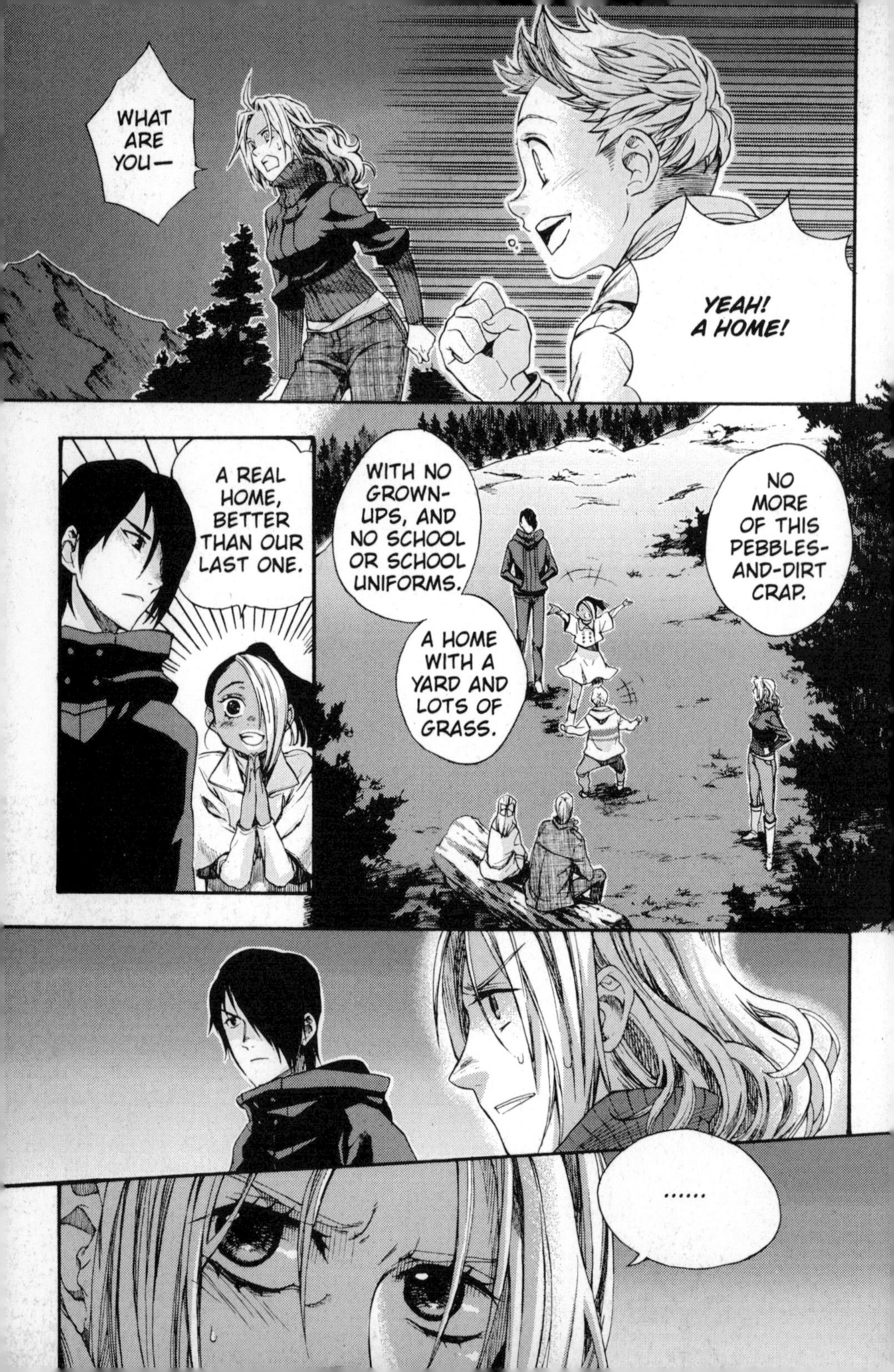

WHAT ARE YOU—
YEAH! A HOME!
A REAL HOME, BETTER THAN OUR LAST ONE.
WITH NO GROWN-UPS, AND NO SCHOOL OR SCHOOL UNIFORMS.
A HOME WITH A YARD AND LOTS OF GRASS.
NO MORE OF THIS PEBBLES-AND-DIRT CRAP.
......

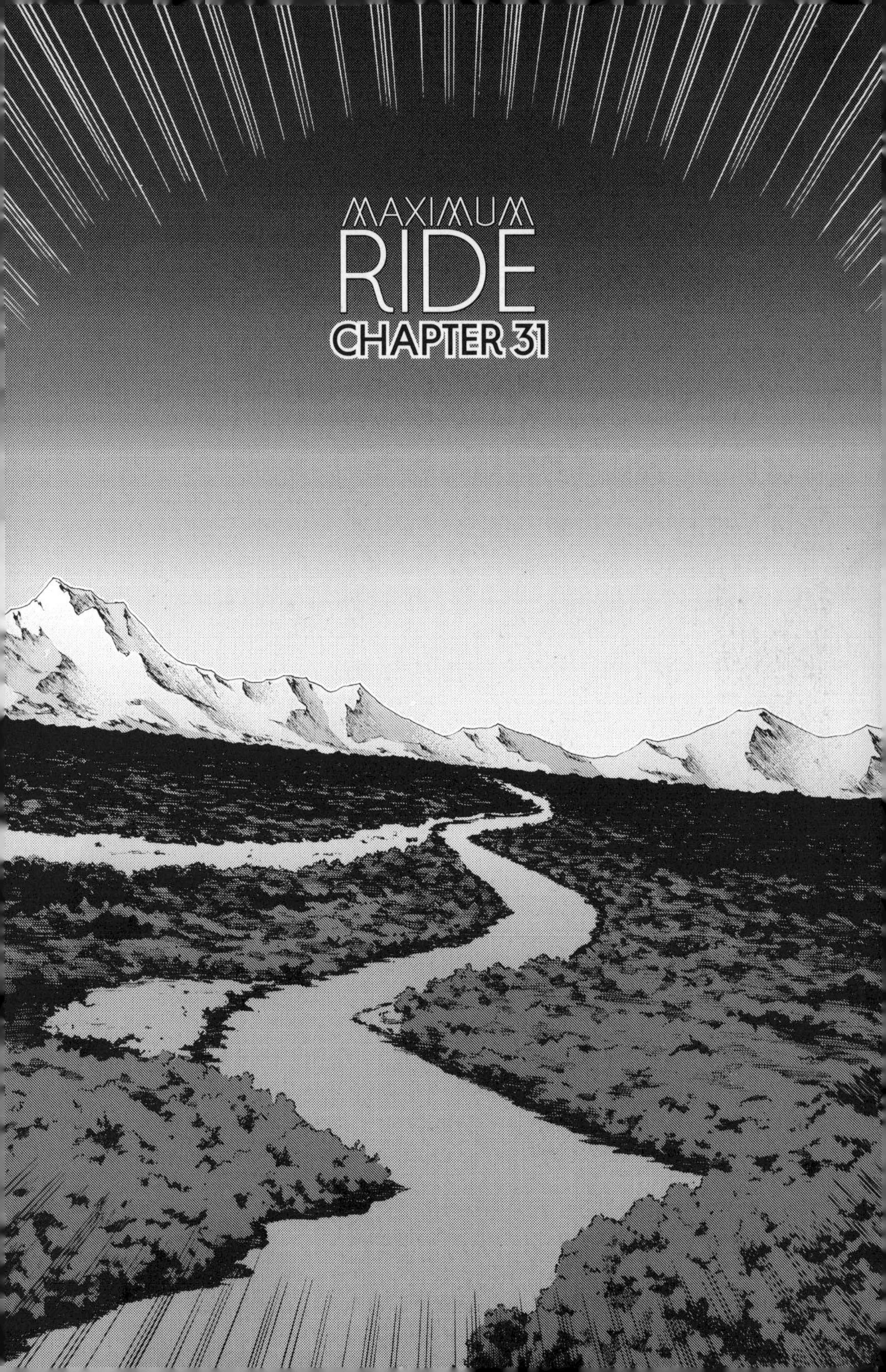
MAXIMUM
RIDE
CHAPTER 31

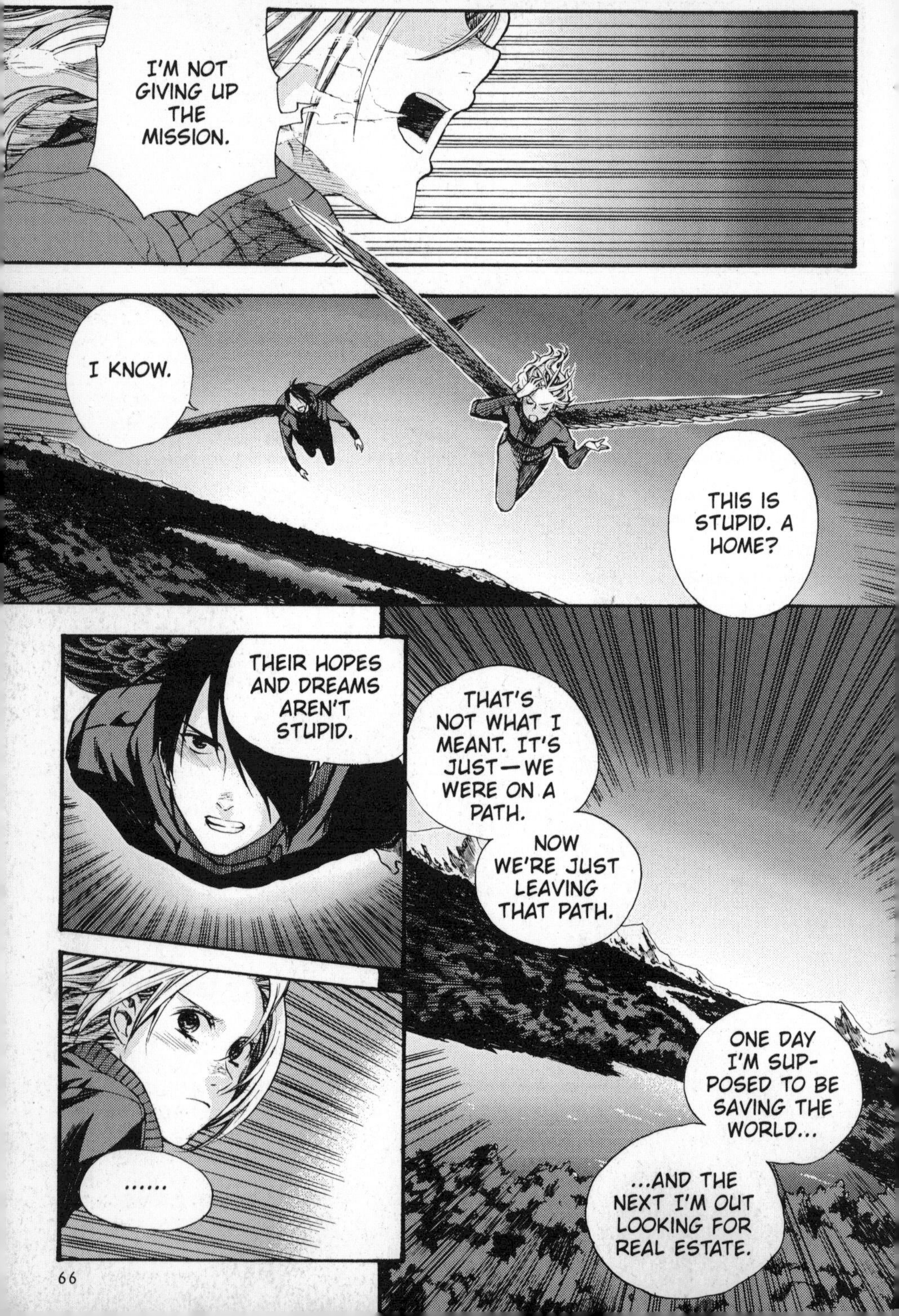
I'M NOT GIVING UP THE MISSION.
I KNOW.
THIS IS STUPID. A HOME?
THEIR HOPES AND DREAMS AREN'T STUPID.
THAT'S NOT WHAT I MEANT. IT'S JUST—WE WERE ON A PATH.
NOW WE'RE JUST LEAVING THAT PATH.
......
ONE DAY I'M SUP-POSED TO BE SAVING THE WORLD...
...AND THE NEXT I'M OUT LOOKING FOR REAL ESTATE.

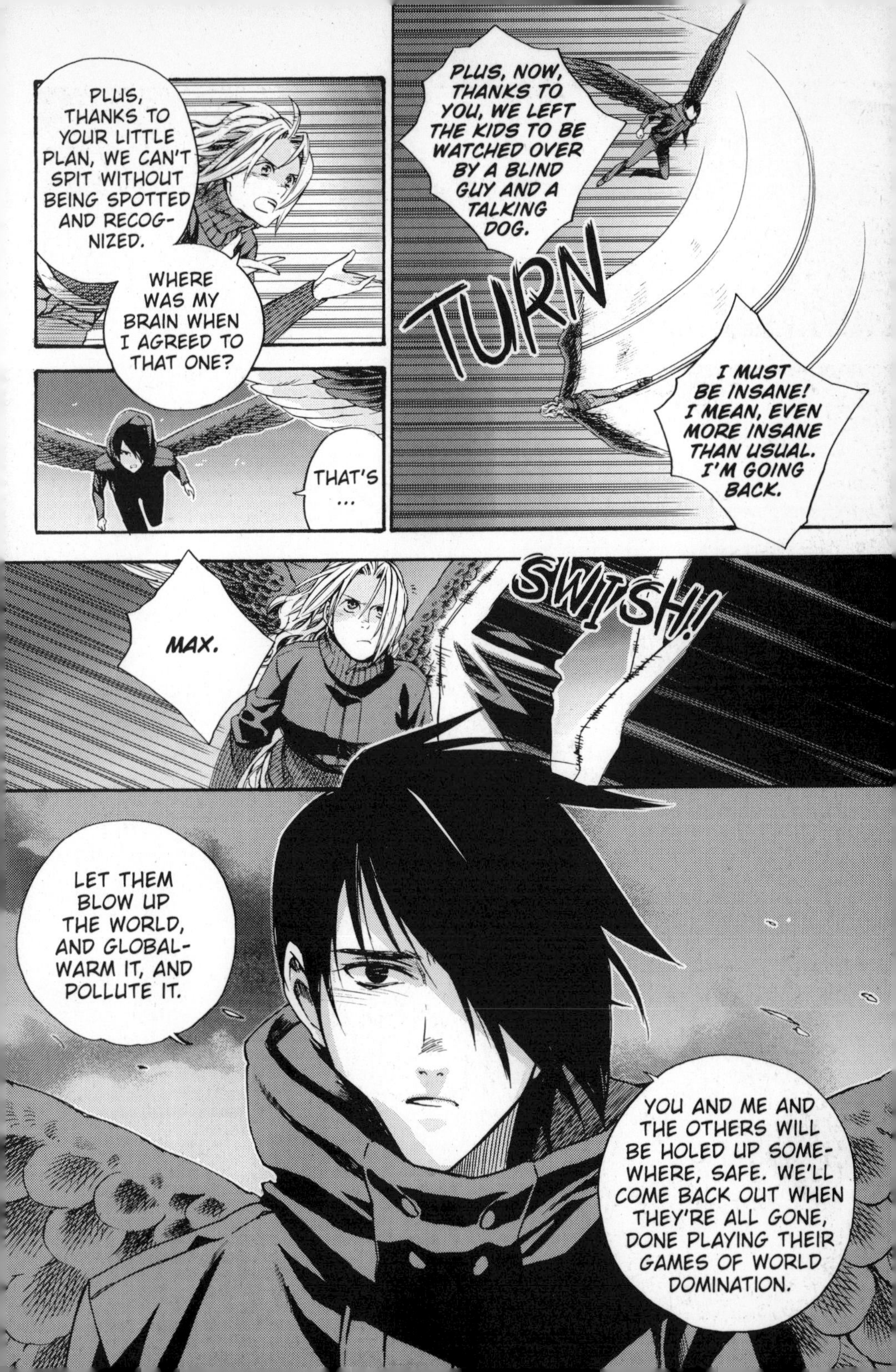
PLUS, THANKS TO YOUR LITTLE PLAN, WE CAN'T SPIT WITHOUT BEING SPOTTED AND RECOG-NIZED.
WHERE WAS MY BRAIN WHEN I AGREED TO THAT ONE?
THAT'S ...
PLUS, NOW, THANKS TO YOU, WE LEFT THE KIDS TO BE WATCHED OVER BY A BLIND GUY AND A TALKING DOG.
TURN
I MUST BE INSANE! I MEAN, EVEN MORE INSANE THAN USUAL. I'M GOING BACK.
MAX.
SWISH!
LET THEM BLOW UP THE WORLD, AND GLOBAL-WARM IT, AND POLLUTE IT.
YOU AND ME AND THE OTHERS WILL BE HOLED UP SOME-WHERE, SAFE. WE'LL COME BACK OUT WHEN THEY'RE ALL GONE, DONE PLAYING THEIR GAMES OF WORLD DOMINATION.

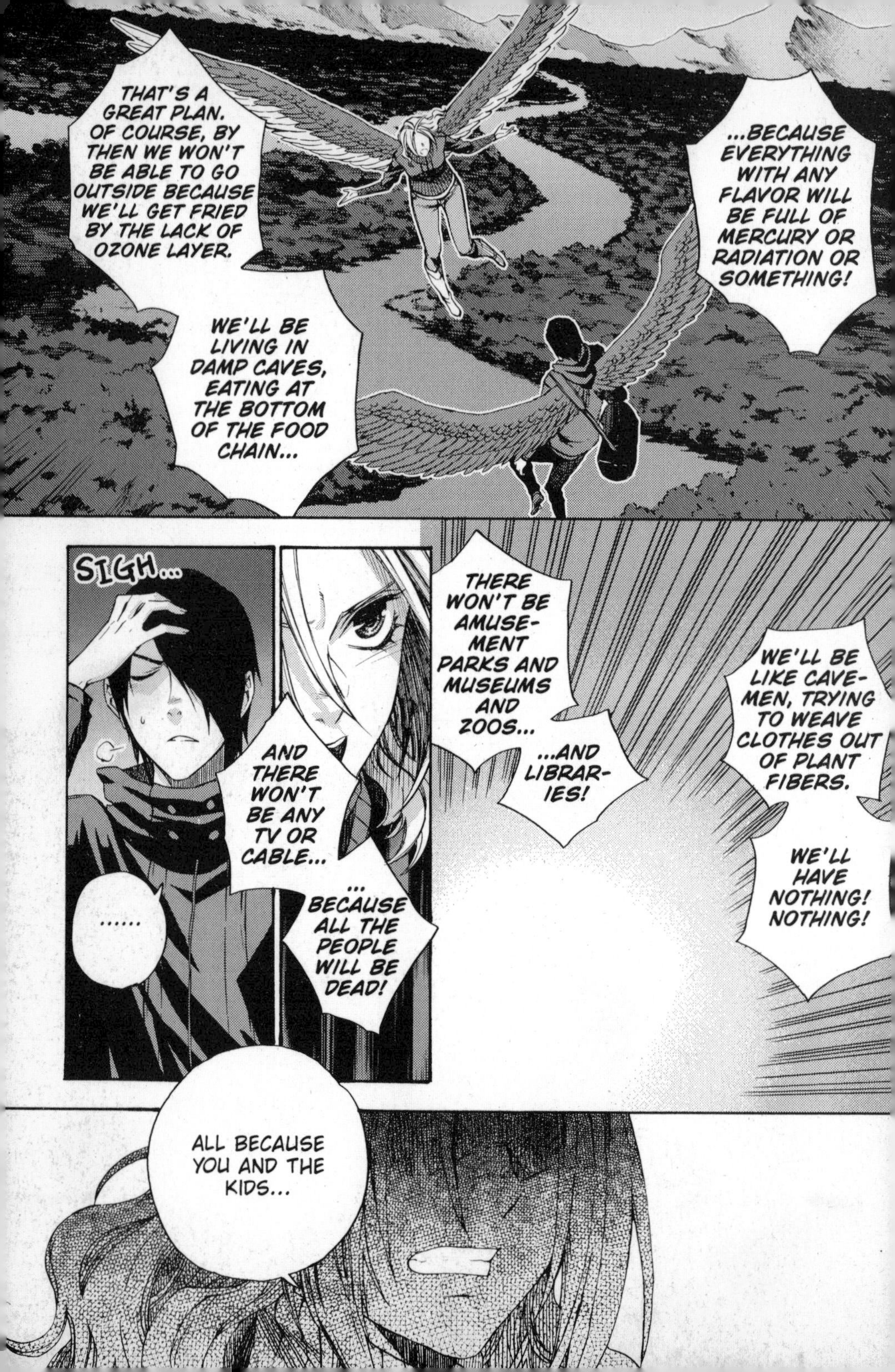
THAT'S A GREAT PLAN. OF COURSE, BY THEN WE WON'T BE ABLE TO GO OUTSIDE BECAUSE WE'LL GET FRIED BY THE LACK OF OZONE LAYER.
WE'LL BE LIVING IN DAMP CAVES, EATING AT THE BOTTOM OF THE FOOD CHAIN...
...BECAUSE EVERYTHING WITH ANY FLAVOR WILL BE FULL OF MERCURY OR RADIATION OR SOMETHING!
SIGH...
......
AND THERE WON'T BE ANY TV OR CABLE...
...BECAUSE ALL THE PEOPLE WILL BE DEAD!
THERE WON'T BE AMUSEMENT PARKS AND MUSEUMS AND ZOOS...
...AND LIBRARIES!
WE'LL BE LIKE CAVEMEN, TRYING TO WEAVE CLOTHES OUT OF PLANT FIBERS.
WE'LL HAVE NOTHING! NOTHING!
ALL BECAUSE YOU AND THE KIDS...

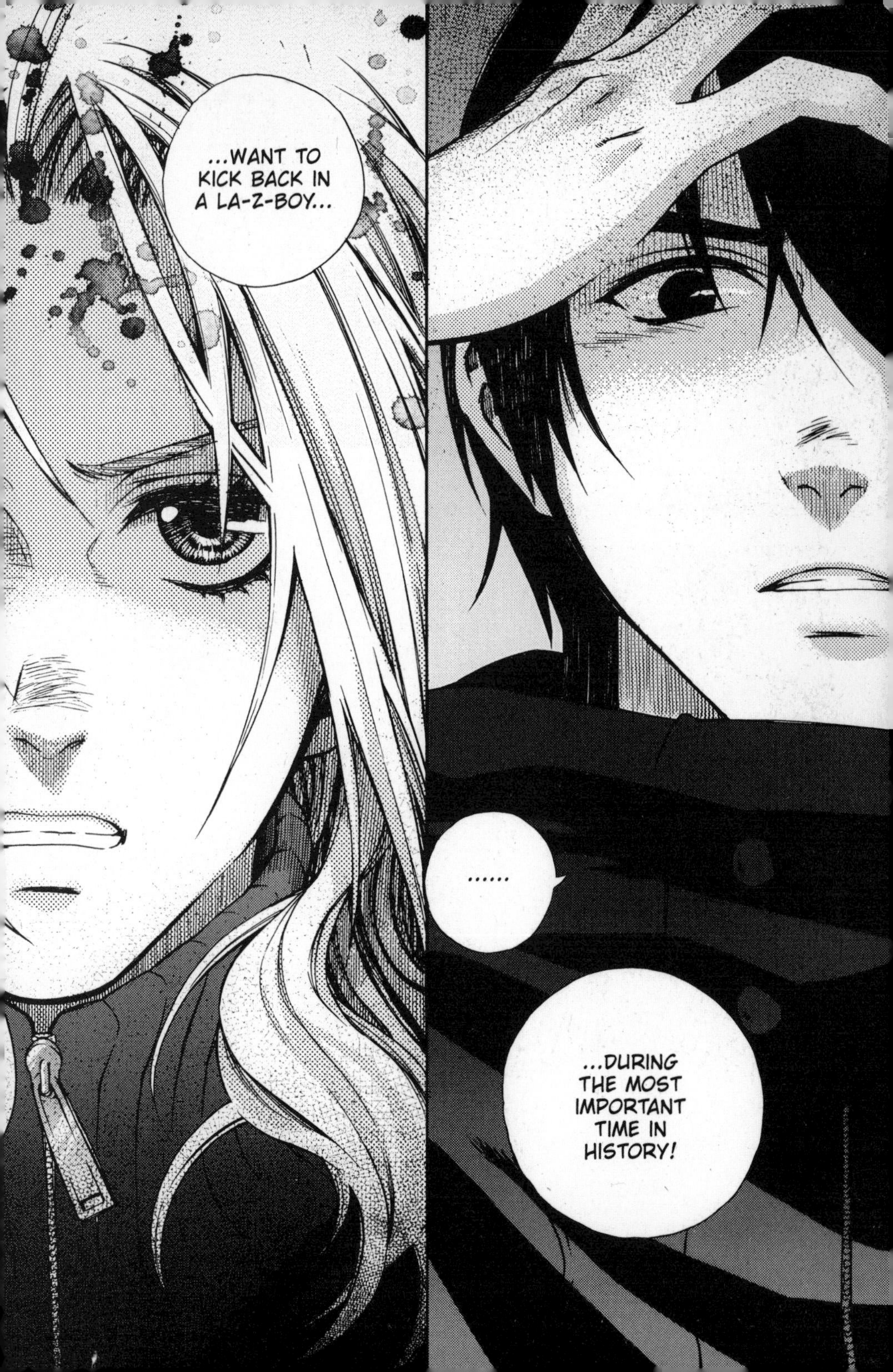

...WANT TO KICK BACK IN A LA-Z-BOY...
......
...DURING THE MOST IMPORTANT TIME IN HISTORY!

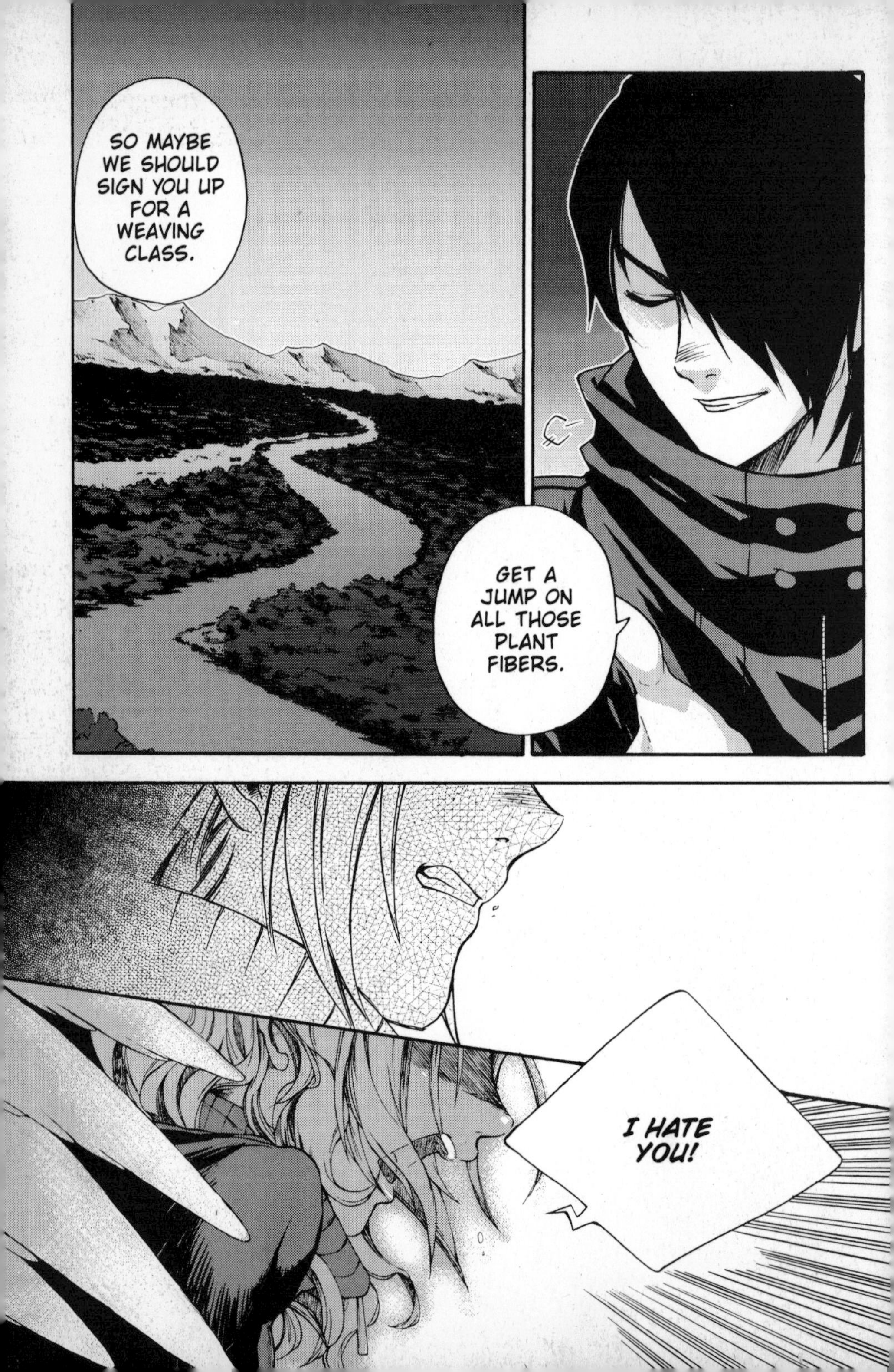
SO MAYBE WE SHOULD SIGN YOU UP FOR A WEAVING CLASS.
GET A JUMP ON ALL THOSE PLANT FIBERS.
I HATE YOU!

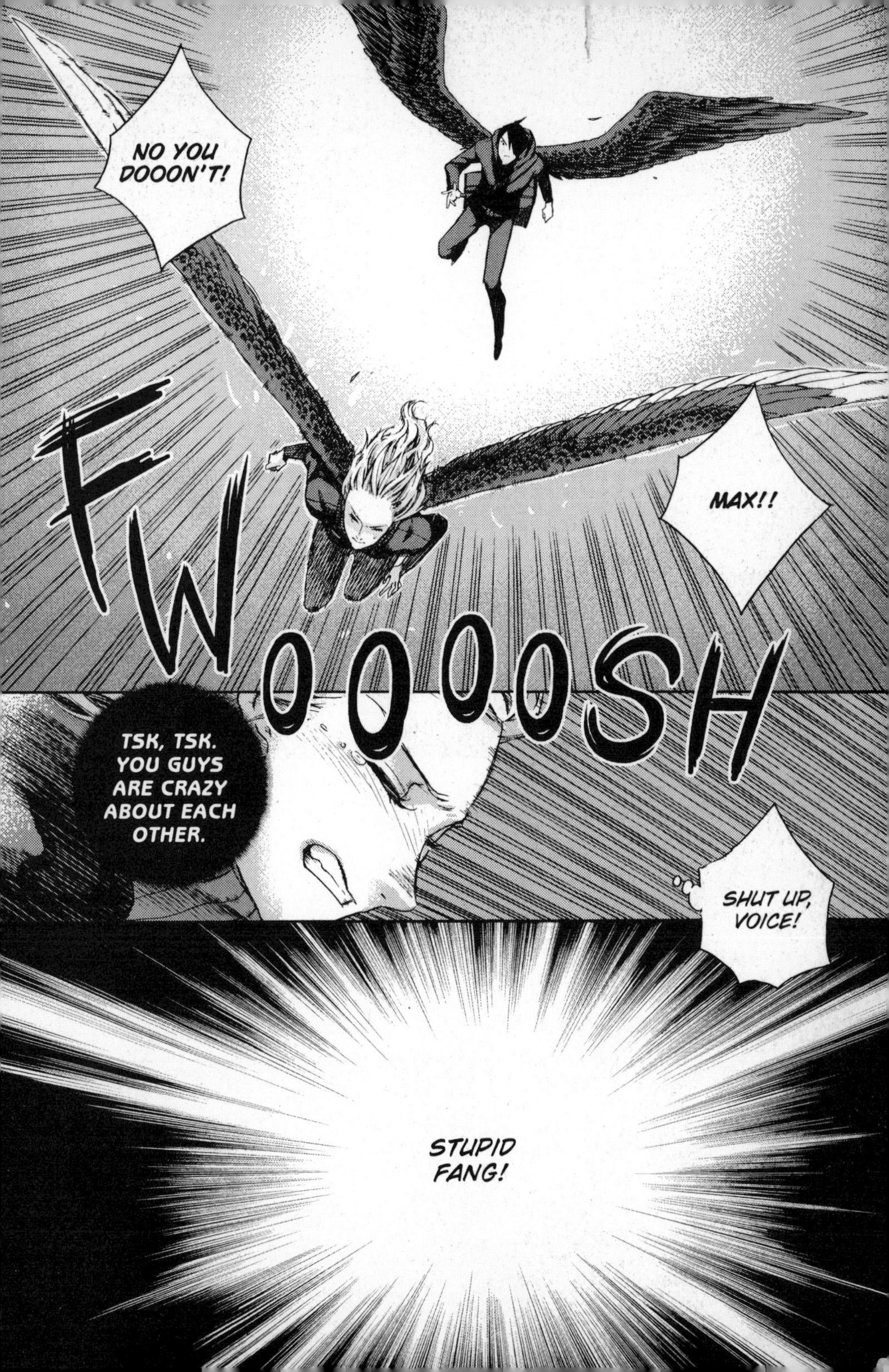
NO YOU DOOON'T!
MAX!!
FWOOOOSH
TSK, TSK. YOU GUYS ARE CRAZY ABOUT EACH OTHER.
SHUT UP, VOICE!
STUPID FANG!

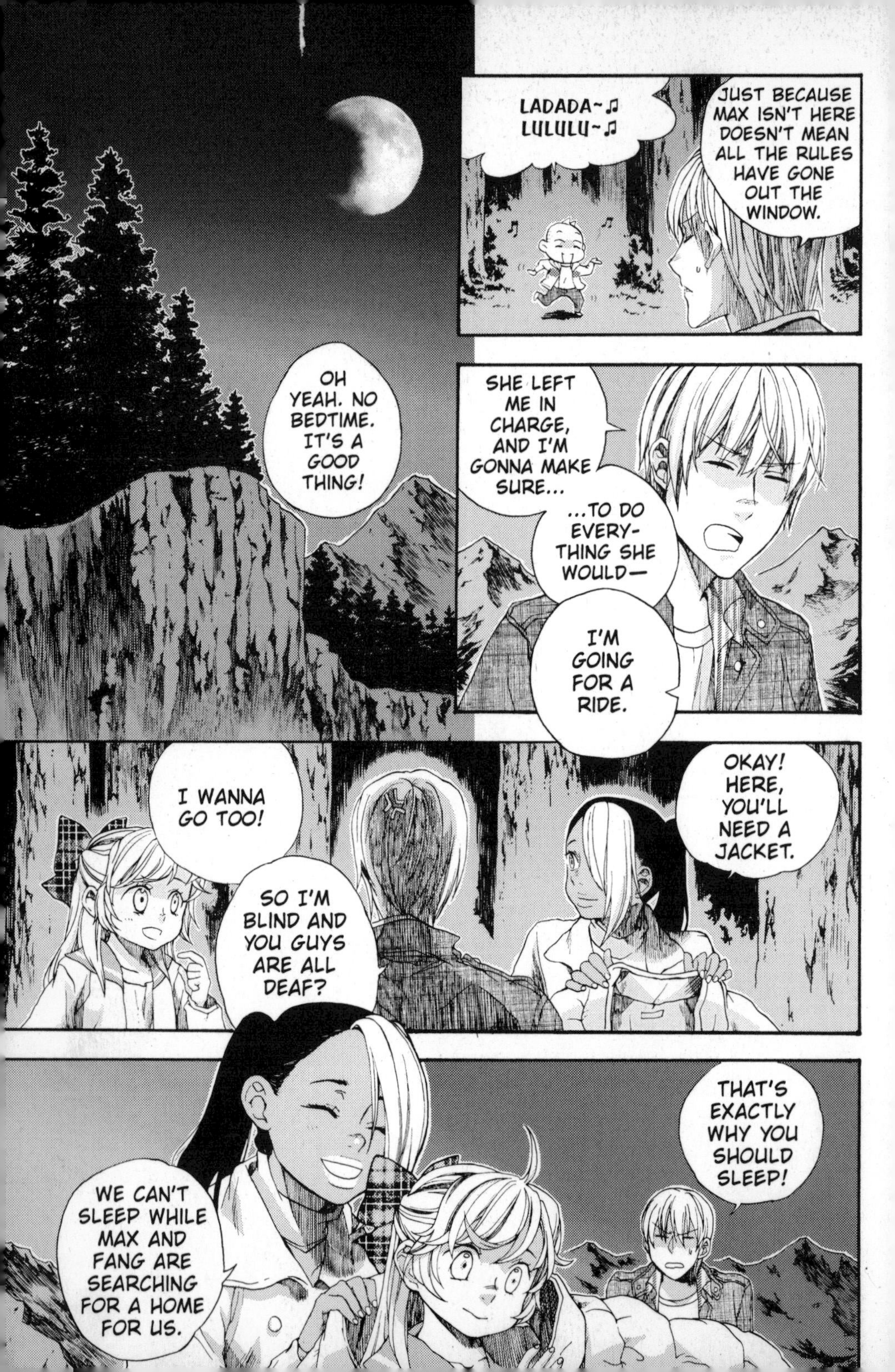
OH YEAH. NO BEDTIME. IT'S A GOOD THING!
LADADA~♫ LULULU~♫
JUST BECAUSE MAX ISN'T HERE DOESN'T MEAN ALL THE RULES HAVE GONE OUT THE WINDOW.
SHE LEFT ME IN CHARGE, AND I'M GONNA MAKE SURE...
...TO DO EVERY-THING SHE WOULD—
I'M GOING FOR A RIDE.
I WANNA GO TOO!
SO I'M BLIND AND YOU GUYS ARE ALL DEAF?
OKAY! HERE, YOU'LL NEED A JACKET.
WE CAN'T SLEEP WHILE MAX AND FANG ARE SEARCHING FOR A HOME FOR US.
THAT'S EXACTLY WHY YOU SHOULD SLEEP!

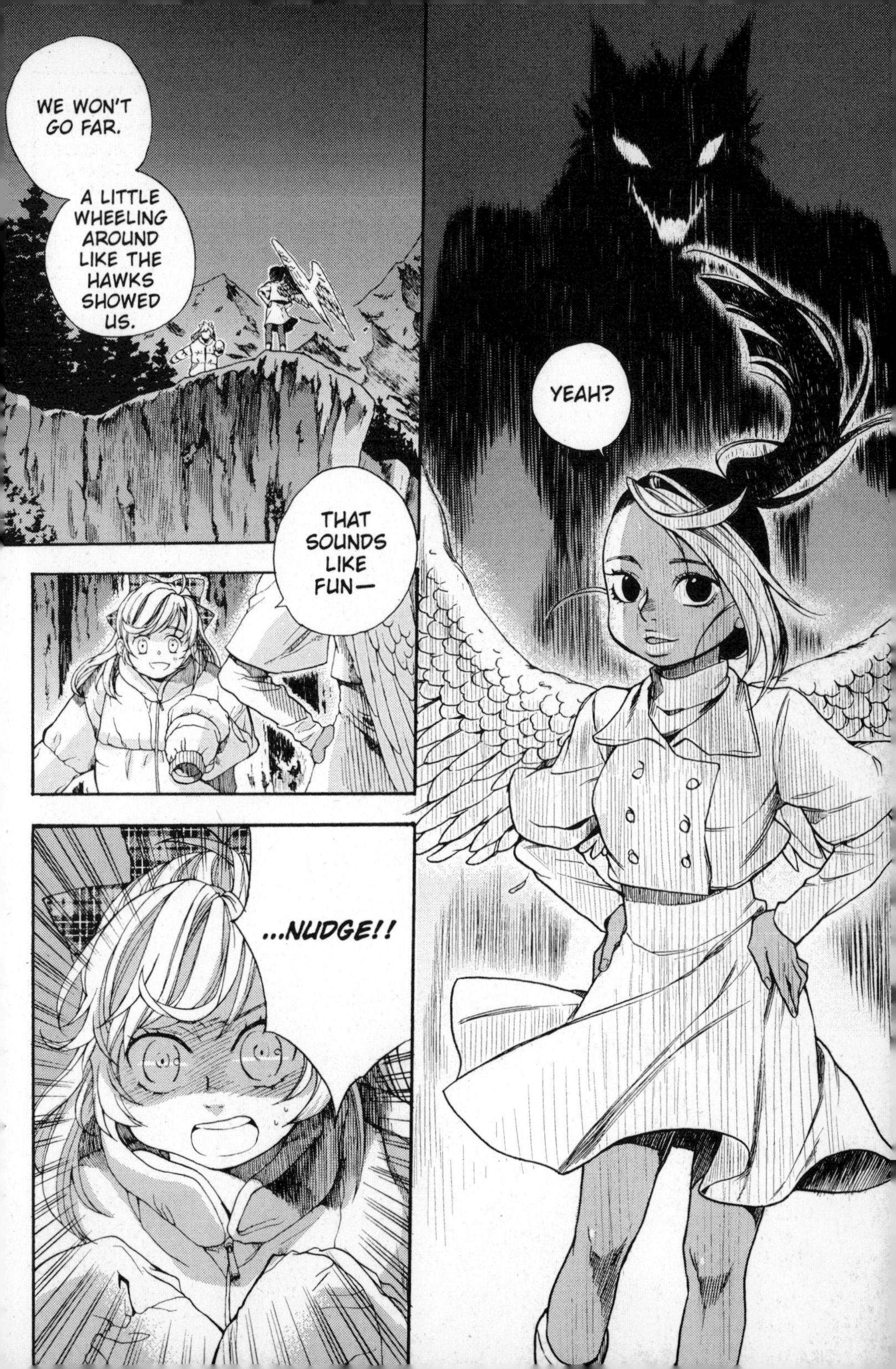
WE WON'T GO FAR.
A LITTLE WHEELING AROUND LIKE THE HAWKS SHOWED US.
THAT SOUNDS LIKE FUN—
...NUDGE!!
YEAH?

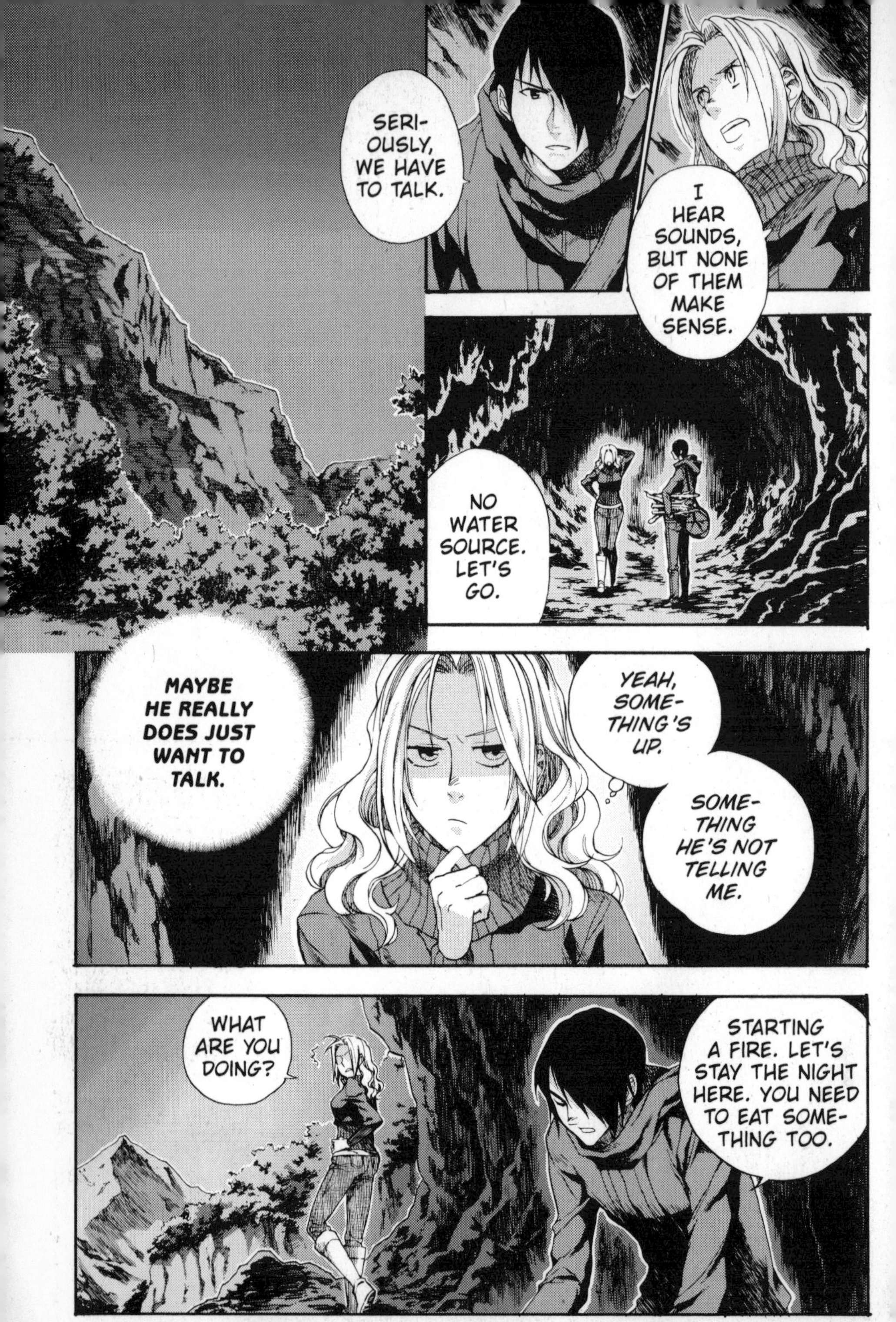
SERIOUSLY, WE HAVE TO TALK.
I HEAR SOUNDS, BUT NONE OF THEM MAKE SENSE.
NO WATER SOURCE. LET'S GO.
MAYBE HE REALLY DOES JUST WANT TO TALK.
YEAH, SOMETHING'S UP.
SOMETHING HE'S NOT TELLING ME.
WHAT ARE YOU DOING?
STARTING A FIRE. LET'S STAY THE NIGHT HERE. YOU NEED TO EAT SOMETHING TOO.

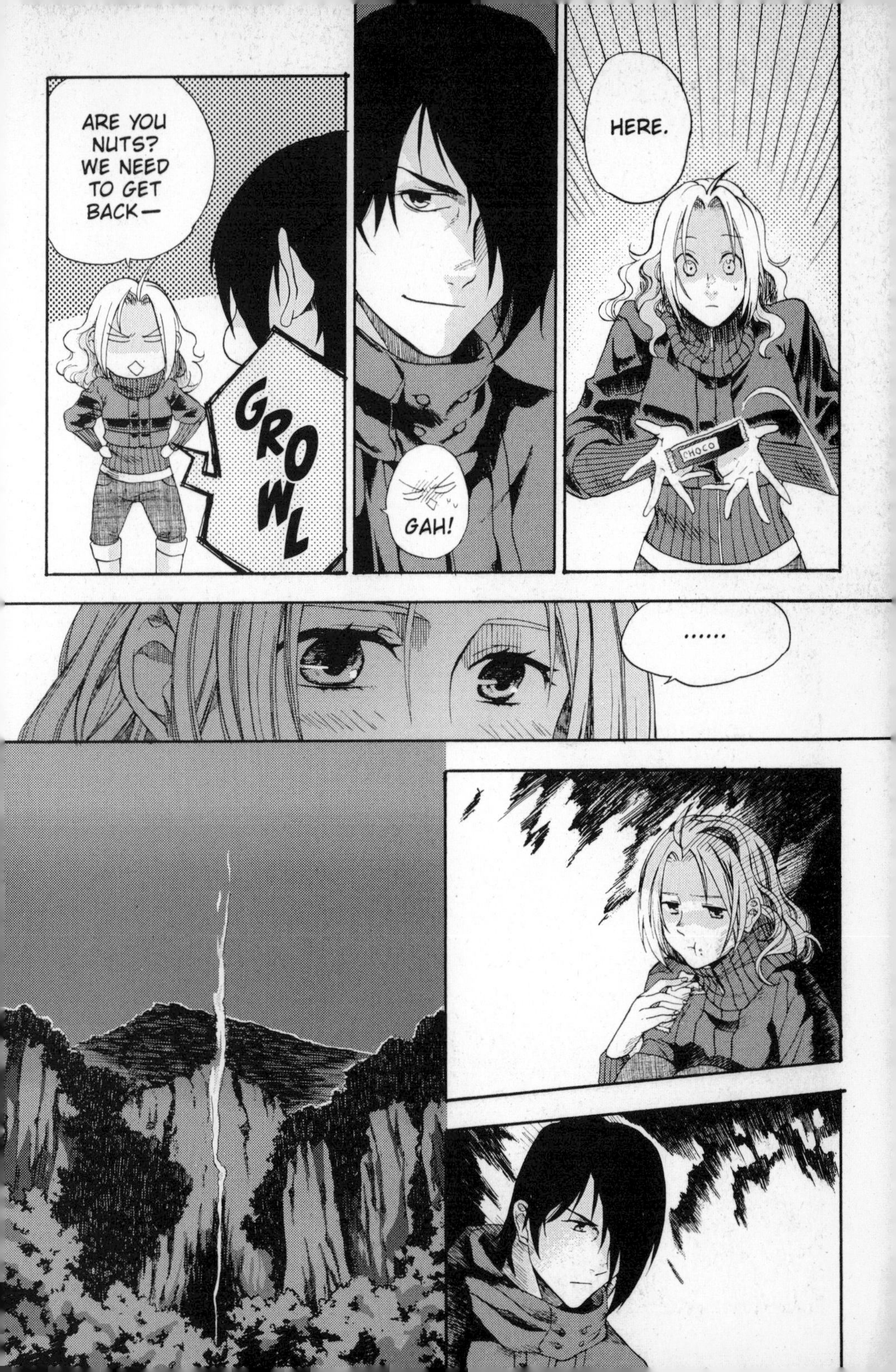
ARE YOU NUTS? WE NEED TO GET BACK—
GROWL
GAH!
HERE.
CHOCO
......

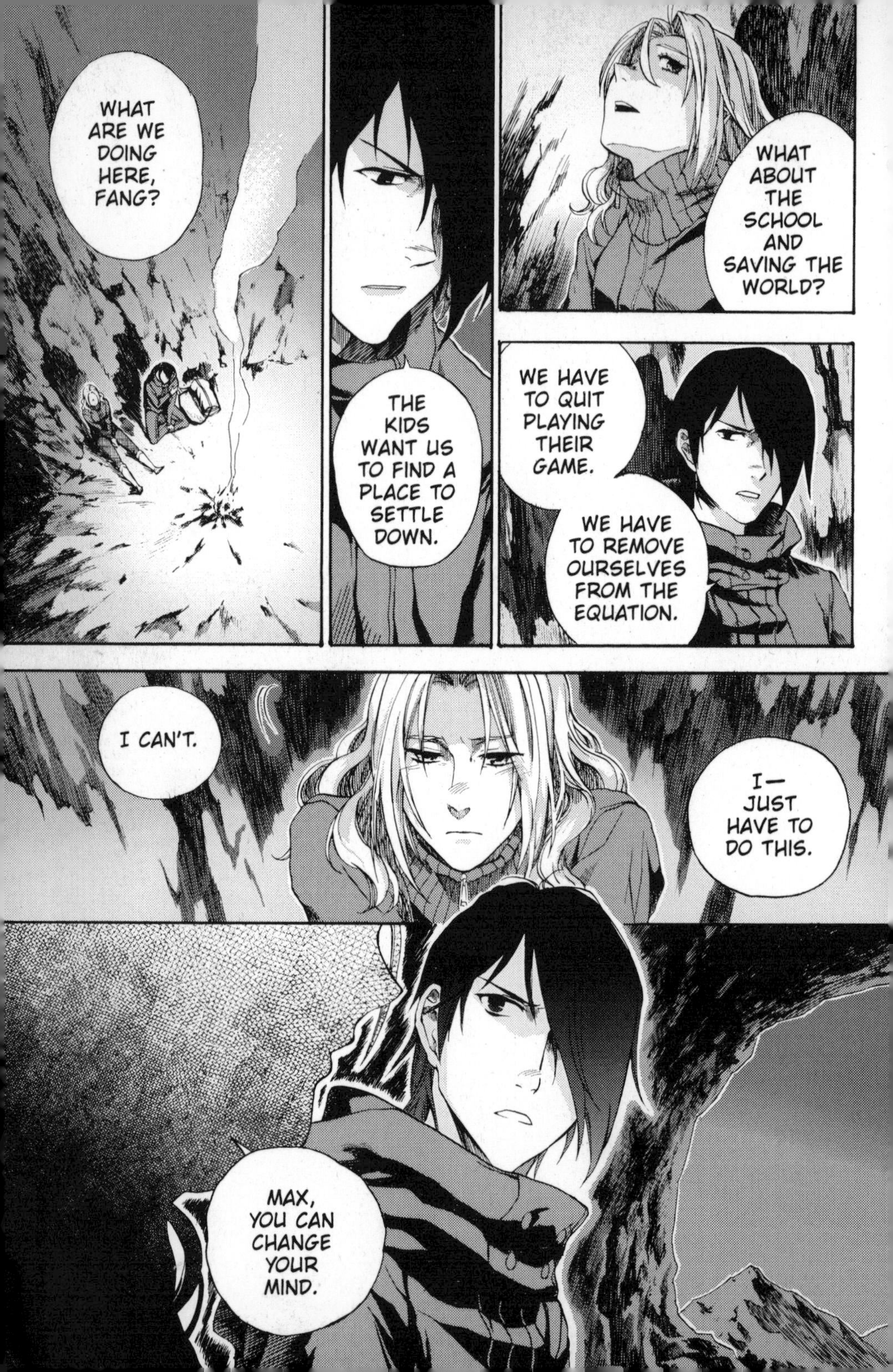
WHAT ARE WE DOING HERE, FANG?
THE KIDS WANT US TO FIND A PLACE TO SETTLE DOWN.
WHAT ABOUT THE SCHOOL AND SAVING THE WORLD?
WE HAVE TO QUIT PLAYING THEIR GAME.
WE HAVE TO REMOVE OURSELVES FROM THE EQUATION.
I CAN'T.
I— JUST HAVE TO DO THIS.
MAX, YOU CAN CHANGE YOUR MIND.

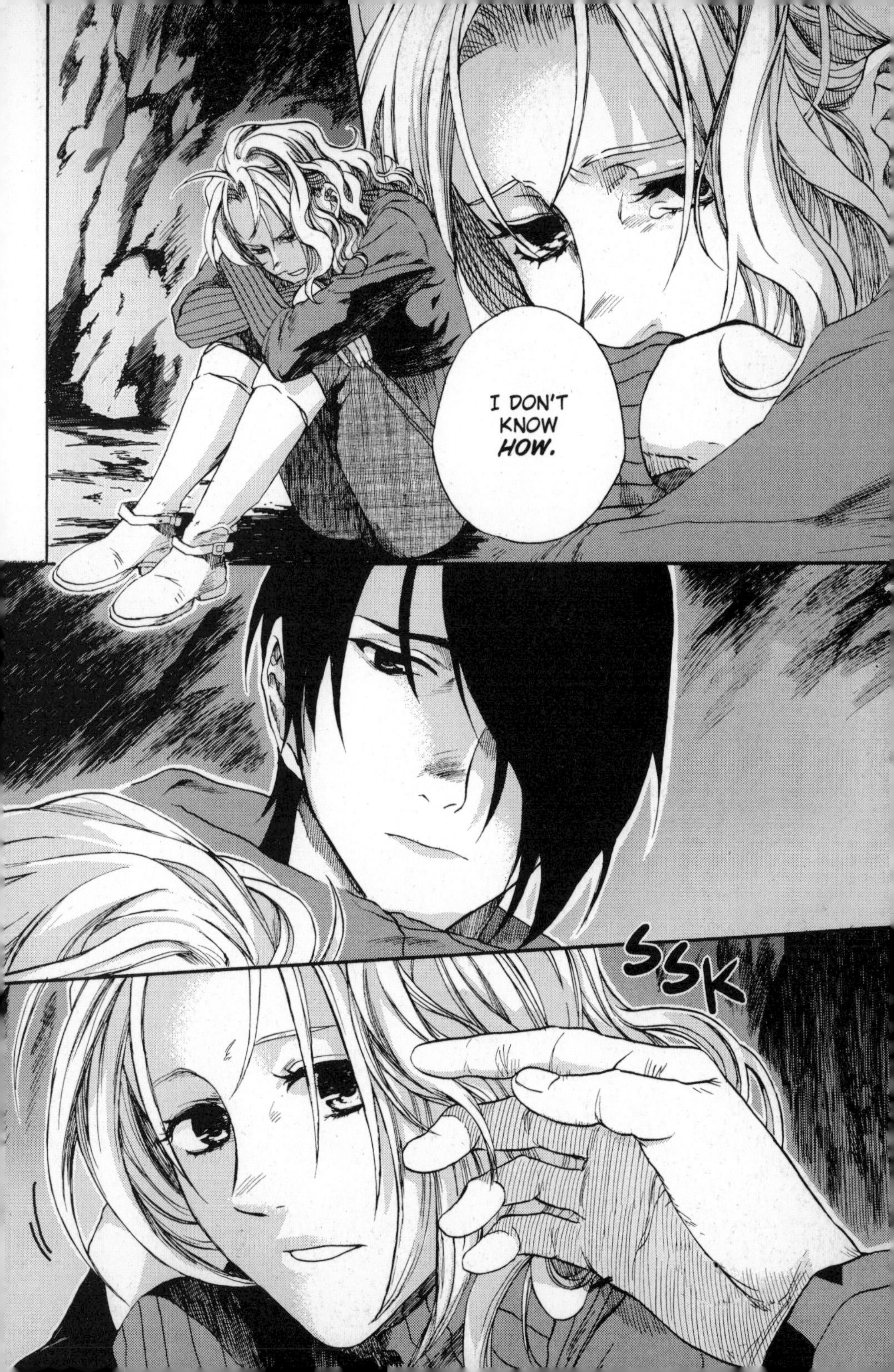
I DON'T KNOW HOW.
SSK

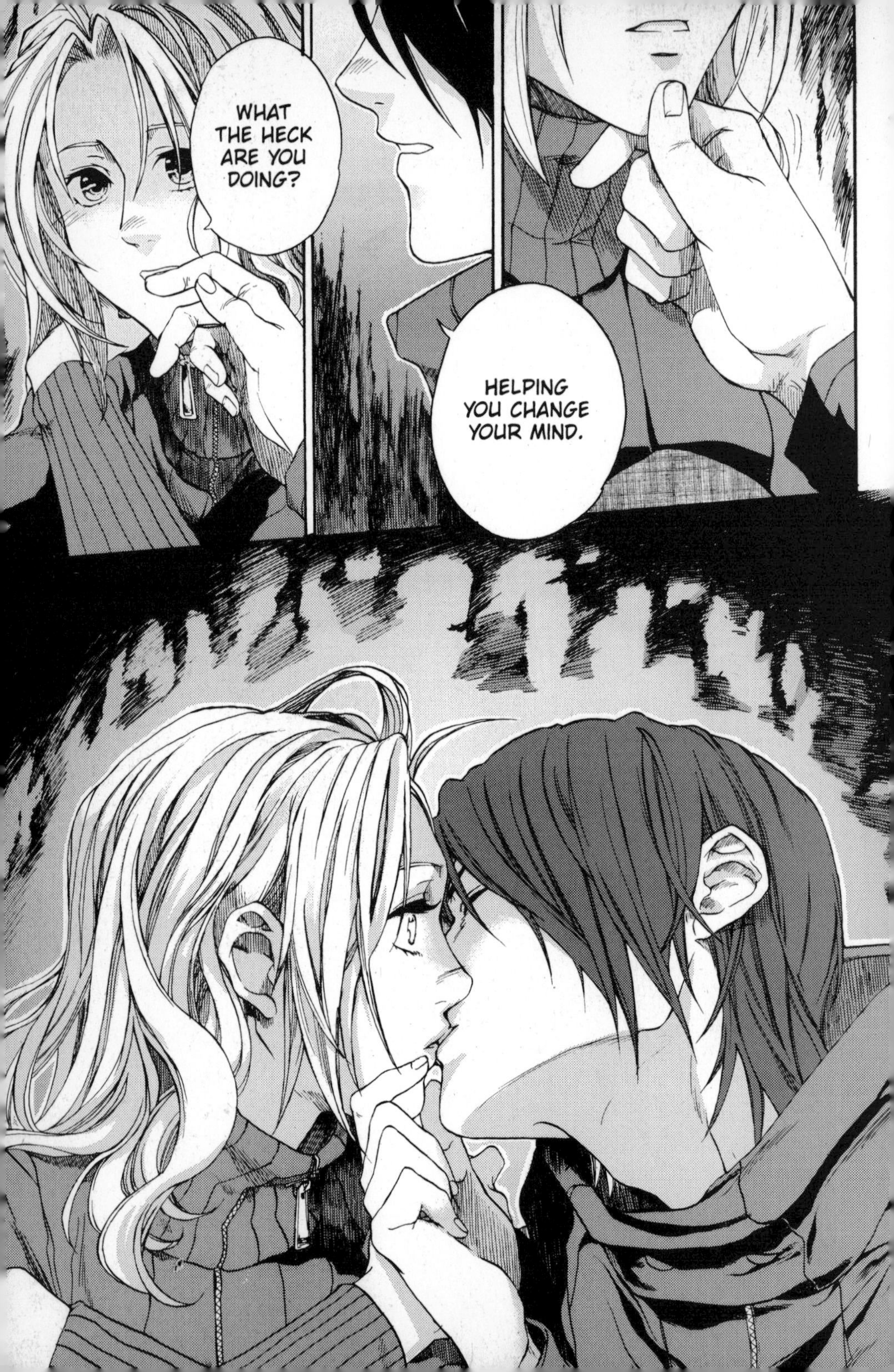
WHAT THE HECK ARE YOU DOING?
HELPING YOU CHANGE YOUR MIND.

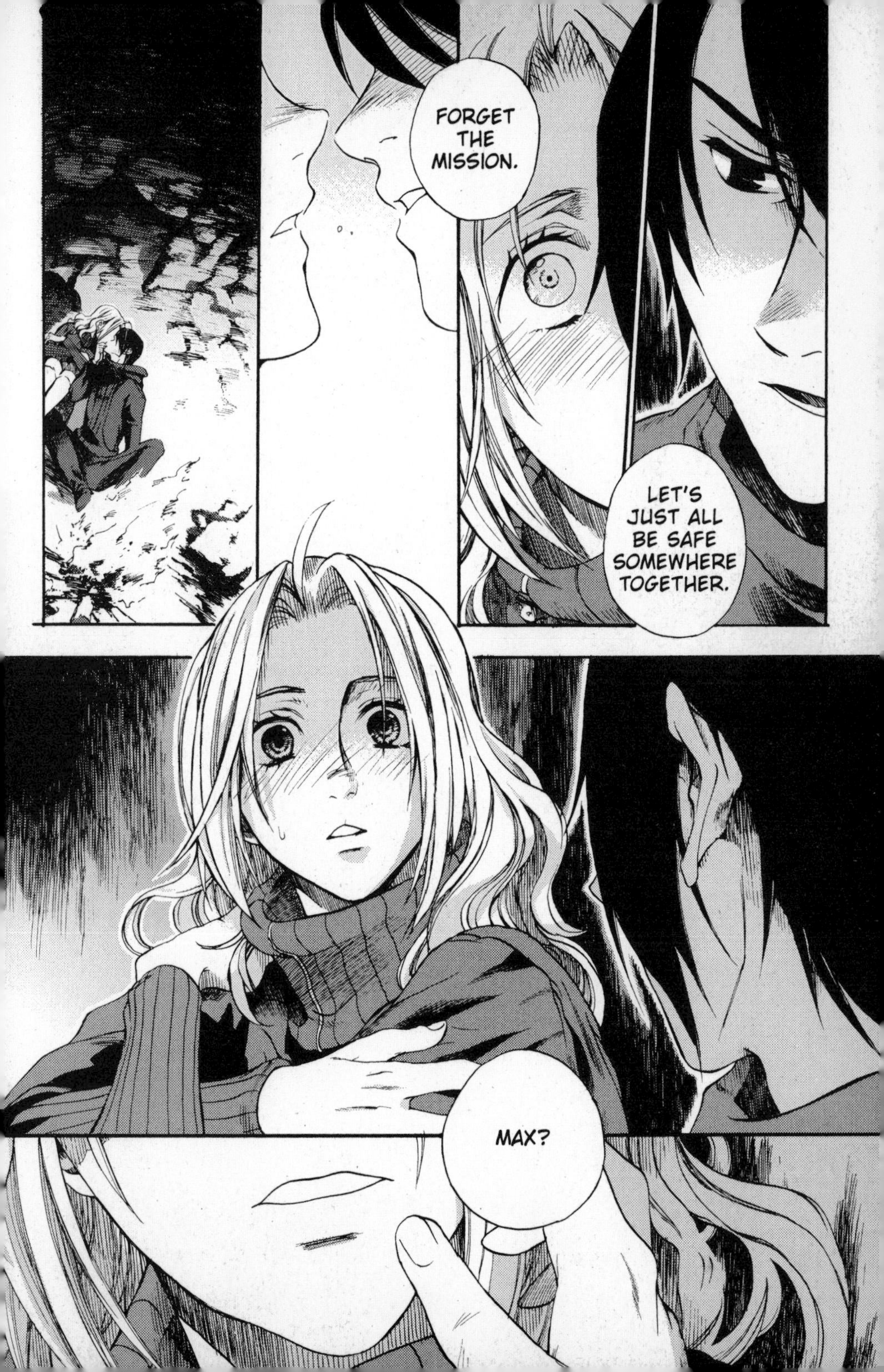
FORGET THE MISSION.
LET'S JUST ALL BE SAFE SOMEWHERE TOGETHER.
MAX?

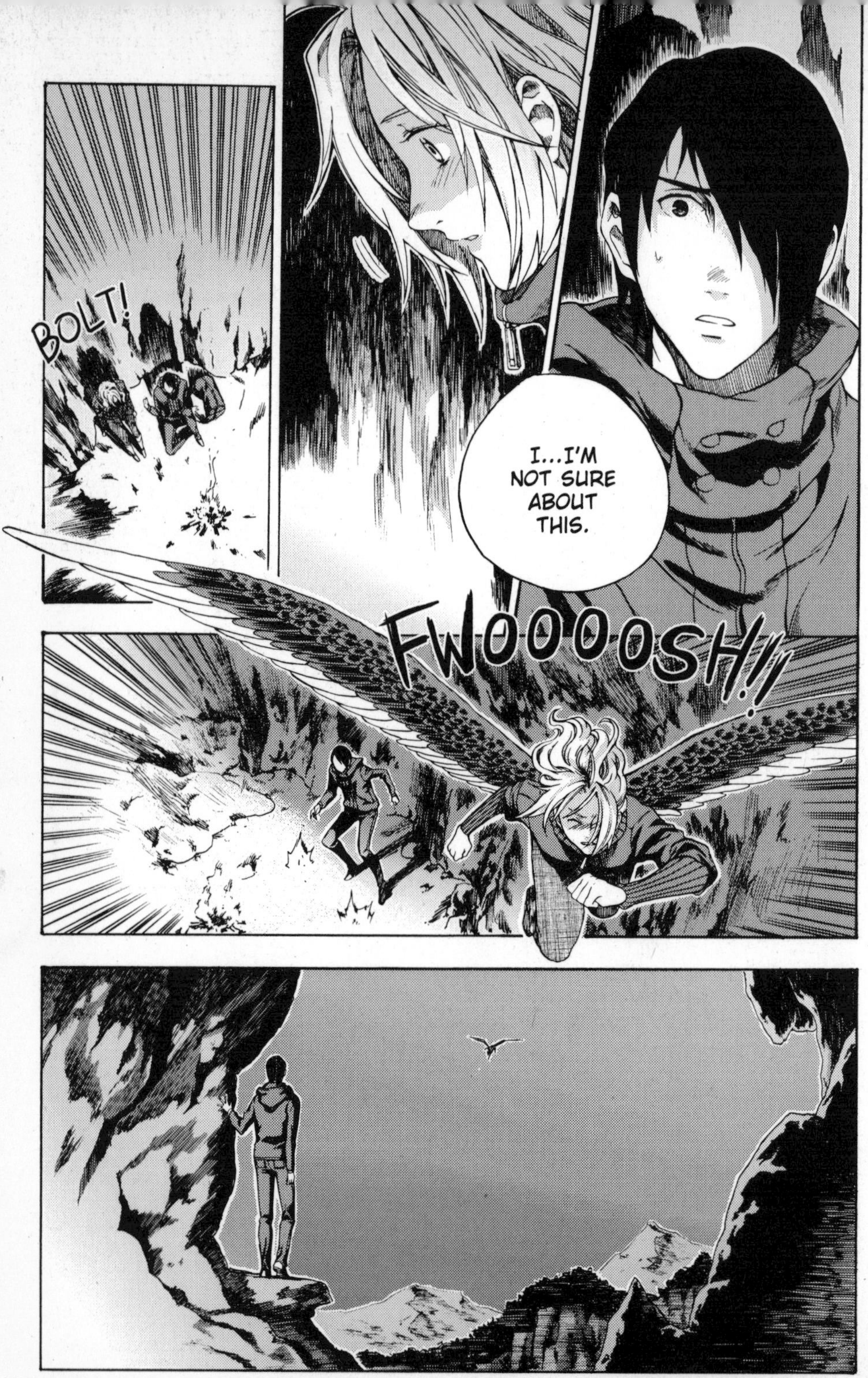
BOLT!
I...I'M NOT SURE ABOUT THIS.
FWOOOOSH!!

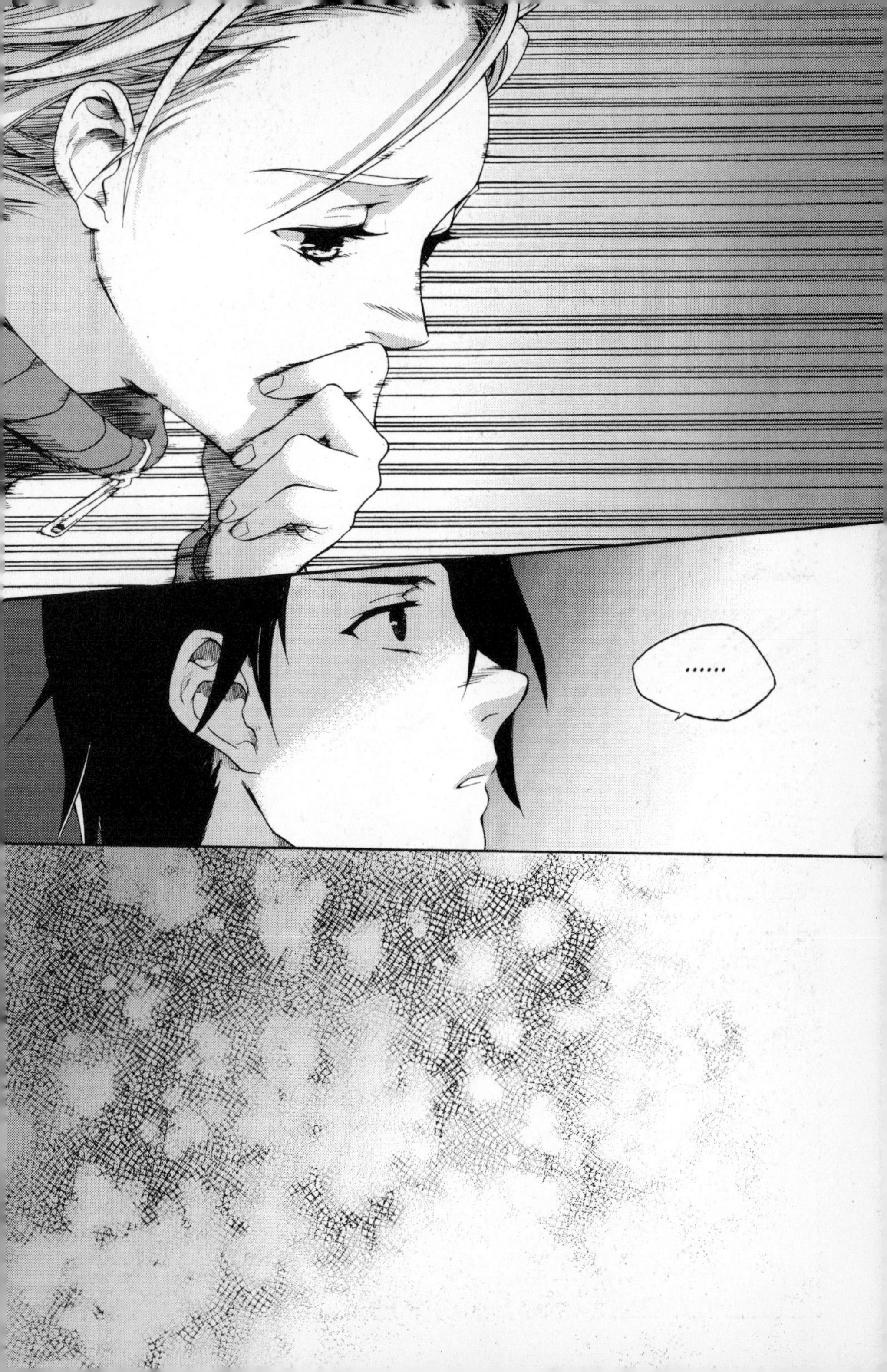
......

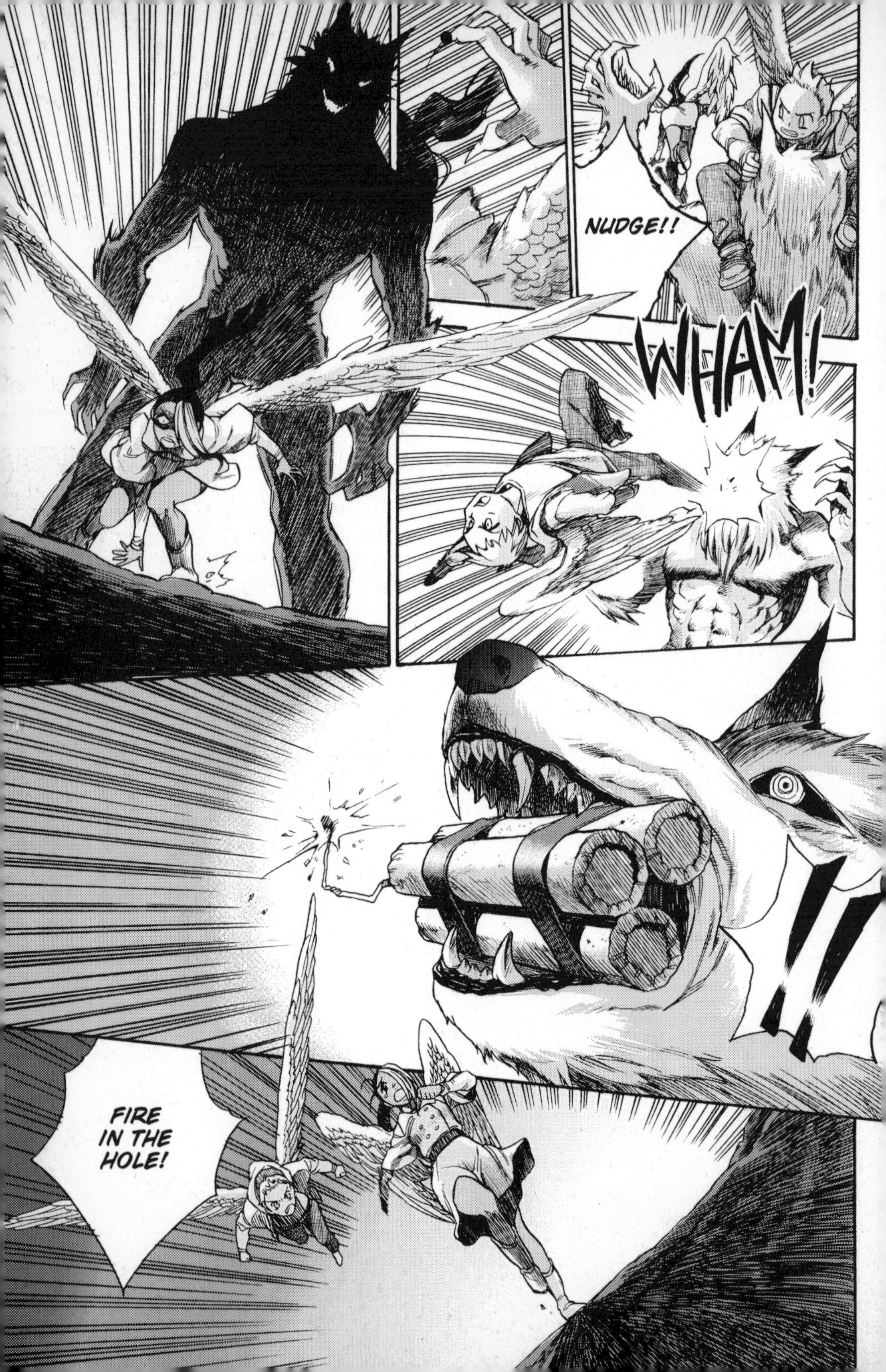
NUDGE!!
WHAM!
FIRE IN THE HOLE!

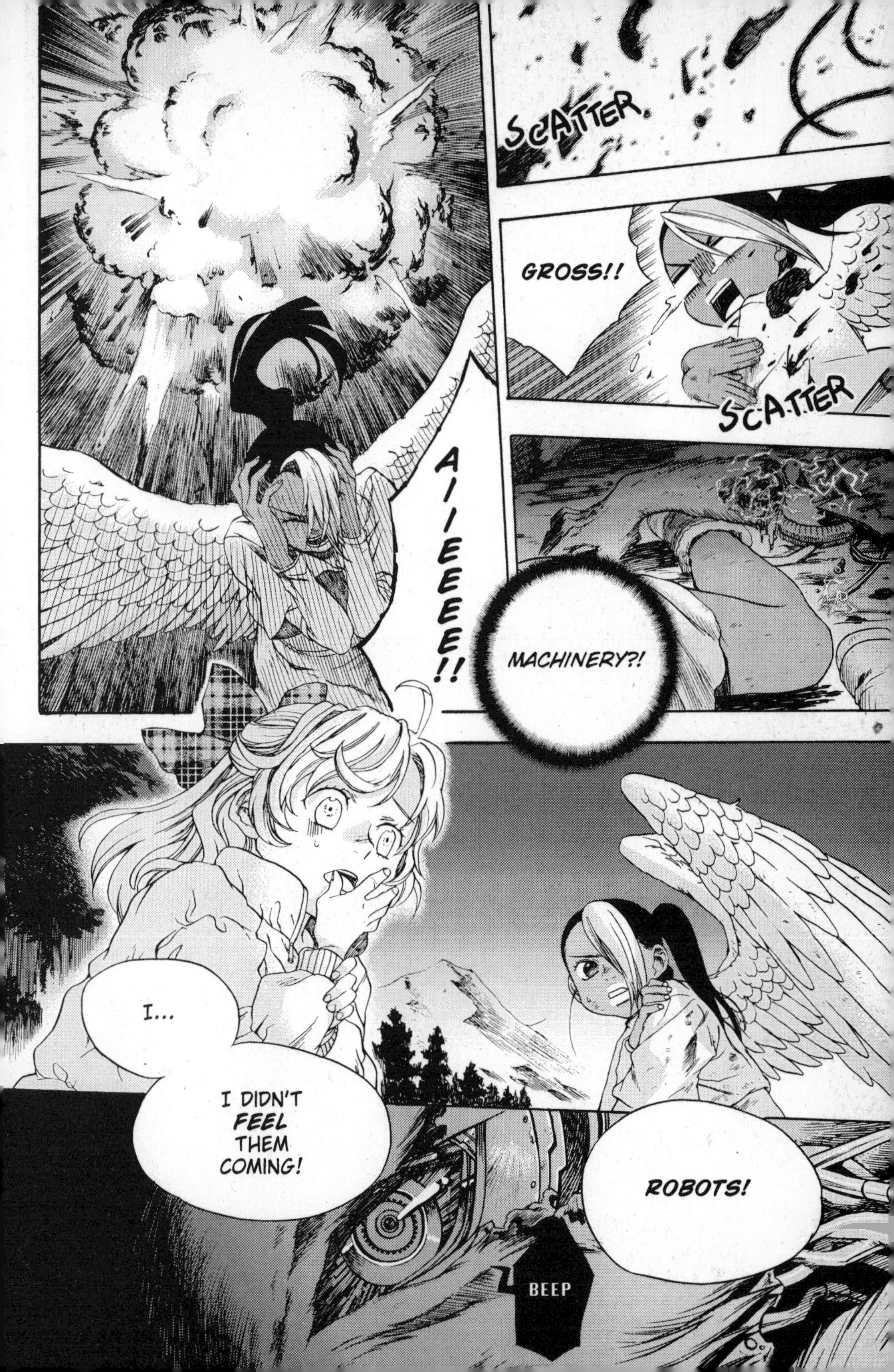
AIIEEEEE!!
SCATTER
GROSS!!
SCATTER
MACHINERY?!
I...
I DIDN'T FEEL THEM COMING!
ROBOTS!
BEEP

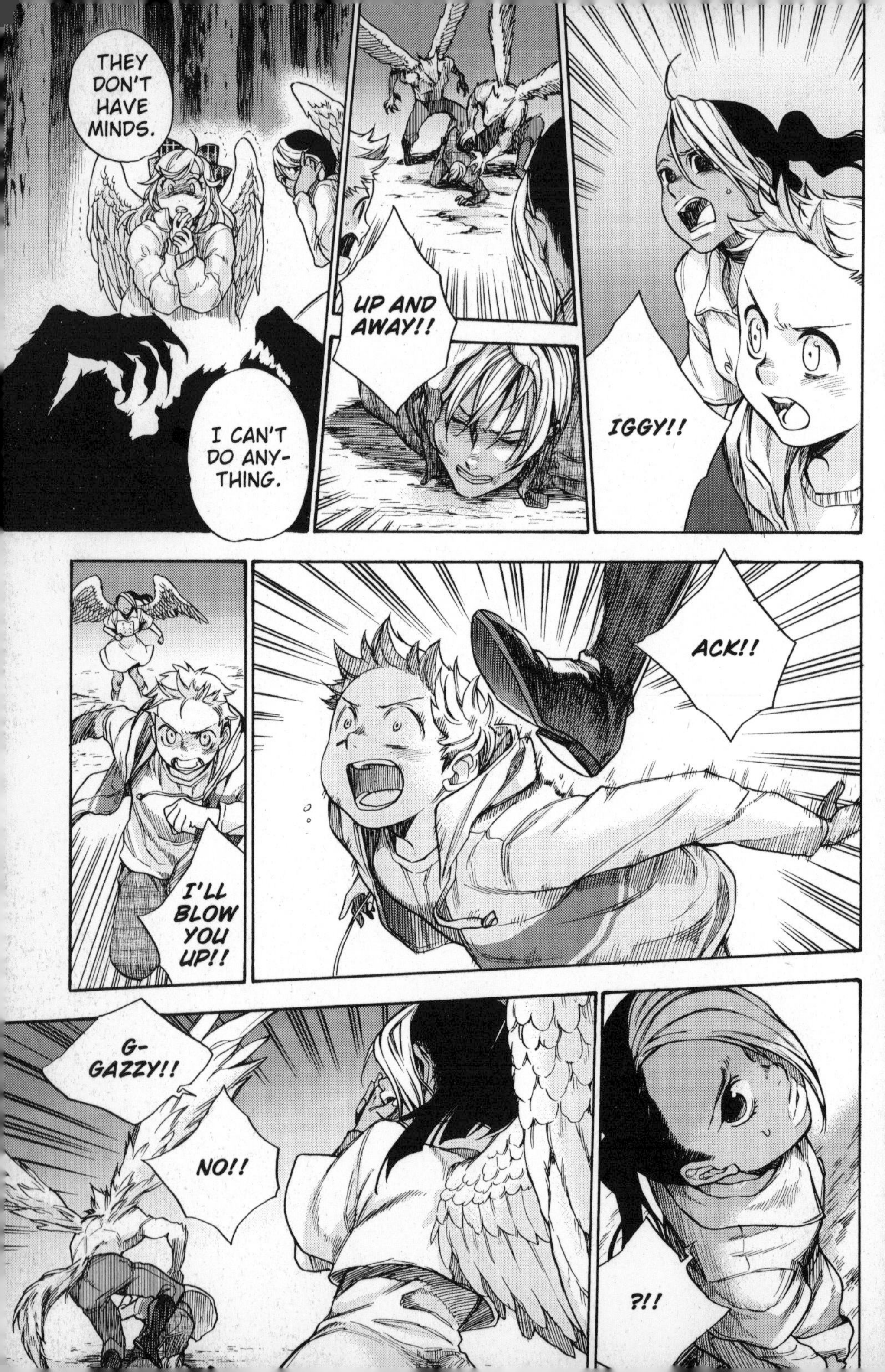
THEY DON'T HAVE MINDS.
I CAN'T DO ANY-THING.
UP AND AWAY!!
IGGY!!
I'LL BLOW YOU UP!!
ACK!!
G-GAZZY!!
NO!!
?!!

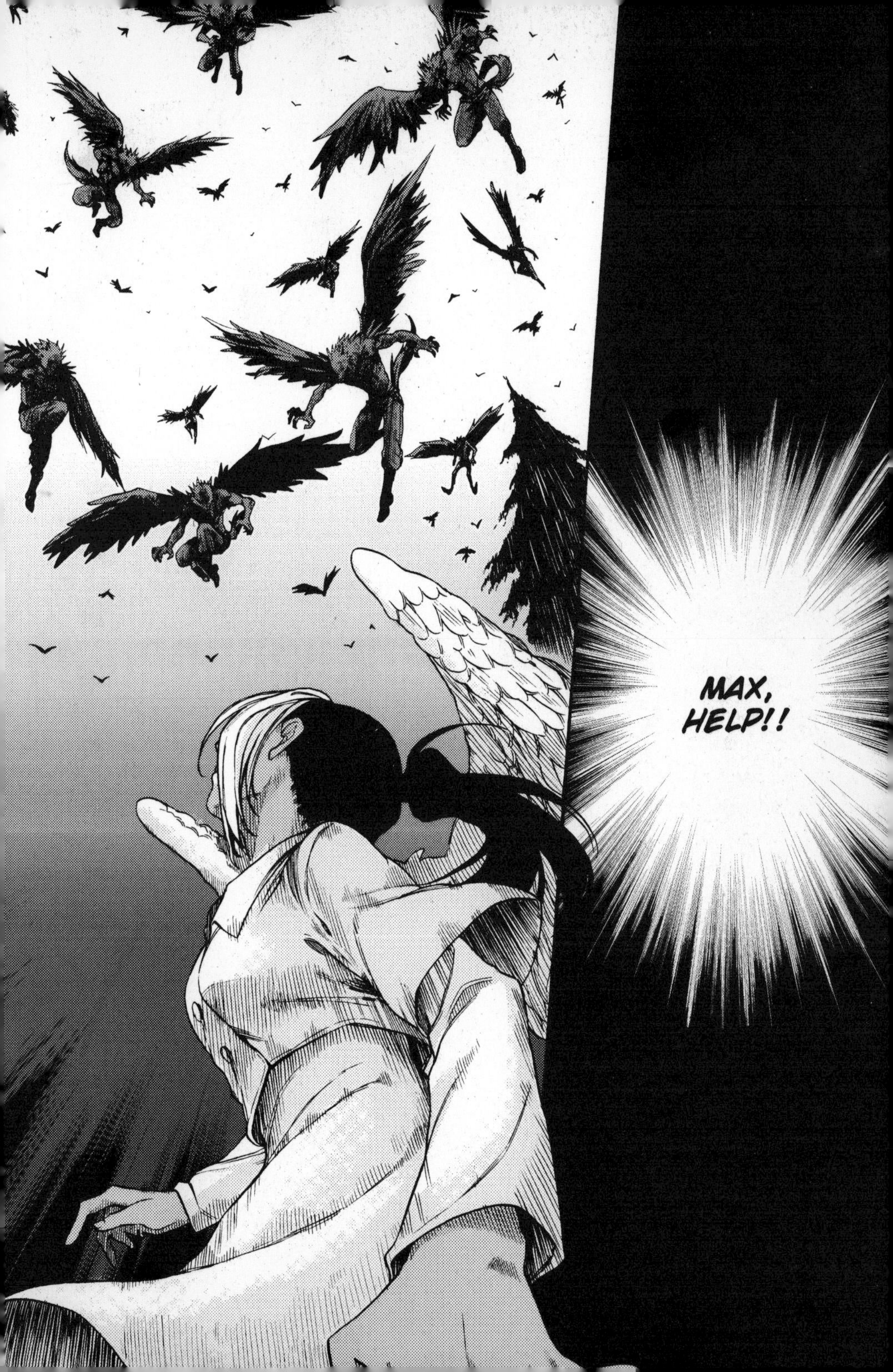
MAX, HELP!!

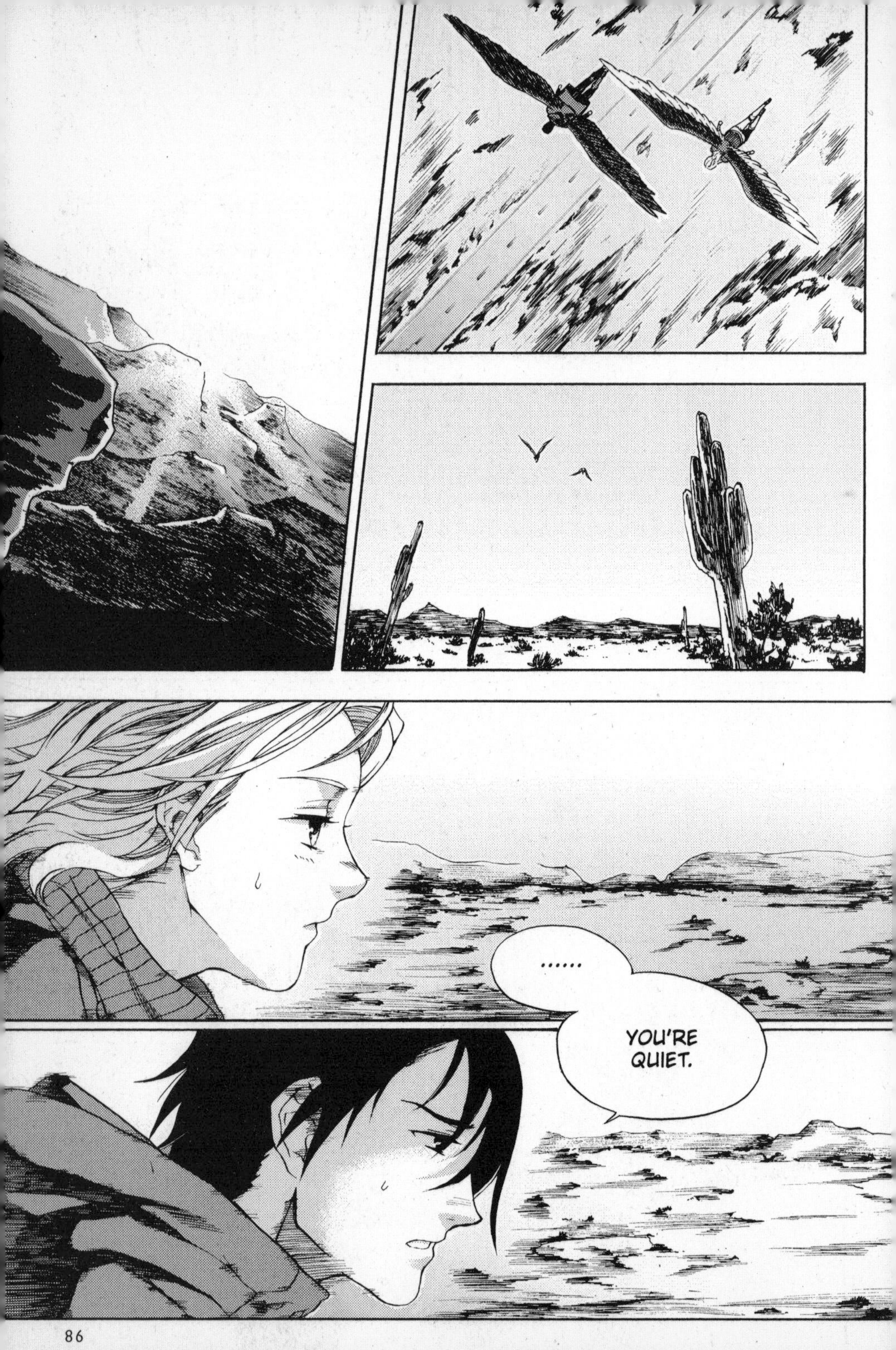
......
YOU'RE QUIET.

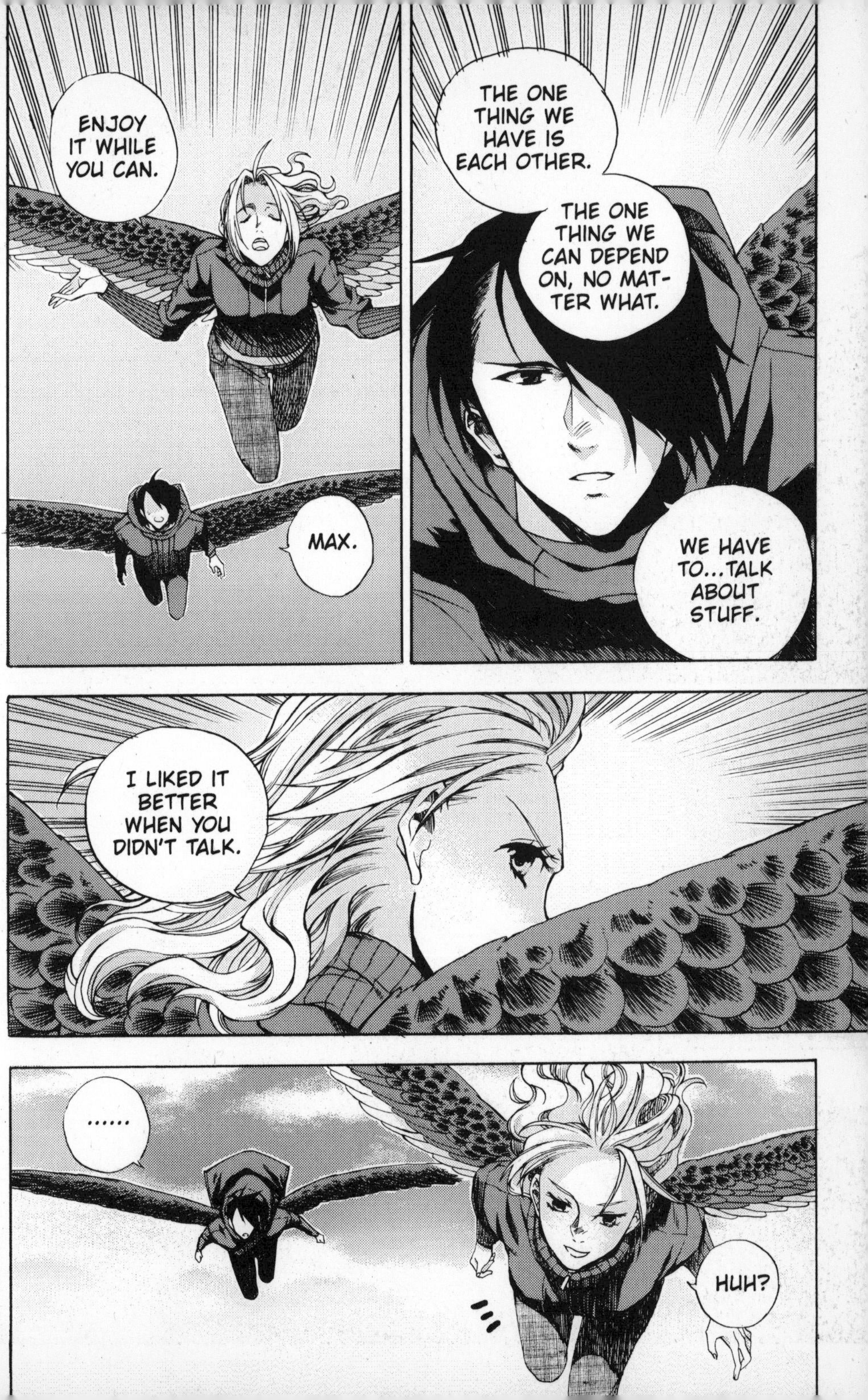
ENJOY IT WHILE YOU CAN.
MAX.
THE ONE THING WE HAVE IS EACH OTHER.
THE ONE THING WE CAN DEPEND ON, NO MAT-TER WHAT.
WE HAVE TO...TALK ABOUT STUFF.
I LIKED IT BETTER WHEN YOU DIDN'T TALK.
......
HUH?

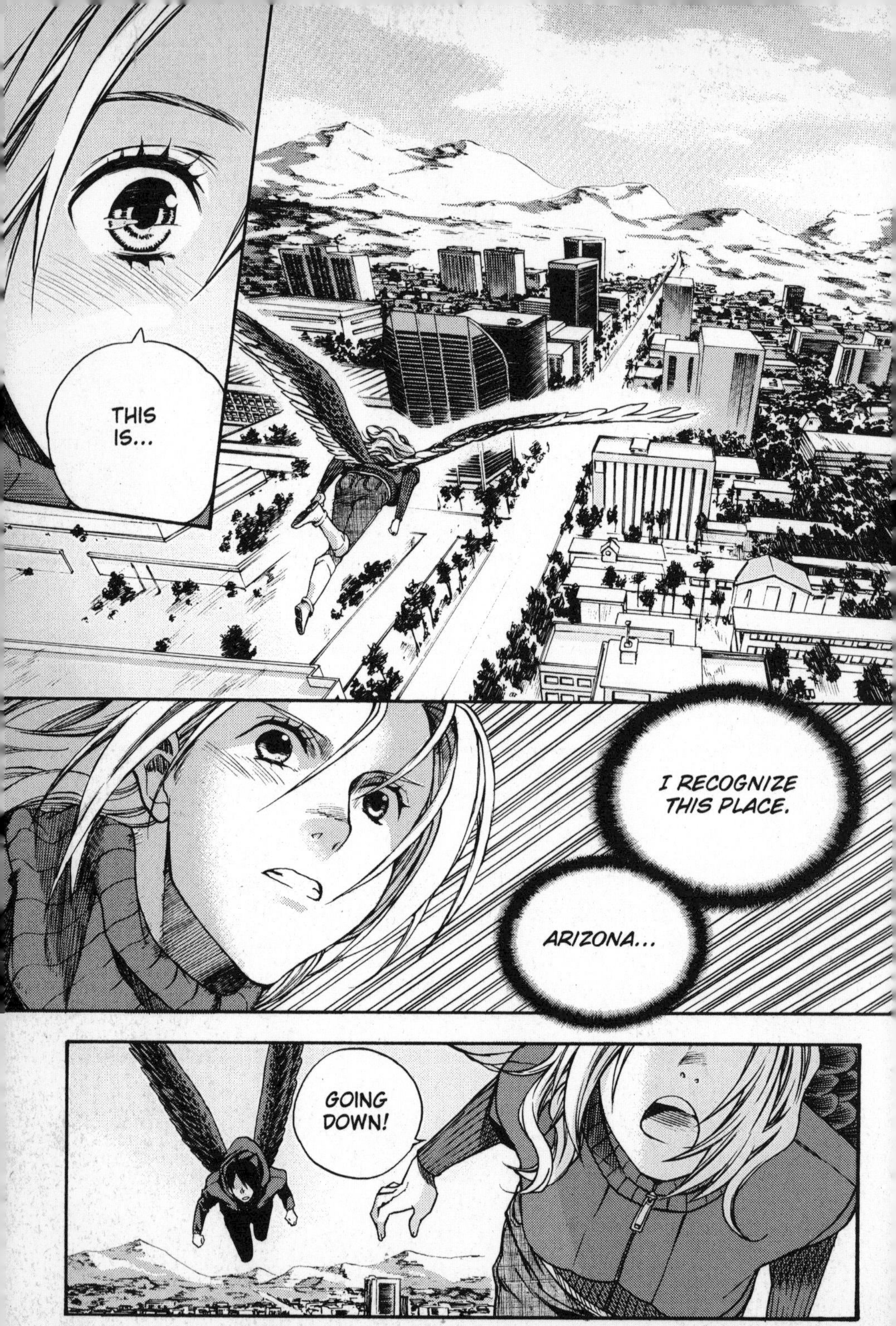
THIS IS...
I RECOGNIZE THIS PLACE.
ARIZONA...
GOING DOWN!

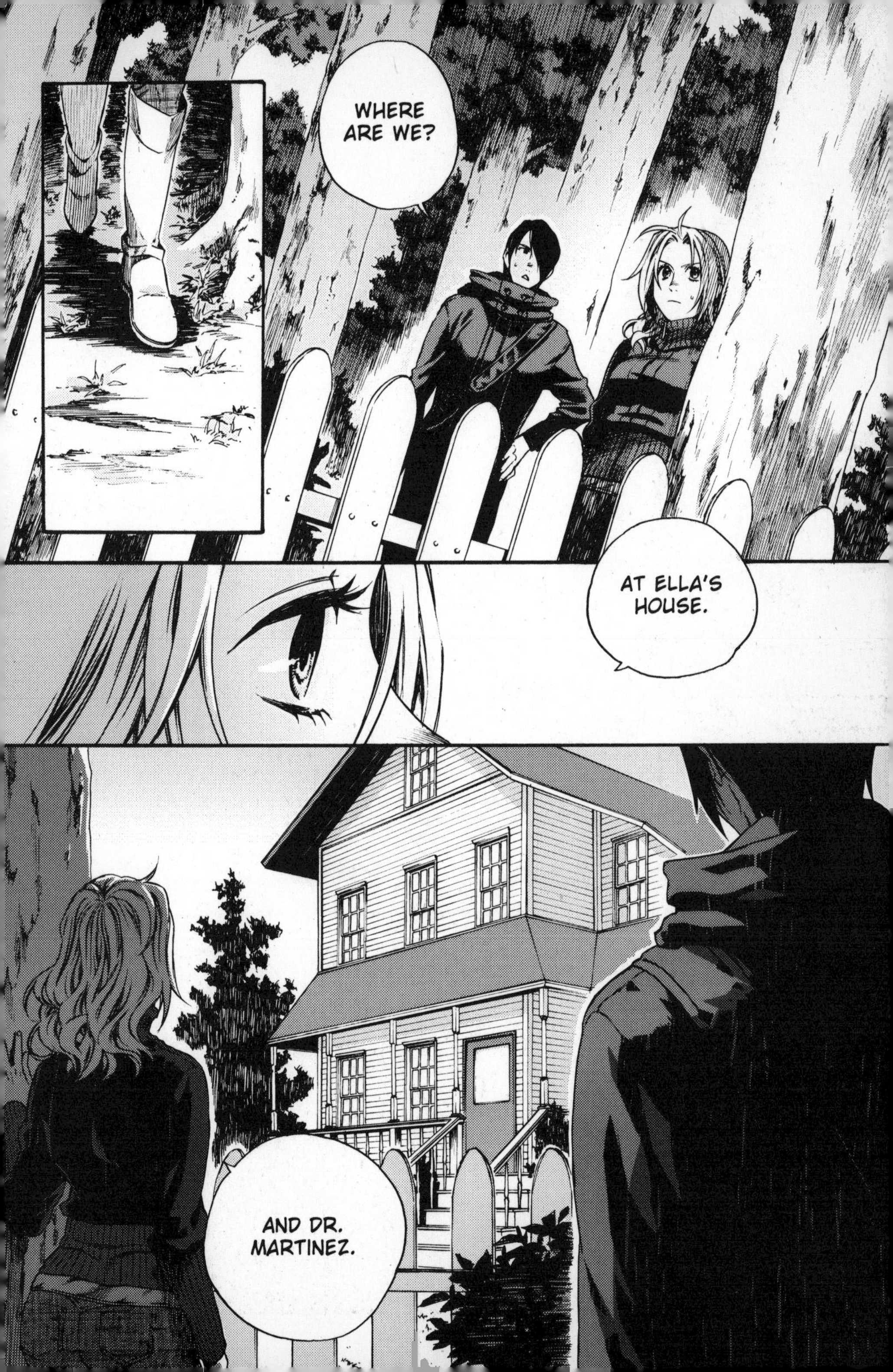
WHERE ARE WE?
AT ELLA'S HOUSE.
AND DR. MARTINEZ.

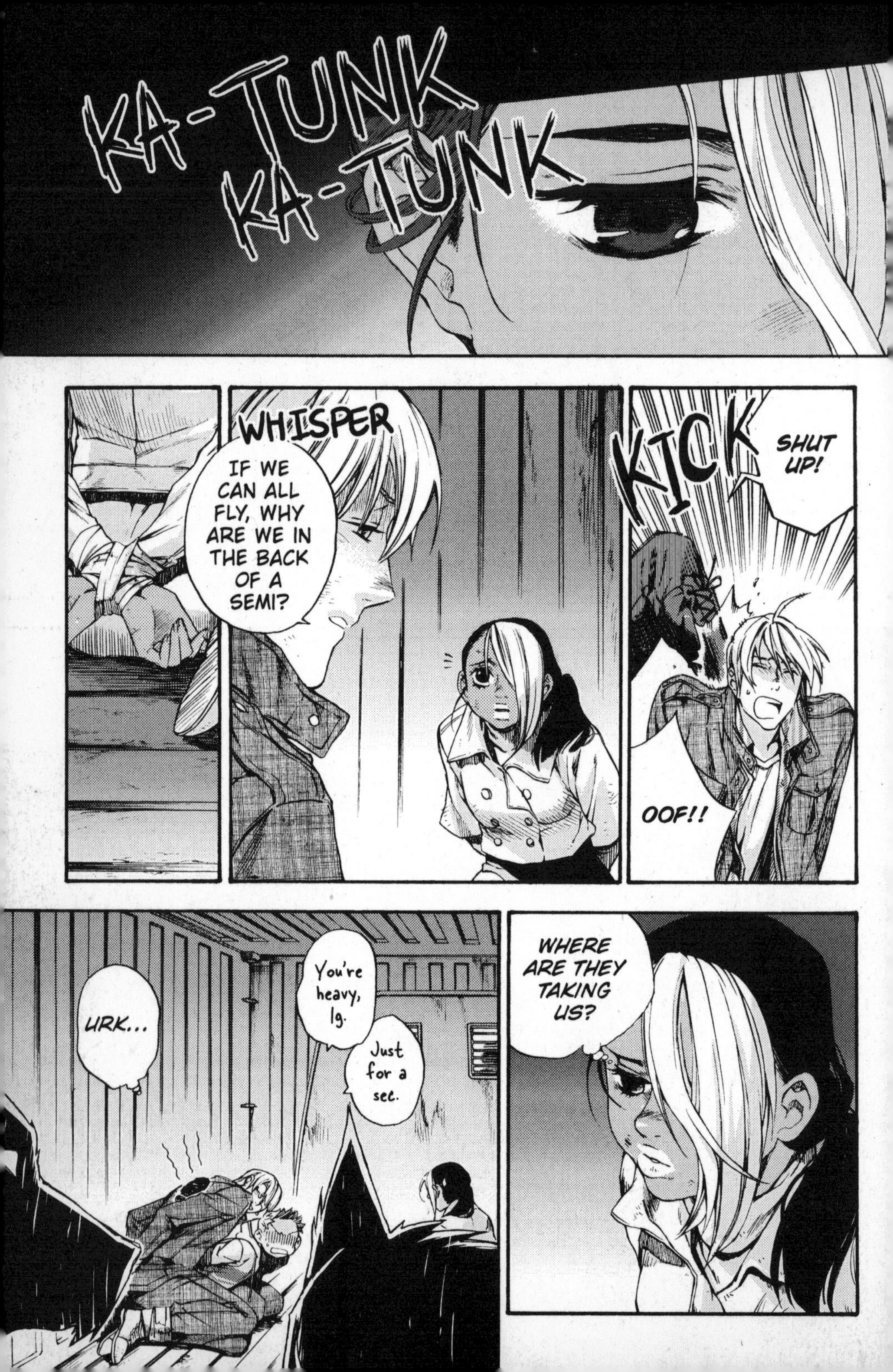
KA-TUNK KA-TUNK
WHISPER
IF WE CAN ALL FLY, WHY ARE WE IN THE BACK OF A SEMI?
KICK
SHUT UP!
OOF!!
URK...
You're heavy, Ig.
Just for a sec.
WHERE ARE THEY TAKING US?

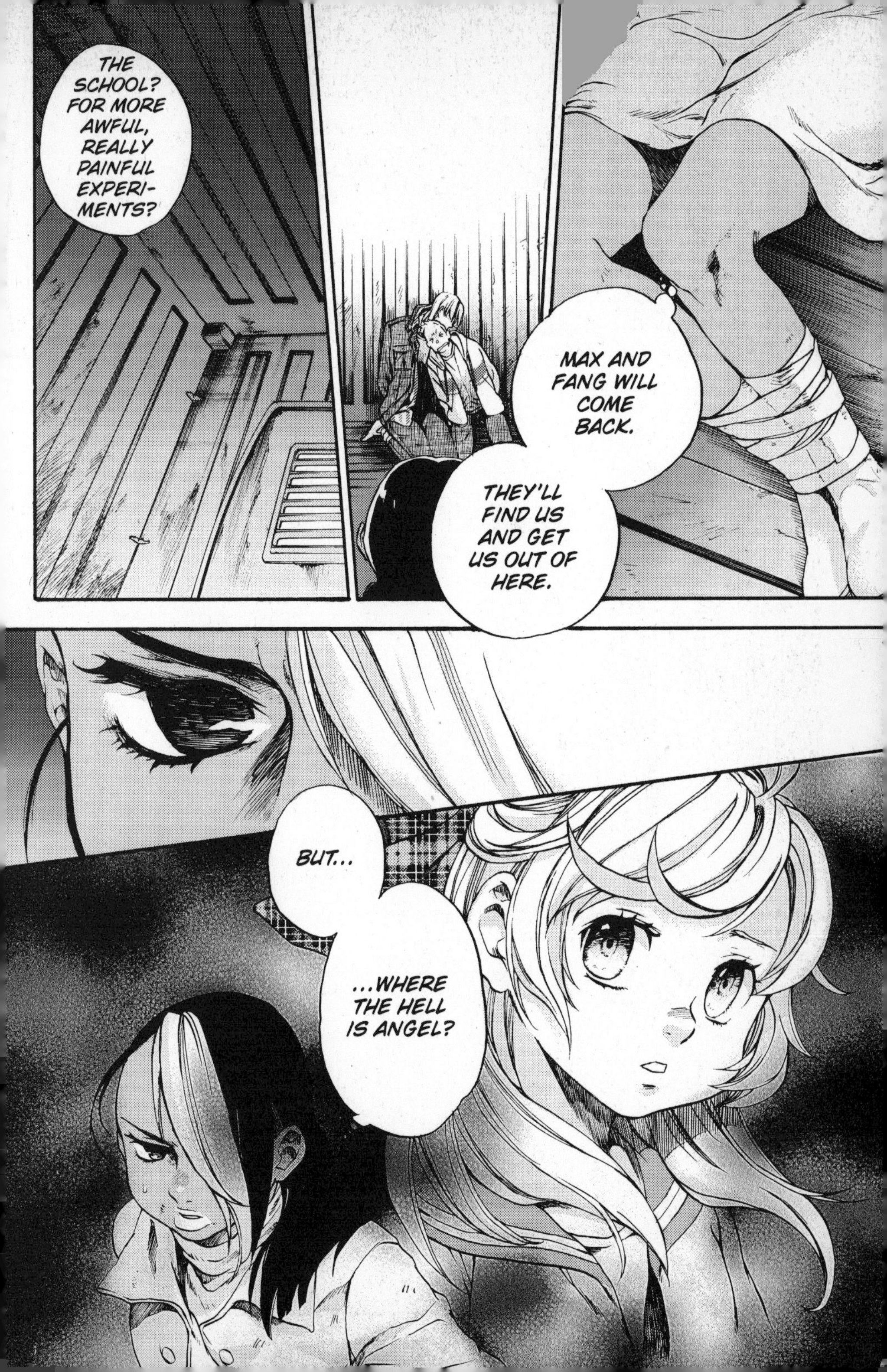
THE SCHOOL? FOR MORE AWFUL, REALLY PAINFUL EXPERIMENTS?
MAX AND FANG WILL COME BACK.
THEY'LL FIND US AND GET US OUT OF HERE.
BUT...
...WHERE THE HELL IS ANGEL?

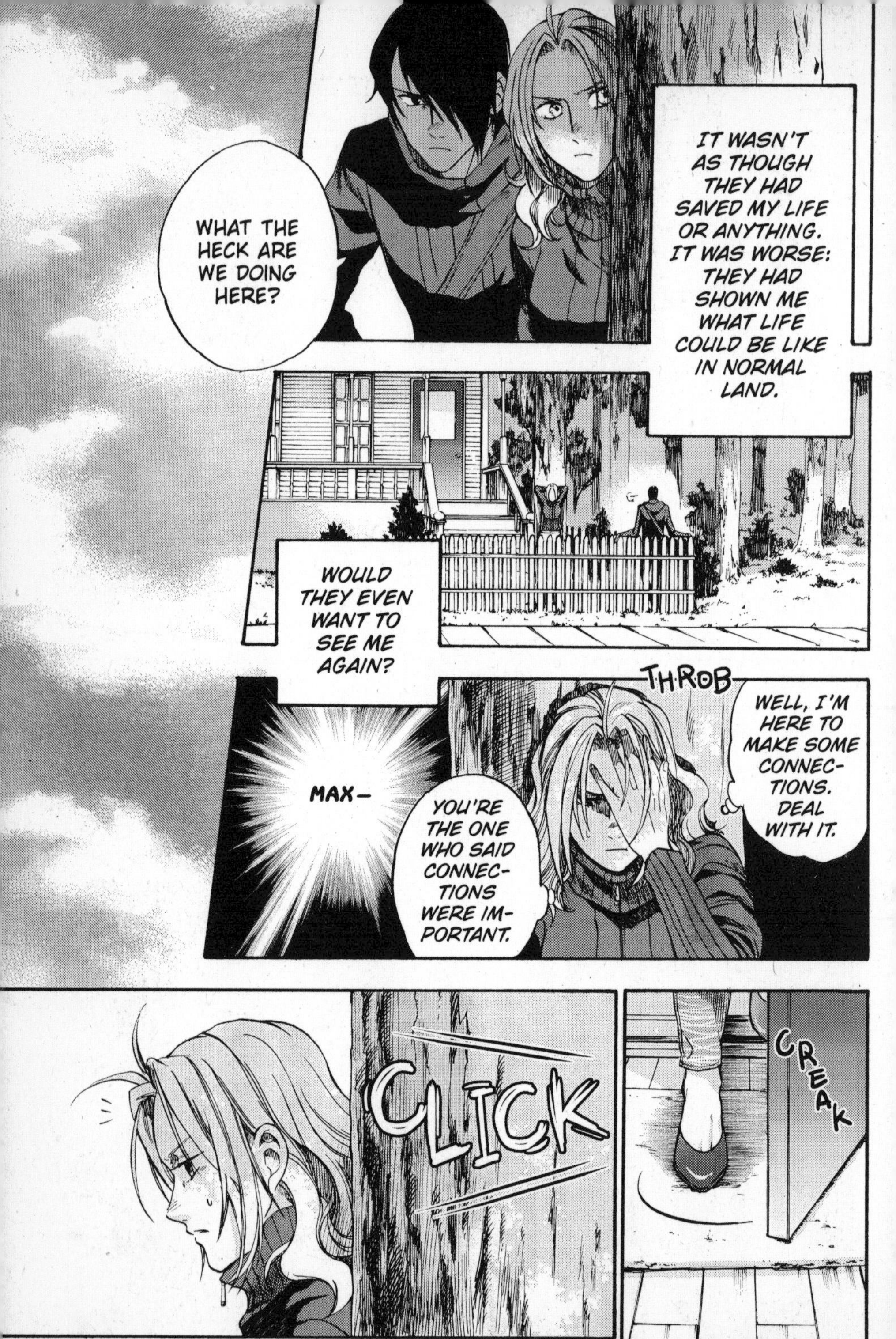
WHAT THE HECK ARE WE DOING HERE?
IT WASN'T AS THOUGH THEY HAD SAVED MY LIFE OR ANYTHING. IT WAS WORSE: THEY HAD SHOWN ME WHAT LIFE COULD BE LIKE IN NORMAL LAND.
WOULD THEY EVEN WANT TO SEE ME AGAIN?
MAX—
YOU'RE THE ONE WHO SAID CONNEC-TIONS WERE IM-PORTANT.
THROB
WELL, I'M HERE TO MAKE SOME CONNEC-TIONS. DEAL WITH IT.
CLICK
CREAK

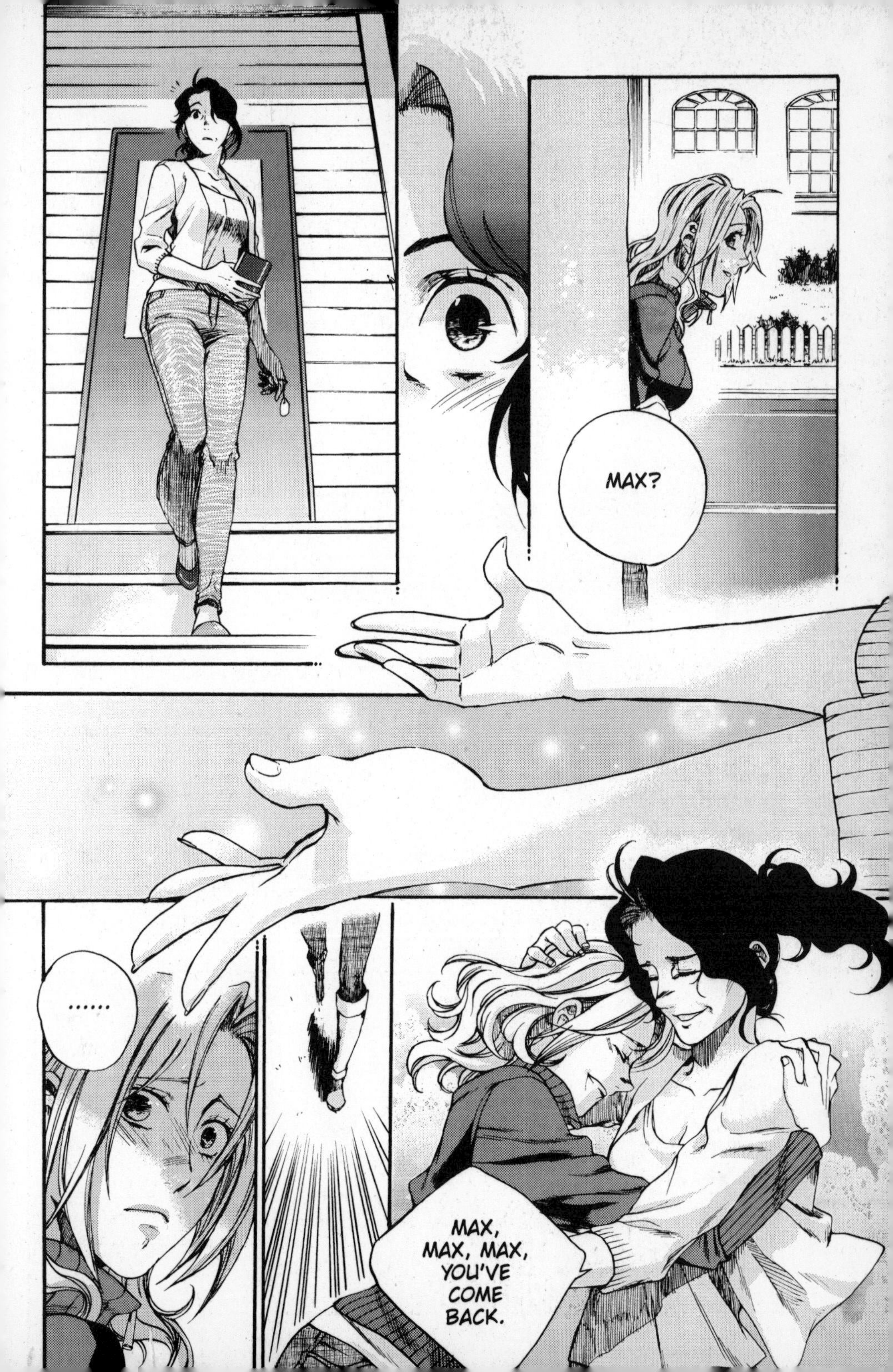
MAX?
......
MAX, MAX, MAX, YOU'VE COME BACK.

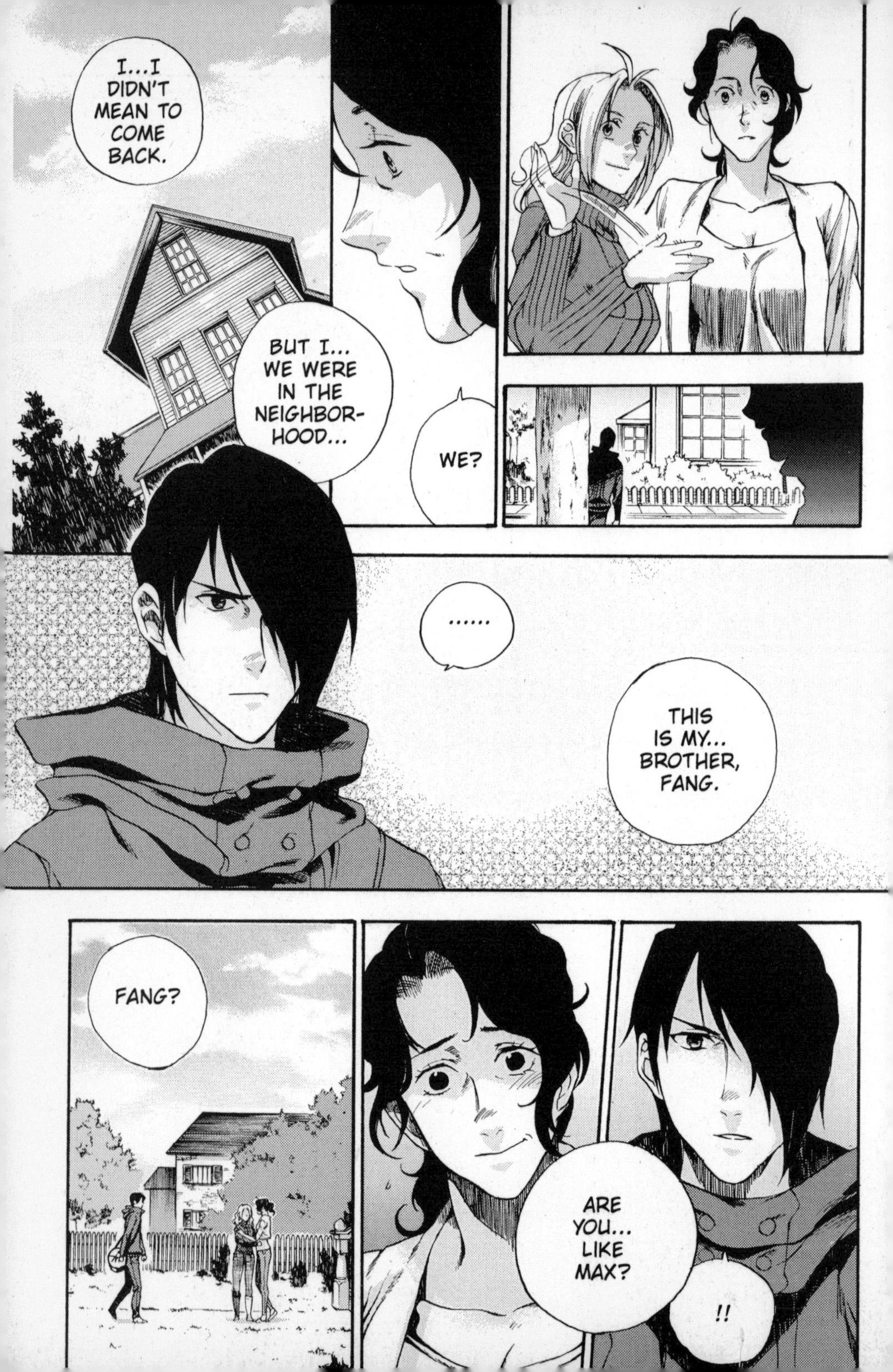
I...I DIDN'T MEAN TO COME BACK.
BUT I... WE WERE IN THE NEIGHBOR-HOOD...
WE?
......
THIS IS MY... BROTHER, FANG.
FANG?
ARE YOU... LIKE MAX?
!!

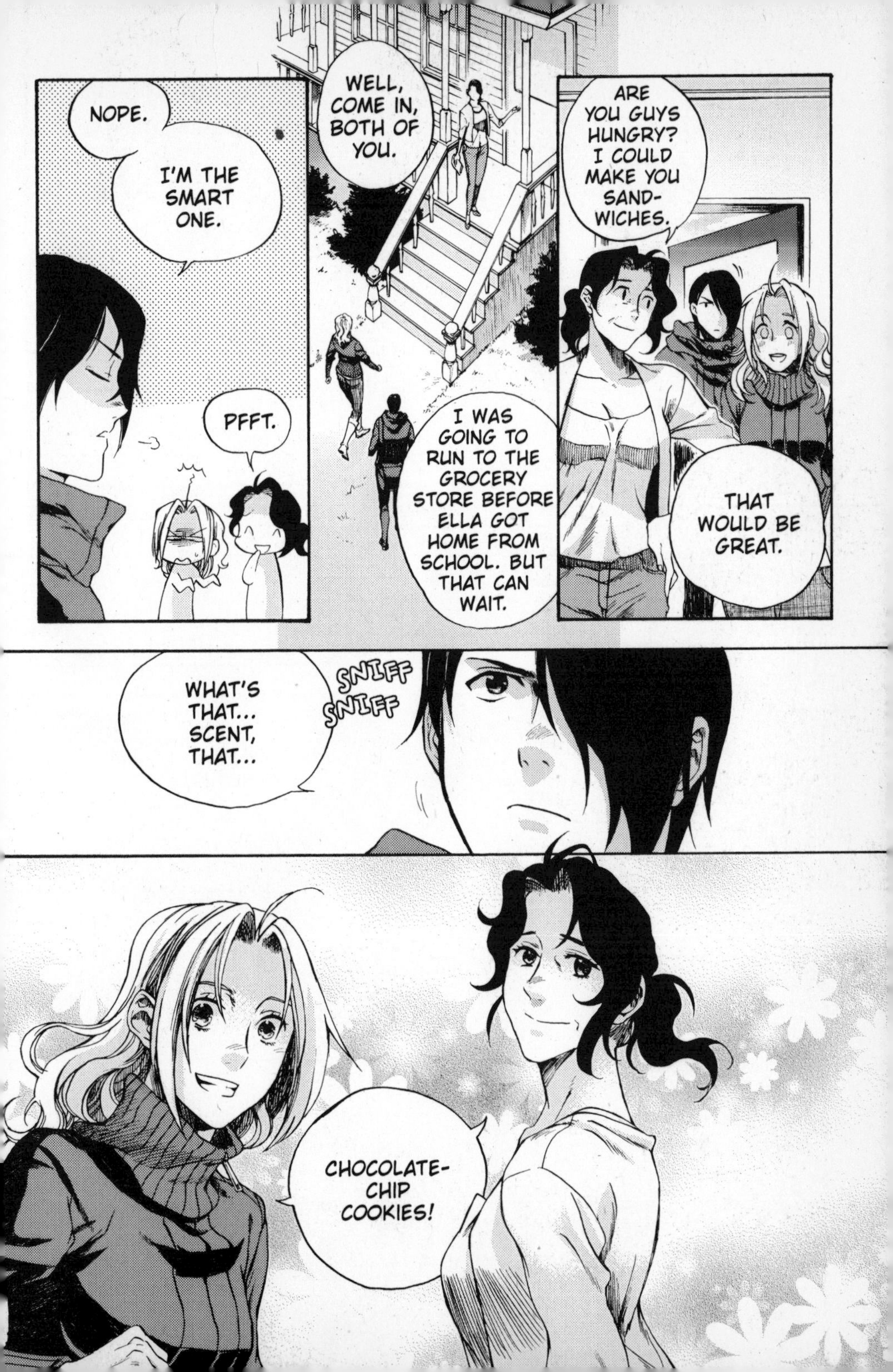
NOPE.
I'M THE SMART ONE.
PFFT.
WELL, COME IN, BOTH OF YOU.
I WAS GOING TO RUN TO THE GROCERY STORE BEFORE ELLA GOT HOME FROM SCHOOL. BUT THAT CAN WAIT.
ARE YOU GUYS HUNGRY? I COULD MAKE YOU SAND-WICHES.
THAT WOULD BE GREAT.
WHAT'S THAT... SCENT, THAT...
SNIFF SNIFF
CHOCOLATE-CHIP COOKIES!

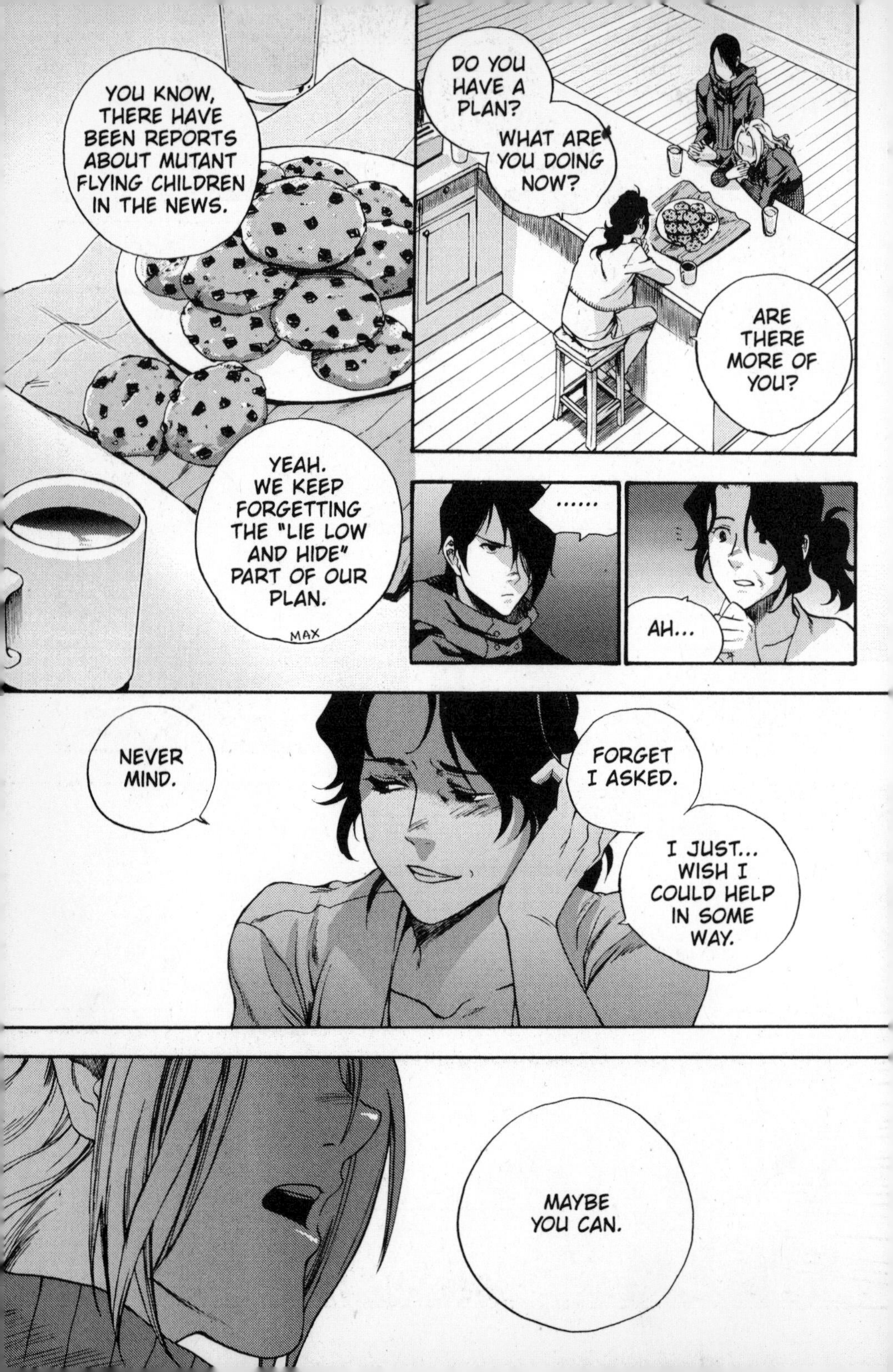
YOU KNOW, THERE HAVE BEEN REPORTS ABOUT MUTANT FLYING CHILDREN IN THE NEWS.
YEAH. WE KEEP FORGETTING THE "LIE LOW AND HIDE" PART OF OUR PLAN.
MAX
DO YOU HAVE A PLAN?
WHAT ARE YOU DOING NOW?
ARE THERE MORE OF YOU?
......
AH...
NEVER MIND.
FORGET I ASKED.
I JUST... WISH I COULD HELP IN SOME WAY.
MAYBE YOU CAN.

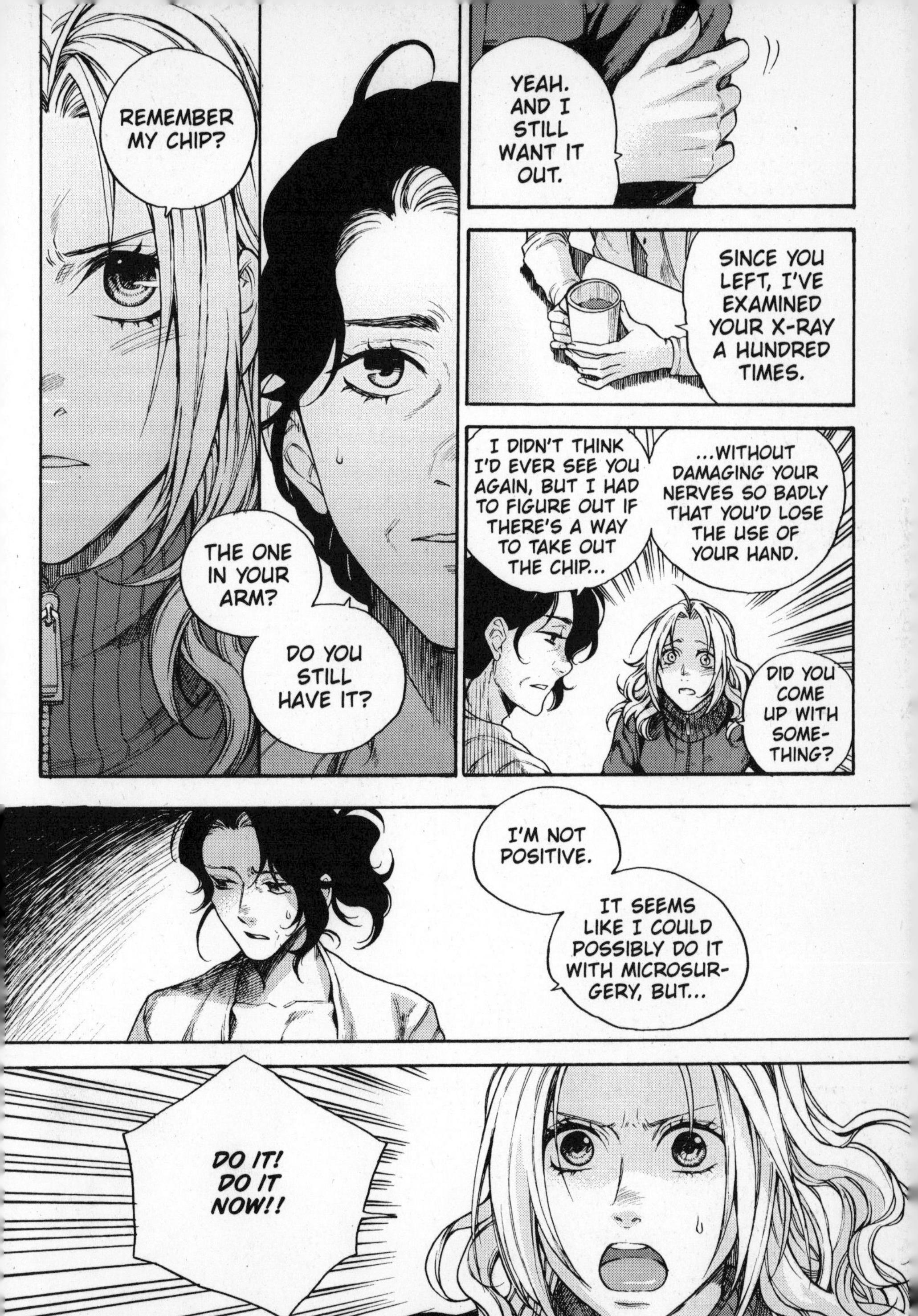
REMEMBER MY CHIP?
THE ONE IN YOUR ARM?
DO YOU STILL HAVE IT?
YEAH. AND I STILL WANT IT OUT.
SINCE YOU LEFT, I'VE EXAMINED YOUR X-RAY A HUNDRED TIMES.
I DIDN'T THINK I'D EVER SEE YOU AGAIN, BUT I HAD TO FIGURE OUT IF THERE'S A WAY TO TAKE OUT THE CHIP...
...WITHOUT DAMAGING YOUR NERVES SO BADLY THAT YOU'D LOSE THE USE OF YOUR HAND.
DID YOU COME UP WITH SOME-THING?
I'M NOT POSITIVE.
IT SEEMS LIKE I COULD POSSIBLY DO IT WITH MICROSUR-GERY, BUT...
DO IT! DO IT NOW!!

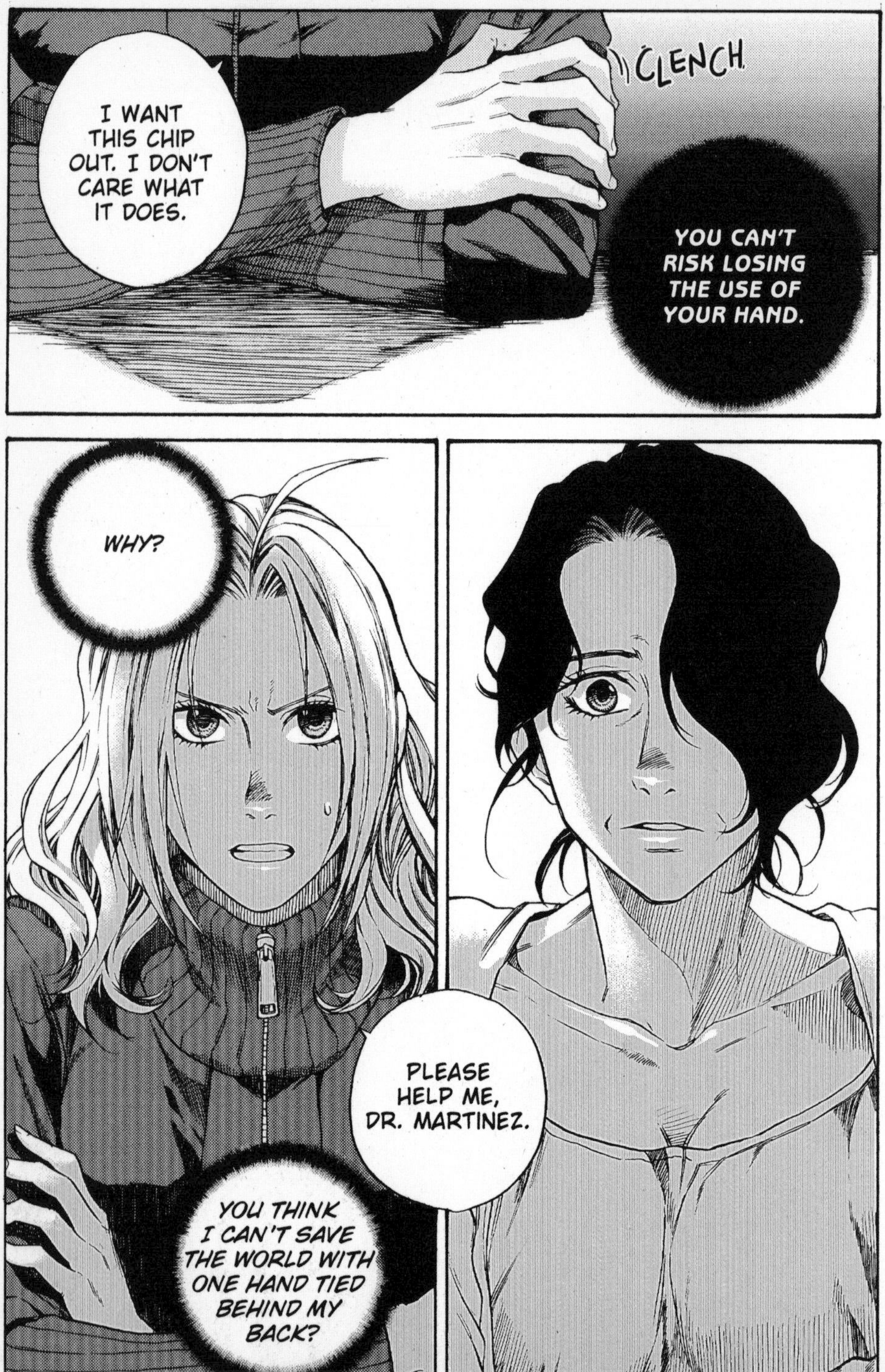
I WANT THIS CHIP OUT. I DON'T CARE WHAT IT DOES.
CLENCH
YOU CAN'T RISK LOSING THE USE OF YOUR HAND.
WHY?
YOU THINK I CAN'T SAVE THE WORLD WITH ONE HAND TIED BEHIND MY BACK?
PLEASE HELP ME, DR. MARTINEZ.

MAXIMUM

RIDE

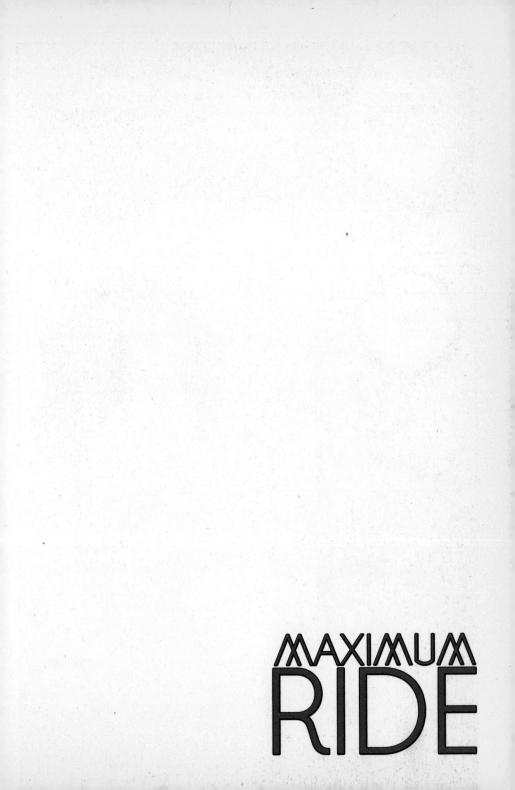

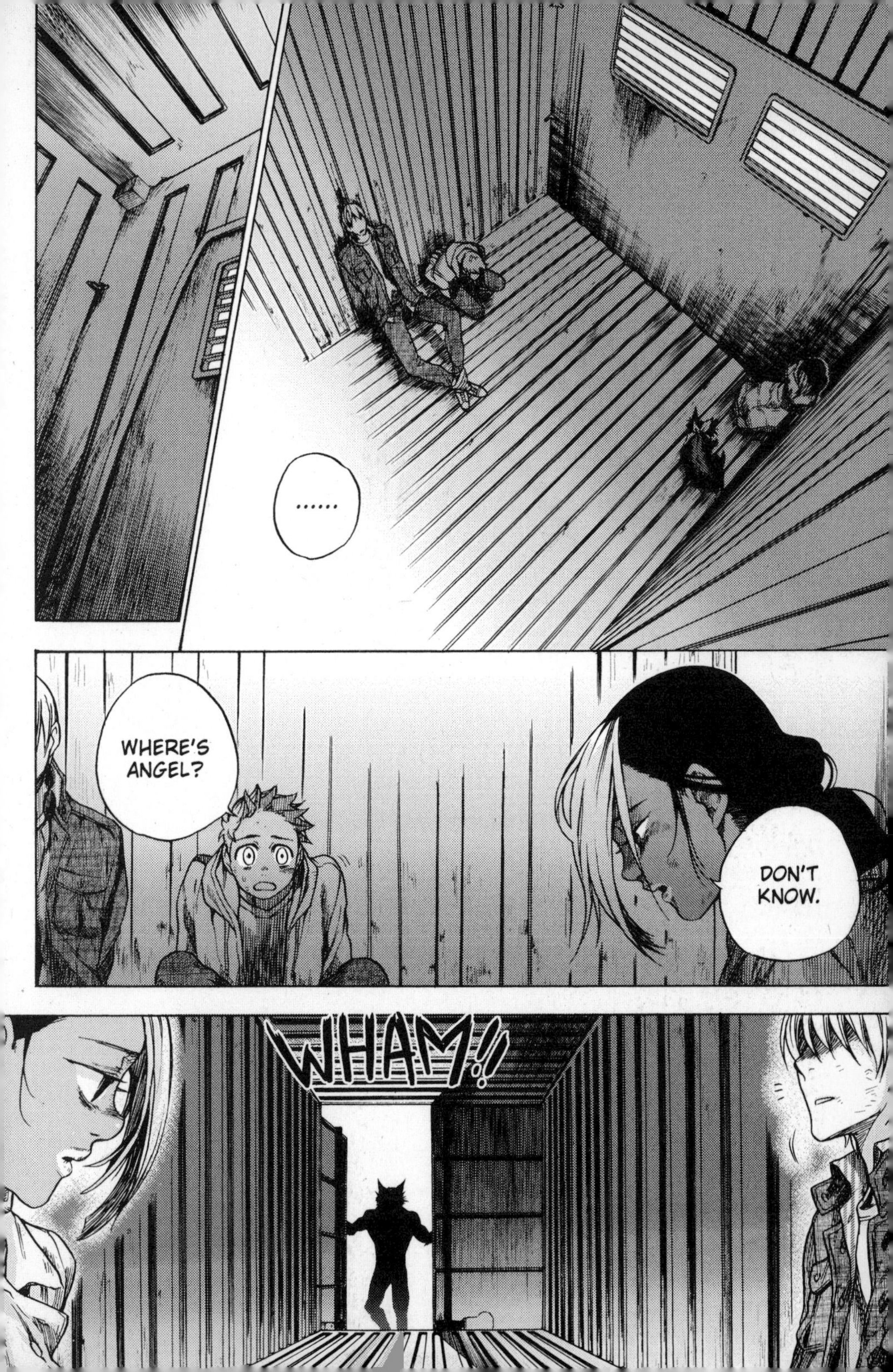
......
WHERE'S ANGEL?
DON'T KNOW.
WHAM!!

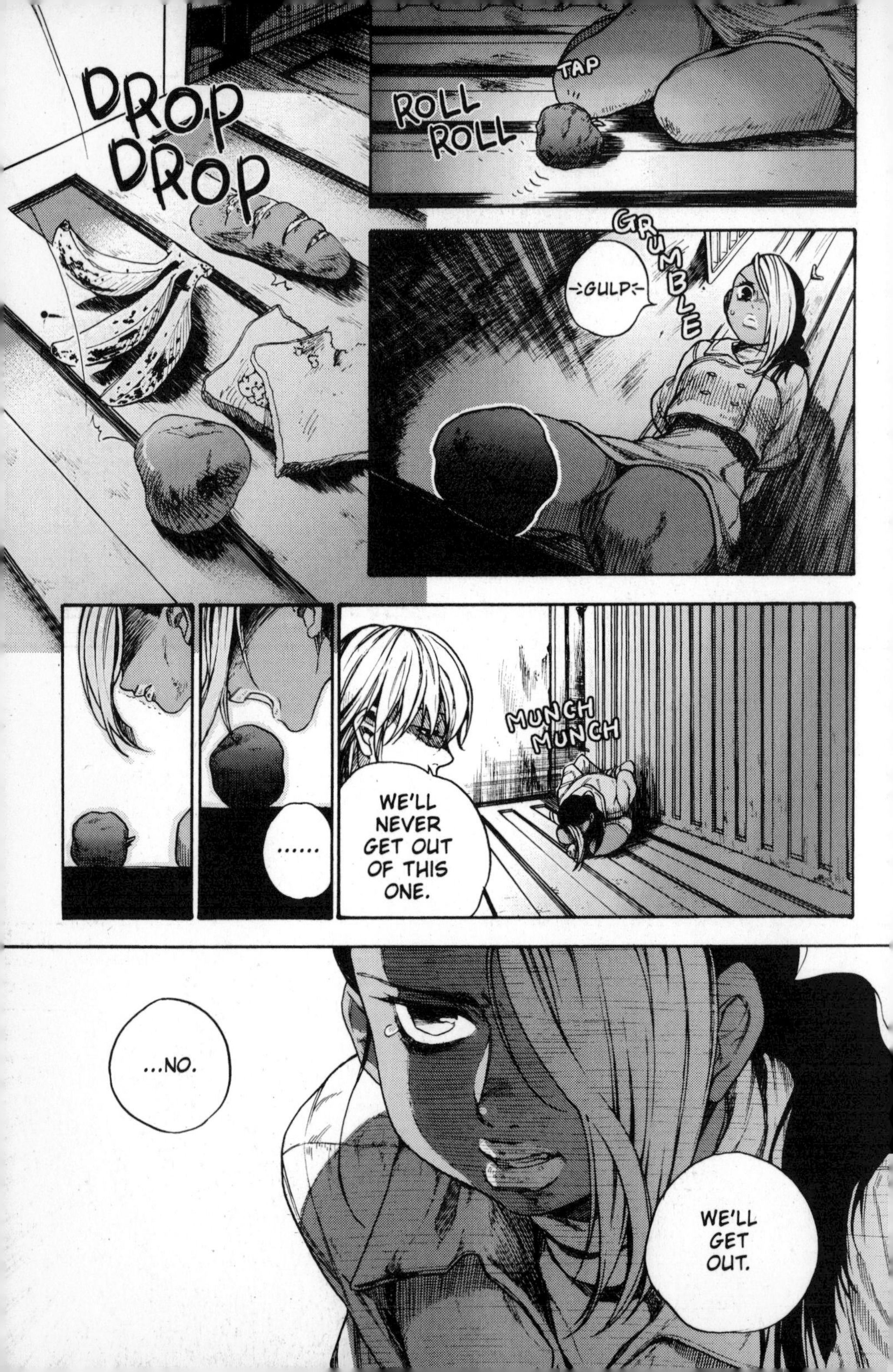
DROP DROP
TAP
ROLL ROLL
GRUMBLE
-GULP-
......
MUNCH MUNCH
WE'LL NEVER GET OUT OF THIS ONE.
...NO.
WE'LL GET OUT.

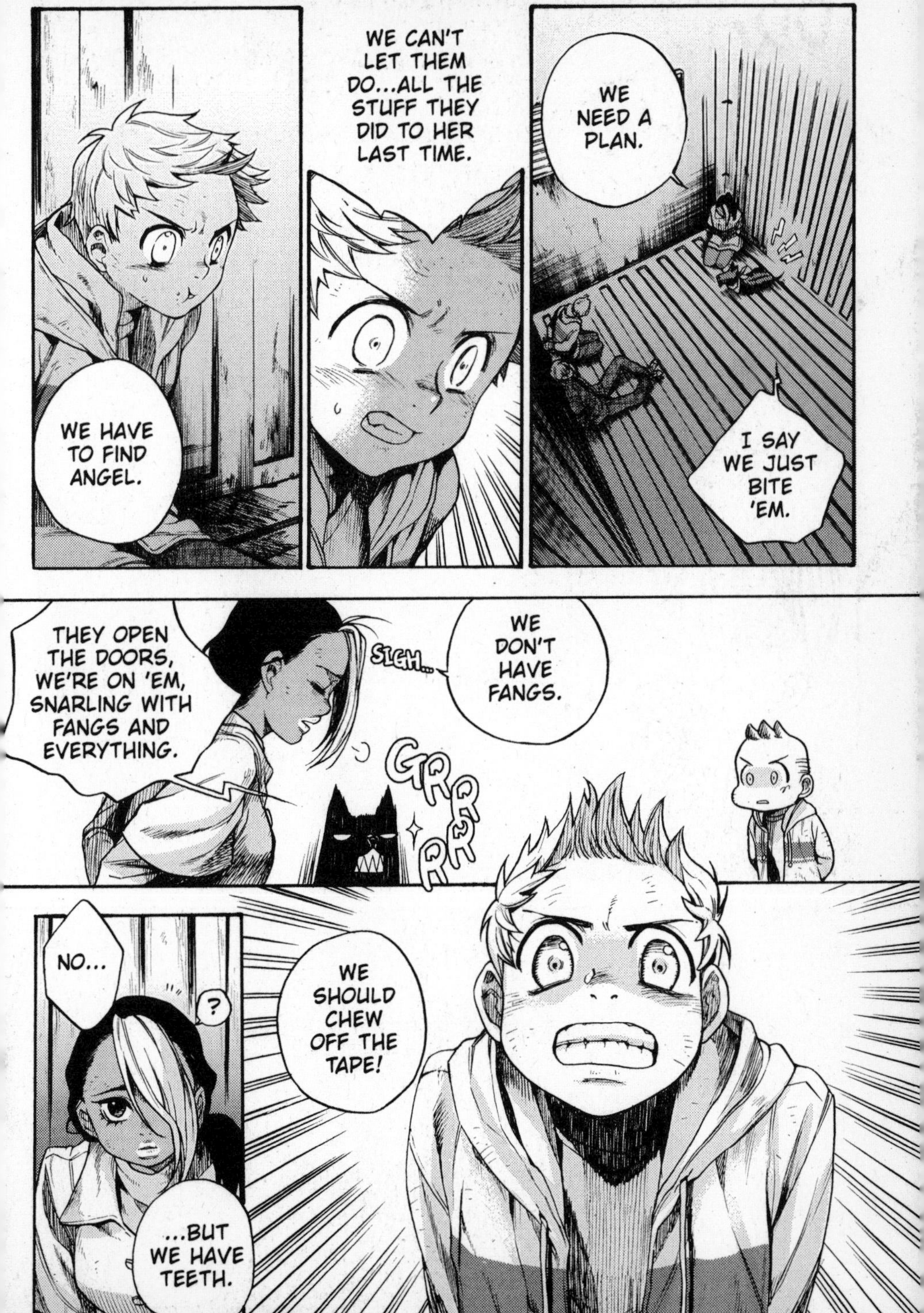
WE HAVE TO FIND ANGEL.
WE CAN'T LET THEM DO...ALL THE STUFF THEY DID TO HER LAST TIME.
WE NEED A PLAN.
I SAY WE JUST BITE 'EM.
THEY OPEN THE DOORS, WE'RE ON 'EM, SNARLING WITH FANGS AND EVERYTHING.
SIGH...
WE DON'T HAVE FANGS.
GRRRRR
NO...
?
...BUT WE HAVE TEETH.
WE SHOULD CHEW OFF THE TAPE!

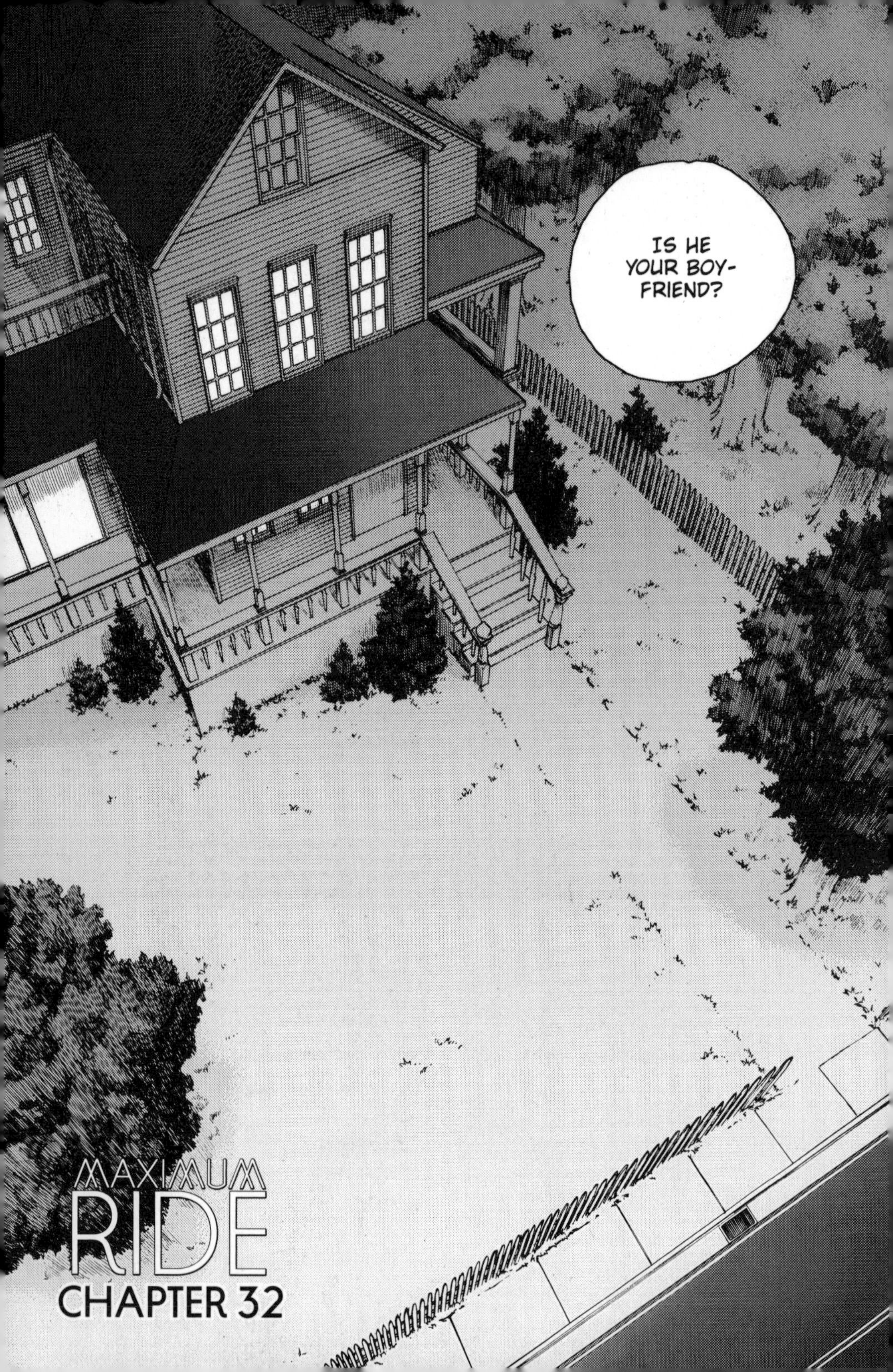
IS HE
YOUR BOY-
FRIEND?
MAXIMUM RIDE
CHAPTER 32

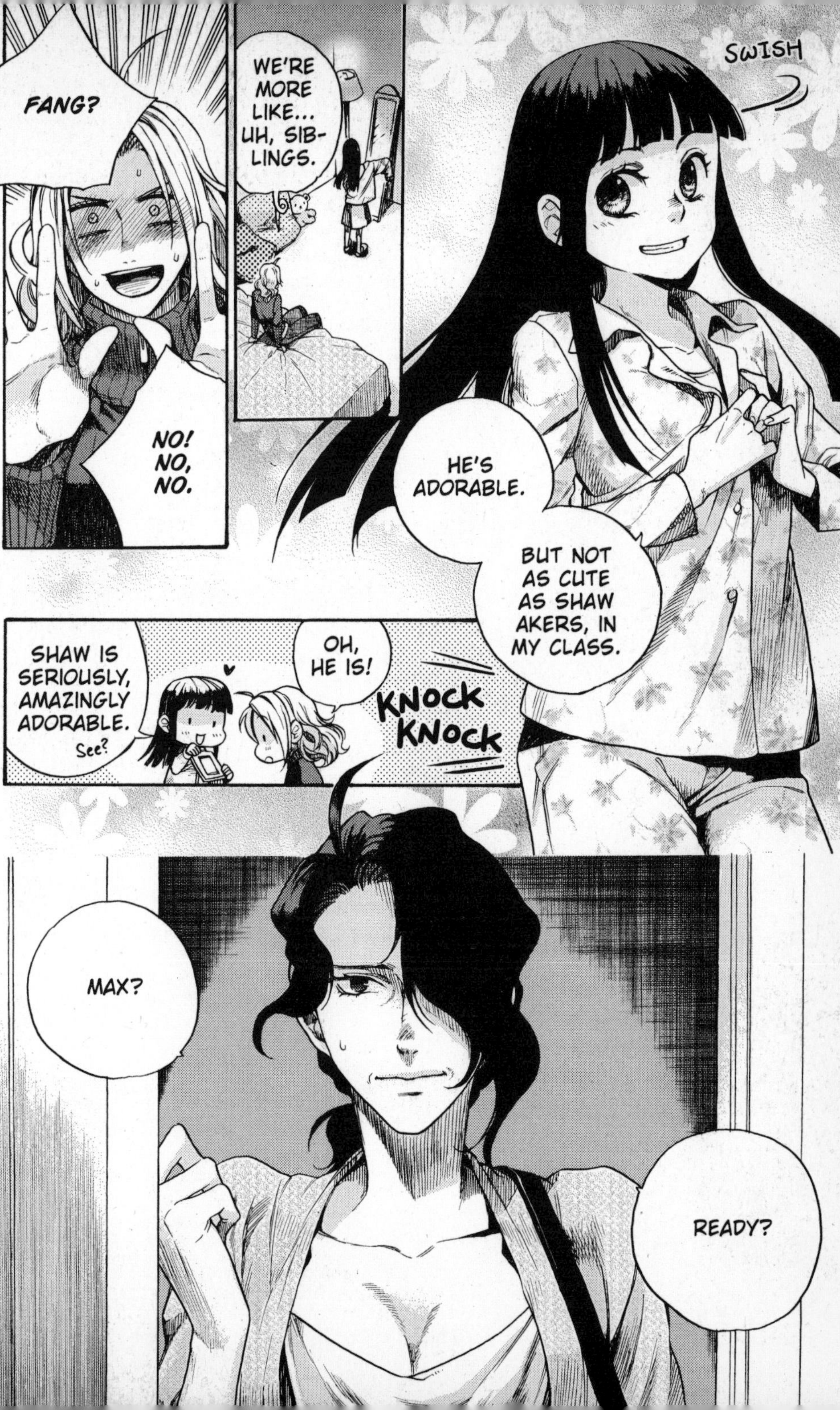

FANG?
NO! NO, NO.
WE'RE MORE LIKE... UH, SIB-LINGS.
SWISH
HE'S ADORABLE.
BUT NOT AS CUTE AS SHAW AKERS, IN MY CLASS.
SHAW IS SERIOUSLY, AMAZINGLY ADORABLE.
See?
OH, HE IS!
KNOCK KNOCK
MAX?
READY?

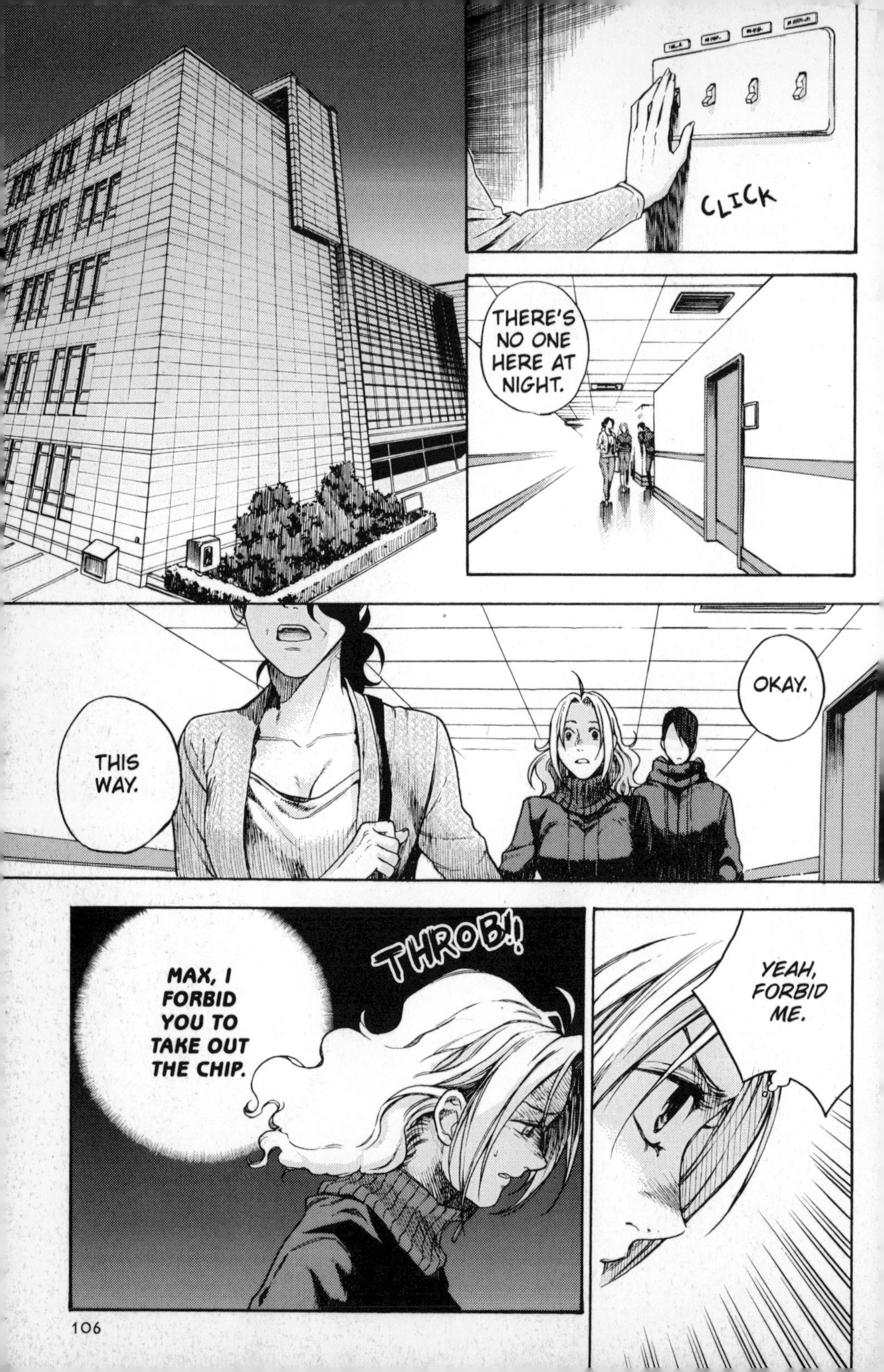
CLICK
THERE'S NO ONE HERE AT NIGHT.
THIS WAY.
OKAY.
MAX, I FORBID YOU TO TAKE OUT THE CHIP.
THROB!!
YEAH, FORBID ME.

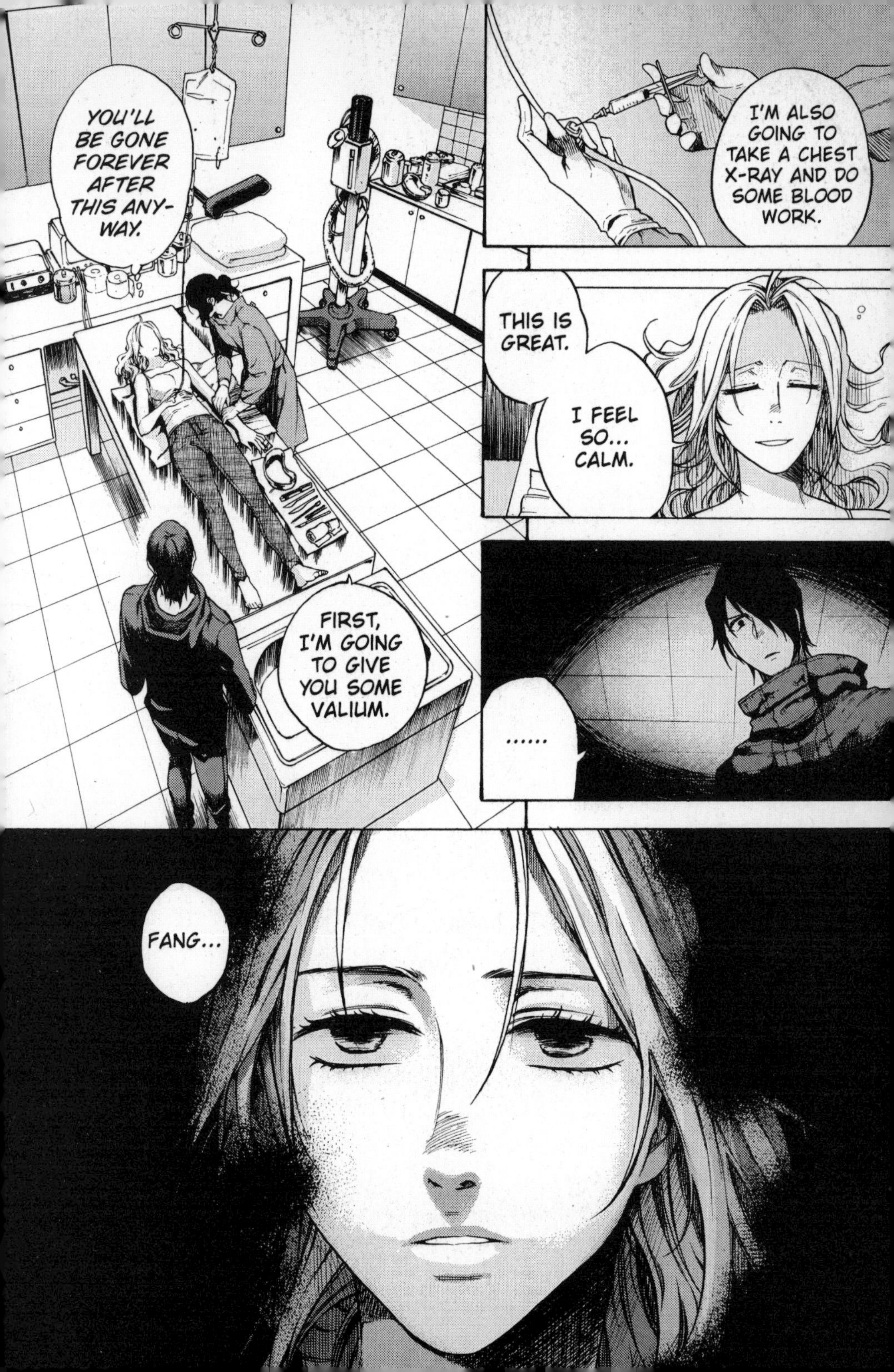
YOU'LL BE GONE FOREVER AFTER THIS ANYWAY.
FIRST, I'M GOING TO GIVE YOU SOME VALIUM.
I'M ALSO GOING TO TAKE A CHEST X-RAY AND DO SOME BLOOD WORK.
THIS IS GREAT.
I FEEL SO... CALM.
......
FANG...

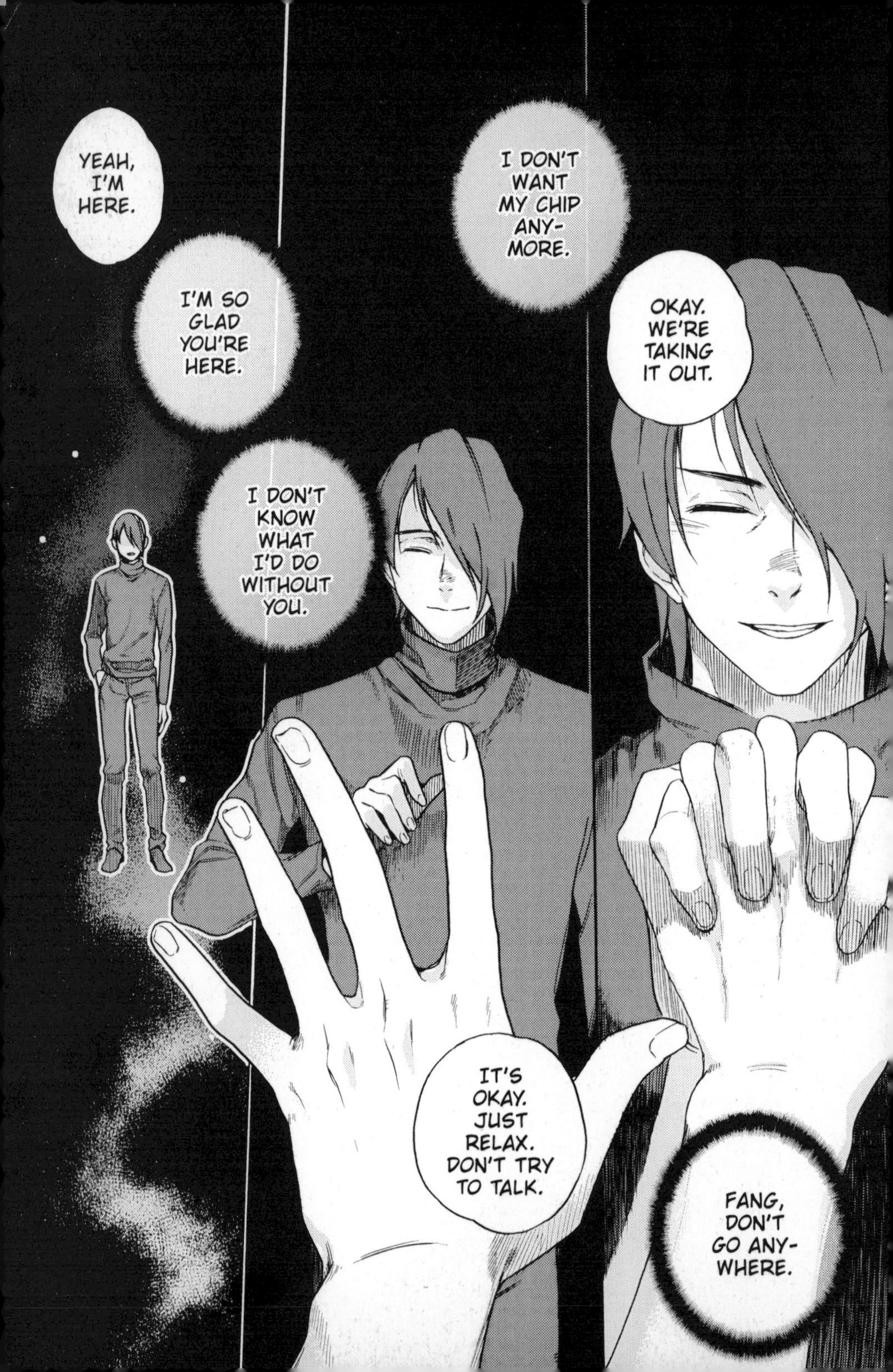
YEAH, I'M HERE.
I'M SO GLAD YOU'RE HERE.
I DON'T KNOW WHAT I'D DO WITHOUT YOU.
I DON'T WANT MY CHIP ANY-MORE.
IT'S OKAY. JUST RELAX. DON'T TRY TO TALK.
OKAY. WE'RE TAKING IT OUT.
FANG, DON'T GO ANY-WHERE.

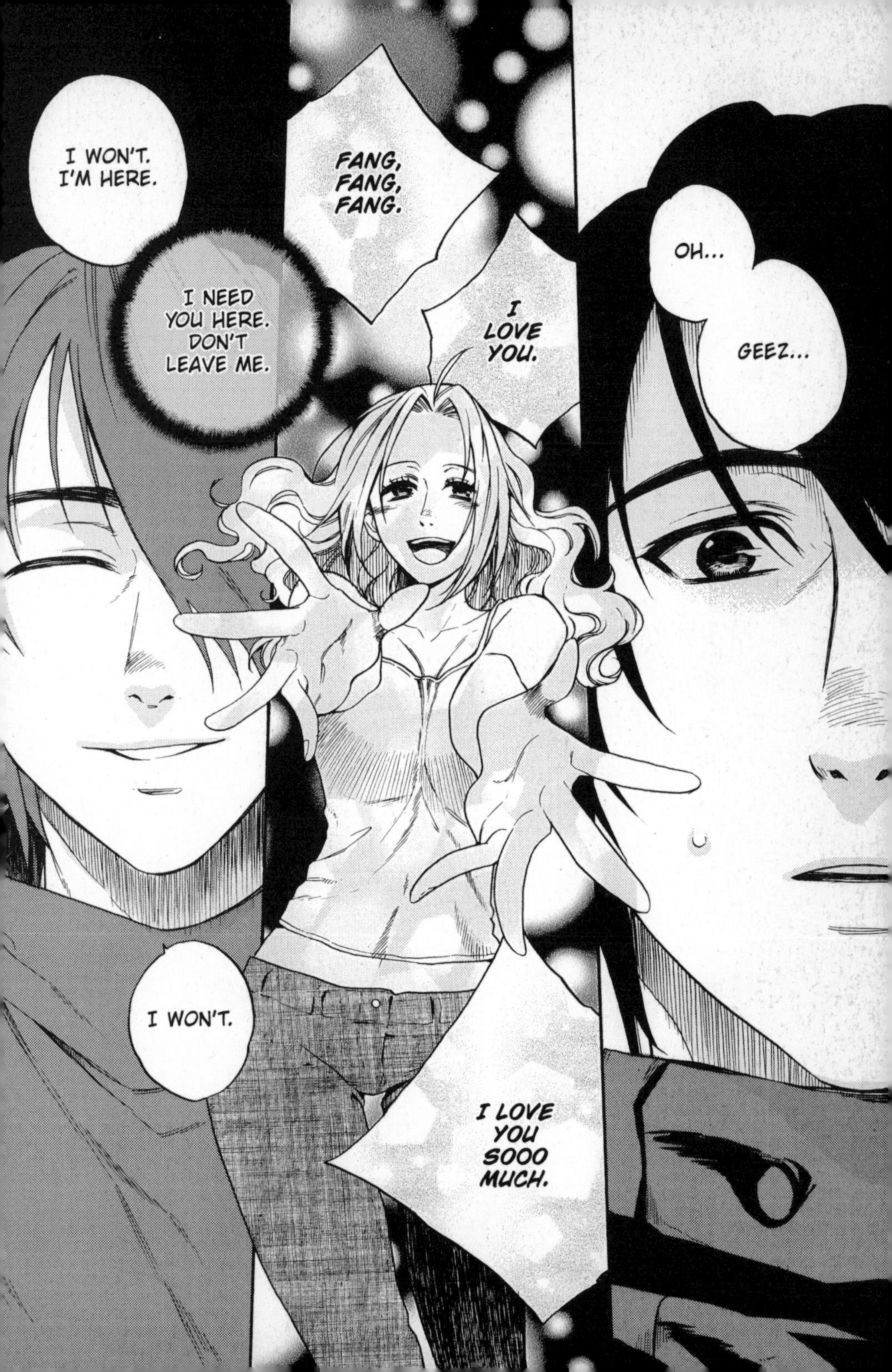
I WON'T. I'M HERE.
I NEED YOU HERE. DON'T LEAVE ME.
I WON'T.
FANG, FANG, FANG.
I LOVE YOU.
I LOVE YOU SOOO MUCH.
OH...
GEEZ...

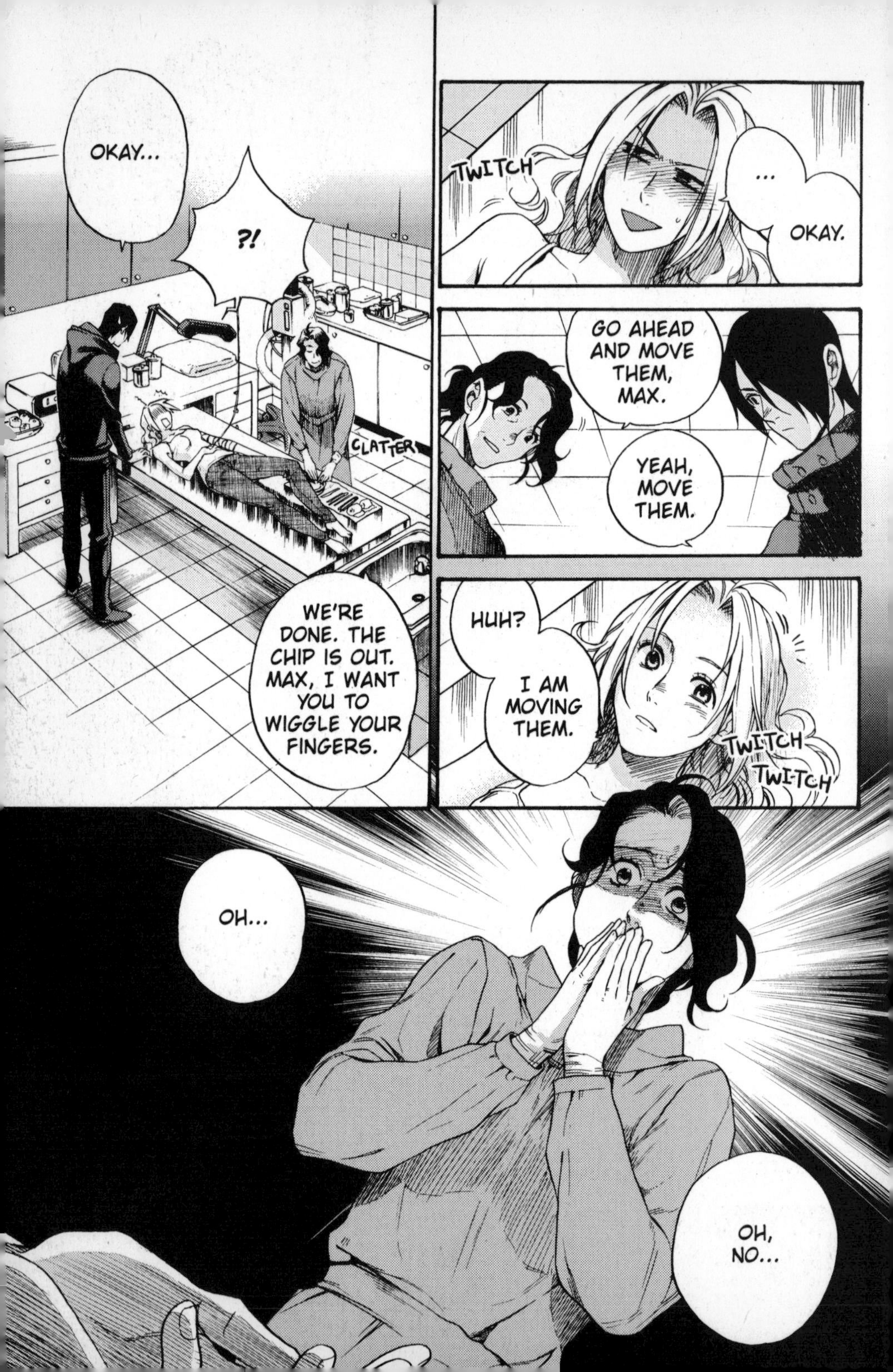
OKAY...
?!
CLATTER
WE'RE DONE. THE CHIP IS OUT. MAX, I WANT YOU TO WIGGLE YOUR FINGERS.
TWITCH
... OKAY.
GO AHEAD AND MOVE THEM, MAX.
YEAH, MOVE THEM.
HUH?
I AM MOVING THEM.
TWITCH TWITCH
OH...
OH, NO...

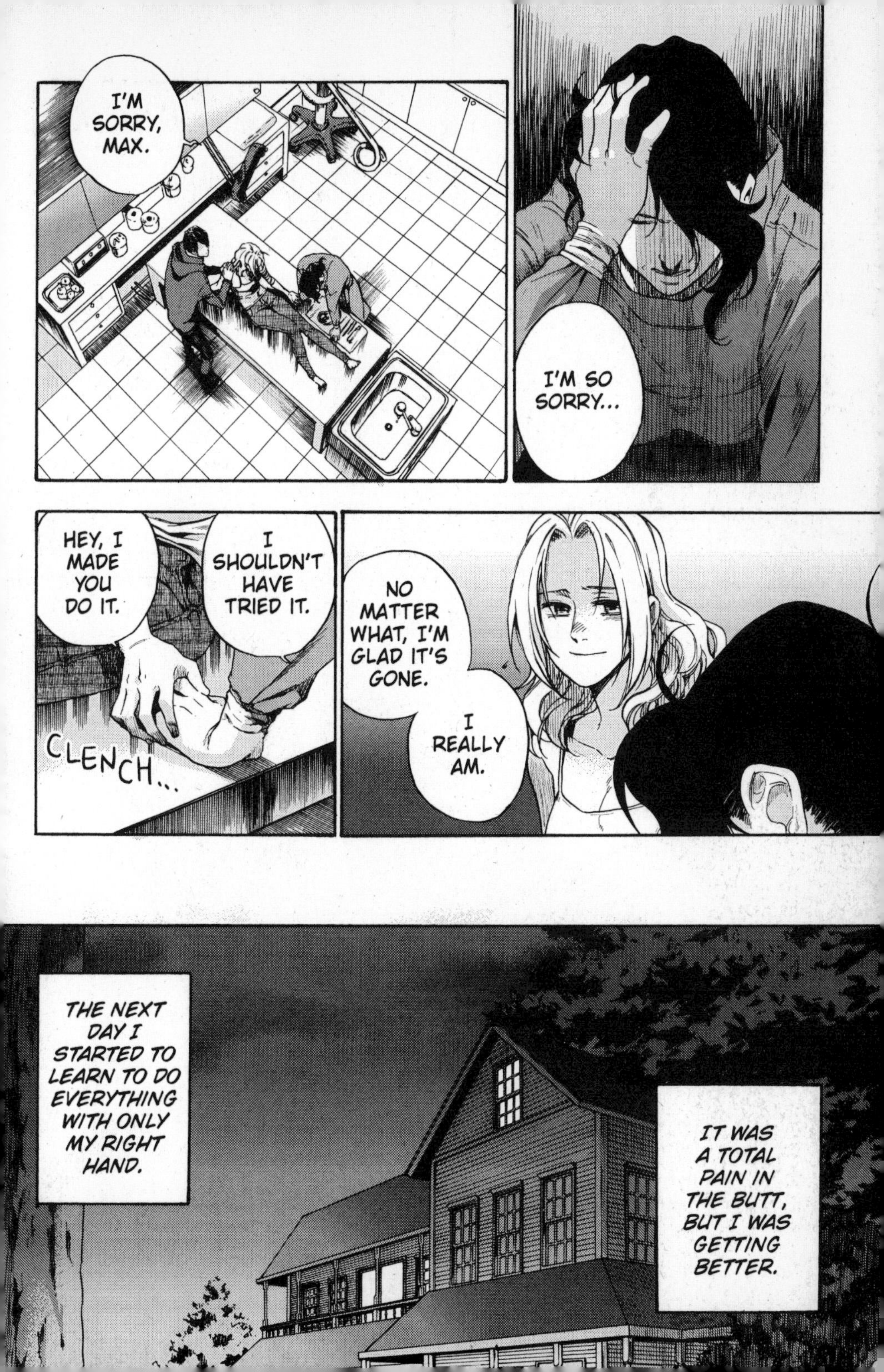
I'M SORRY, MAX.
I'M SO SORRY...
HEY, I MADE YOU DO IT.
I SHOULDN'T HAVE TRIED IT.
CLENCH...
NO MATTER WHAT, I'M GLAD IT'S GONE.
I REALLY AM.
THE NEXT DAY I STARTED TO LEARN TO DO EVERYTHING WITH ONLY MY RIGHT HAND.
IT WAS A TOTAL PAIN IN THE BUTT, BUT I WAS GETTING BETTER.

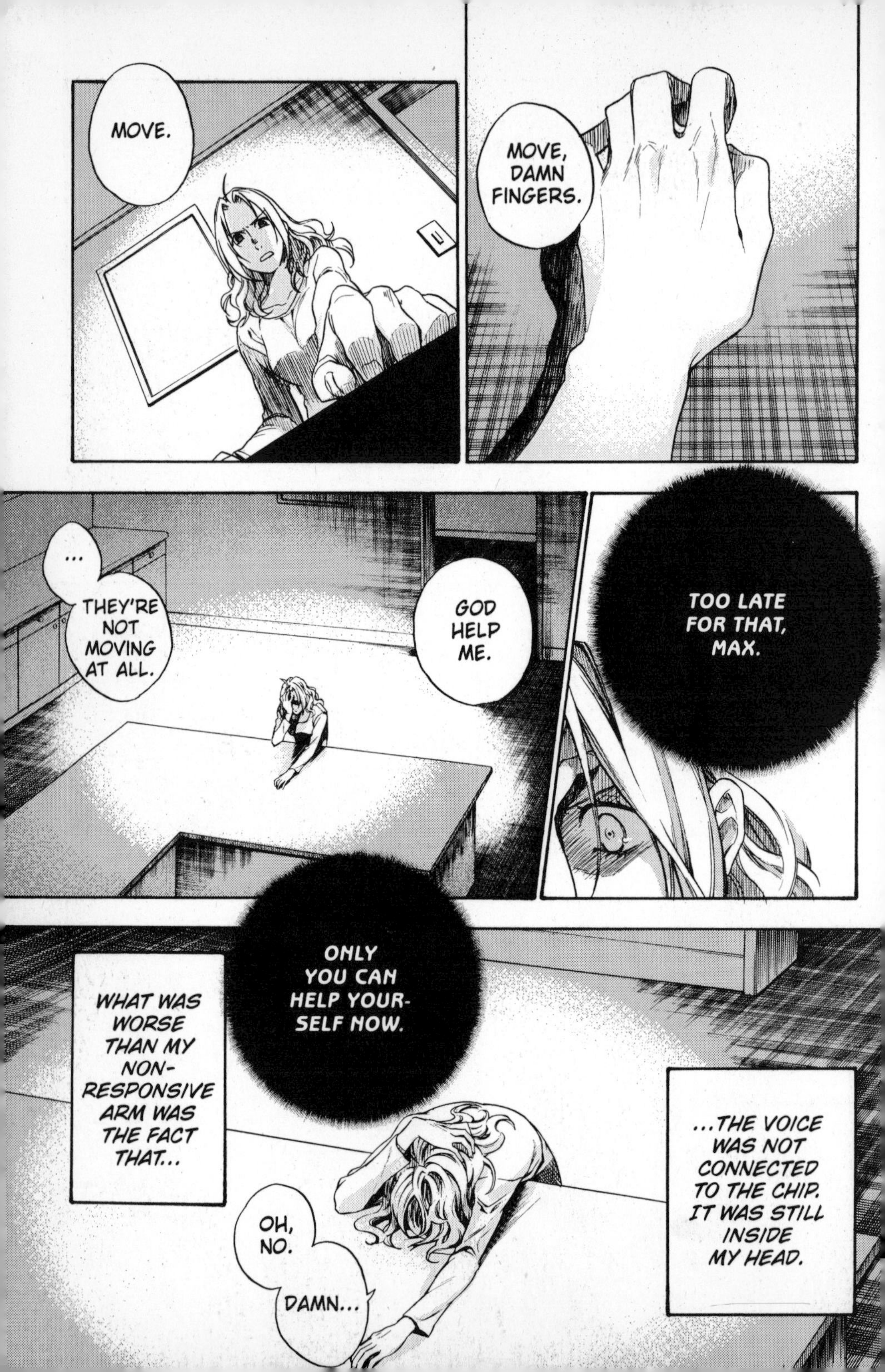
MOVE.
MOVE, DAMN FINGERS.
...
THEY'RE NOT MOVING AT ALL.
GOD HELP ME.
TOO LATE FOR THAT, MAX.
WHAT WAS WORSE THAN MY NON-RESPONSIVE ARM WAS THE FACT THAT...
ONLY YOU CAN HELP YOUR-SELF NOW.
OH, NO.
DAMN...
...THE VOICE WAS NOT CONNECTED TO THE CHIP. IT WAS STILL INSIDE MY HEAD.

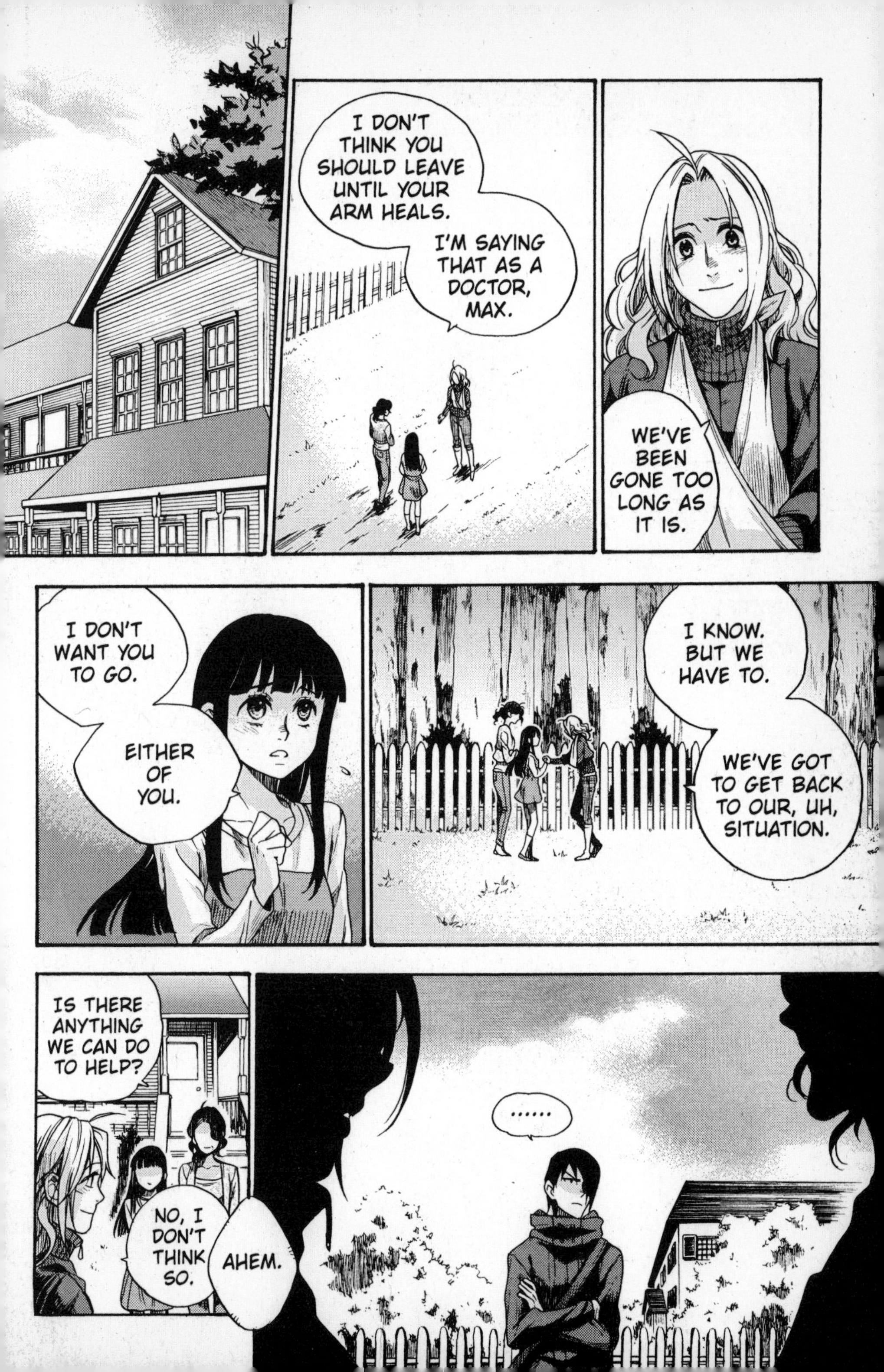
I DON'T THINK YOU SHOULD LEAVE UNTIL YOUR ARM HEALS.
I'M SAYING THAT AS A DOCTOR, MAX.
WE'VE BEEN GONE TOO LONG AS IT IS.
I DON'T WANT YOU TO GO.
EITHER OF YOU.
I KNOW. BUT WE HAVE TO.
WE'VE GOT TO GET BACK TO OUR, UH, SITUATION.
IS THERE ANYTHING WE CAN DO TO HELP?
NO, I DON'T THINK SO.
AHEM.
......

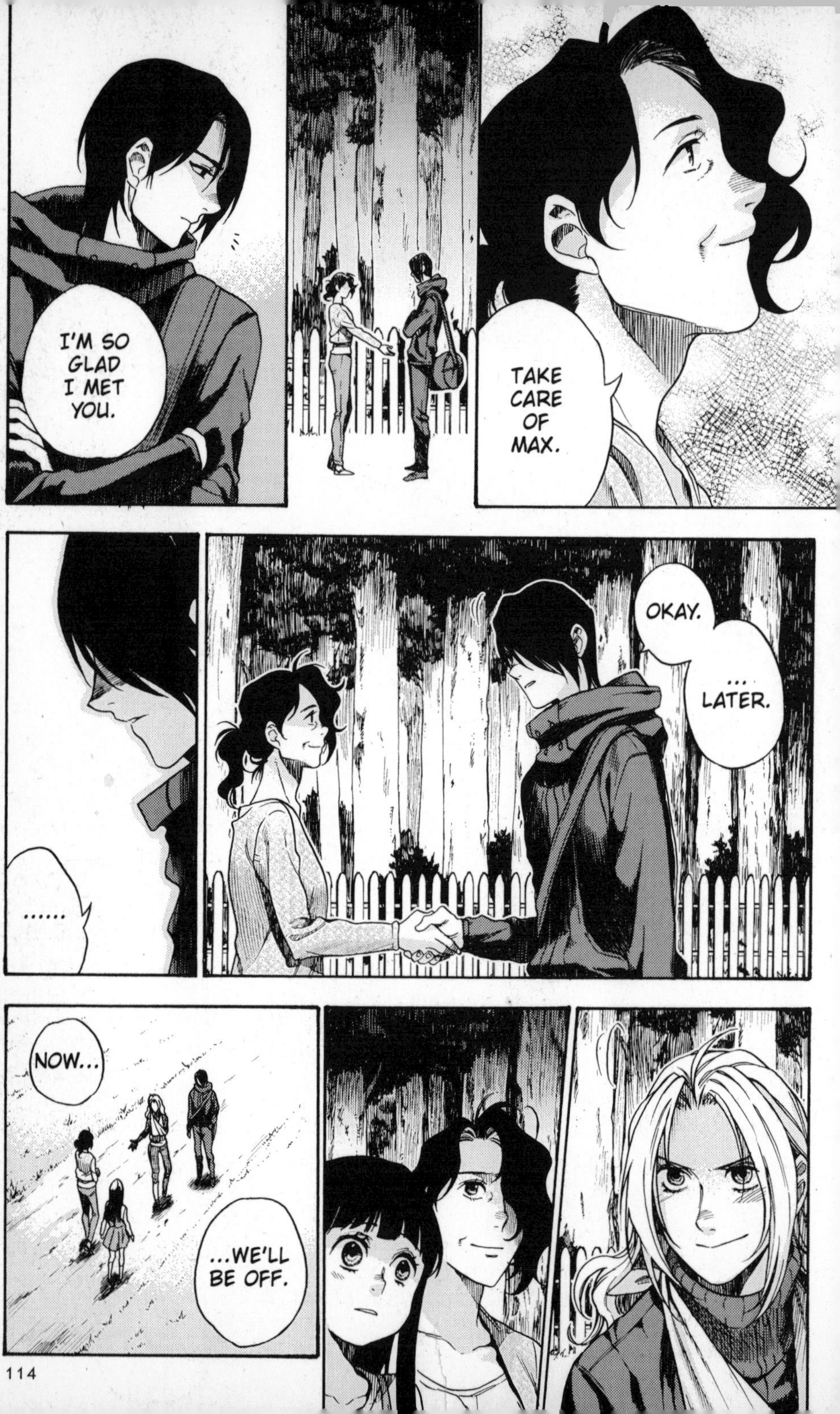
I'M SO GLAD I MET YOU.
TAKE CARE OF MAX.
......
OKAY.
...LATER.
NOW...
...WE'LL BE OFF.

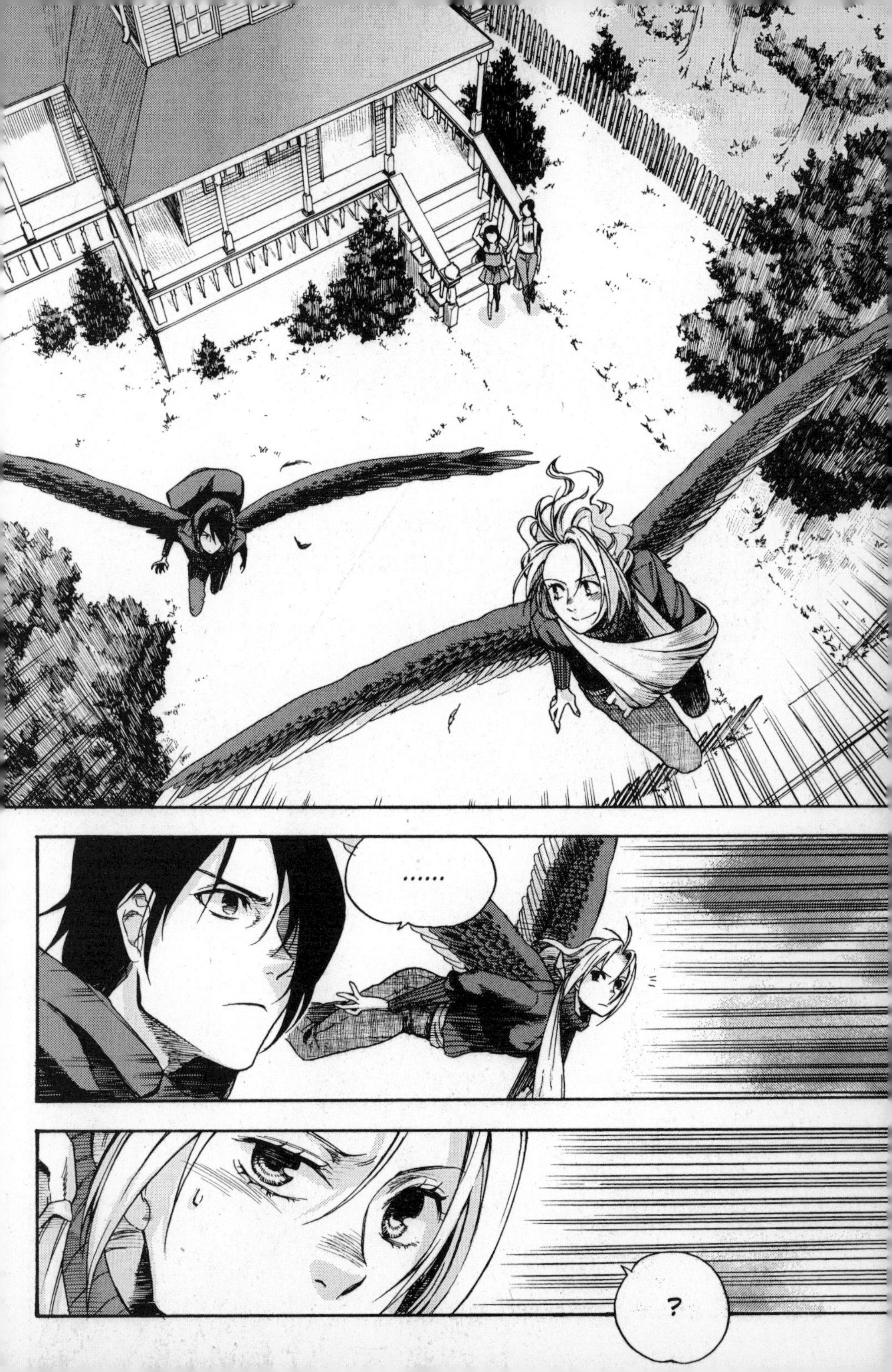
......
?

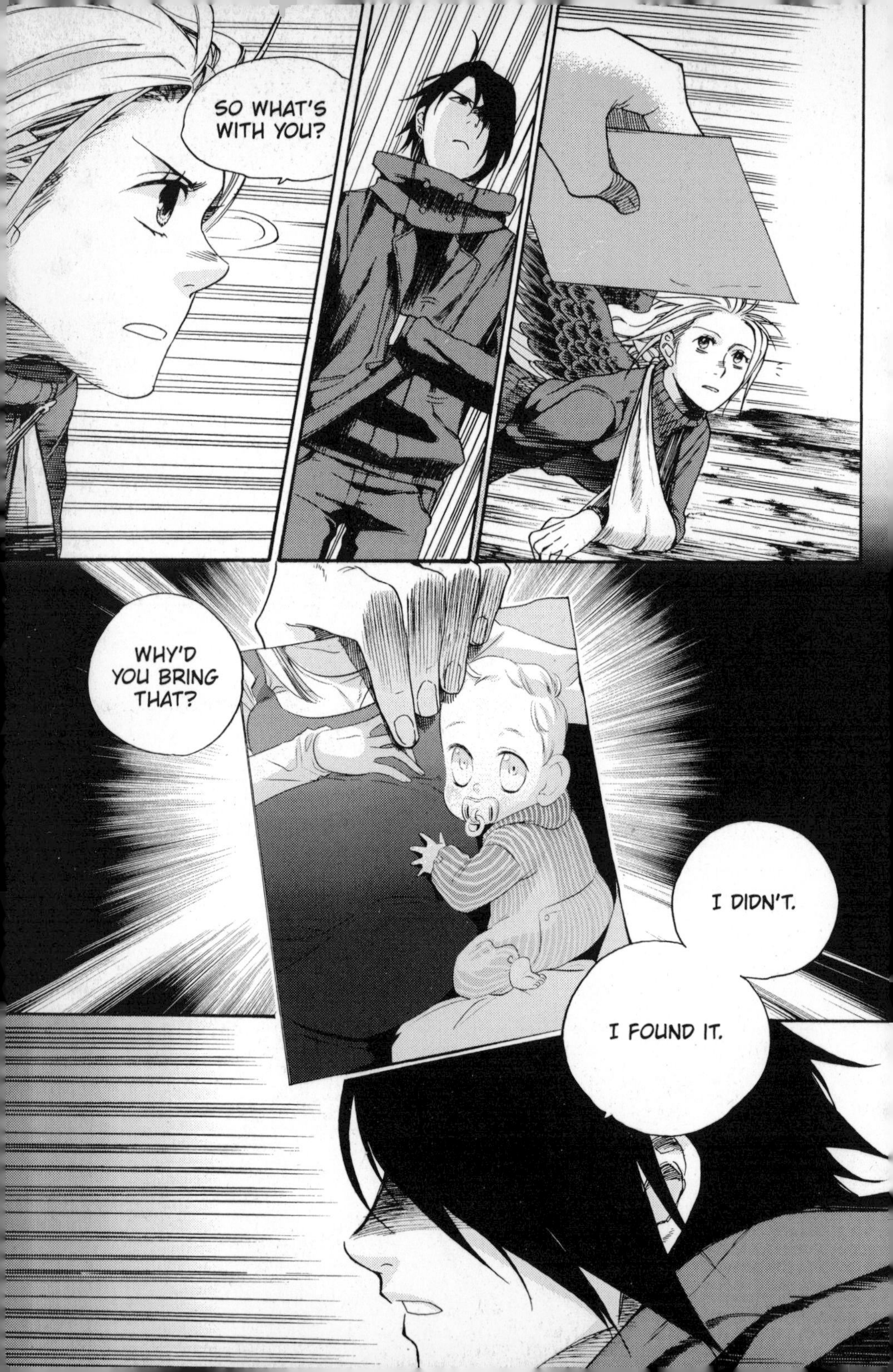
SO WHAT'S WITH YOU?
WHY'D YOU BRING THAT?
I DIDN'T.
I FOUND IT.

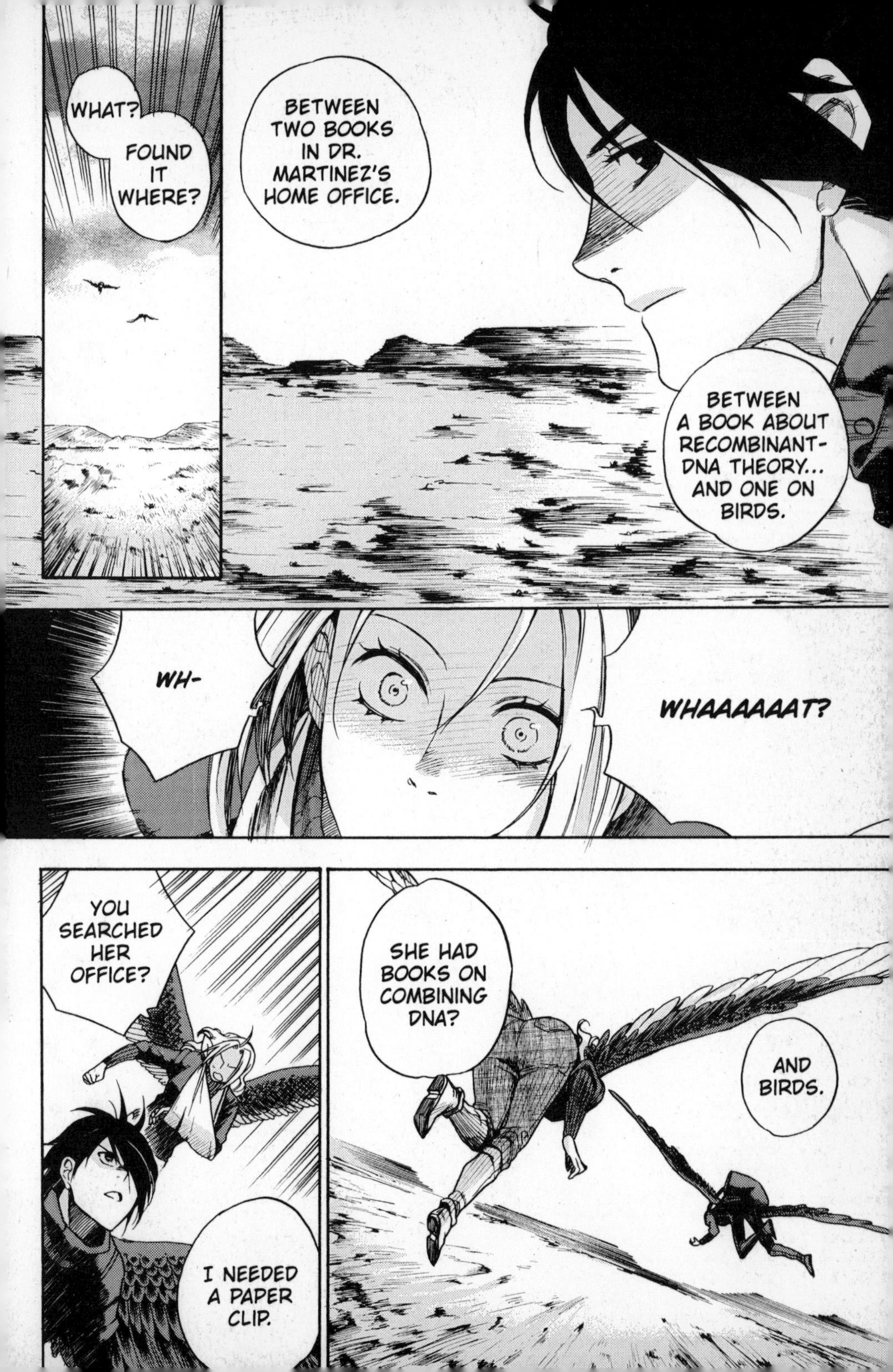
WHAT?
FOUND IT WHERE?
BETWEEN TWO BOOKS IN DR. MARTINEZ'S HOME OFFICE.
BETWEEN A BOOK ABOUT RECOMBINANT-DNA THEORY... AND ONE ON BIRDS.
WH-
WHAAAAAAT?
YOU SEARCHED HER OFFICE?
I NEEDED A PAPER CLIP.
SHE HAD BOOKS ON COMBINING DNA?
AND BIRDS.

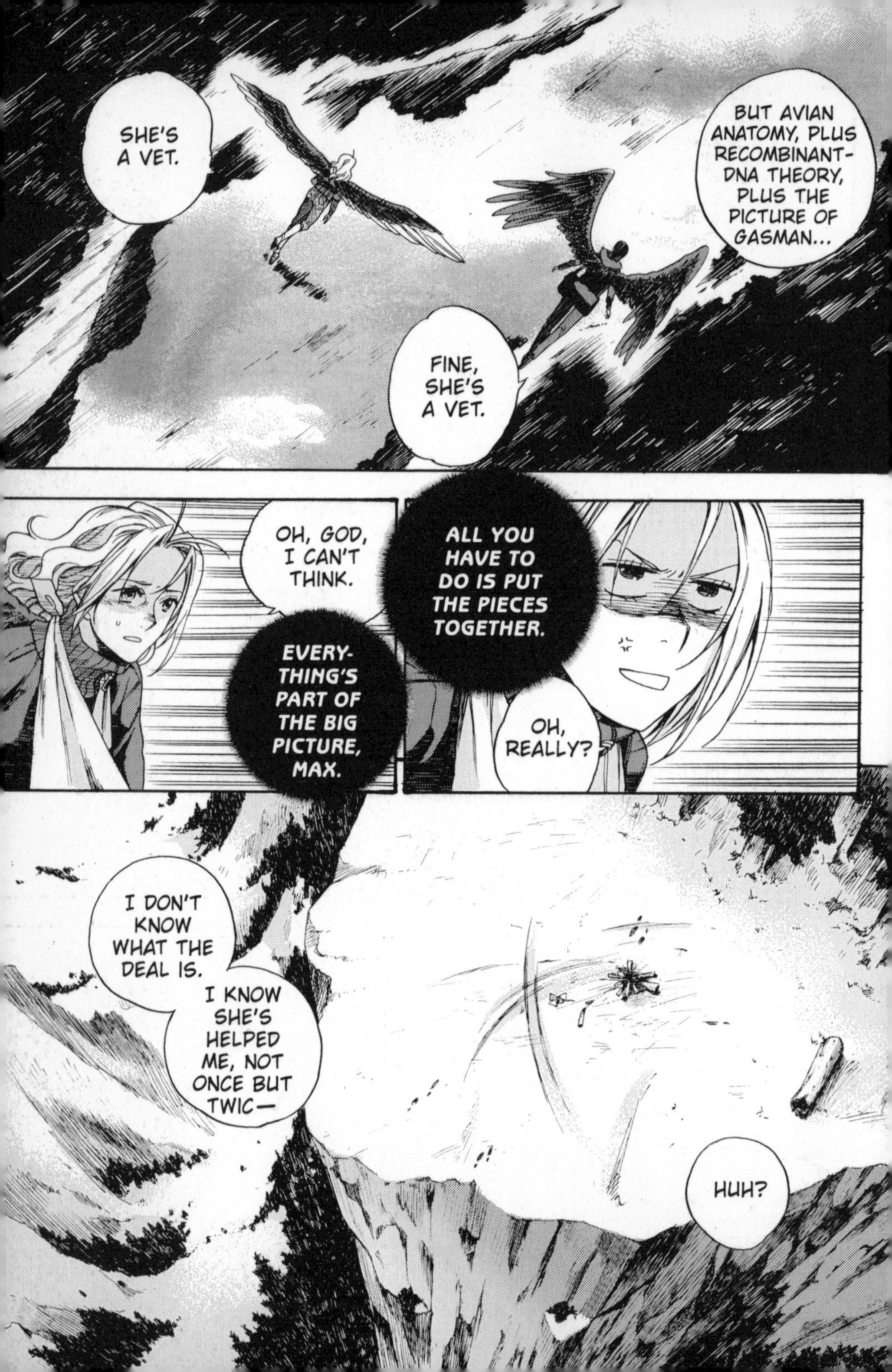
SHE'S A VET.
BUT AVIAN ANATOMY, PLUS RECOMBINANT-DNA THEORY, PLUS THE PICTURE OF GASMAN...
FINE, SHE'S A VET.
OH, GOD, I CAN'T THINK.
EVERY-THING'S PART OF THE BIG PICTURE, MAX.
ALL YOU HAVE TO DO IS PUT THE PIECES TOGETHER.
OH, REALLY?
I DON'T KNOW WHAT THE DEAL IS.
I KNOW SHE'S HELPED ME, NOT ONCE BUT TWIC—
HUH?

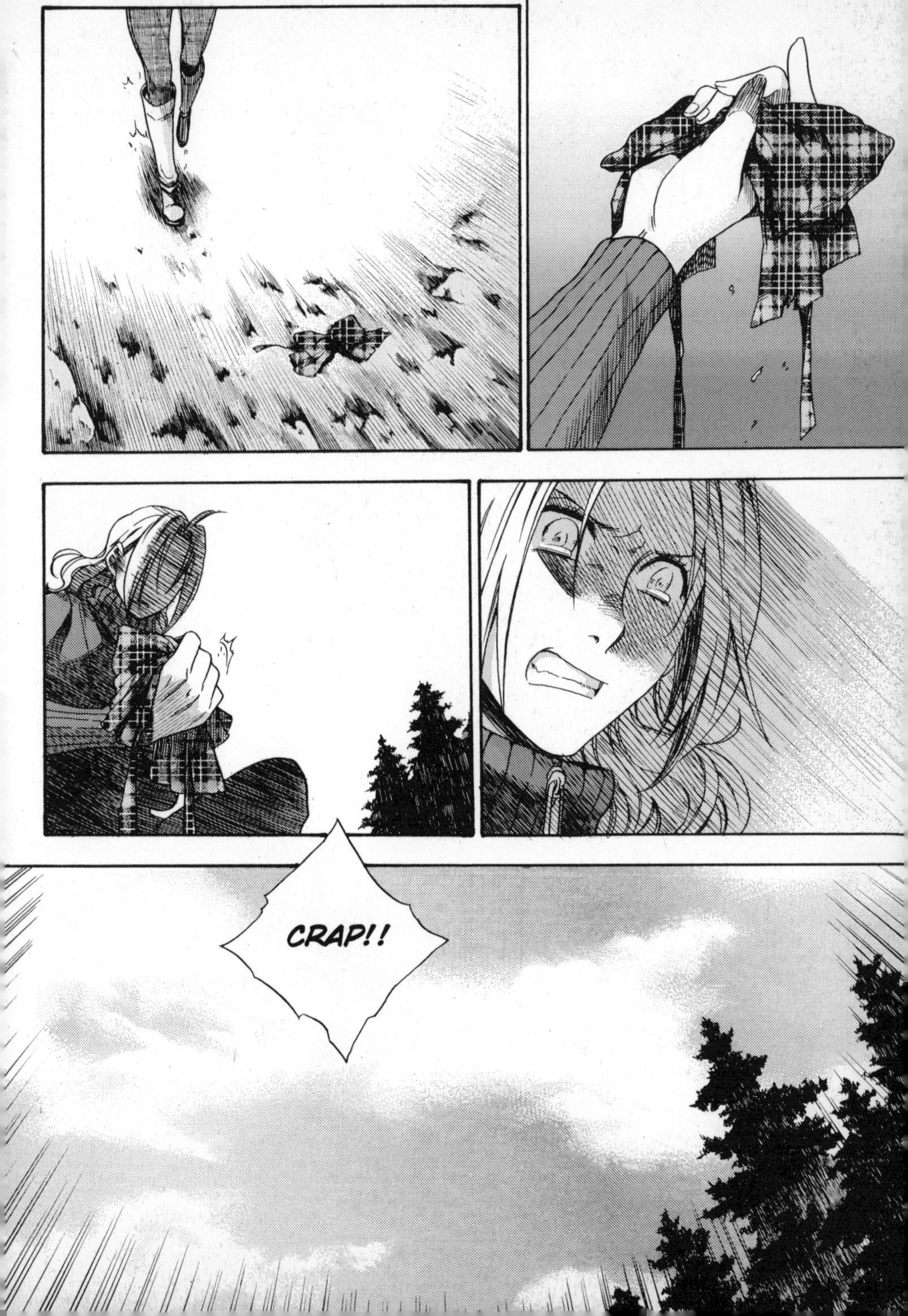
CRAP!!

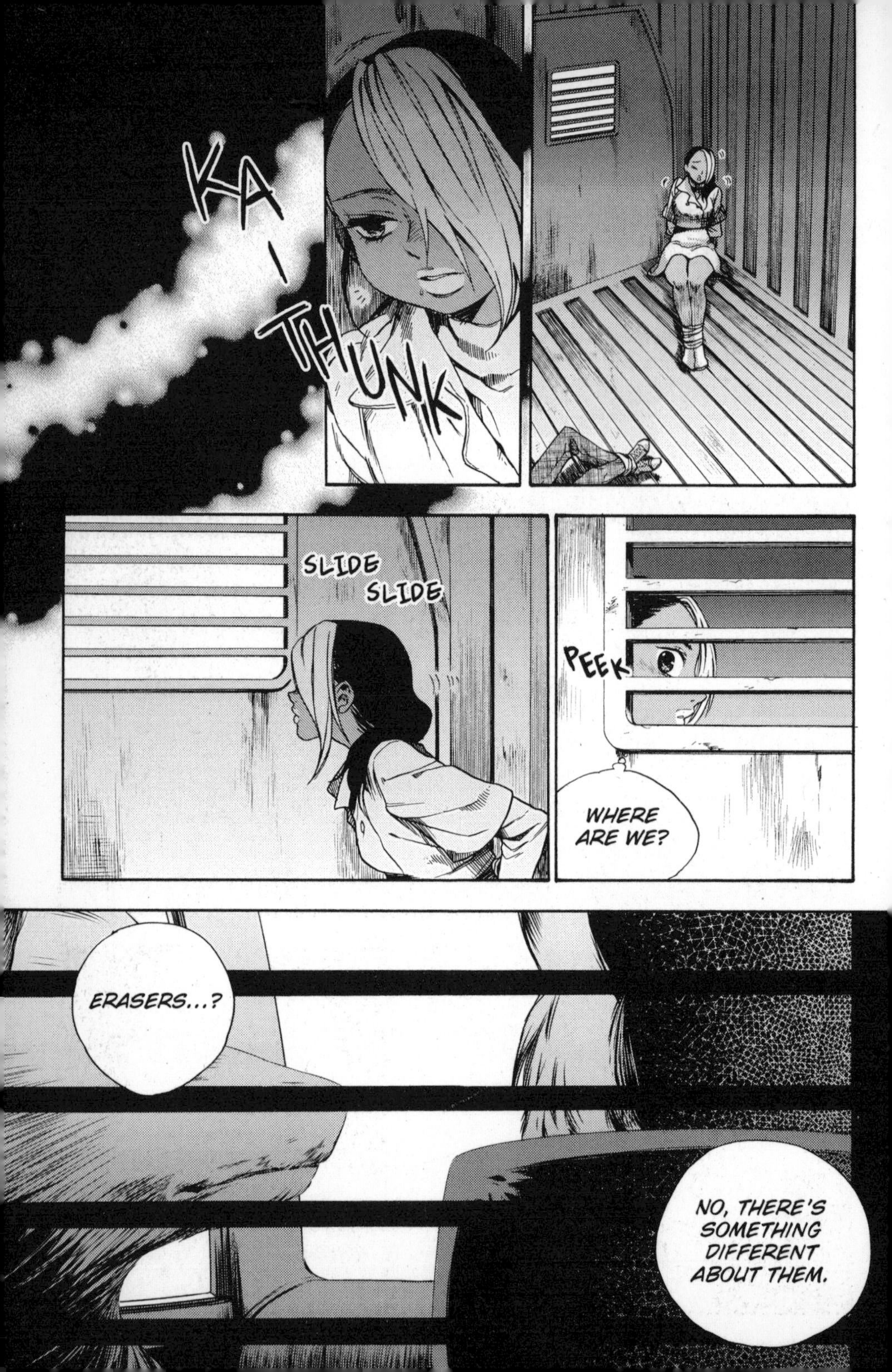
KA-THUNK
SLIDE SLIDE
PEEK
WHERE ARE WE?
ERASERS...?
NO, THERE'S SOMETHING DIFFERENT ABOUT THEM.

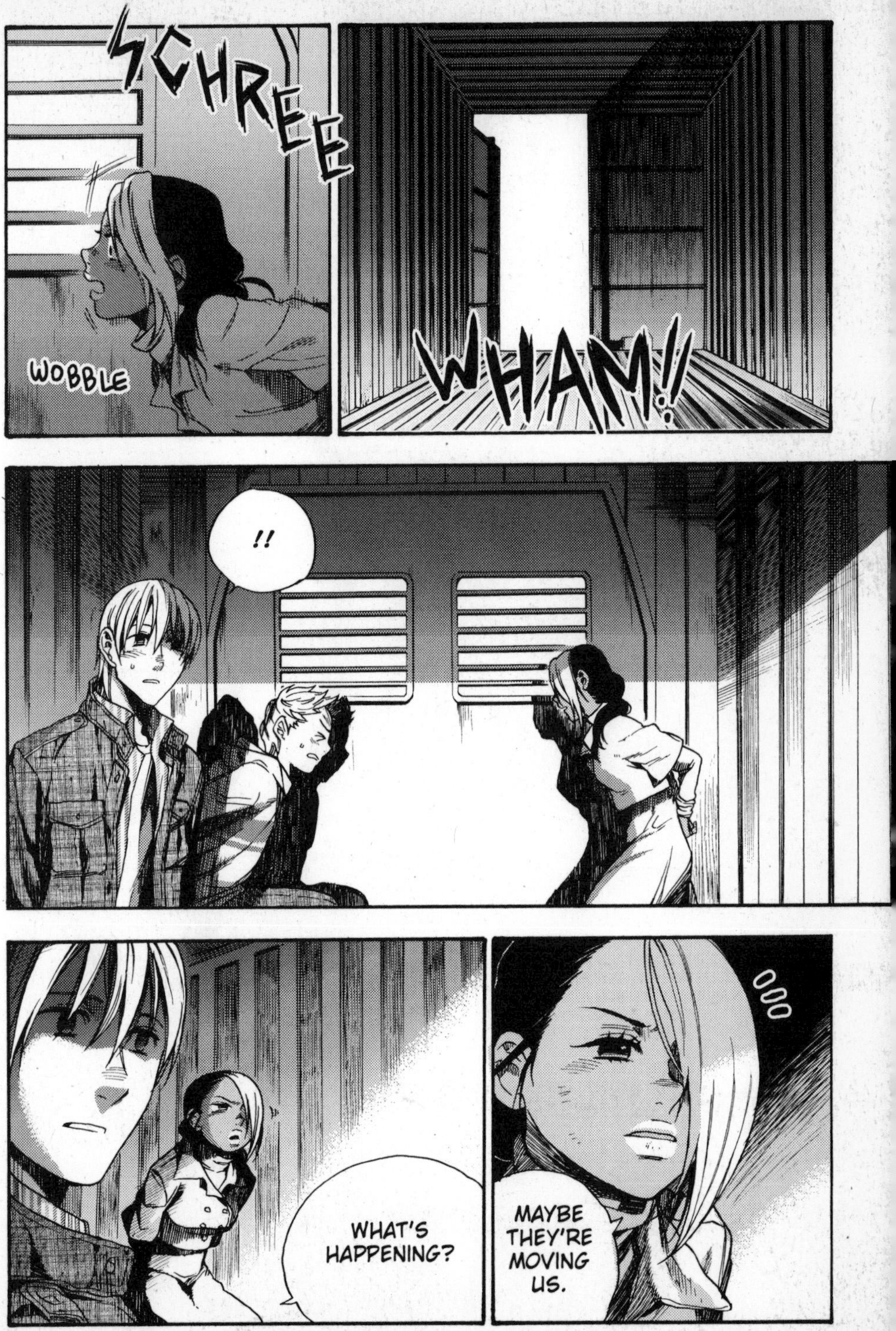
SCHREE
WOBBLE
WHAM!!
!!
WHAT'S HAPPENING?
OOO
MAYBE THEY'RE MOVING US.

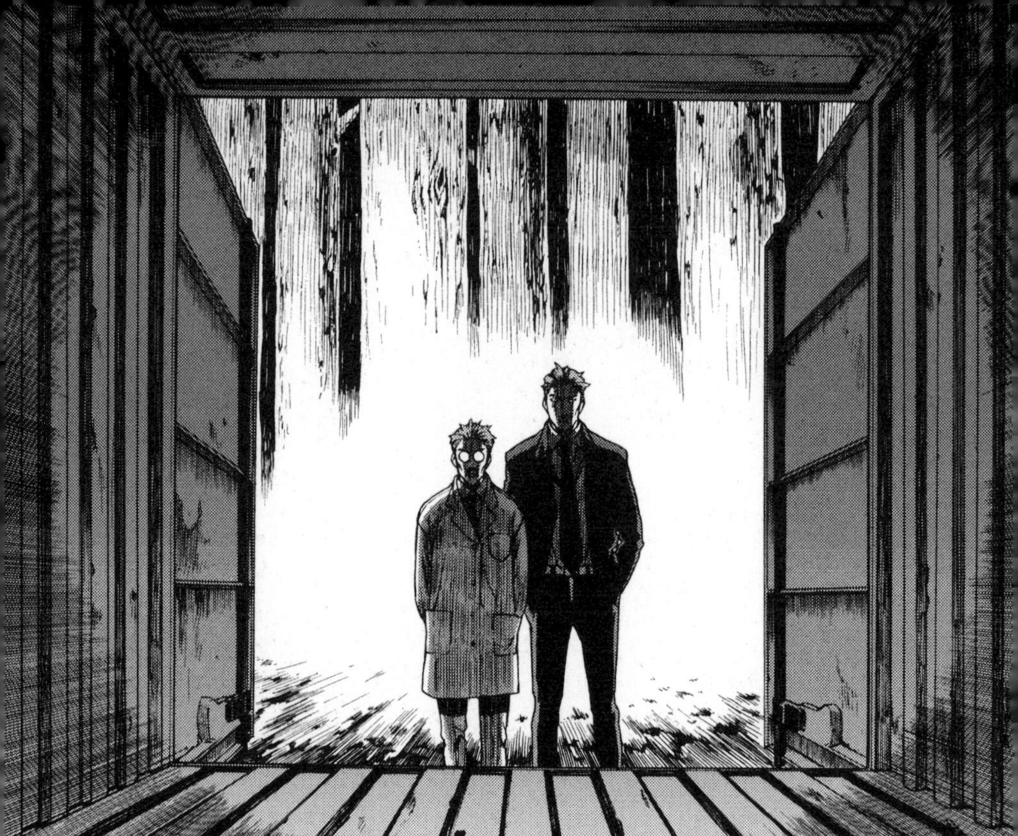

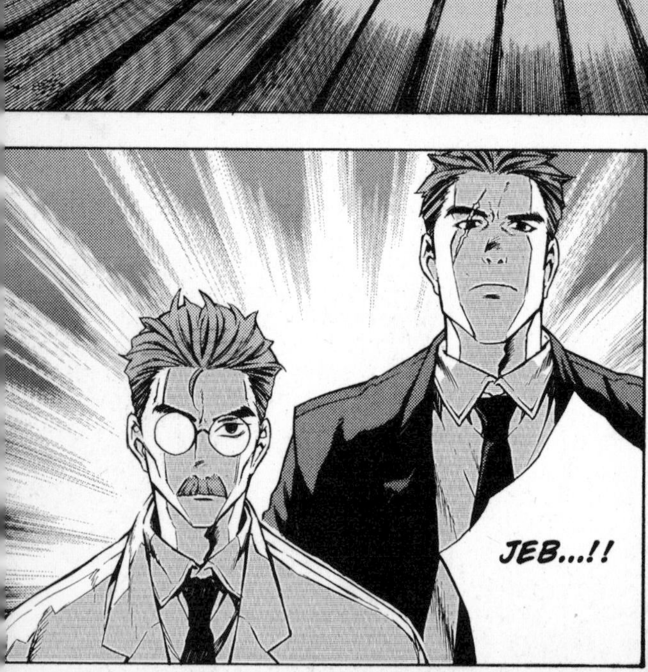
JEB...!!

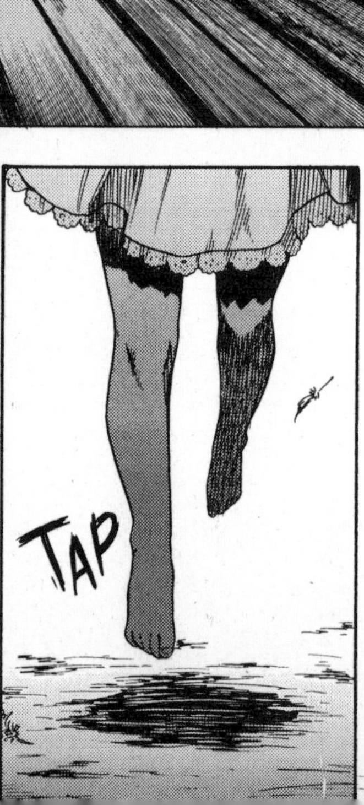
TAP

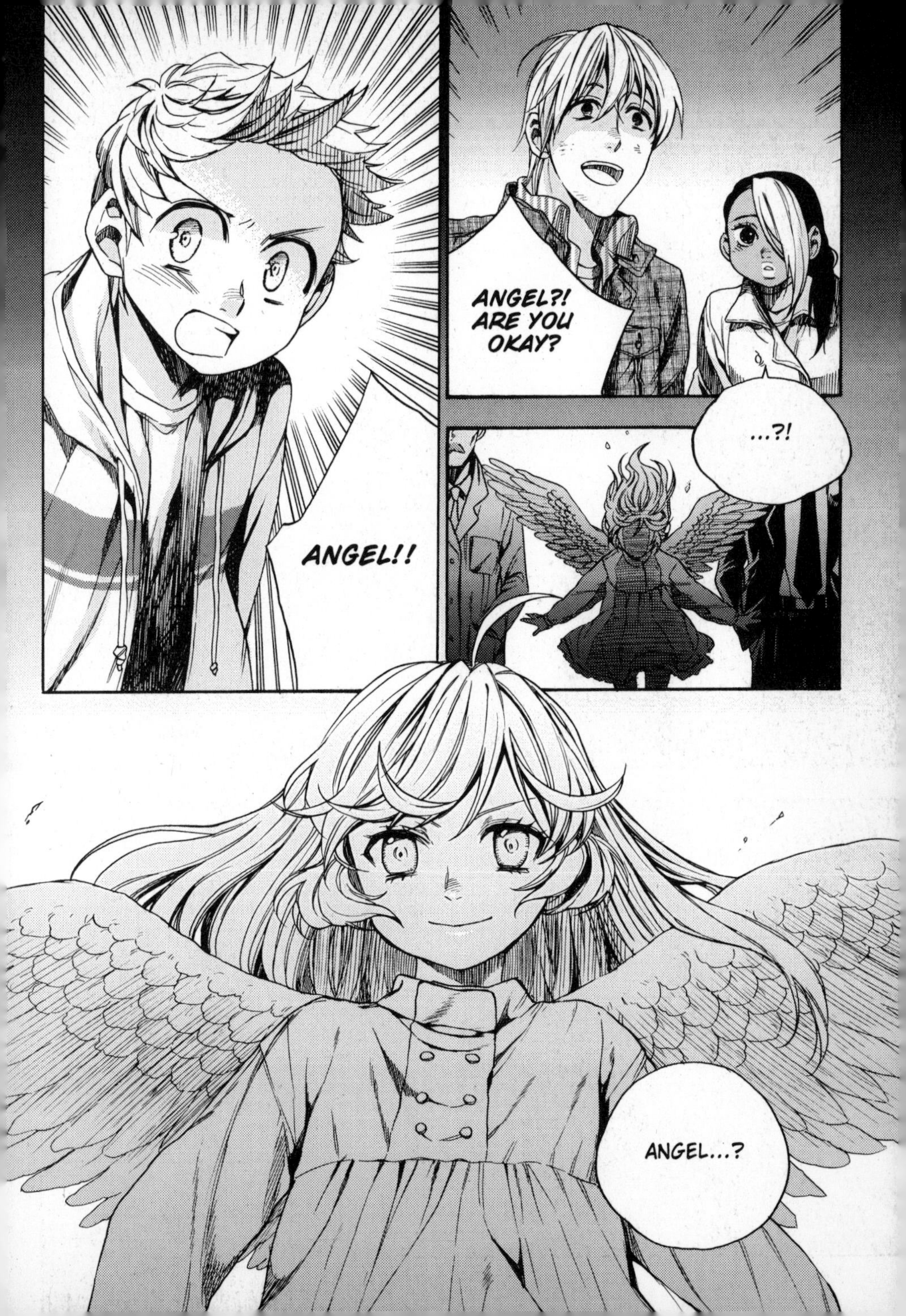
ANGEL!!
ANGEL?! ARE YOU OKAY?
...?!
ANGEL...?

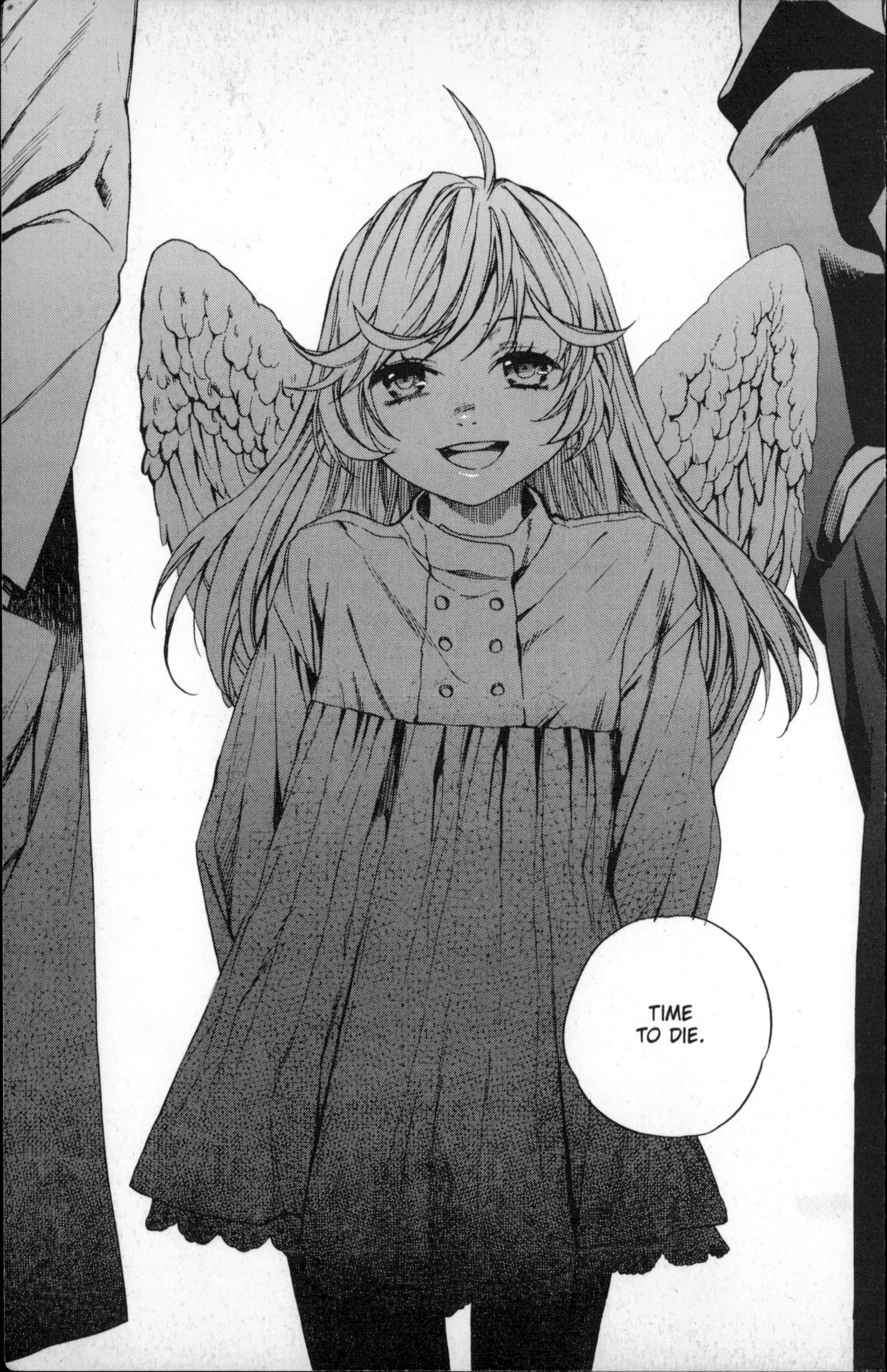
TIME TO DIE.

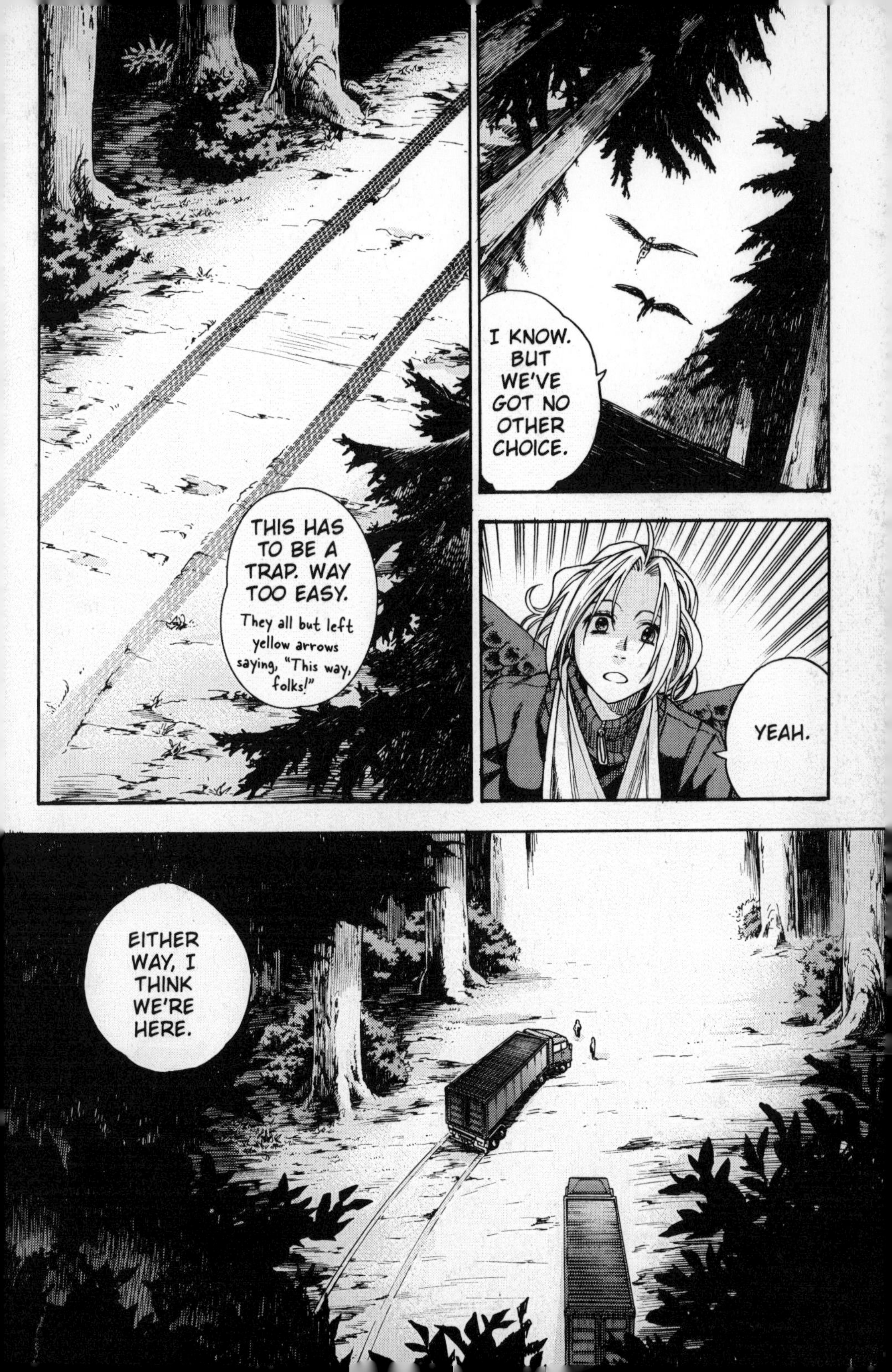
THIS HAS TO BE A TRAP. WAY TOO EASY.
They all but left yellow arrows saying, "This way, folks!"
I KNOW. BUT WE'VE GOT NO OTHER CHOICE.
YEAH.
EITHER WAY, I THINK WE'RE HERE.

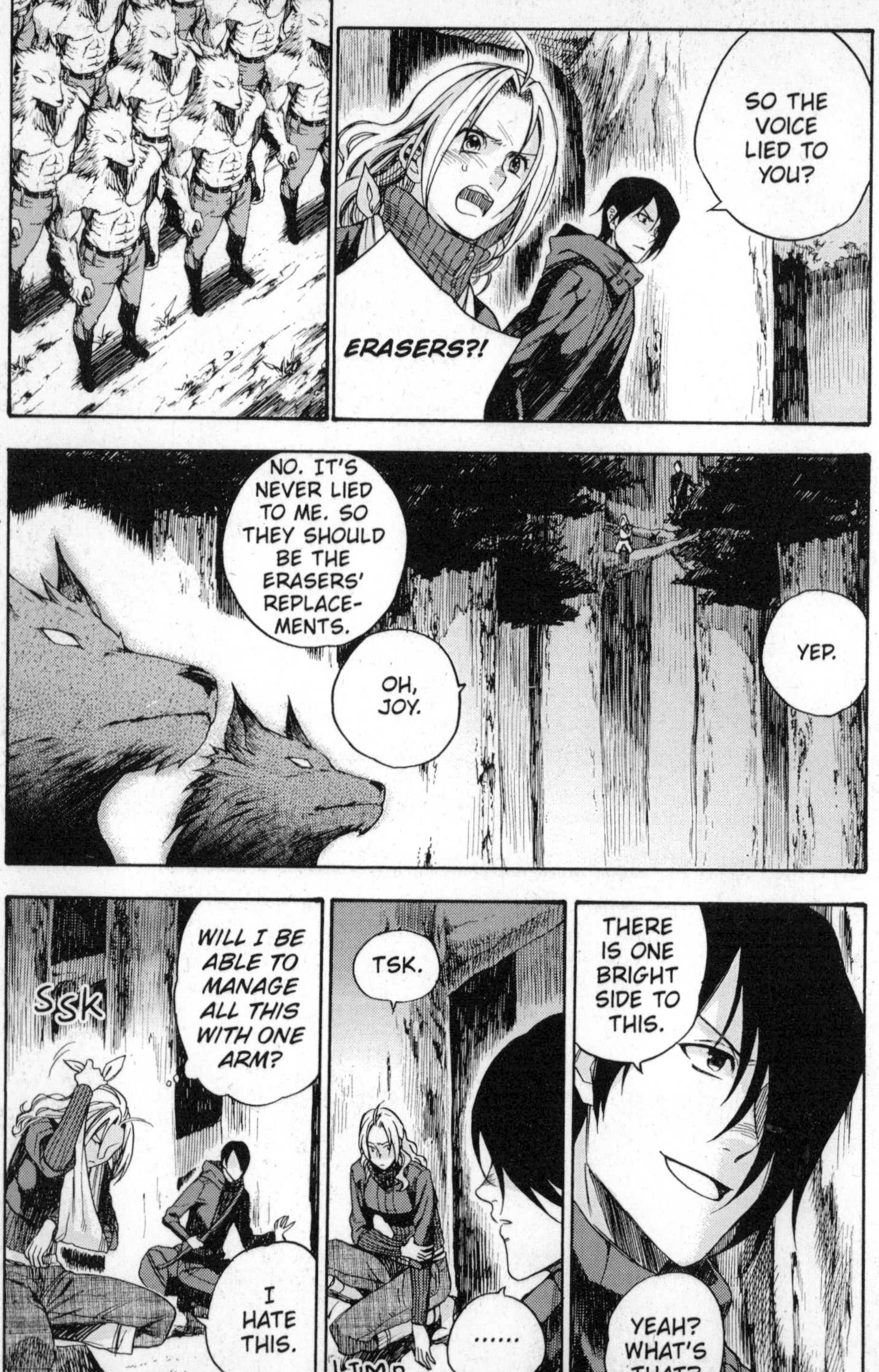
ERASERS?!
SO THE VOICE LIED TO YOU?
NO. IT'S NEVER LIED TO ME. SO THEY SHOULD BE THE ERASERS' REPLACE-MENTS.
OH, JOY.
YEP.
SSK
WILL I BE ABLE TO MANAGE ALL THIS WITH ONE ARM?
I HATE THIS.
TSK.
......
LIMP...
THERE IS ONE BRIGHT SIDE TO THIS.
YEAH? WHAT'S THAT?

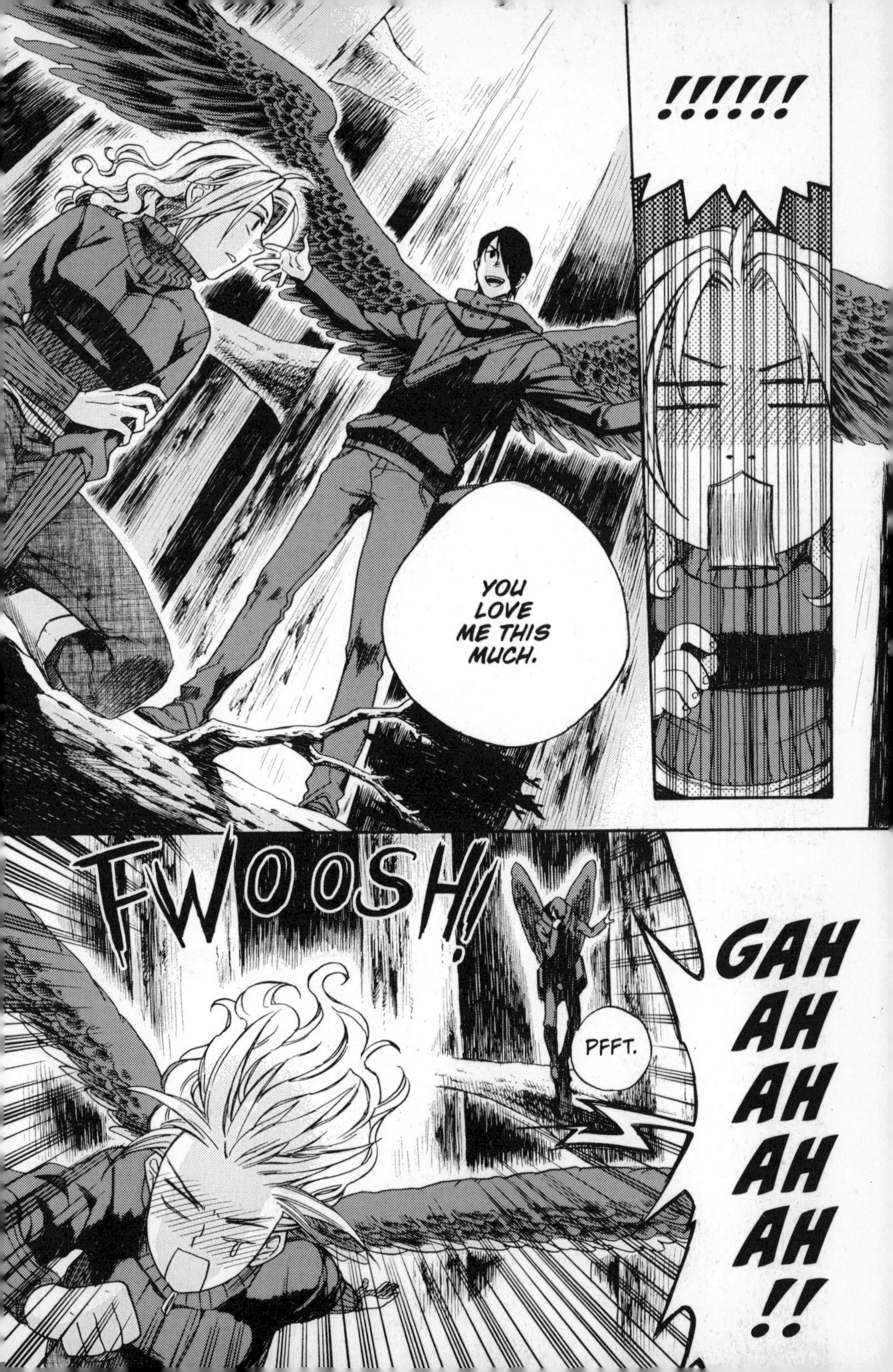
YOU LOVE ME THIS MUCH.
!!!!!!
FWOOSH!
PFFT.
GAH AH AH AH AH AH!!

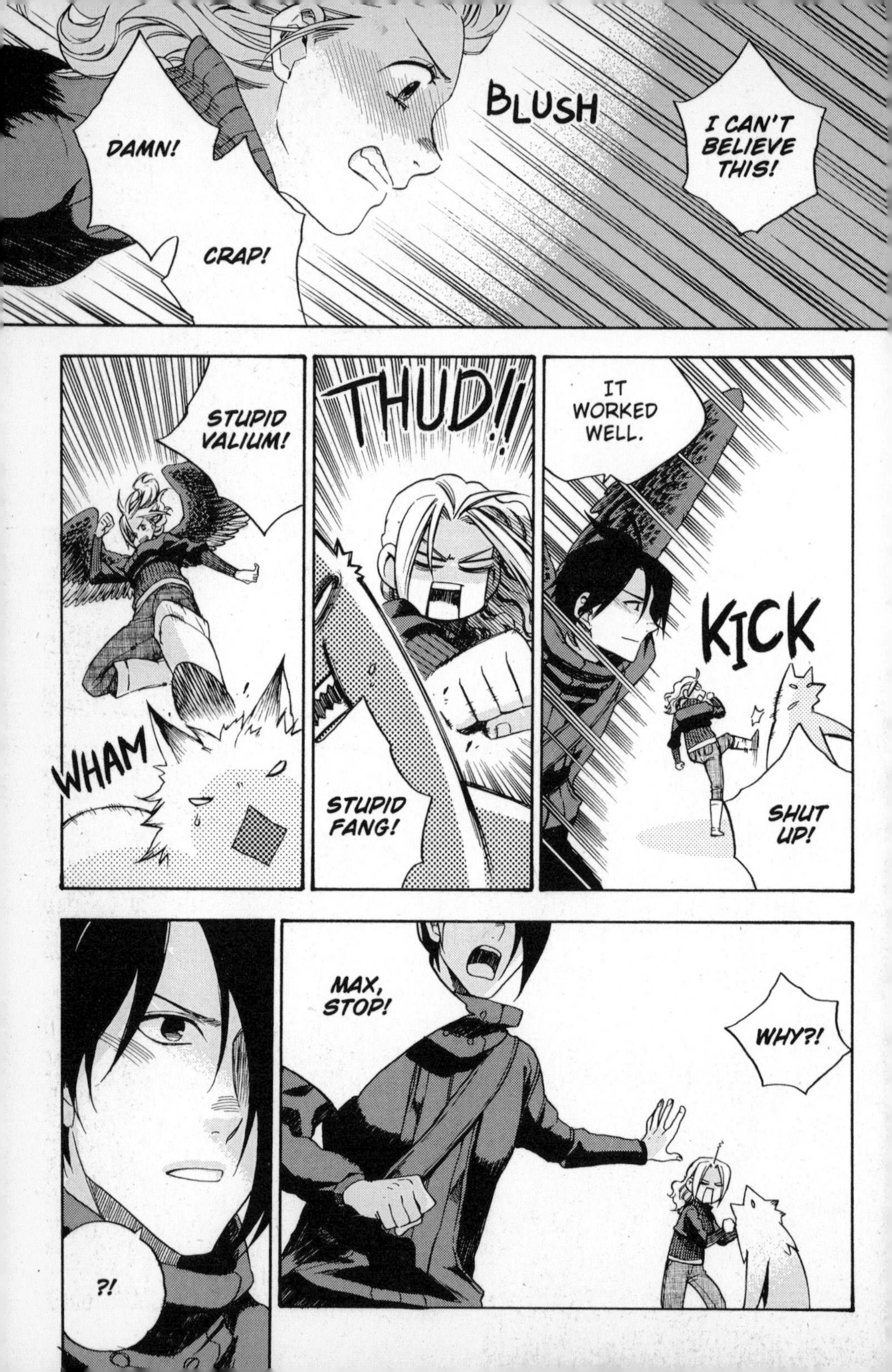
DAMN!
CRAP!
BLUSH
I CAN'T BELIEVE THIS!
STUPID VALIUM!
WHAM
THUD!!
STUPID FANG!
IT WORKED WELL.
KICK
SHUT UP!
?!
MAX, STOP!
WHY?!

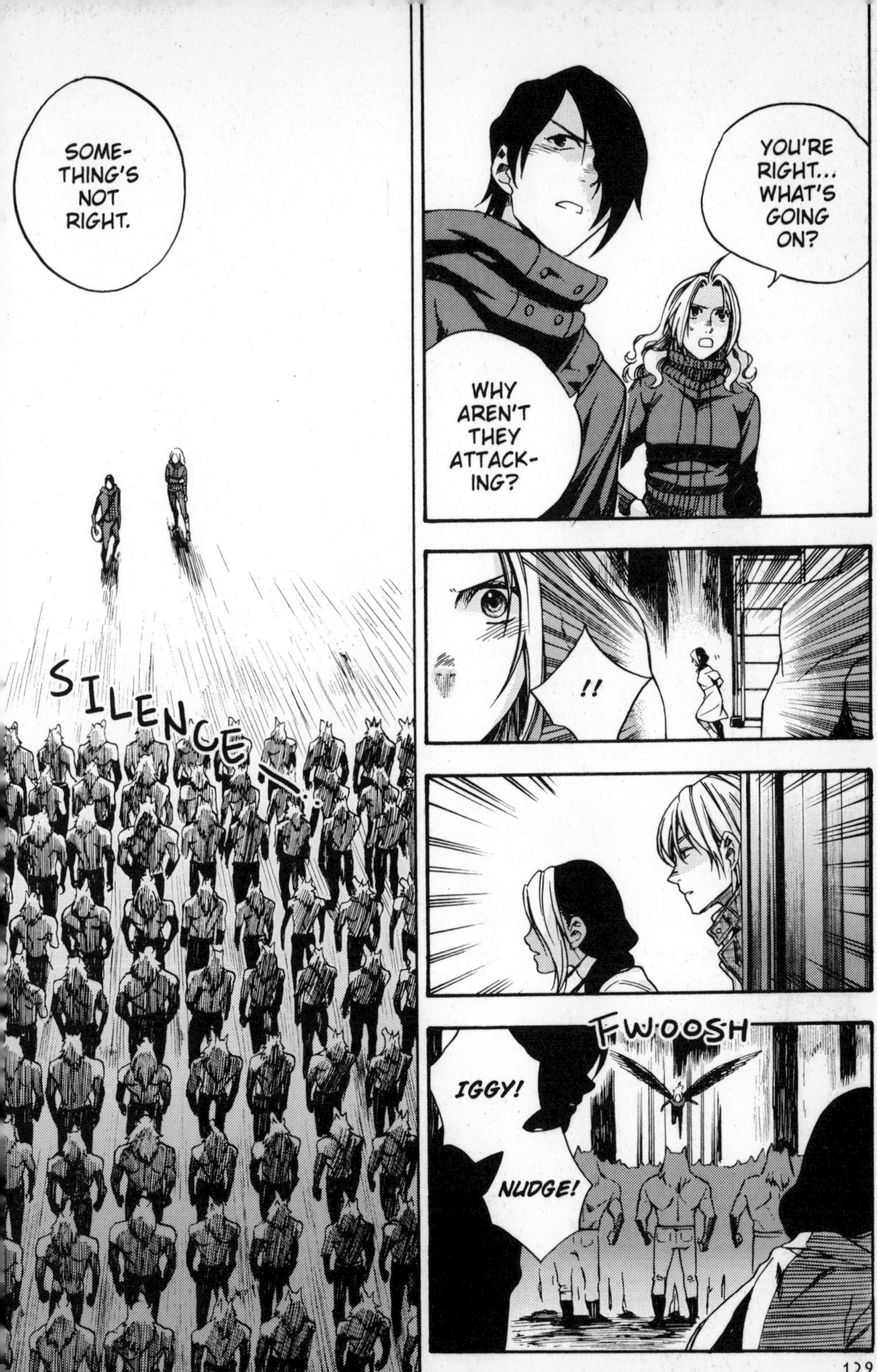
SOME-THING'S NOT RIGHT.
SILENCE...
YOU'RE RIGHT... WHAT'S GOING ON?
WHY AREN'T THEY ATTACK-ING?
!!
FWOOSH
IGGY!
NUDGE!

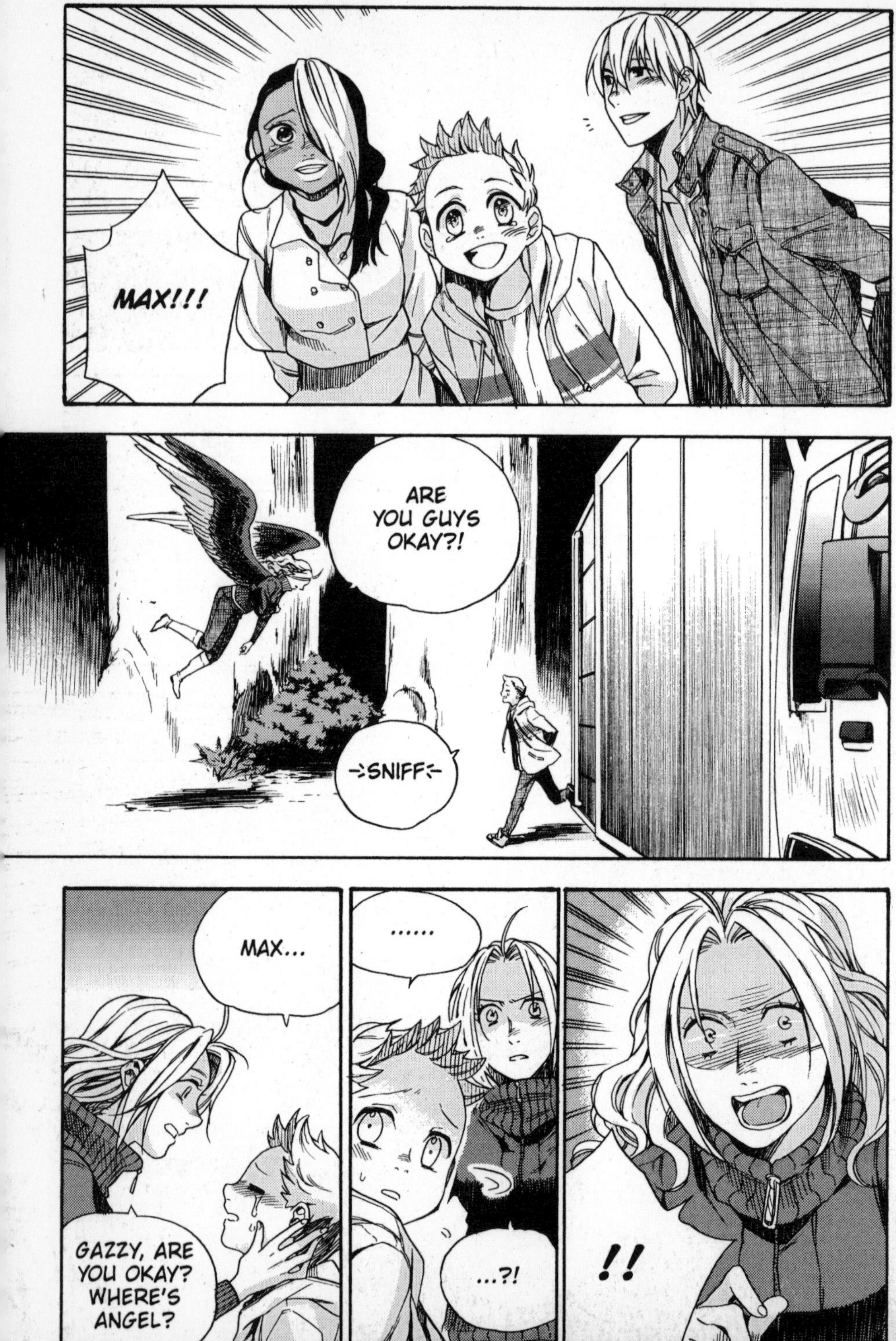
MAX!!!
ARE YOU GUYS OKAY?!
-SNIFF-
MAX...
GAZZY, ARE YOU OKAY? WHERE'S ANGEL?
......
...?!
!!

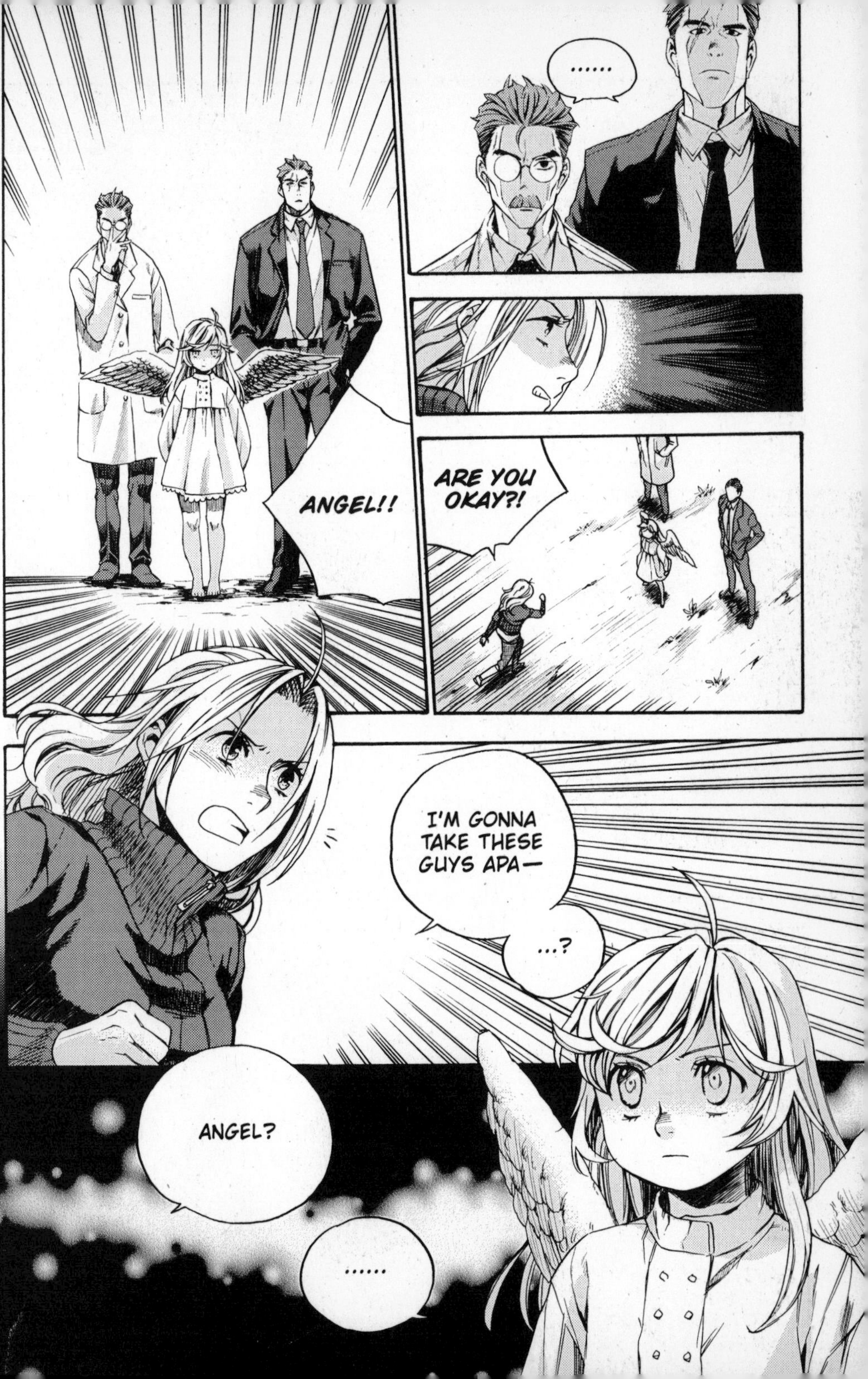
ANGEL!!
......
ARE YOU OKAY?!
I'M GONNA TAKE THESE GUYS APA—
...?
ANGEL?
......

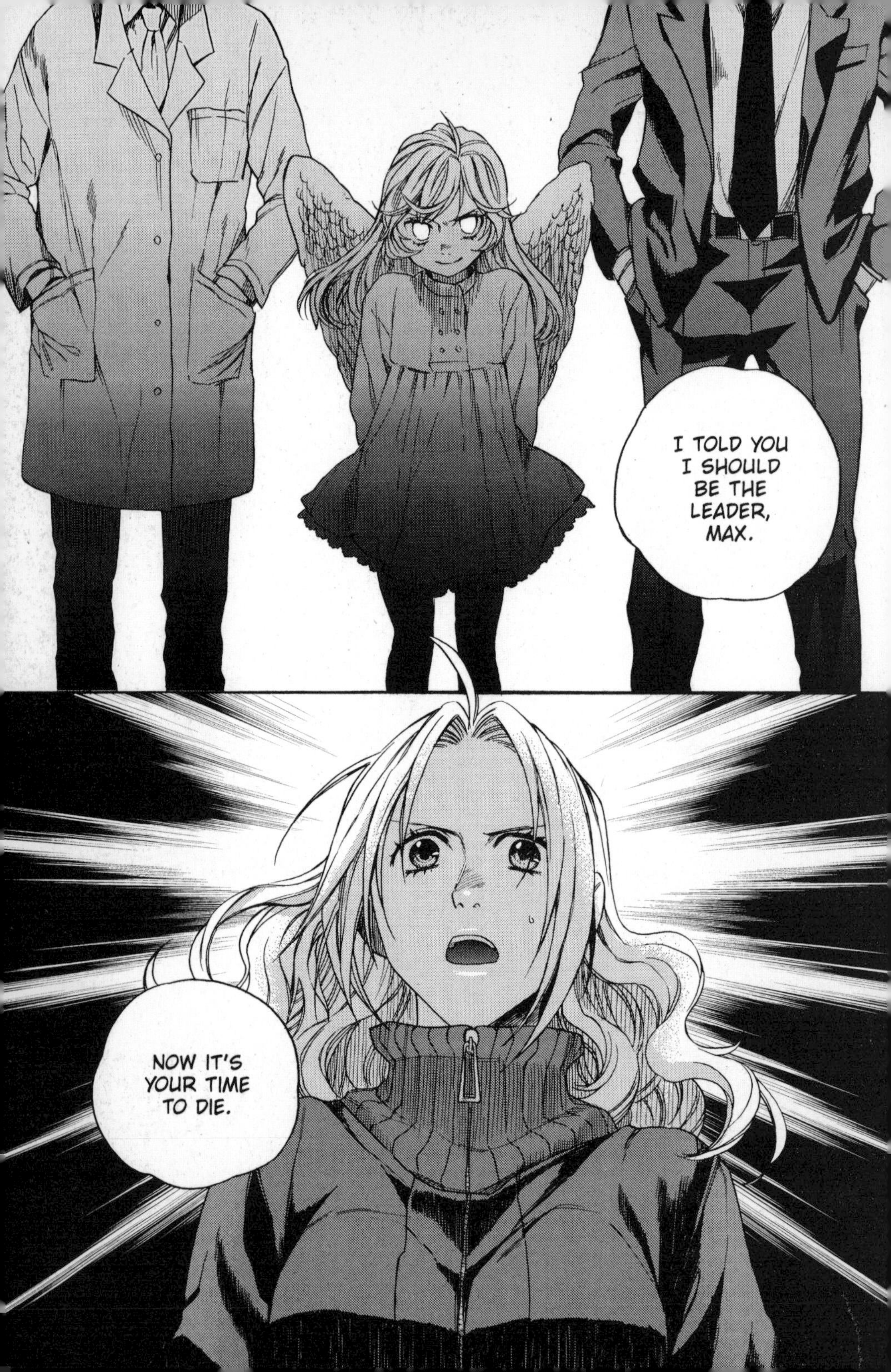
I TOLD YOU I SHOULD BE THE LEADER, MAX.
NOW IT'S YOUR TIME TO DIE.

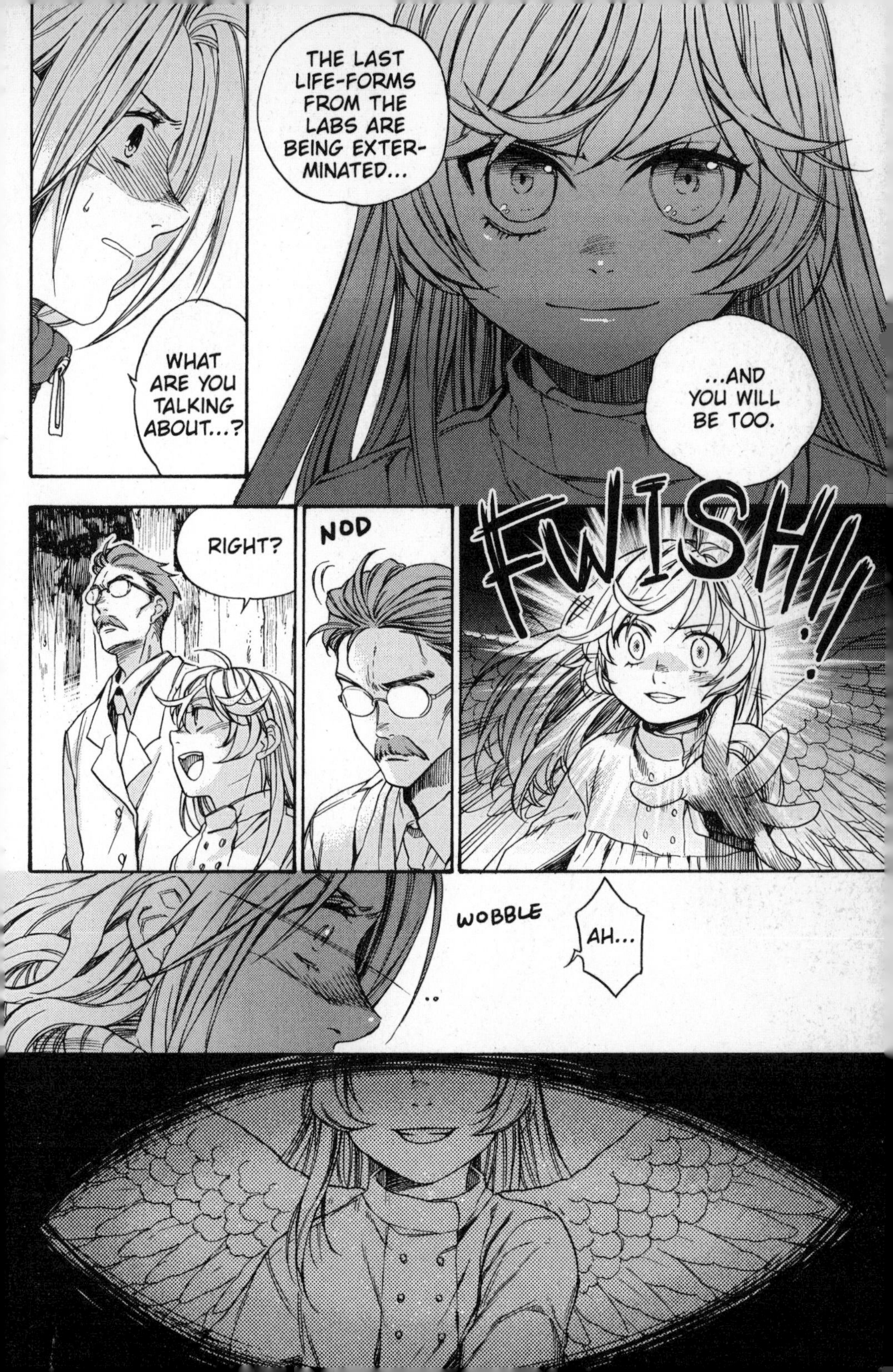
THE LAST LIFE-FORMS FROM THE LABS ARE BEING EXTERMINATED...
WHAT ARE YOU TALKING ABOUT...?
...AND YOU WILL BE TOO.
RIGHT?
NOD
FWISH!!
WOBBLE
AH...

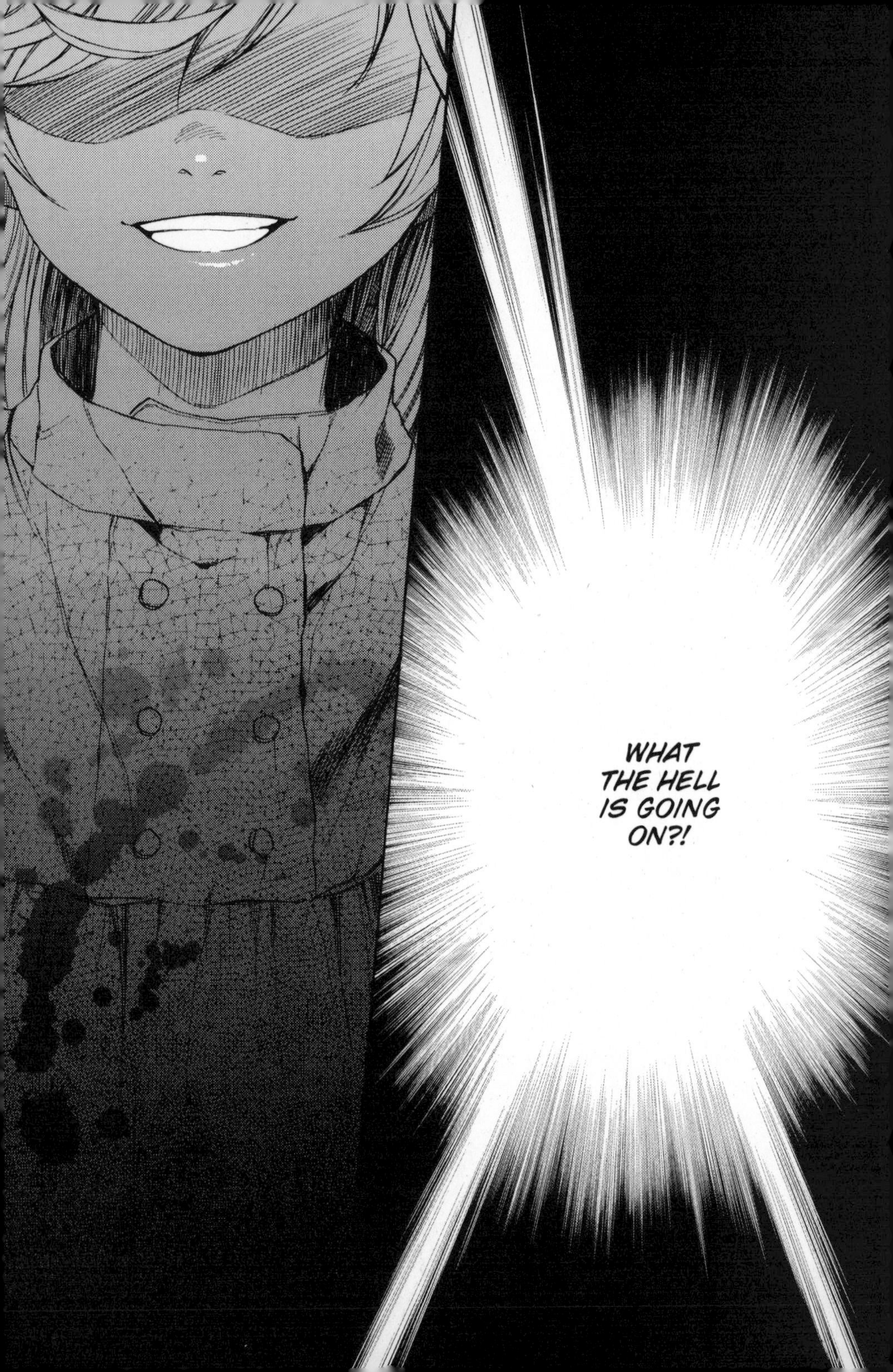
WHAT THE HELL IS GOING ON?!

MAXIMUM
RIDE

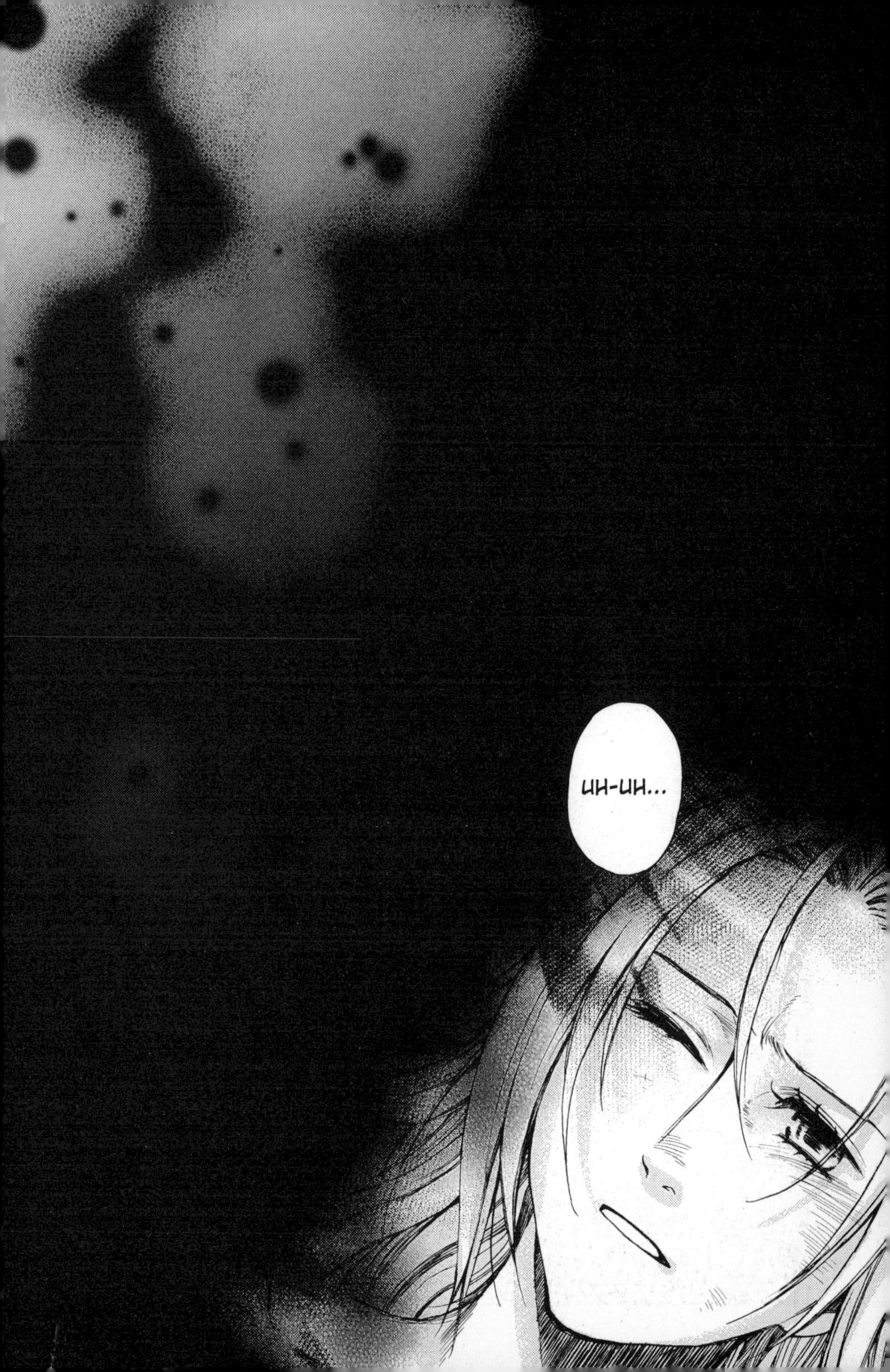
UH-UH...

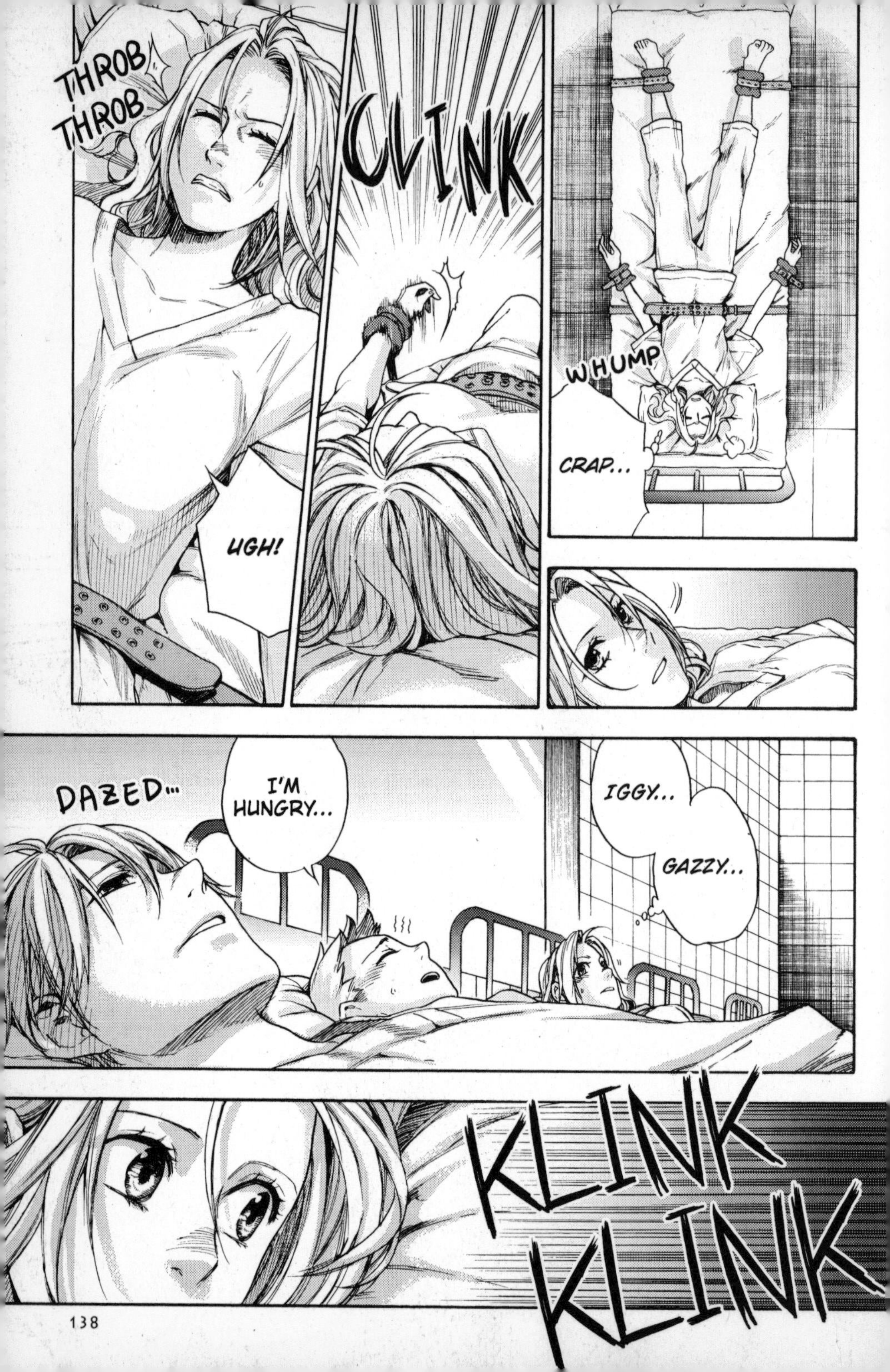
THROB THROB
UGH!
CLINK
WHUMP
CRAP...
DAZED...
I'M HUNGRY...
IGGY...
GAZZY...
KLINK KLINK

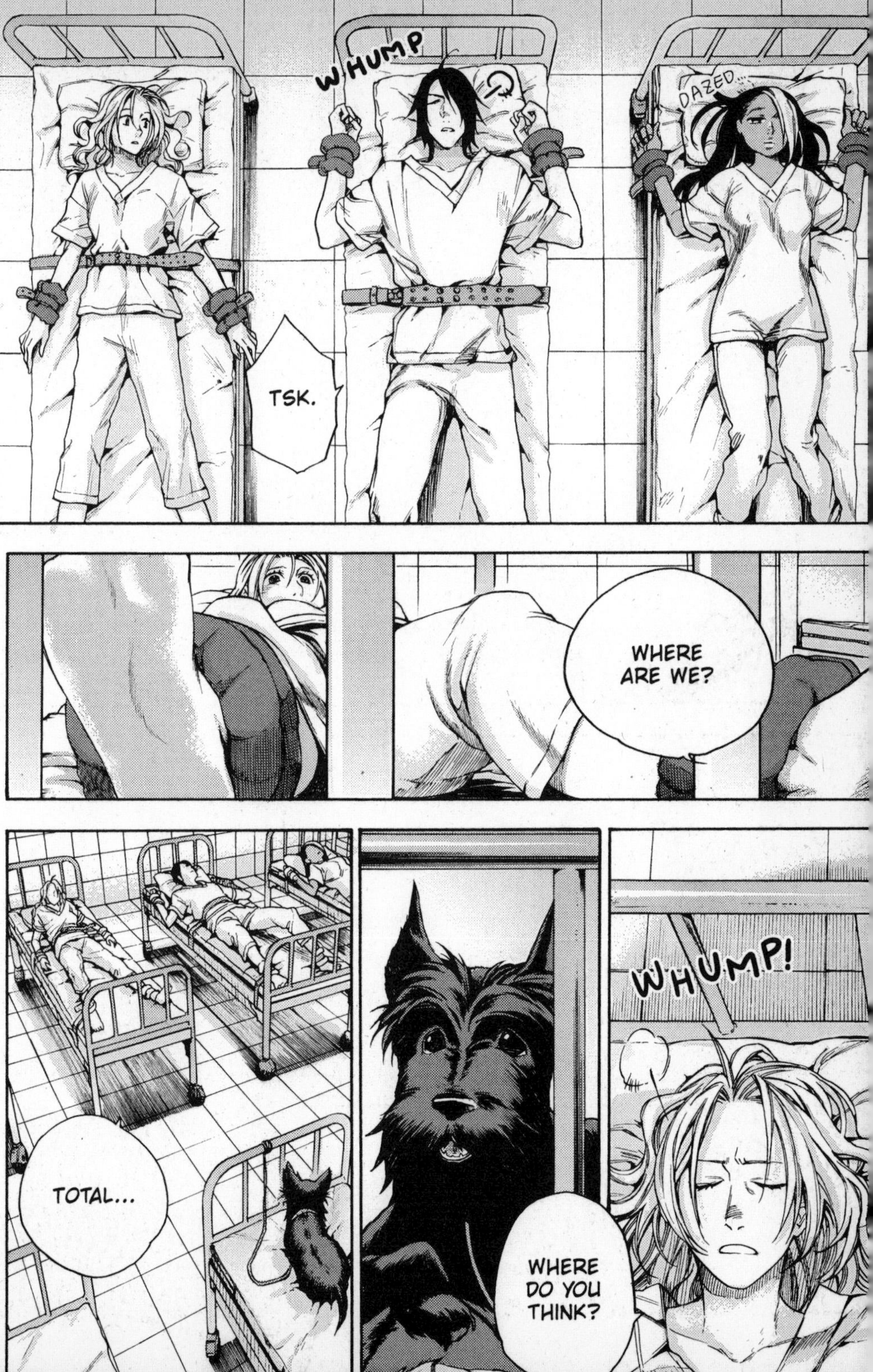

WHUMP
DAZED...
TSK.
WHERE ARE WE?
TOTAL...
WHERE DO YOU THINK?
WHUMP!

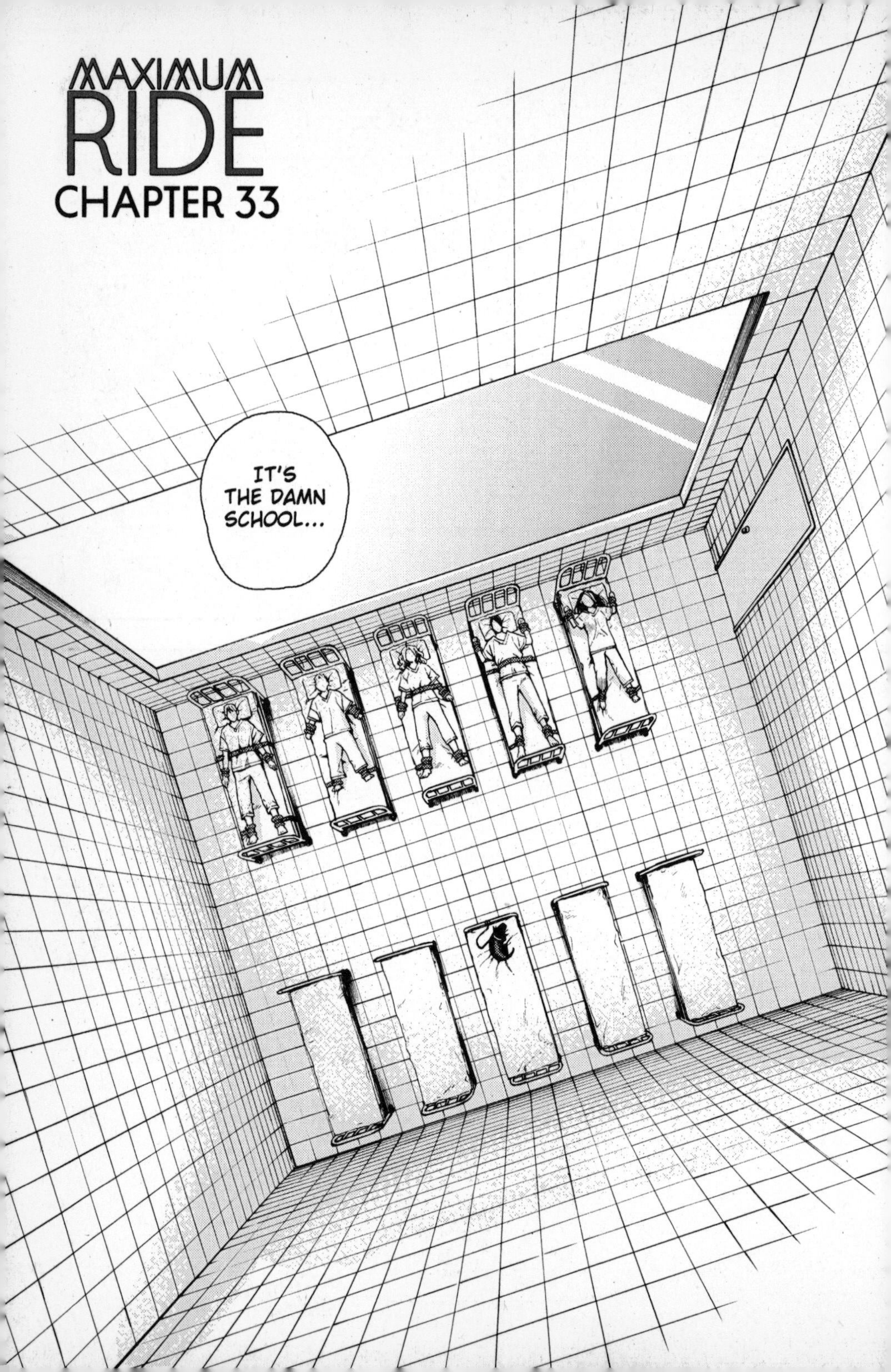
MAXIMUM RIDE
CHAPTER 33
IT'S THE DAMN SCHOOL...

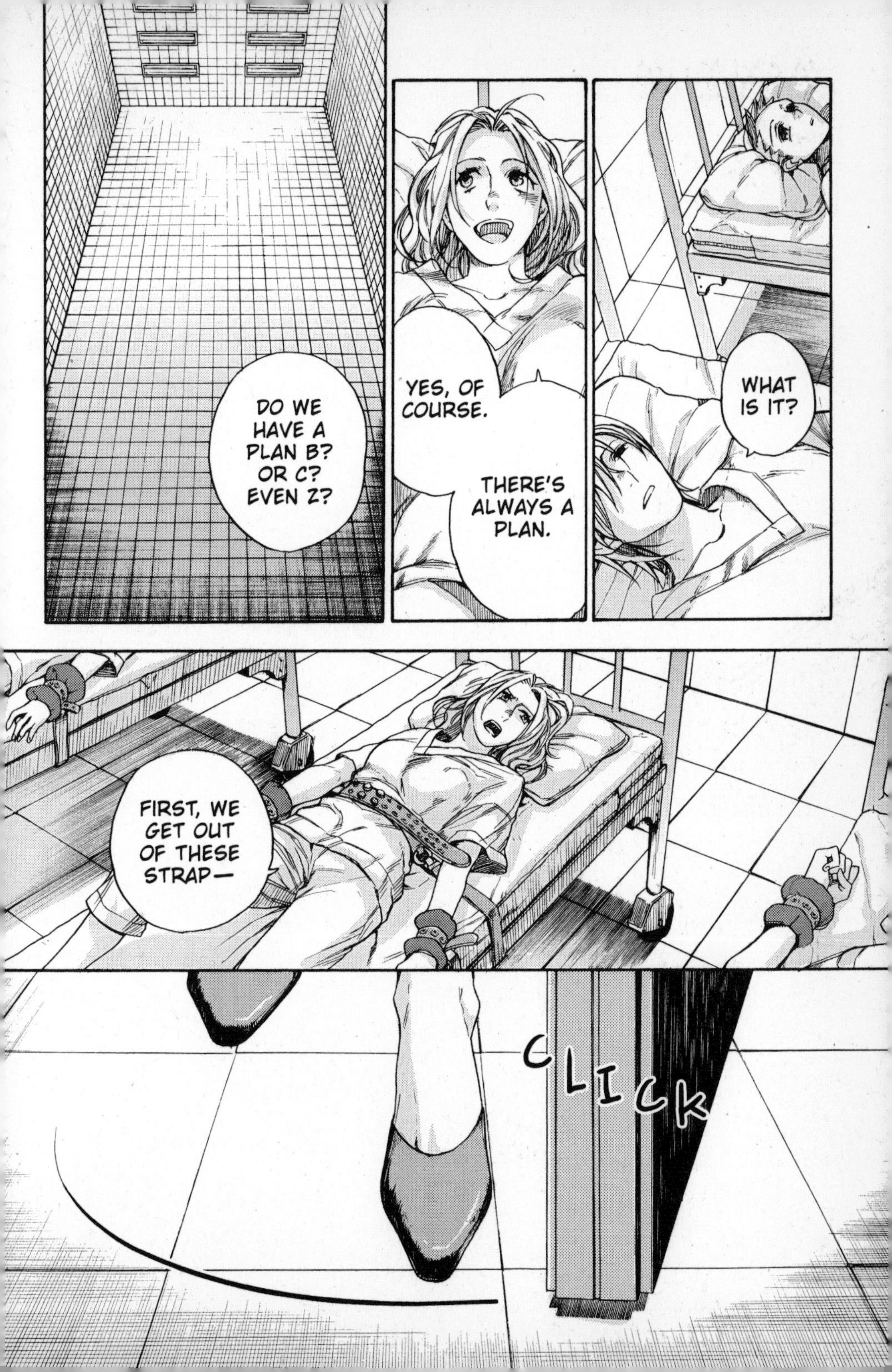
DO WE HAVE A PLAN B? OR C? EVEN Z?
YES, OF COURSE.
THERE'S ALWAYS A PLAN.
WHAT IS IT?
FIRST, WE GET OUT OF THESE STRAP—
CLICK

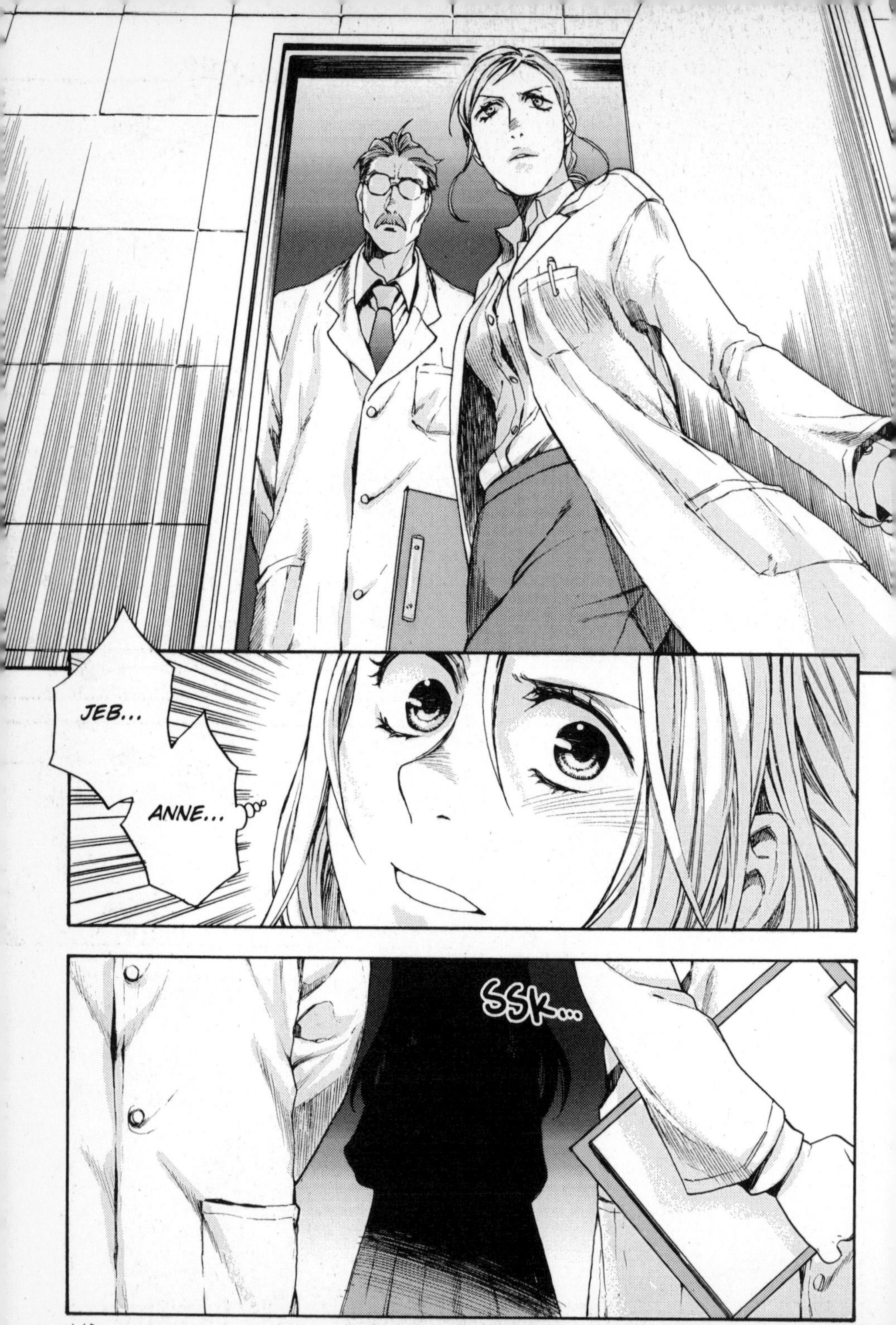
JEB...
ANNE...
SSK...

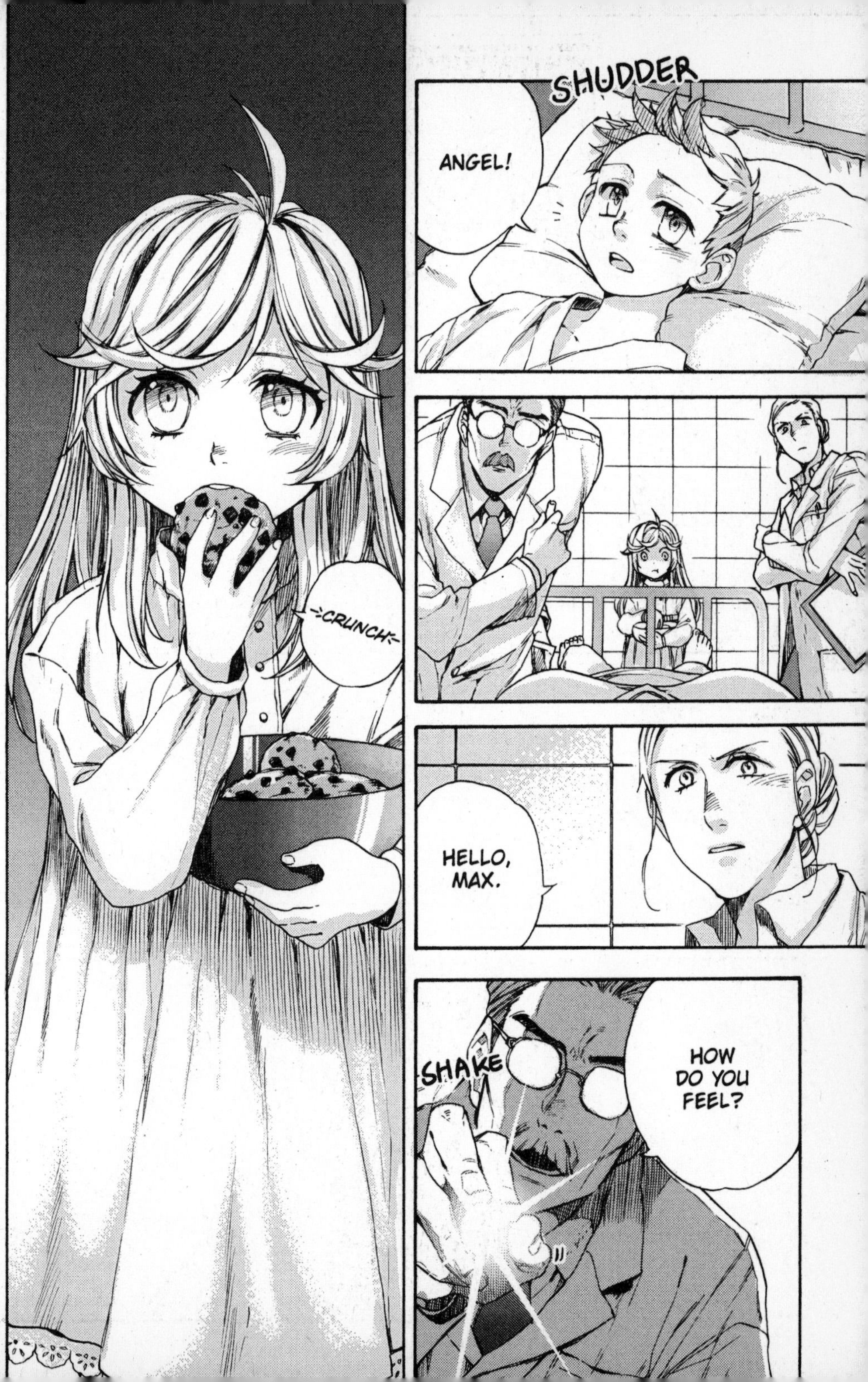
CRUNCH
SHUDDER
ANGEL!
HELLO, MAX.
SHAKE
HOW DO YOU FEEL?

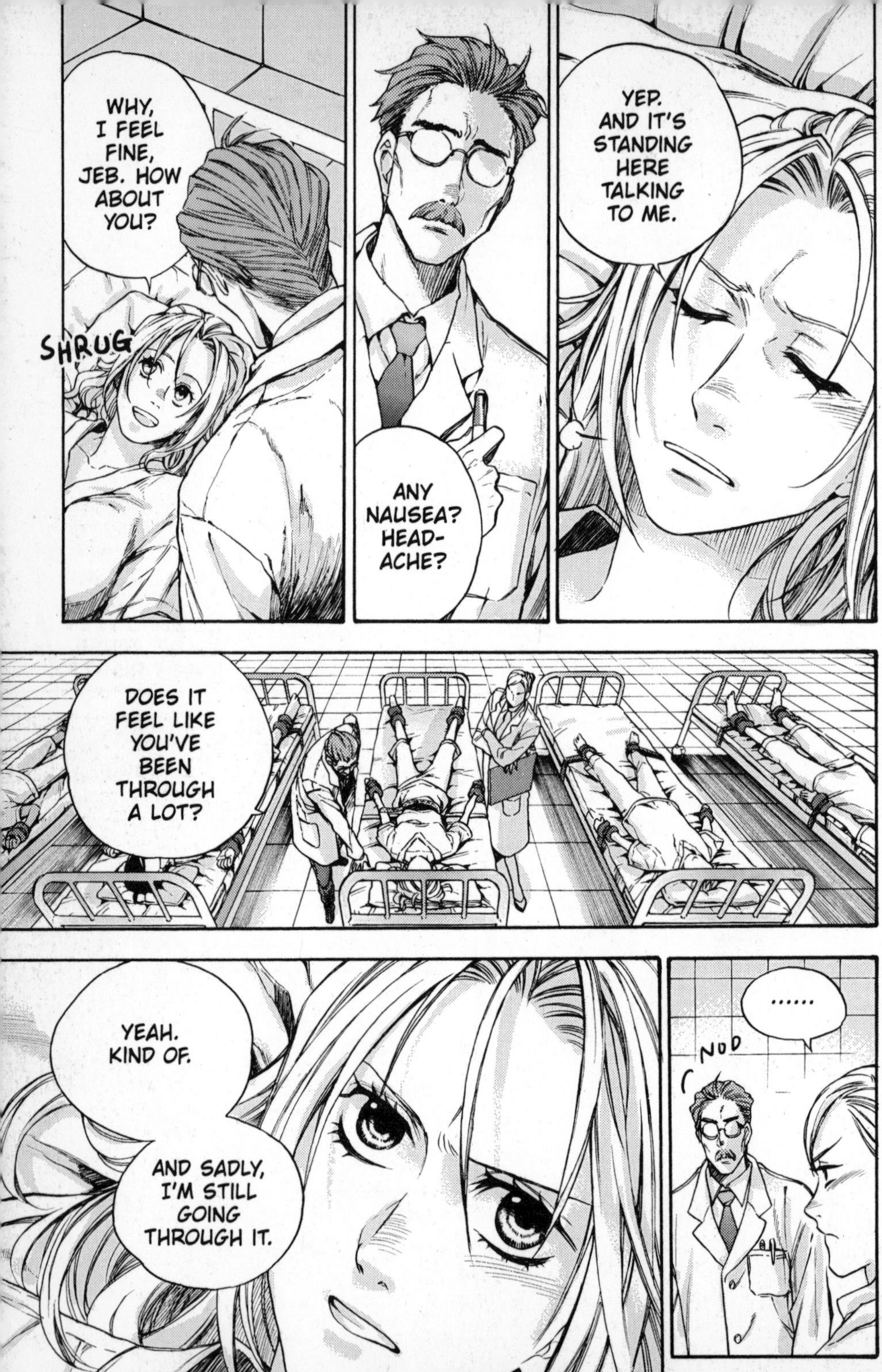
WHY, I FEEL FINE, JEB. HOW ABOUT YOU?
SHRUG
ANY NAUSEA? HEAD-ACHE?
YEP. AND IT'S STANDING HERE TALKING TO ME.
DOES IT FEEL LIKE YOU'VE BEEN THROUGH A LOT?
YEAH. KIND OF.
AND SADLY, I'M STILL GOING THROUGH IT.
......
NOD

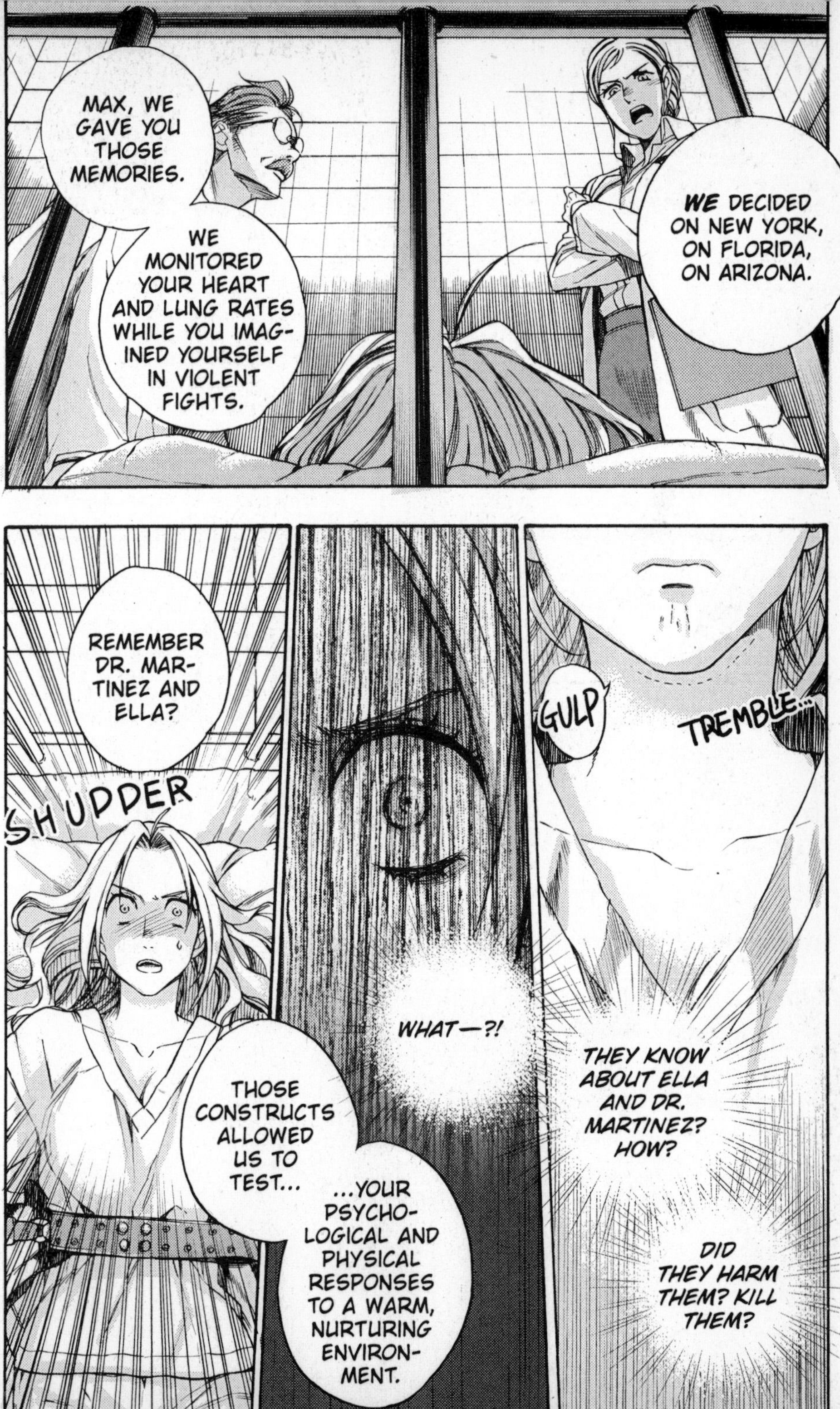
MAX, WE GAVE YOU THOSE MEMORIES.
WE MONITORED YOUR HEART AND LUNG RATES WHILE YOU IMAG-INED YOURSELF IN VIOLENT FIGHTS.
WE DECIDED ON NEW YORK, ON FLORIDA, ON ARIZONA.
REMEMBER DR. MAR-TINEZ AND ELLA?
SHUDDER
THOSE CONSTRUCTS ALLOWED US TO TEST...
...YOUR PSYCHO-LOGICAL AND PHYSICAL RESPONSES TO A WARM, NURTURING ENVIRON-MENT.
WHAT—?!
GULP
TREMBLE...
THEY KNOW ABOUT ELLA AND DR. MARTINEZ? HOW?
DID THEY HARM THEM? KILL THEM?

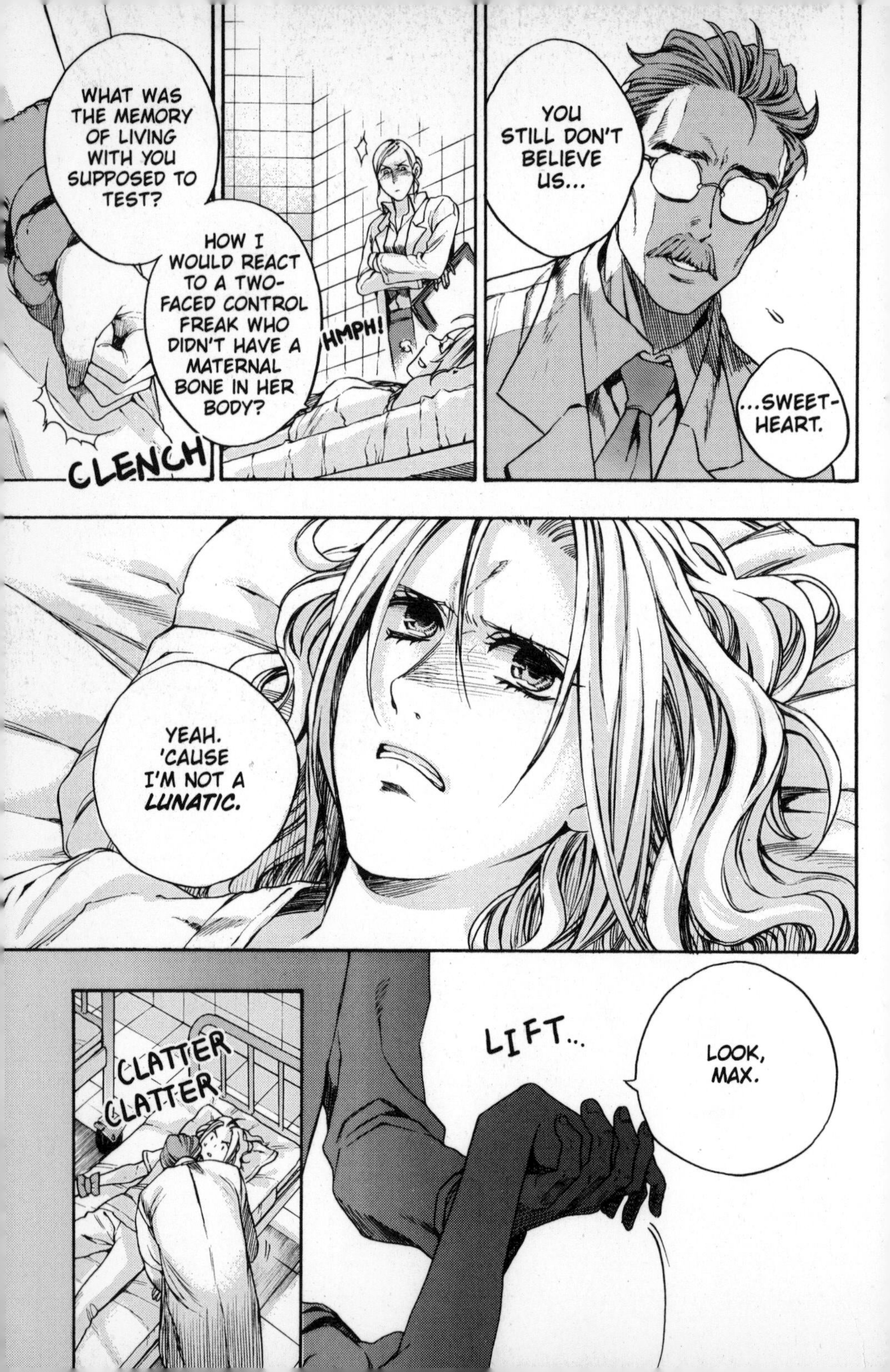
WHAT WAS THE MEMORY OF LIVING WITH YOU SUPPOSED TO TEST?
HOW I WOULD REACT TO A TWO-FACED CONTROL FREAK WHO DIDN'T HAVE A MATERNAL BONE IN HER BODY?
CLENCH
HMPH!
YOU STILL DON'T BELIEVE US...
...SWEET-HEART.
YEAH. 'CAUSE I'M NOT A *LUNATIC.*
CLATTER CLATTER
LIFT...
LOOK, MAX.

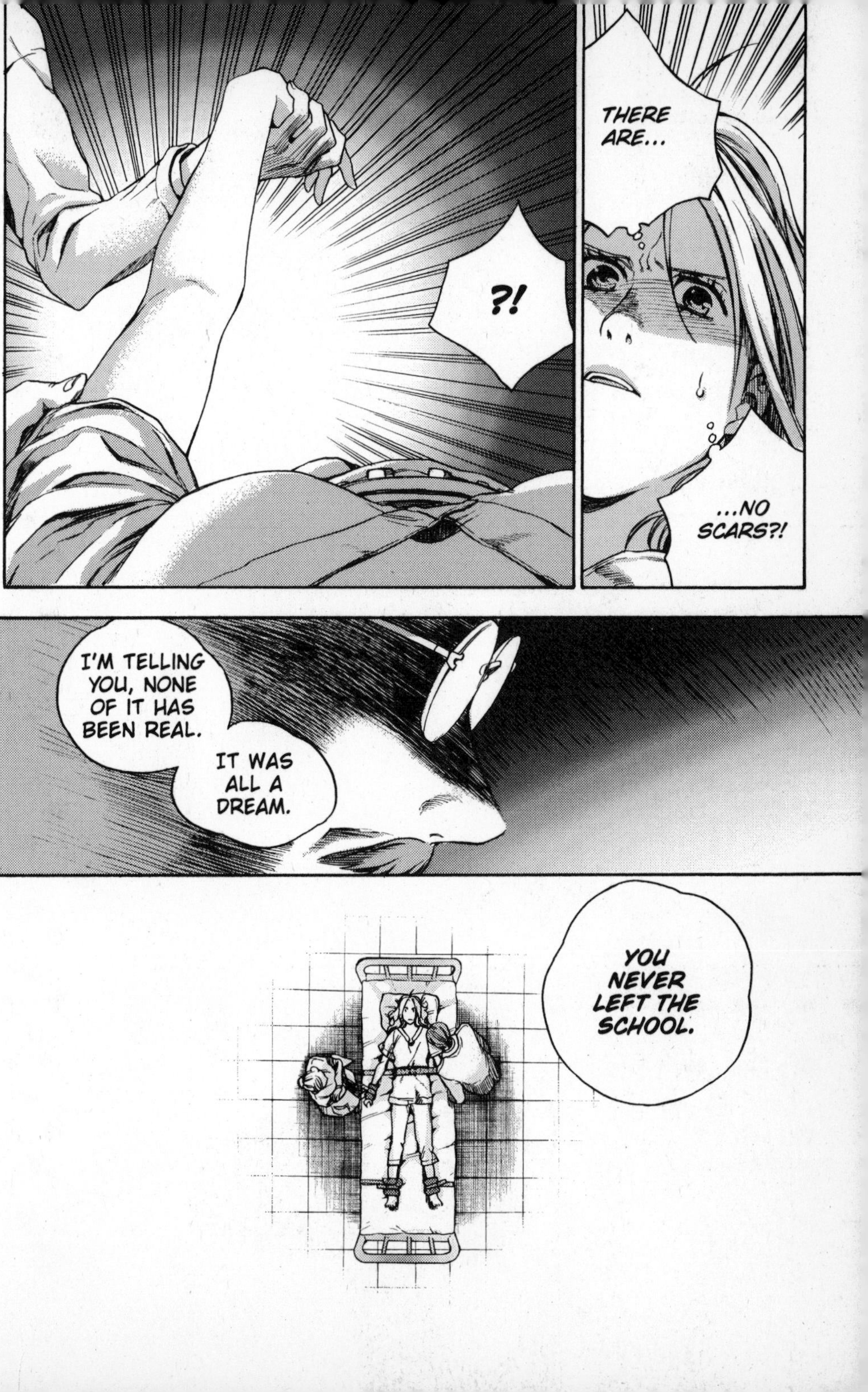
?!
THERE ARE...
...NO SCARS?!
I'M TELLING YOU, NONE OF IT HAS BEEN REAL.
IT WAS ALL A DREAM.
YOU NEVER LEFT THE SCHOOL.

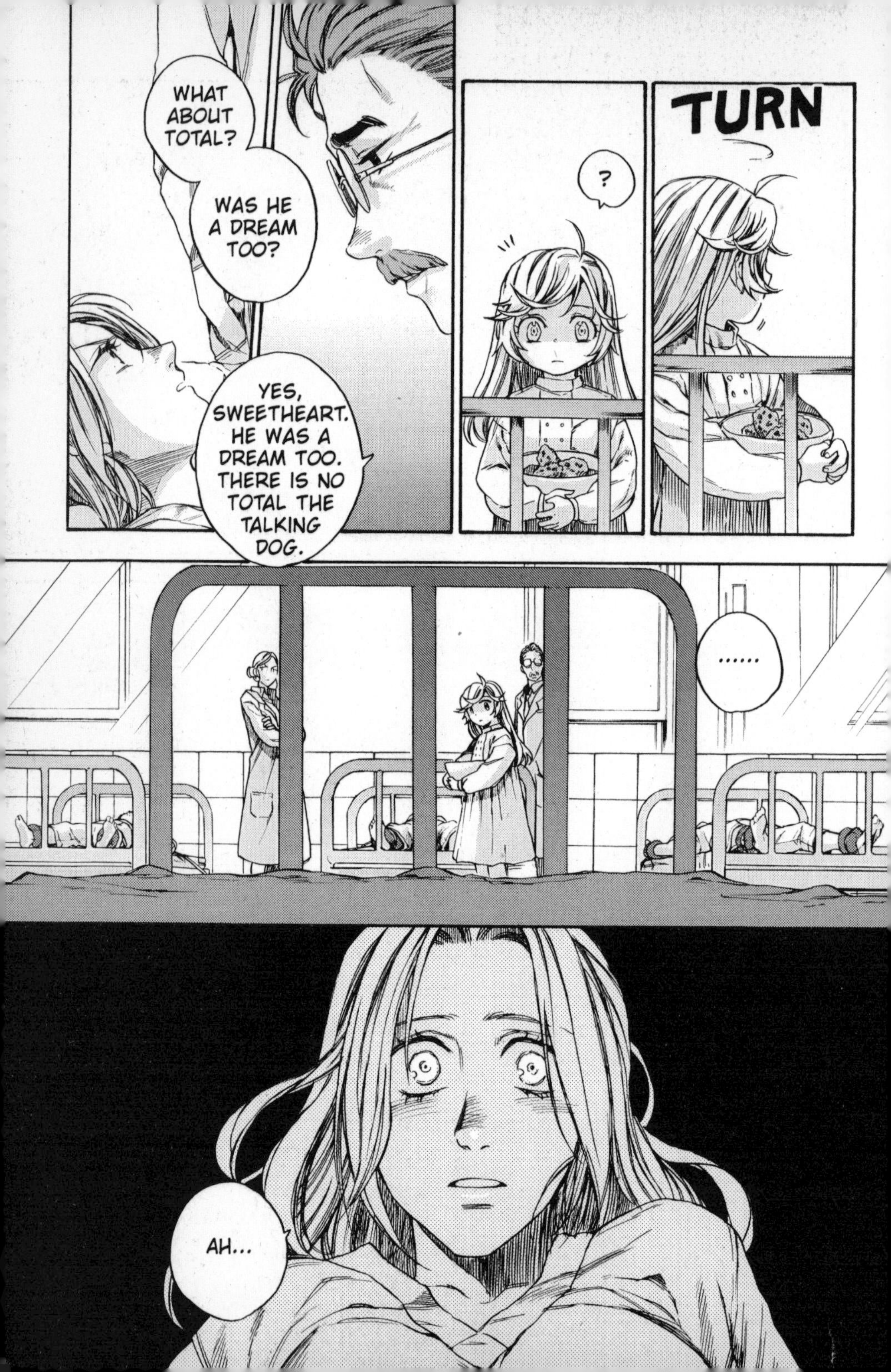
WHAT ABOUT TOTAL?
WAS HE A DREAM TOO?
YES, SWEETHEART. HE WAS A DREAM TOO. THERE IS NO TOTAL THE TALKING DOG.
?
TURN
......
AH...

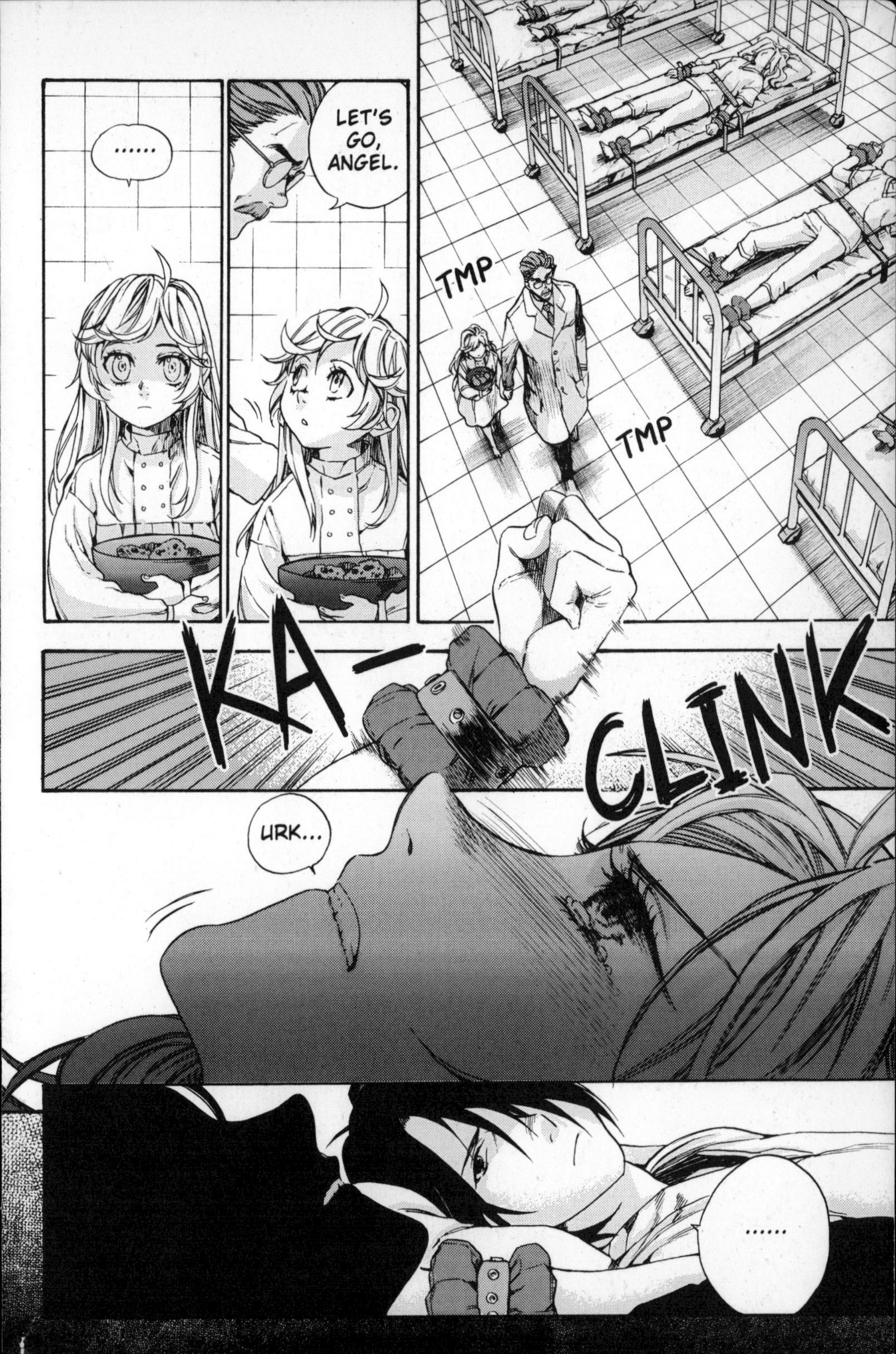
......
LET'S GO, ANGEL.
TMP
TMP
KA-CLINK
URK...
......

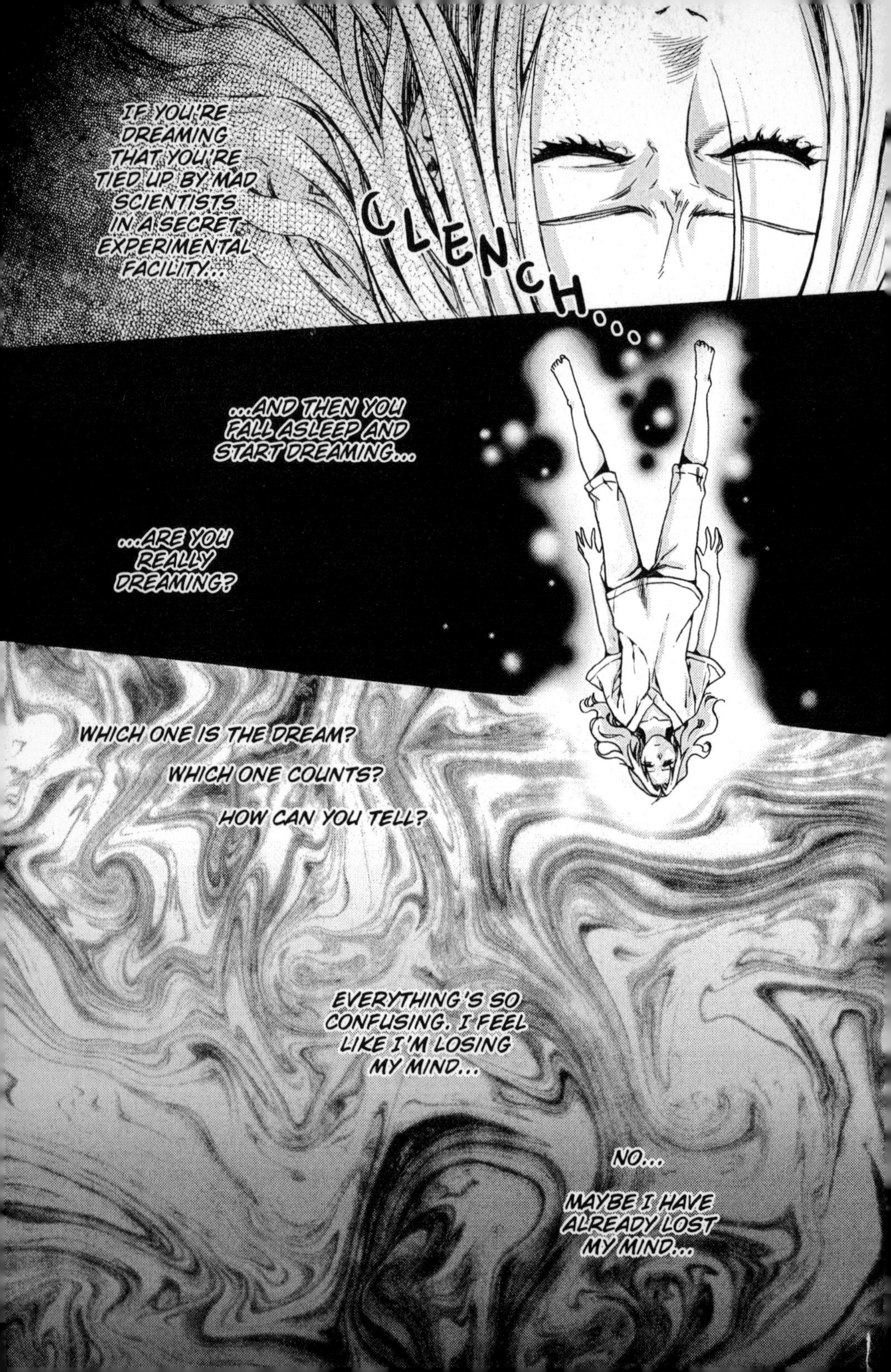
IF YOU'RE DREAMING THAT YOU'RE TIED UP BY MAD SCIENTISTS IN A SECRET EXPERIMENTAL FACILITY...
CLENCH...
...AND THEN YOU FALL ASLEEP AND START DREAMING...
...ARE YOU REALLY DREAMING?
WHICH ONE IS THE DREAM?
WHICH ONE COUNTS?
HOW CAN YOU TELL?
EVERYTHING'S SO CONFUSING. I FEEL LIKE I'M LOSING MY MIND...
NO...
MAYBE I HAVE ALREADY LOST MY MIND...

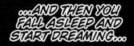

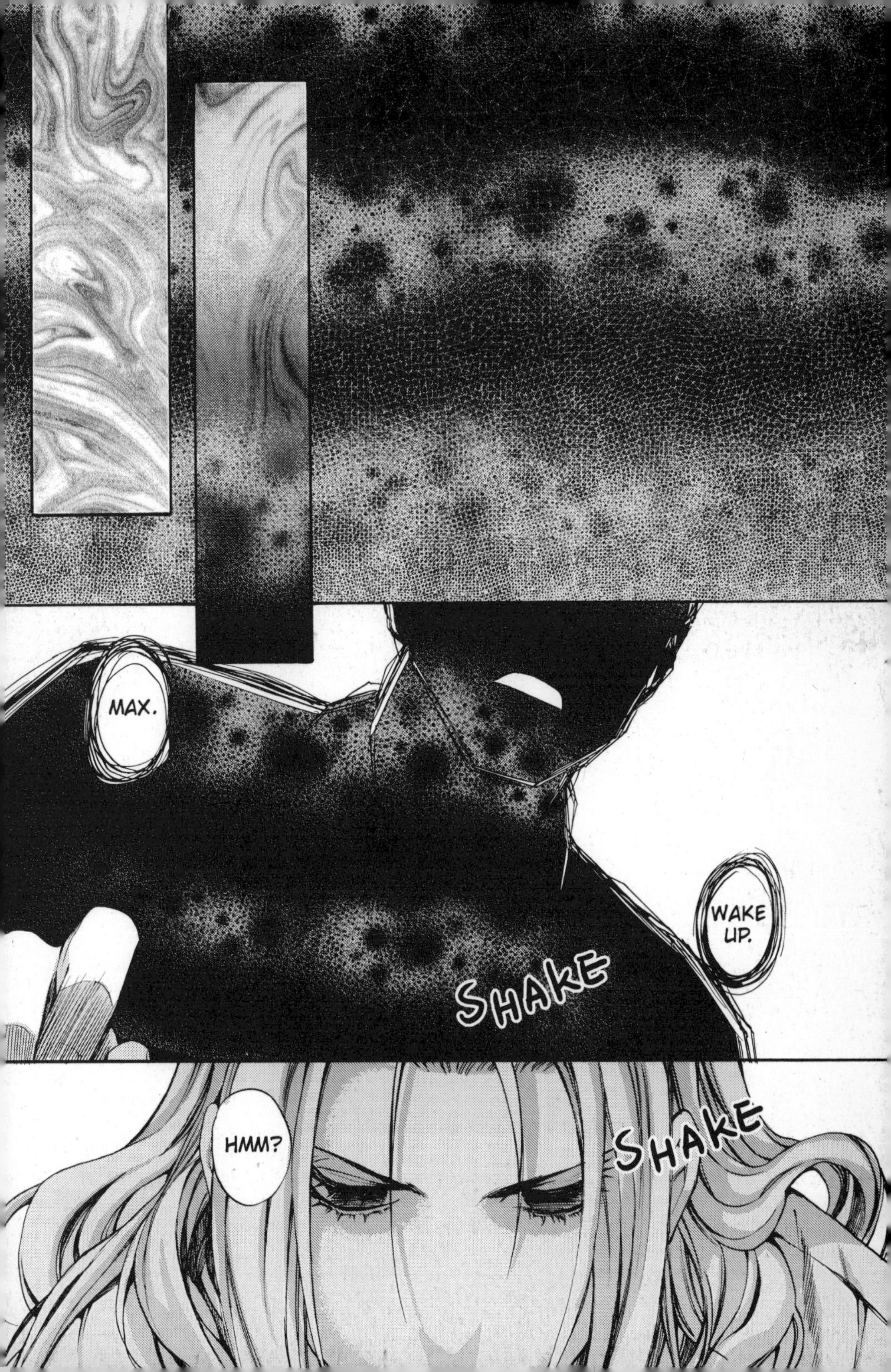
MAX.
WAKE UP.
SHAKE
HMM?
SHAKE

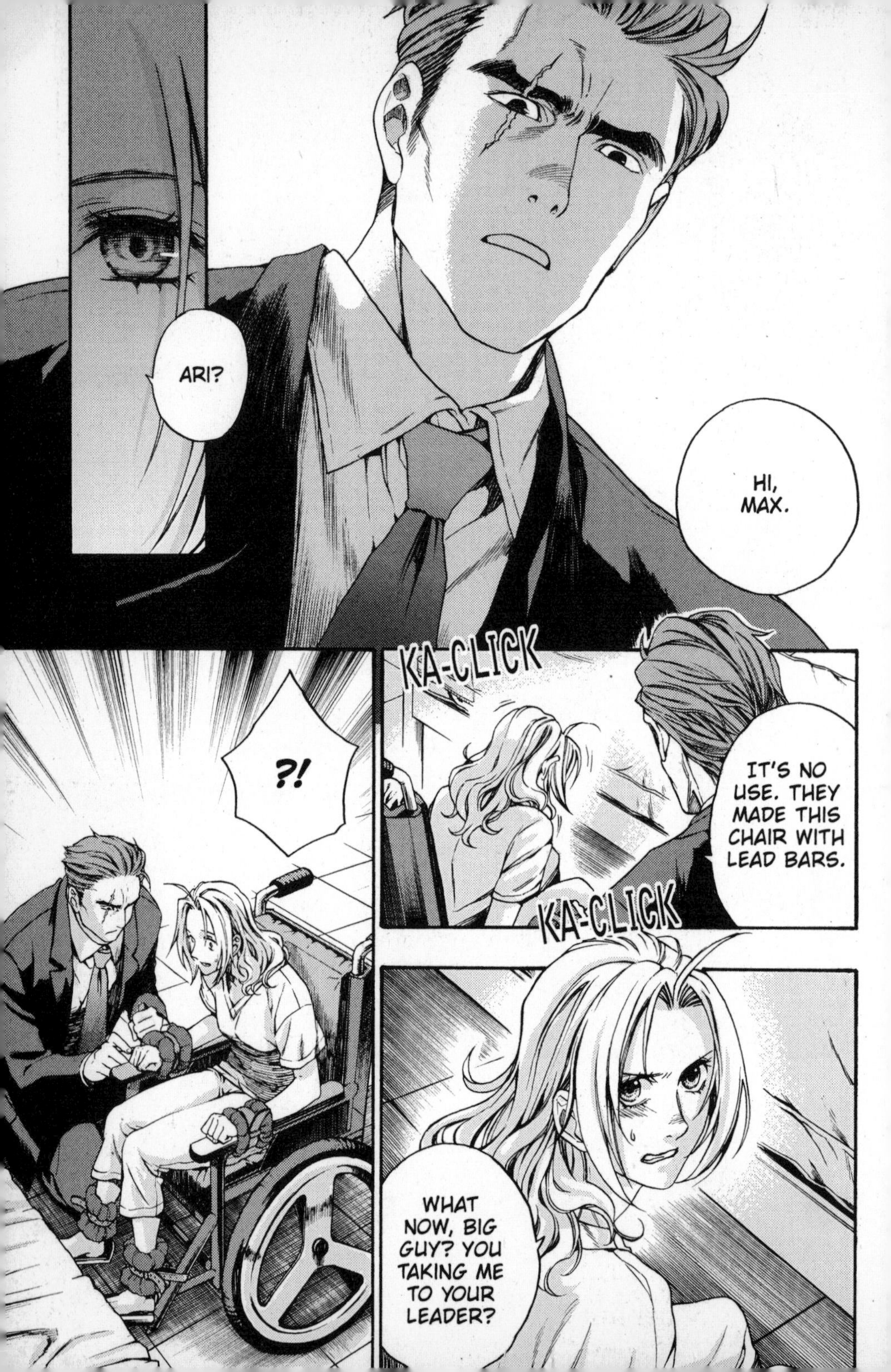
ARI?
HI, MAX.
?!
KA-CLICK
IT'S NO USE. THEY MADE THIS CHAIR WITH LEAD BARS.
KA-CLICK
WHAT NOW, BIG GUY? YOU TAKING ME TO YOUR LEADER?

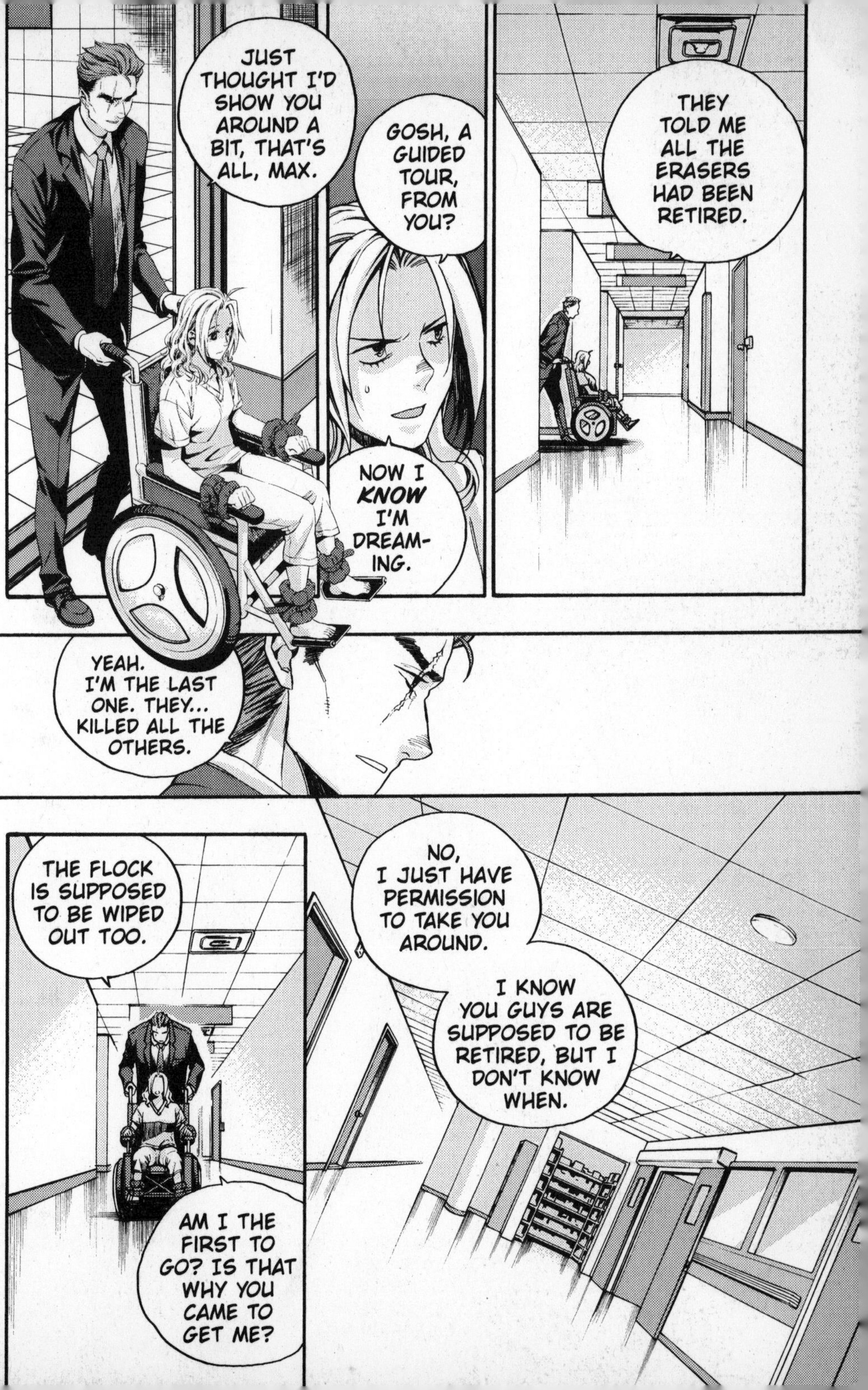
JUST THOUGHT I'D SHOW YOU AROUND A BIT, THAT'S ALL, MAX.
GOSH, A GUIDED TOUR, FROM YOU?
NOW I *KNOW* I'M DREAMING.
THEY TOLD ME ALL THE ERASERS HAD BEEN RETIRED.
YEAH. I'M THE LAST ONE. THEY... KILLED ALL THE OTHERS.
THE FLOCK IS SUPPOSED TO BE WIPED OUT TOO.
AM I THE FIRST TO GO? IS THAT WHY YOU CAME TO GET ME?
NO, I JUST HAVE PERMISSION TO TAKE YOU AROUND.
I KNOW YOU GUYS ARE SUPPOSED TO BE RETIRED, BUT I DON'T KNOW WHEN.

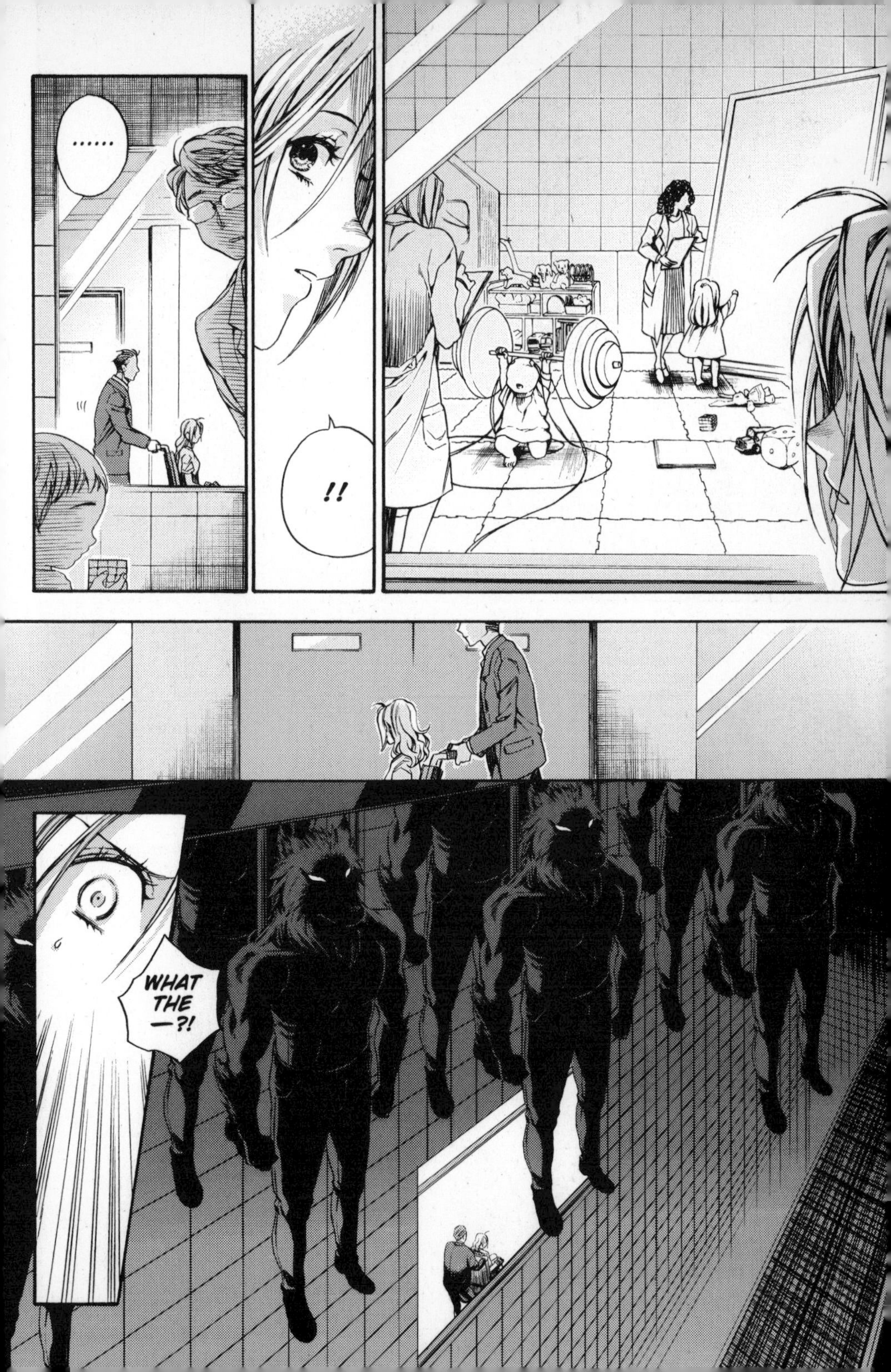
......
!!
WHAT THE —?!

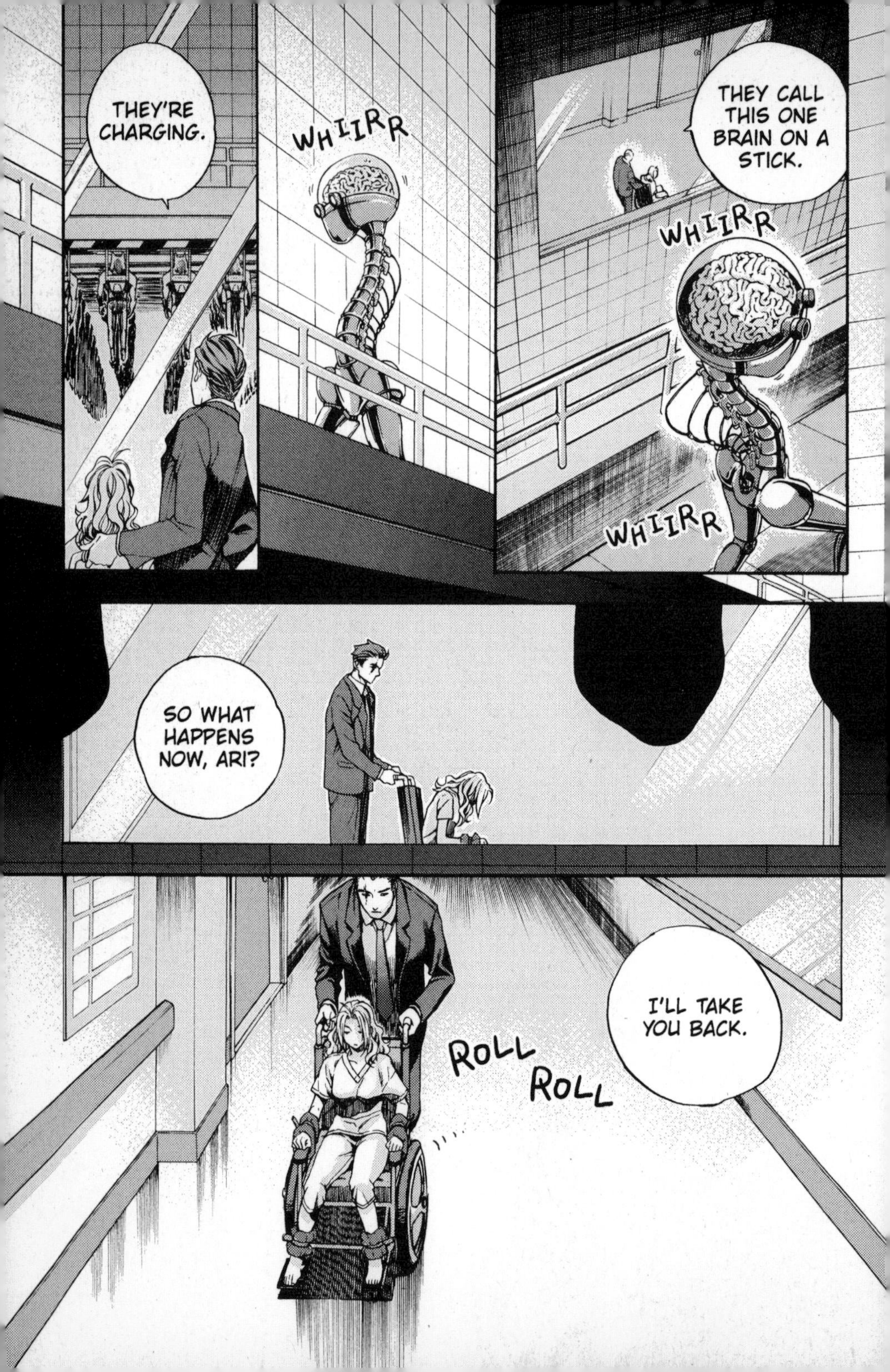
THEY'RE CHARGING.
WHIIRR
THEY CALL THIS ONE BRAIN ON A STICK.
WHIIRR
WHIIRR
SO WHAT HAPPENS NOW, ARI?
ROLL ROLL
I'LL TAKE YOU BACK.

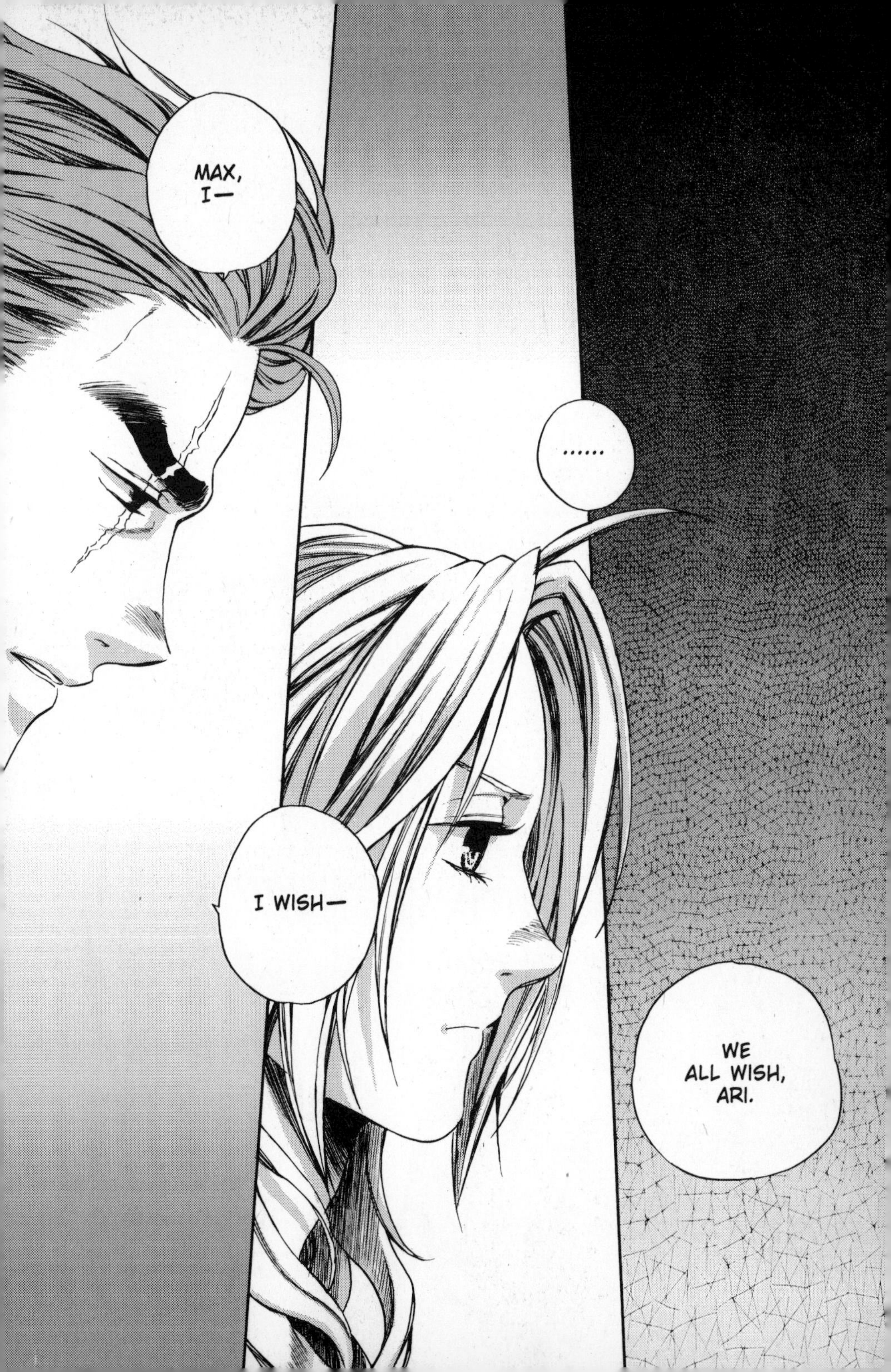
MAX, I—
......
I WISH—
WE ALL WISH, ARI.

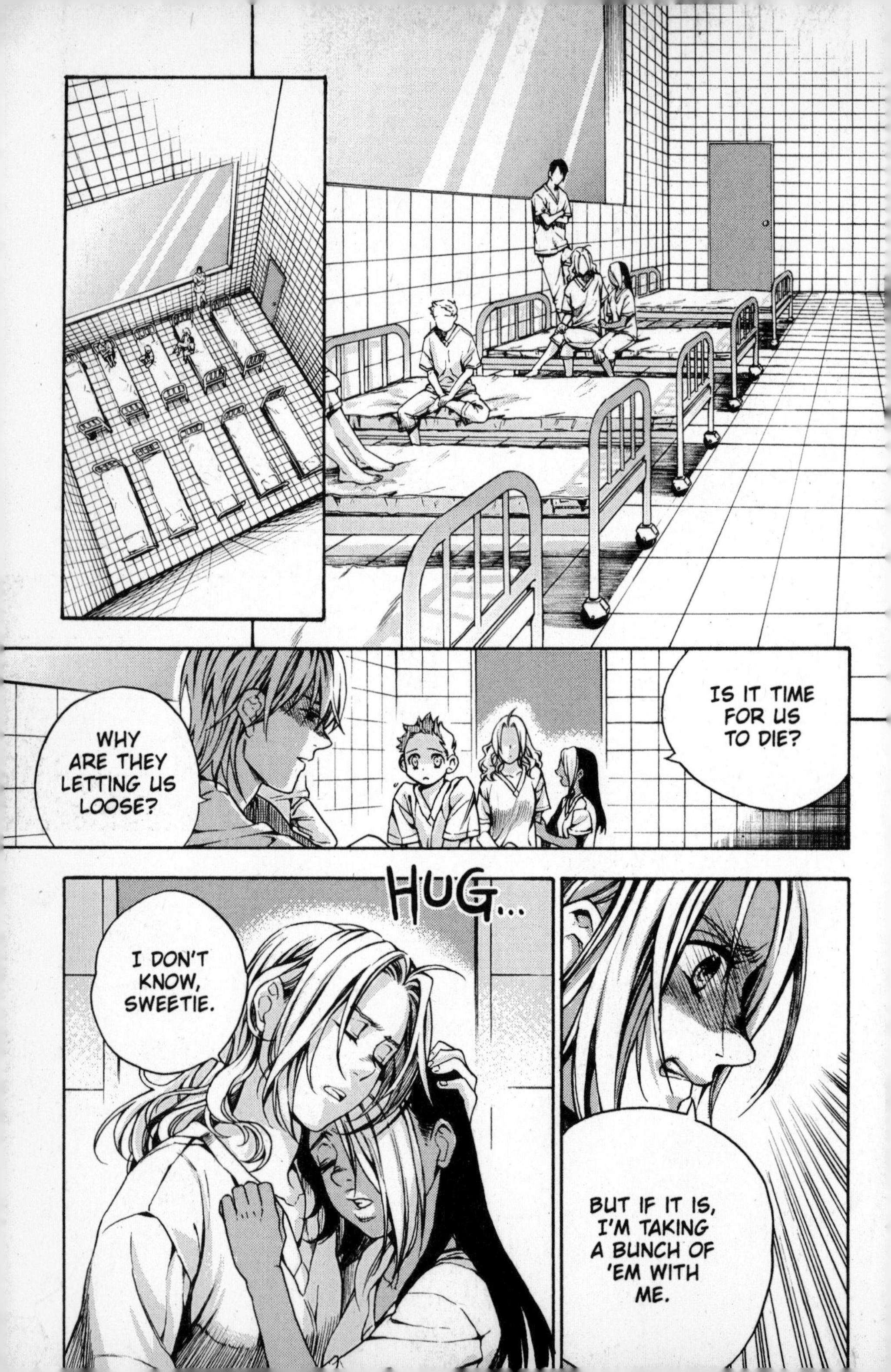
WHY ARE THEY LETTING US LOOSE?
IS IT TIME FOR US TO DIE?
HUG...
I DON'T KNOW, SWEETIE.
BUT IF IT IS, I'M TAKING A BUNCH OF 'EM WITH ME.

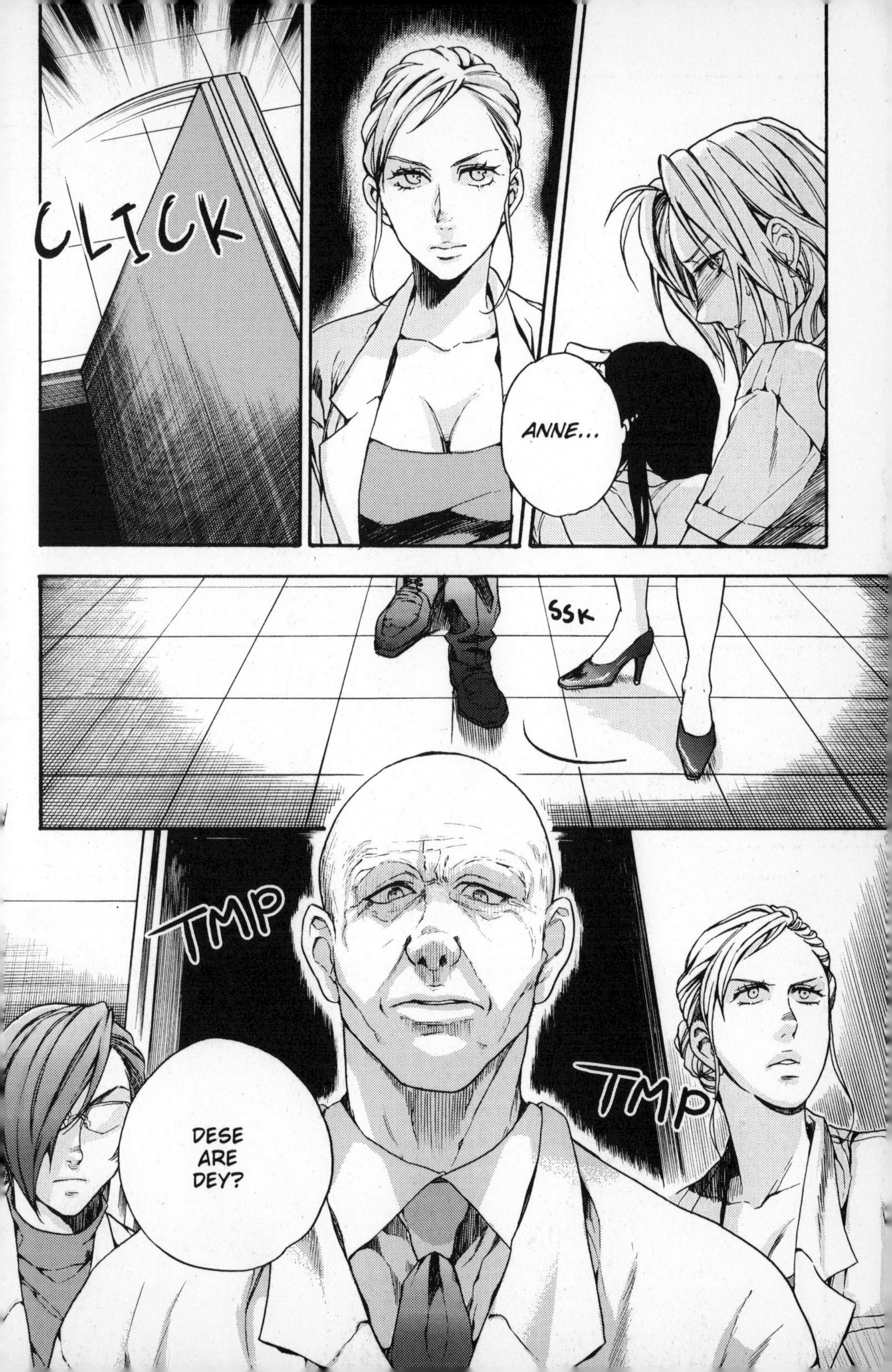
CLICK
ANNE...
SSK
TMP
DESE ARE DEY?
TMP

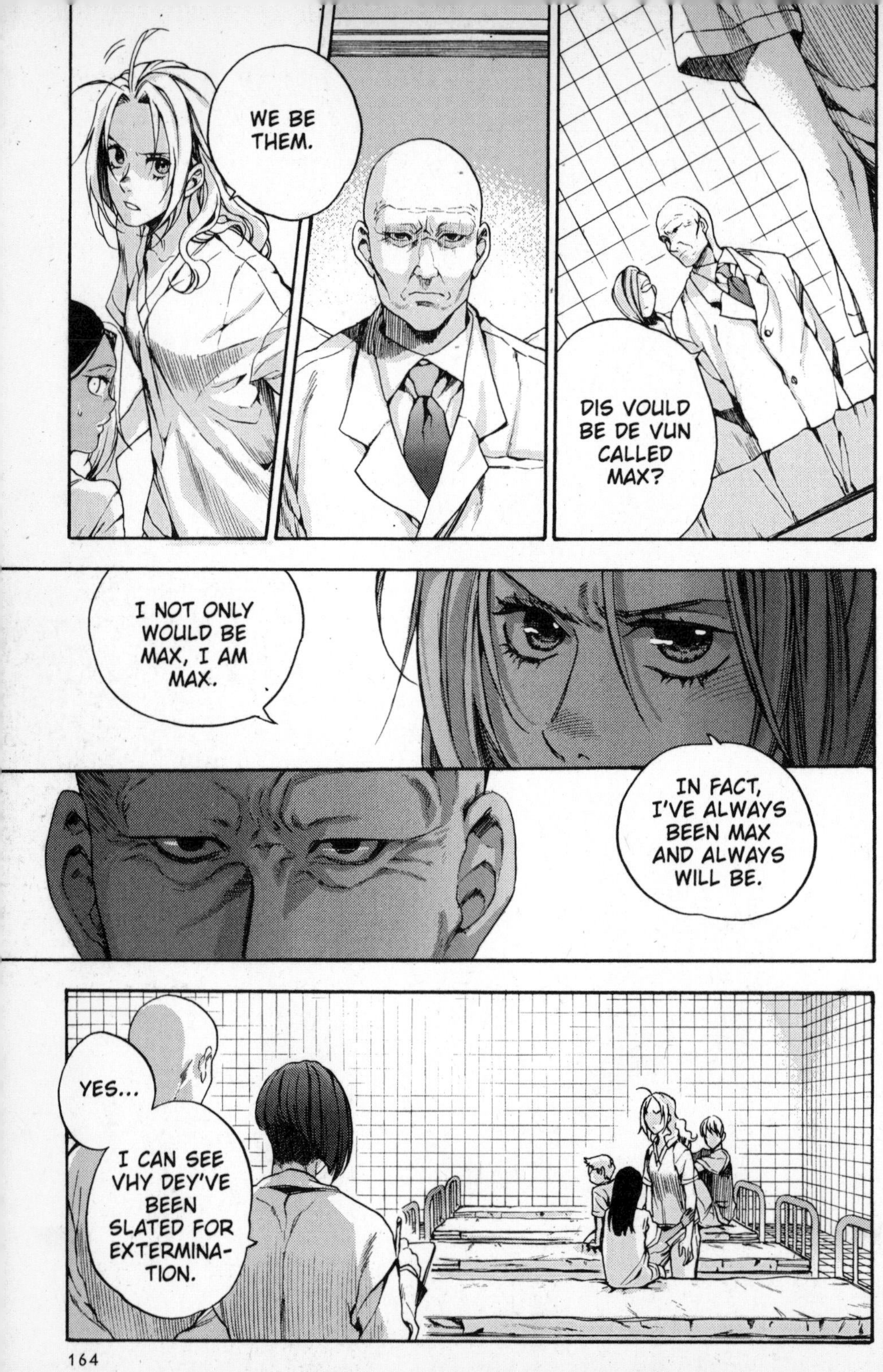
WE BE THEM.
DIS VOULD BE DE VUN CALLED MAX?
I NOT ONLY WOULD BE MAX, I AM MAX.
IN FACT, I'VE ALWAYS BEEN MAX AND ALWAYS WILL BE.
YES...
I CAN SEE VHY DEY'VE BEEN SLATED FOR EXTERMINA-TION.

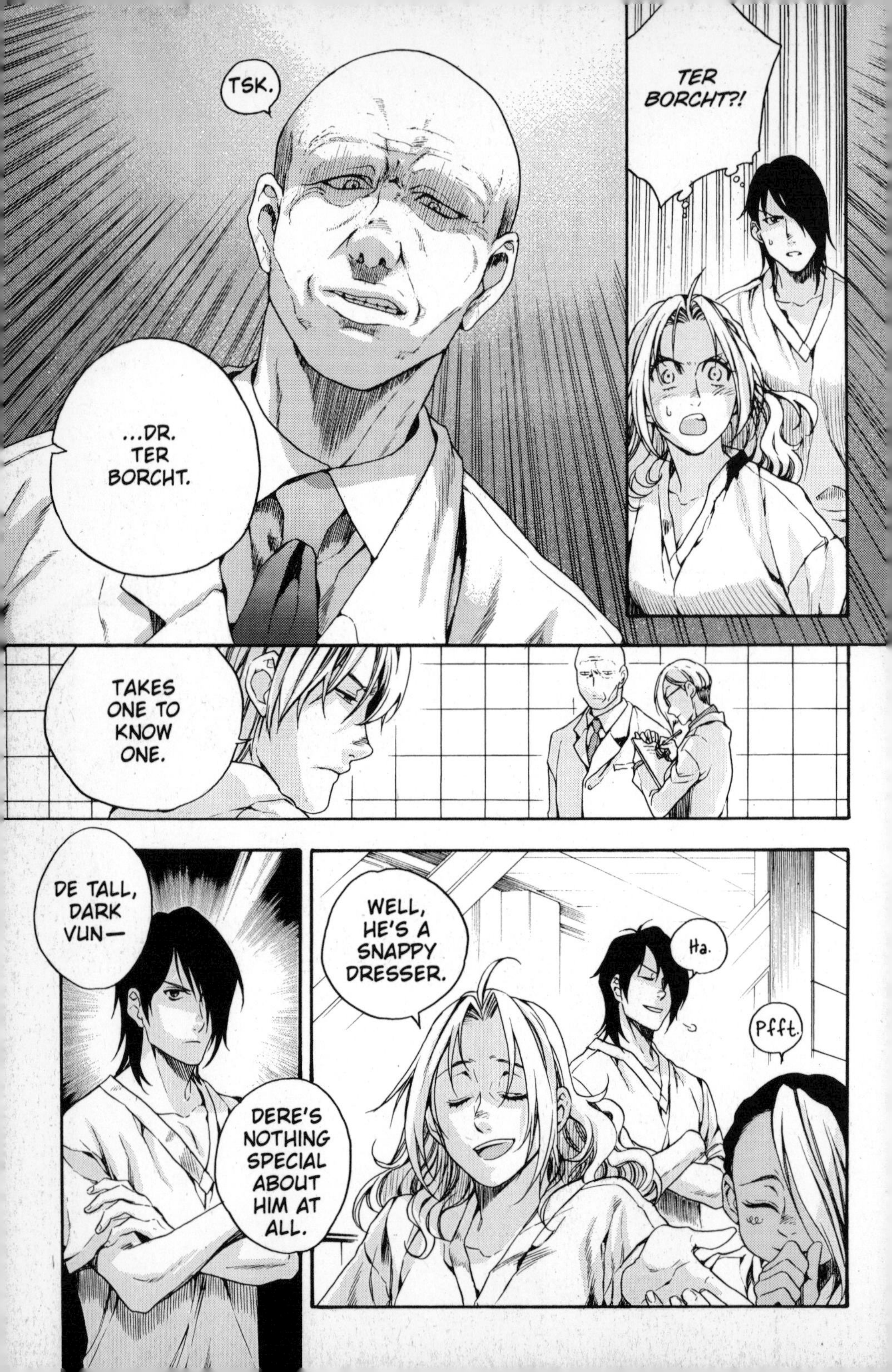
TSK.
...DR. TER BORCHT.
TER BORCHT?!
TAKES ONE TO KNOW ONE.
DE TALL, DARK VUN—
DERE'S NOTHING SPECIAL ABOUT HIM AT ALL.
WELL, HE'S A SNAPPY DRESSER.
Ha.
Pfft.

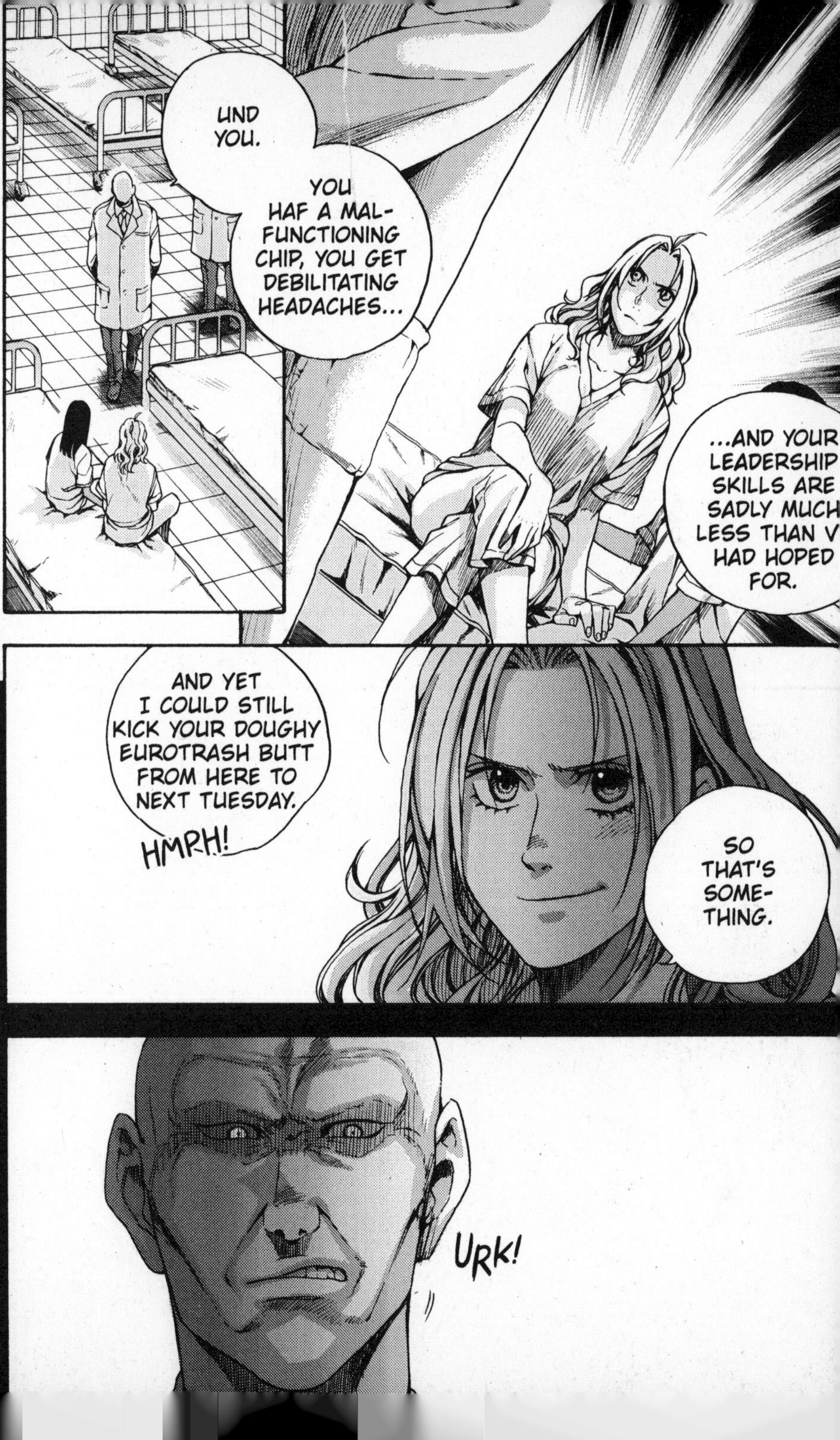
UND YOU.
YOU HAF A MAL-FUNCTIONING CHIP, YOU GET DEBILITATING HEADACHES...
...AND YOUR LEADERSHIP SKILLS ARE SADLY MUCH LESS THAN V HAD HOPED FOR.
AND YET I COULD STILL KICK YOUR DOUGHY EUROTRASH BUTT FROM HERE TO NEXT TUESDAY.
HMPH!
SO THAT'S SOME-THING.
URK!

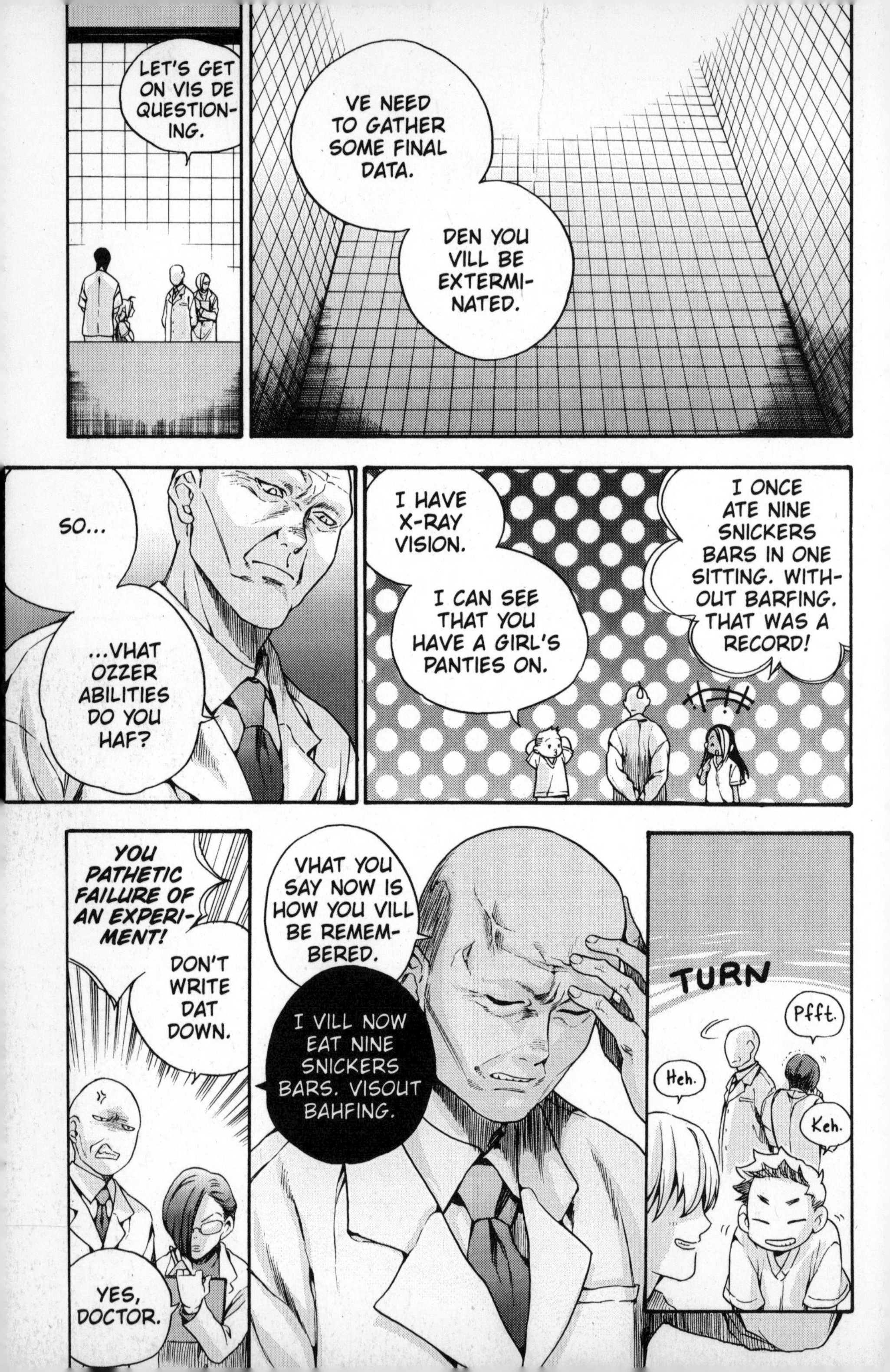
LET'S GET ON VIS DE QUESTION-ING.
VE NEED TO GATHER SOME FINAL DATA.
DEN YOU VILL BE EXTERMI-NATED.
SO...
...VHAT OZZER ABILITIES DO YOU HAF?
I HAVE X-RAY VISION.
I CAN SEE THAT YOU HAVE A GIRL'S PANTIES ON.
I ONCE ATE NINE SNICKERS BARS IN ONE SITTING. WITH-OUT BARFING. THAT WAS A RECORD!
YOU PATHETIC FAILURE OF AN EXPERI-MENT!
DON'T WRITE DAT DOWN.
YES, DOCTOR.
VHAT YOU SAY NOW IS HOW YOU VILL BE REMEM-BERED.
I VILL NOW EAT NINE SNICKERS BARS. VISOUT BAHFING.
TURN
Pfft.
Heh.
Keh.

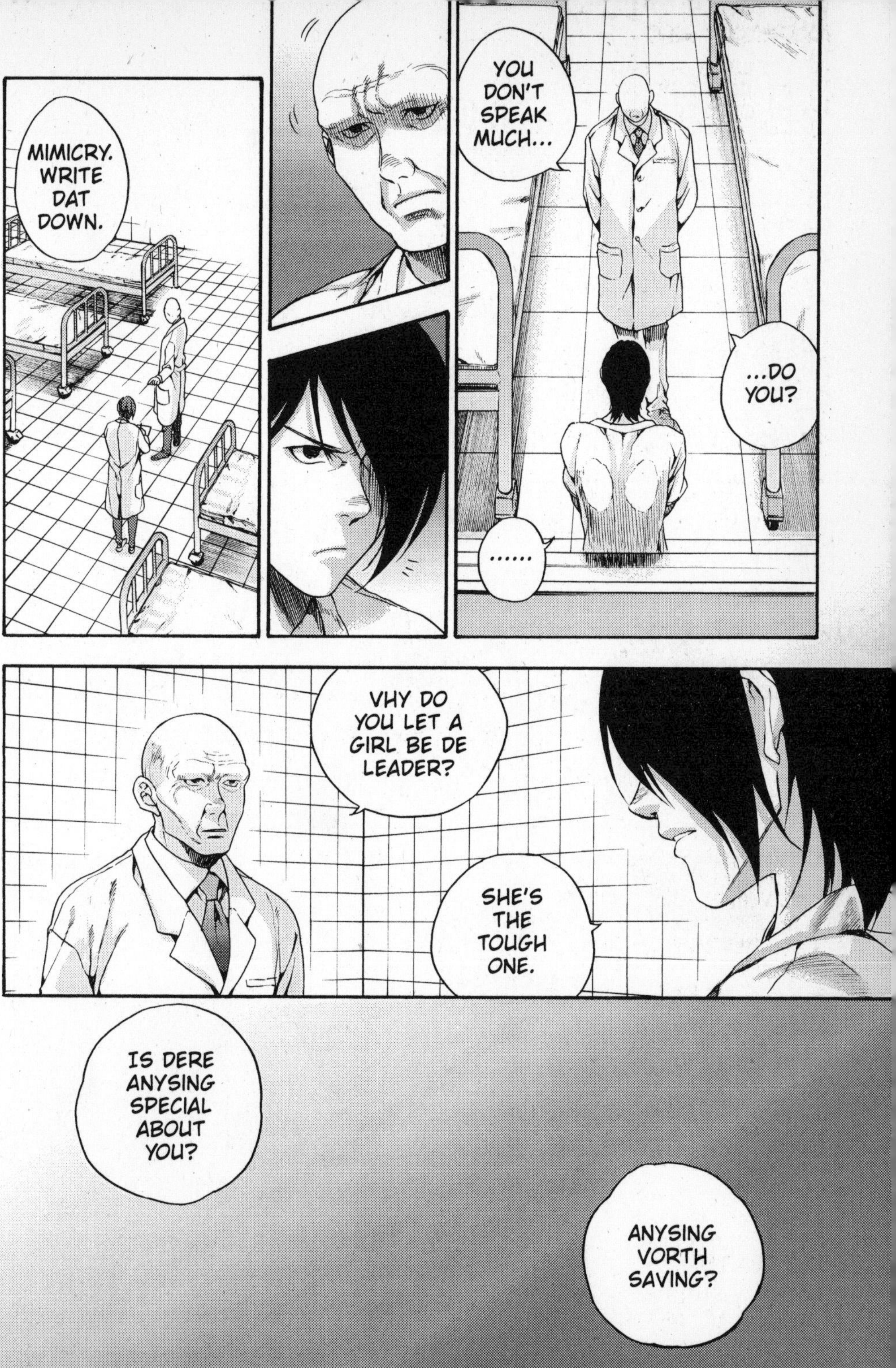
MIMICRY. WRITE DAT DOWN.
YOU DON'T SPEAK MUCH...
...DO YOU?
......
VHY DO YOU LET A GIRL BE DE LEADER?
SHE'S THE TOUGH ONE.
IS DERE ANYSING SPECIAL ABOUT YOU?
ANYSING VORTH SAVING?

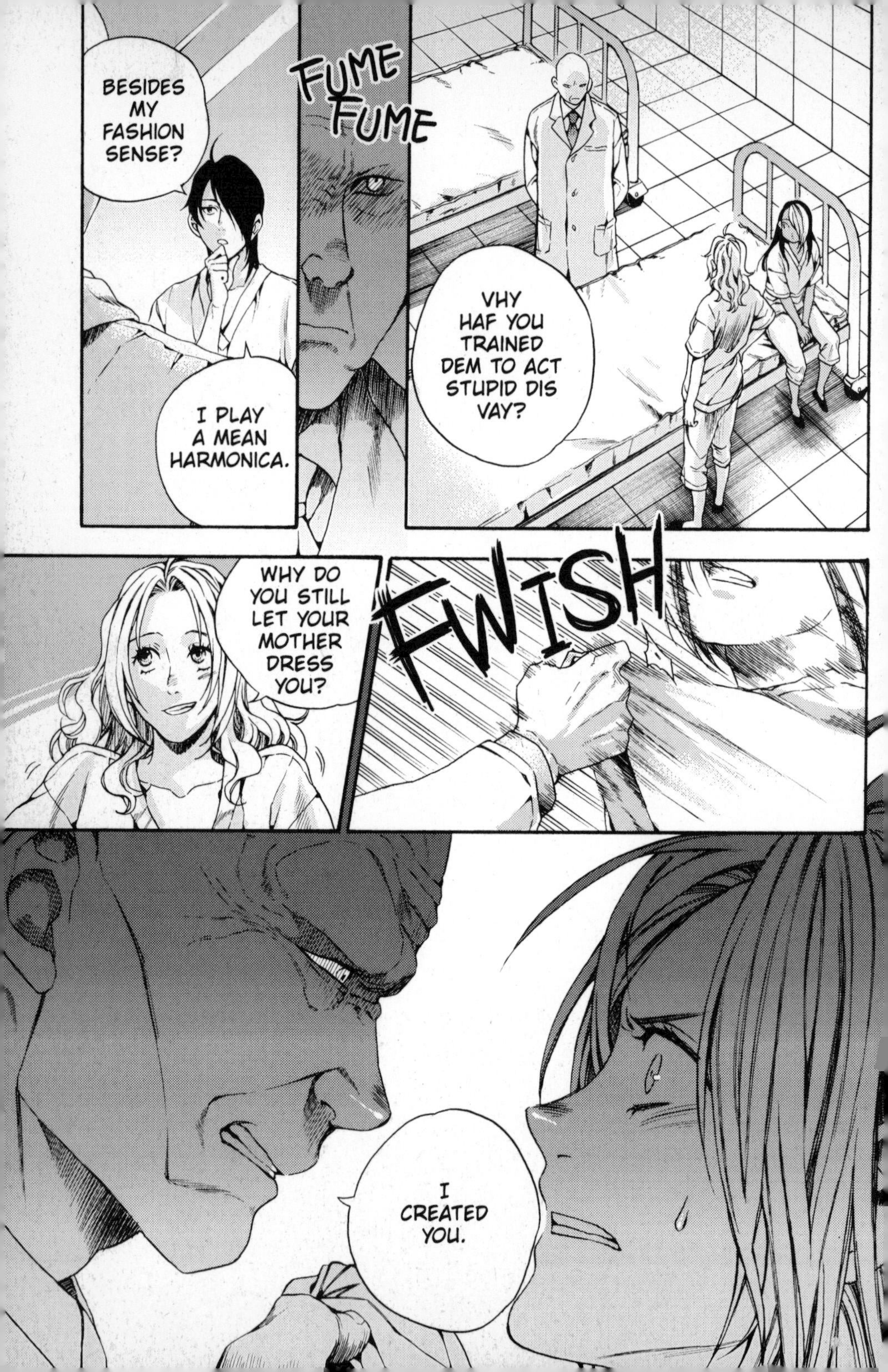
BESIDES MY FASHION SENSE?
I PLAY A MEAN HARMONICA.
FUME FUME
VHY HAF YOU TRAINED DEM TO ACT STUPID DIS VAY?
WHY DO YOU STILL LET YOUR MOTHER DRESS YOU?
FWISH
I CREATED YOU.

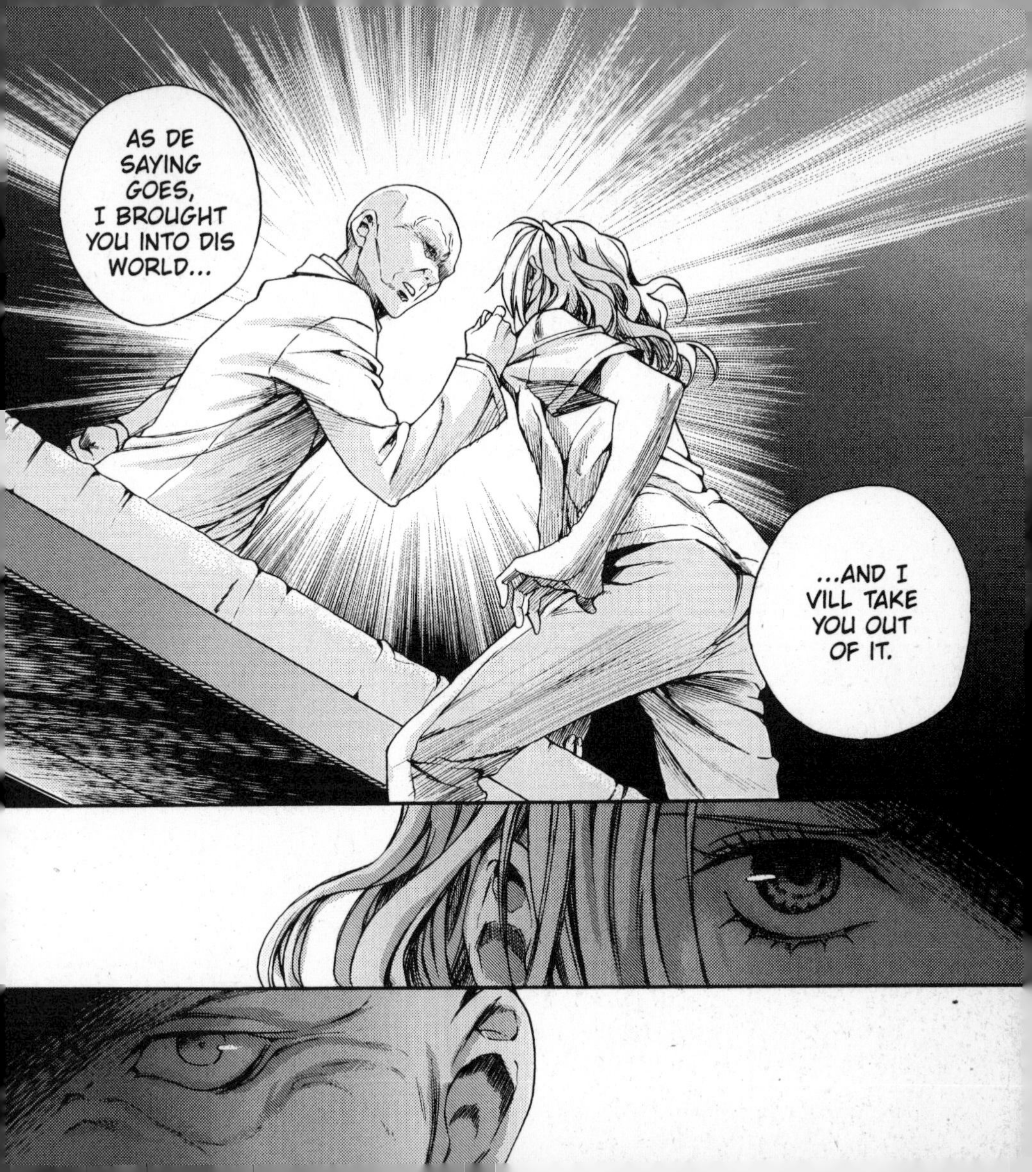
AS DE SAYING GOES, I BROUGHT YOU INTO DIS WORLD...
...AND I VILL TAKE YOU OUT OF IT.

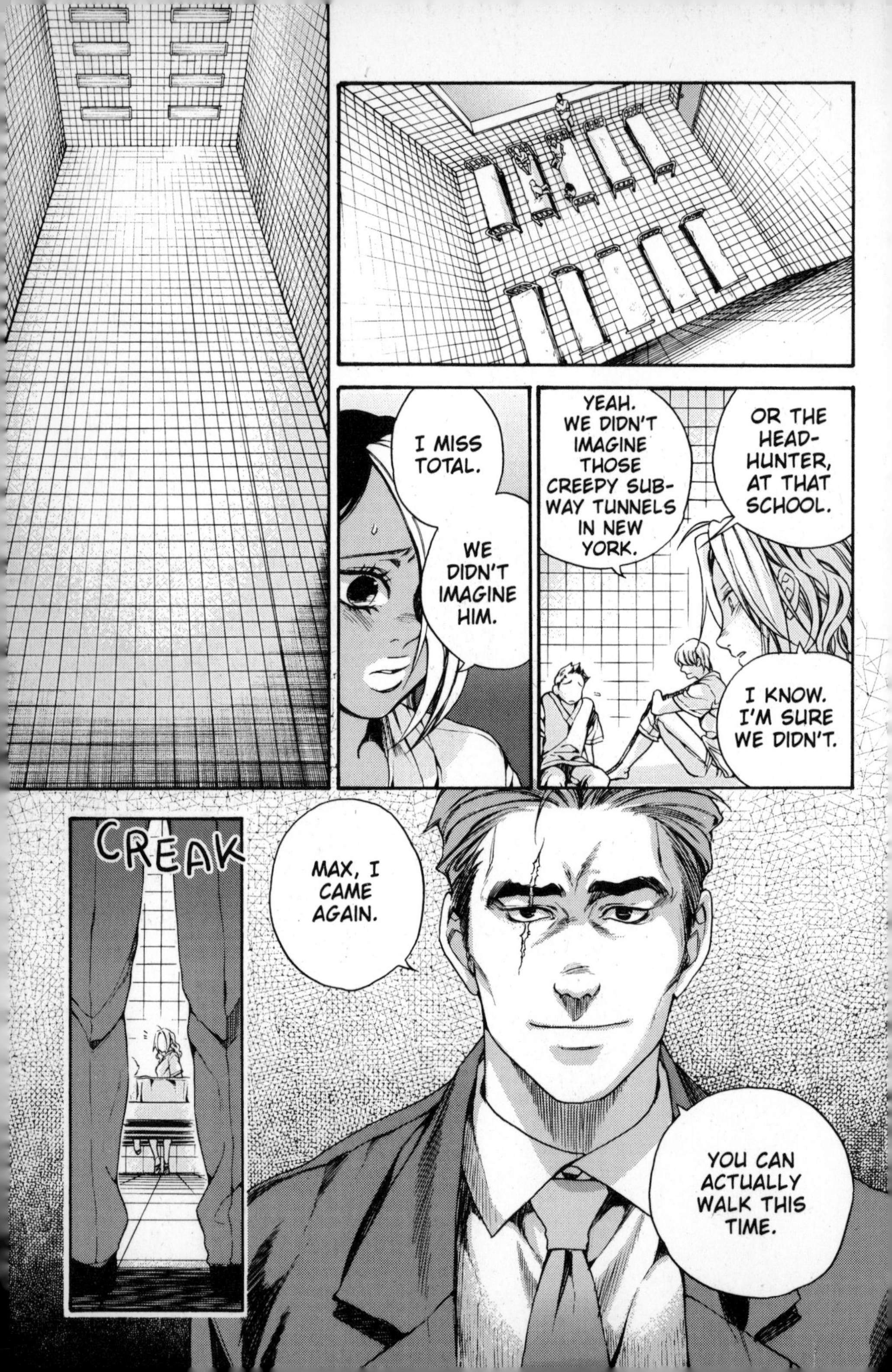
I MISS TOTAL.
WE DIDN'T IMAGINE HIM.
YEAH. WE DIDN'T IMAGINE THOSE CREEPY SUB-WAY TUNNELS IN NEW YORK.
OR THE HEAD-HUNTER, AT THAT SCHOOL.
I KNOW. I'M SURE WE DIDN'T.
CREAK
MAX, I CAME AGAIN.
YOU CAN ACTUALLY WALK THIS TIME.

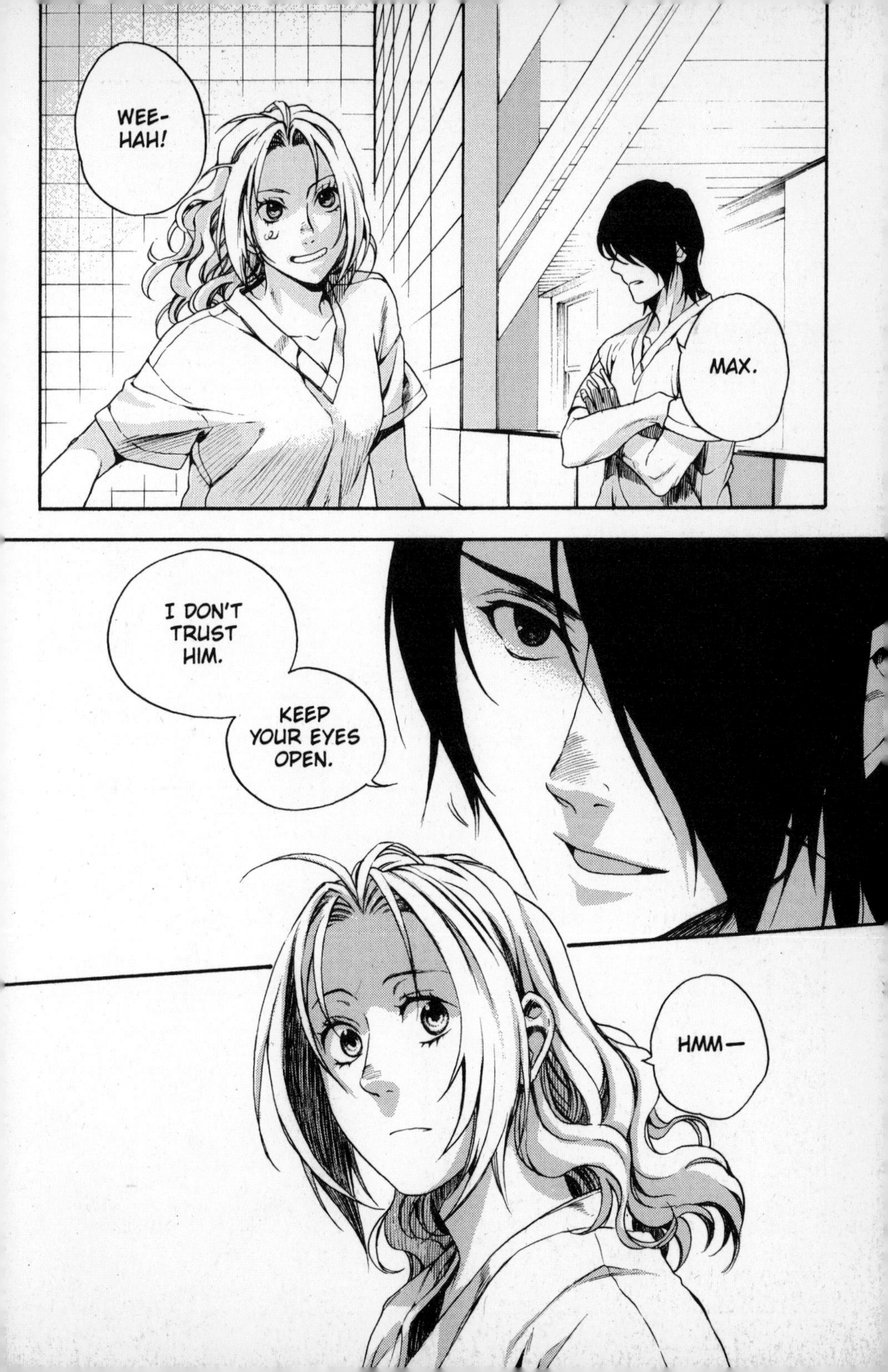
WEE-HAH!
MAX.
I DON'T TRUST HIM.
KEEP YOUR EYES OPEN.
HMM—

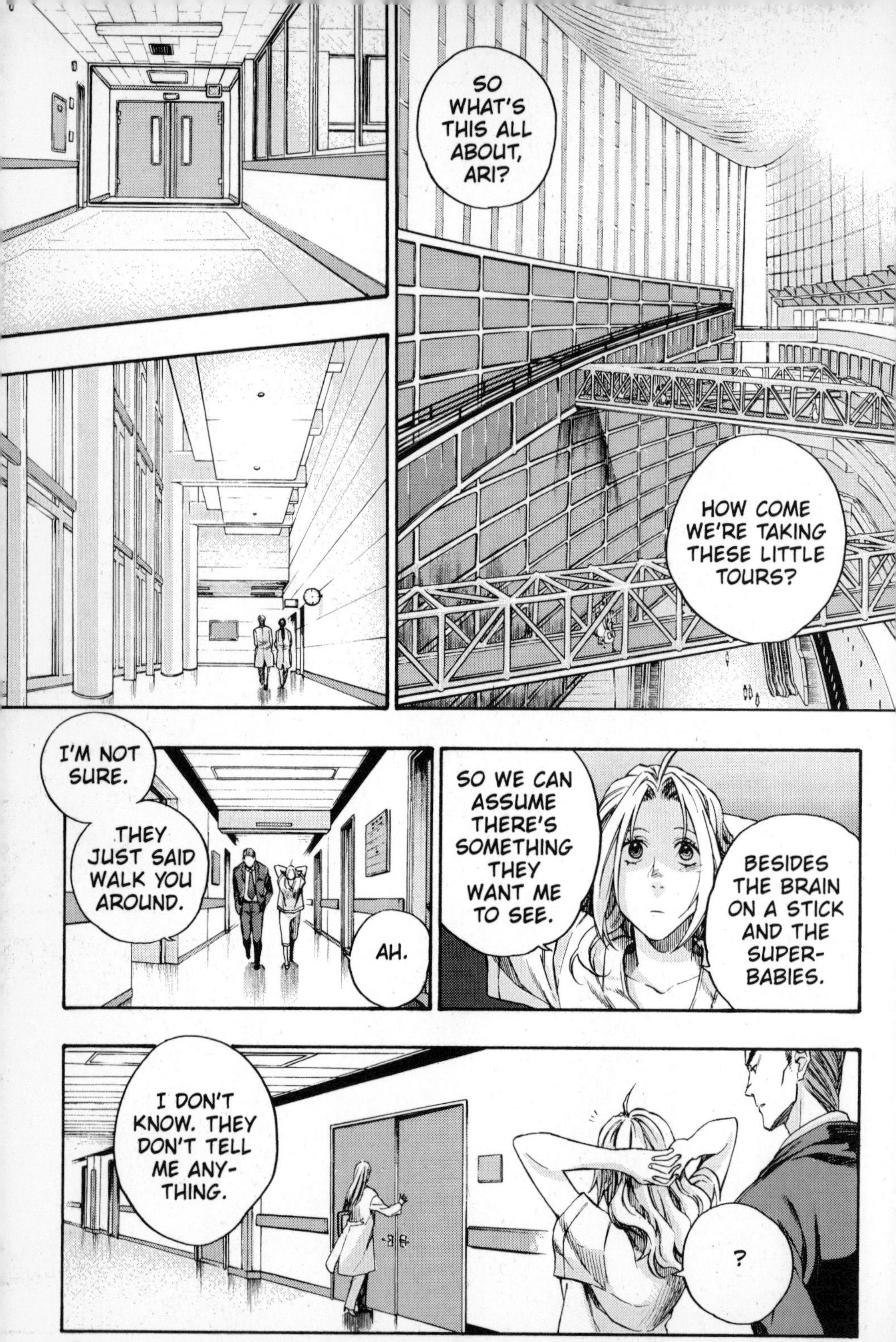
SO WHAT'S THIS ALL ABOUT, ARI?
HOW COME WE'RE TAKING THESE LITTLE TOURS?
I'M NOT SURE.
THEY JUST SAID WALK YOU AROUND.
AH.
SO WE CAN ASSUME THERE'S SOMETHING THEY WANT ME TO SEE.
BESIDES THE BRAIN ON A STICK AND THE SUPER-BABIES.
I DON'T KNOW. THEY DON'T TELL ME ANY-THING.
?

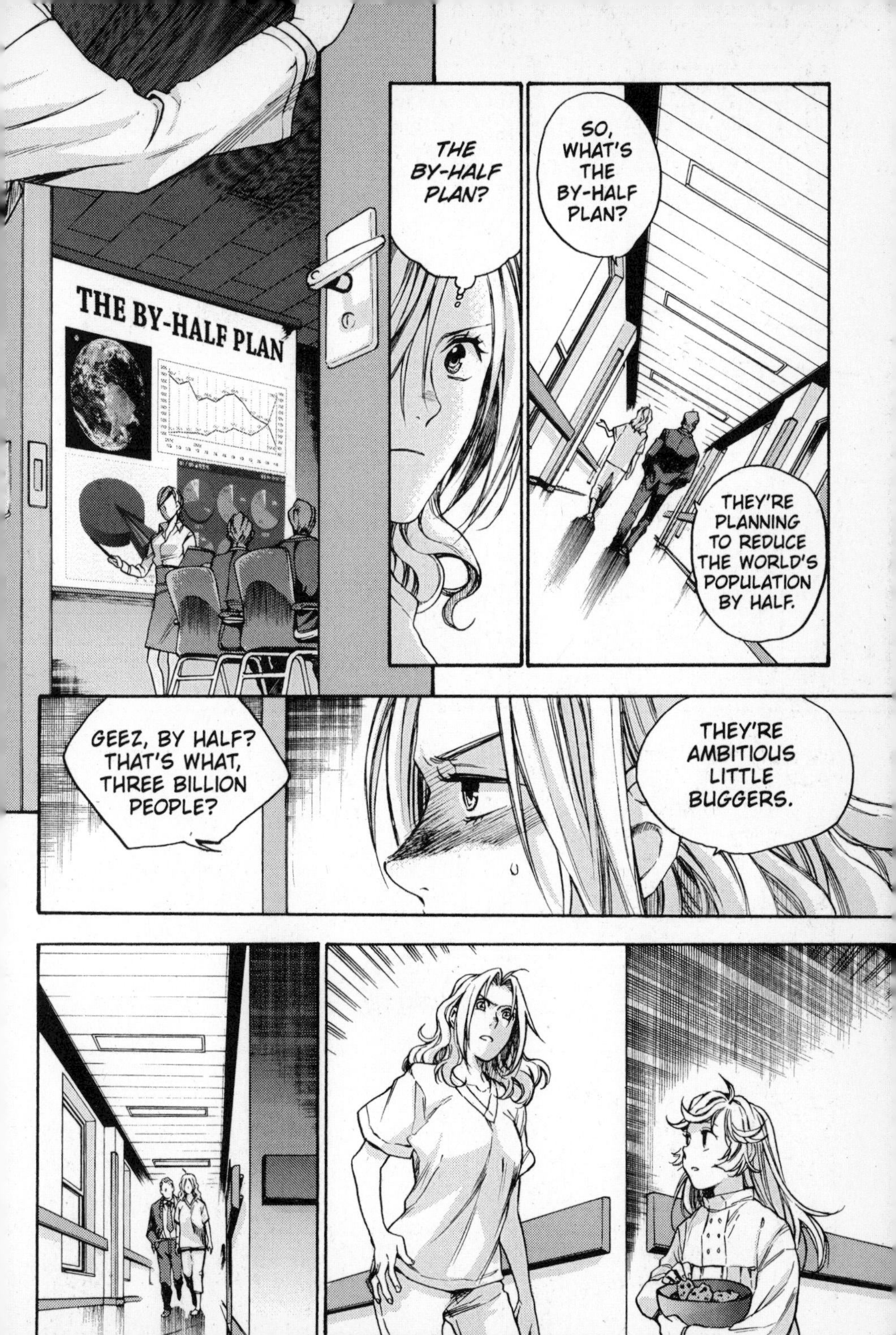
THE BY-HALF PLAN
THE BY-HALF PLAN?
SO, WHAT'S THE BY-HALF PLAN?
THEY'RE PLANNING TO REDUCE THE WORLD'S POPULATION BY HALF.
GEEZ, BY HALF? THAT'S WHAT, THREE BILLION PEOPLE?
THEY'RE AMBITIOUS LITTLE BUGGERS.

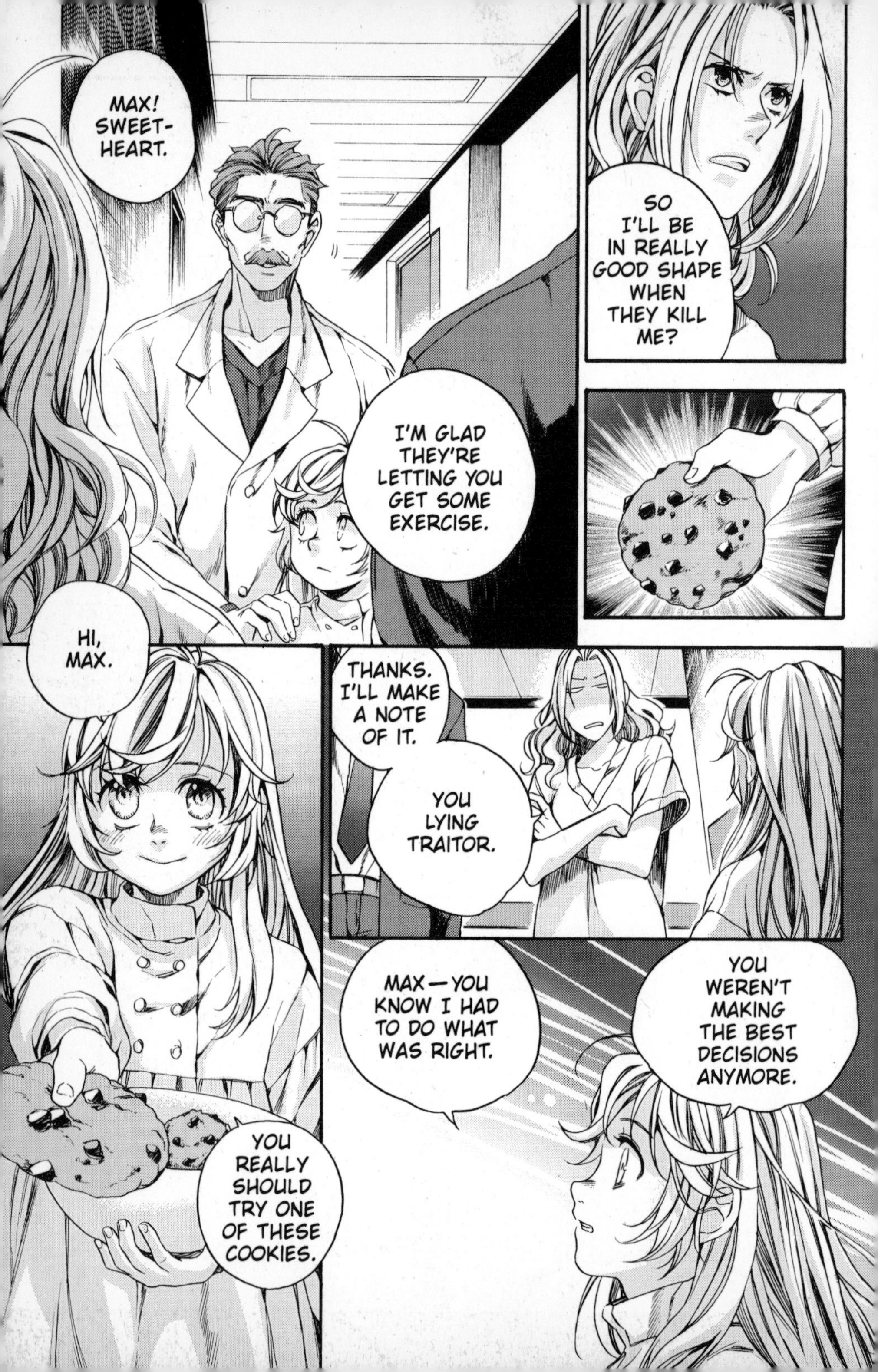
MAX! SWEET-HEART.
I'M GLAD THEY'RE LETTING YOU GET SOME EXERCISE.
SO I'LL BE IN REALLY GOOD SHAPE WHEN THEY KILL ME?
HI, MAX.
YOU REALLY SHOULD TRY ONE OF THESE COOKIES.
THANKS. I'LL MAKE A NOTE OF IT.
YOU LYING TRAITOR.
MAX—YOU KNOW I HAD TO DO WHAT WAS RIGHT.
YOU WEREN'T MAKING THE BEST DECISIONS ANYMORE.

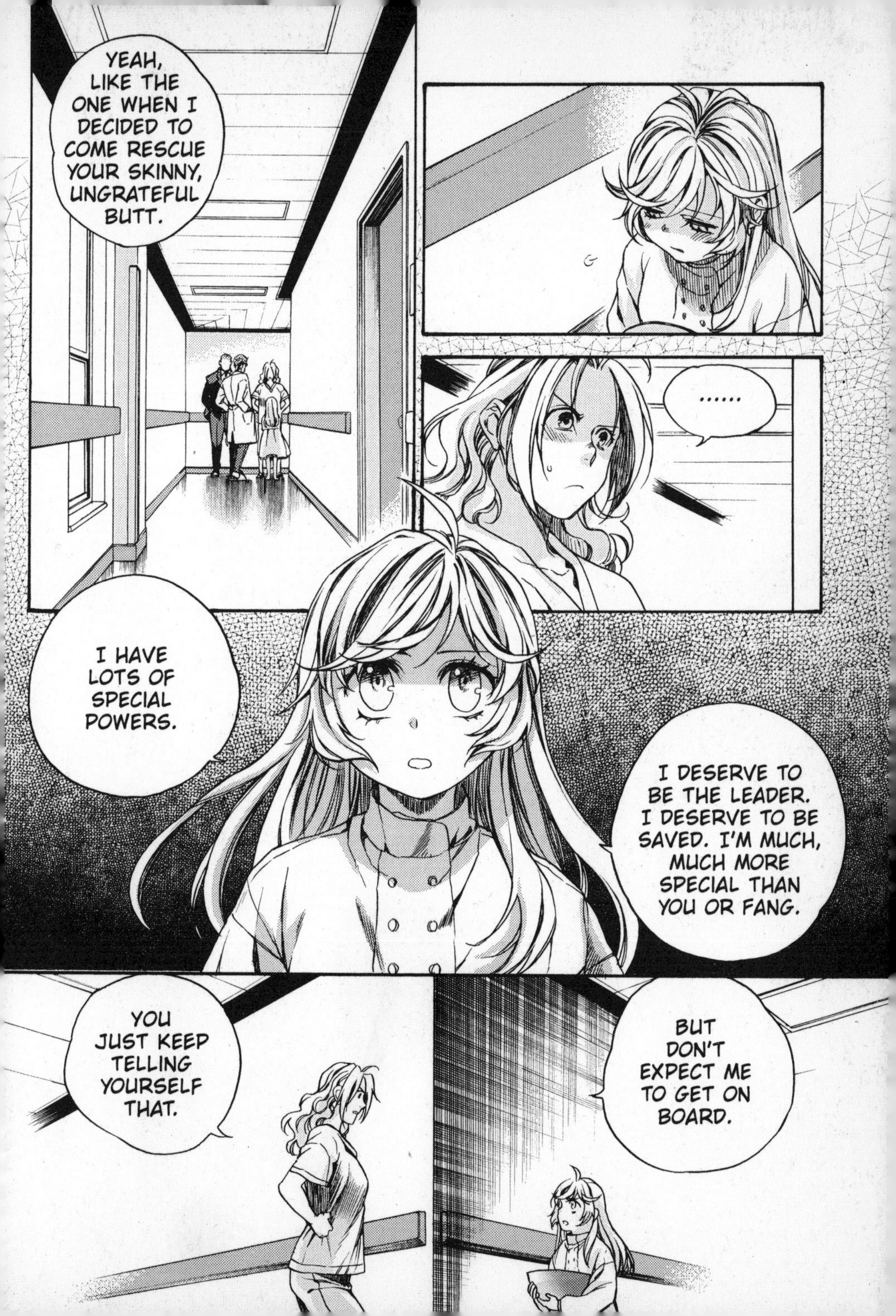
YEAH, LIKE THE ONE WHEN I DECIDED TO COME RESCUE YOUR SKINNY, UNGRATEFUL BUTT.
......
I HAVE LOTS OF SPECIAL POWERS.
I DESERVE TO BE THE LEADER. I DESERVE TO BE SAVED. I'M MUCH, MUCH MORE SPECIAL THAN YOU OR FANG.
YOU JUST KEEP TELLING YOURSELF THAT.
BUT DON'T EXPECT ME TO GET ON BOARD.

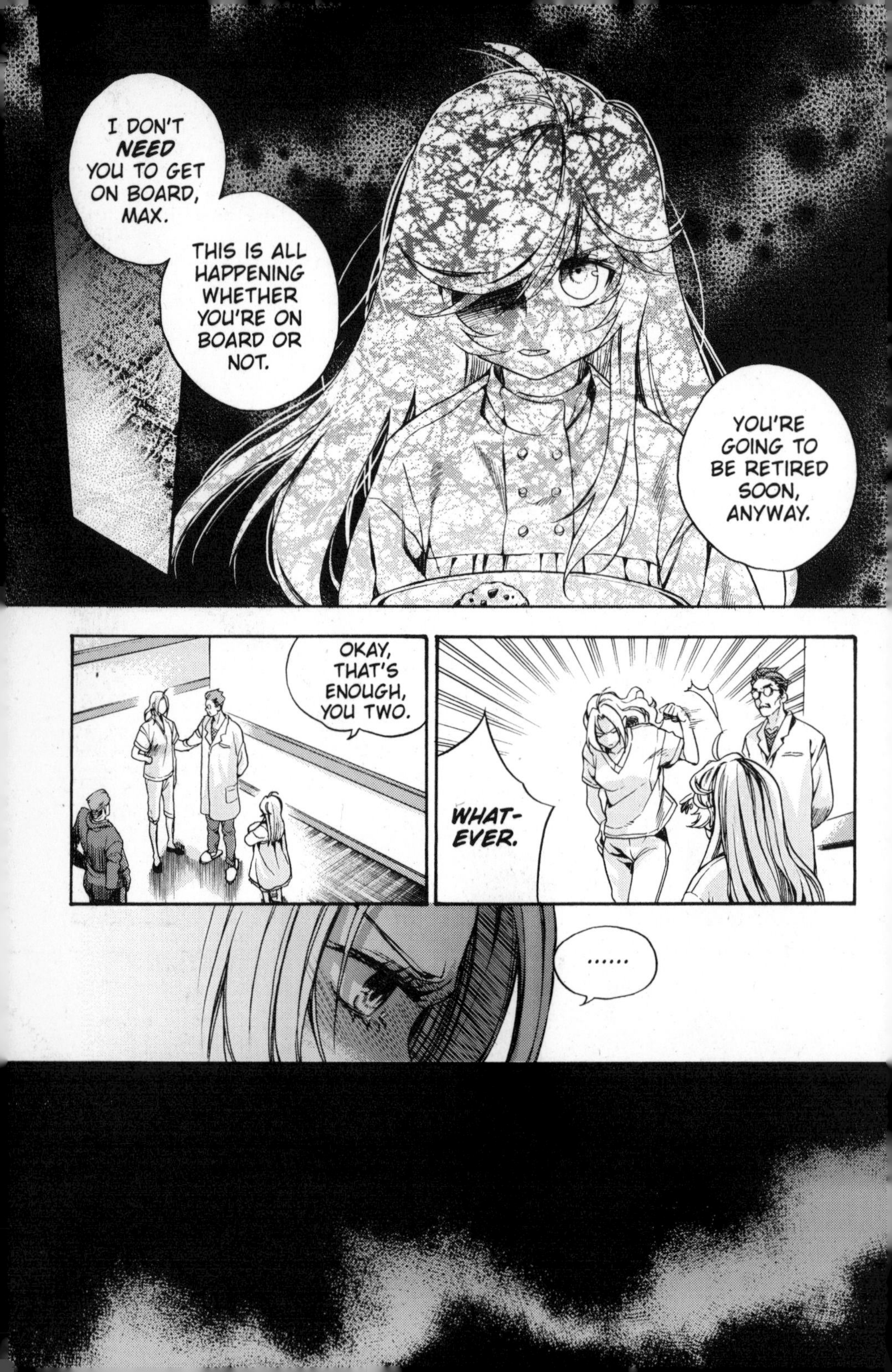
I DON'T **NEED** YOU TO GET ON BOARD, MAX.
THIS IS ALL HAPPENING WHETHER YOU'RE ON BOARD OR NOT.
YOU'RE GOING TO BE RETIRED SOON, ANYWAY.
OKAY, THAT'S ENOUGH, YOU TWO.
WHAT-EVER.
......

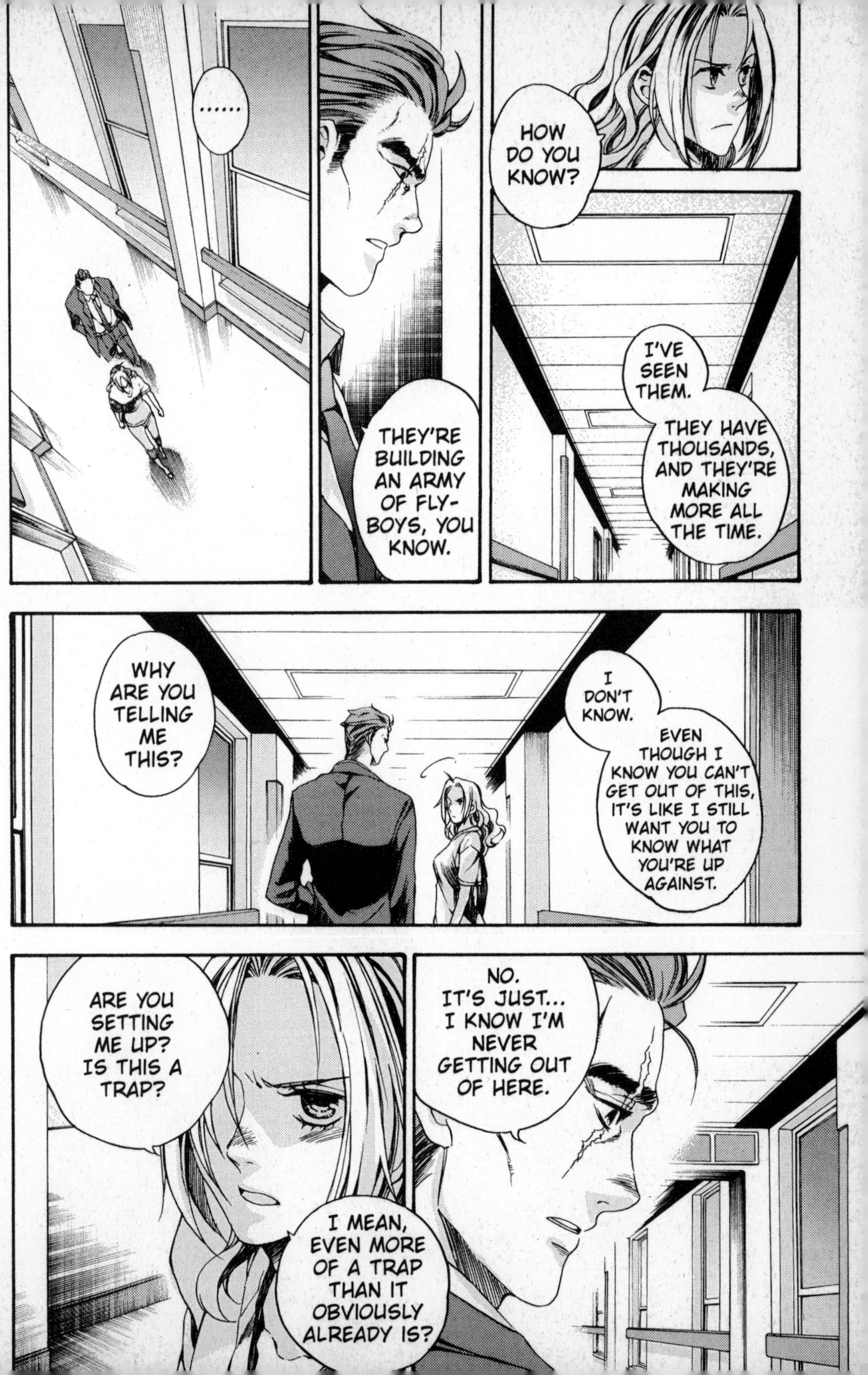
......
THEY'RE BUILDING AN ARMY OF FLY-BOYS, YOU KNOW.
HOW DO YOU KNOW?
I'VE SEEN THEM.
THEY HAVE THOUSANDS, AND THEY'RE MAKING MORE ALL THE TIME.
WHY ARE YOU TELLING ME THIS?
I DON'T KNOW.
EVEN THOUGH I KNOW YOU CAN'T GET OUT OF THIS, IT'S LIKE I STILL WANT YOU TO KNOW WHAT YOU'RE UP AGAINST.
ARE YOU SETTING ME UP? IS THIS A TRAP?
I MEAN, EVEN MORE OF A TRAP THAN IT OBVIOUSLY ALREADY IS?
NO. IT'S JUST... I KNOW I'M NEVER GETTING OUT OF HERE.

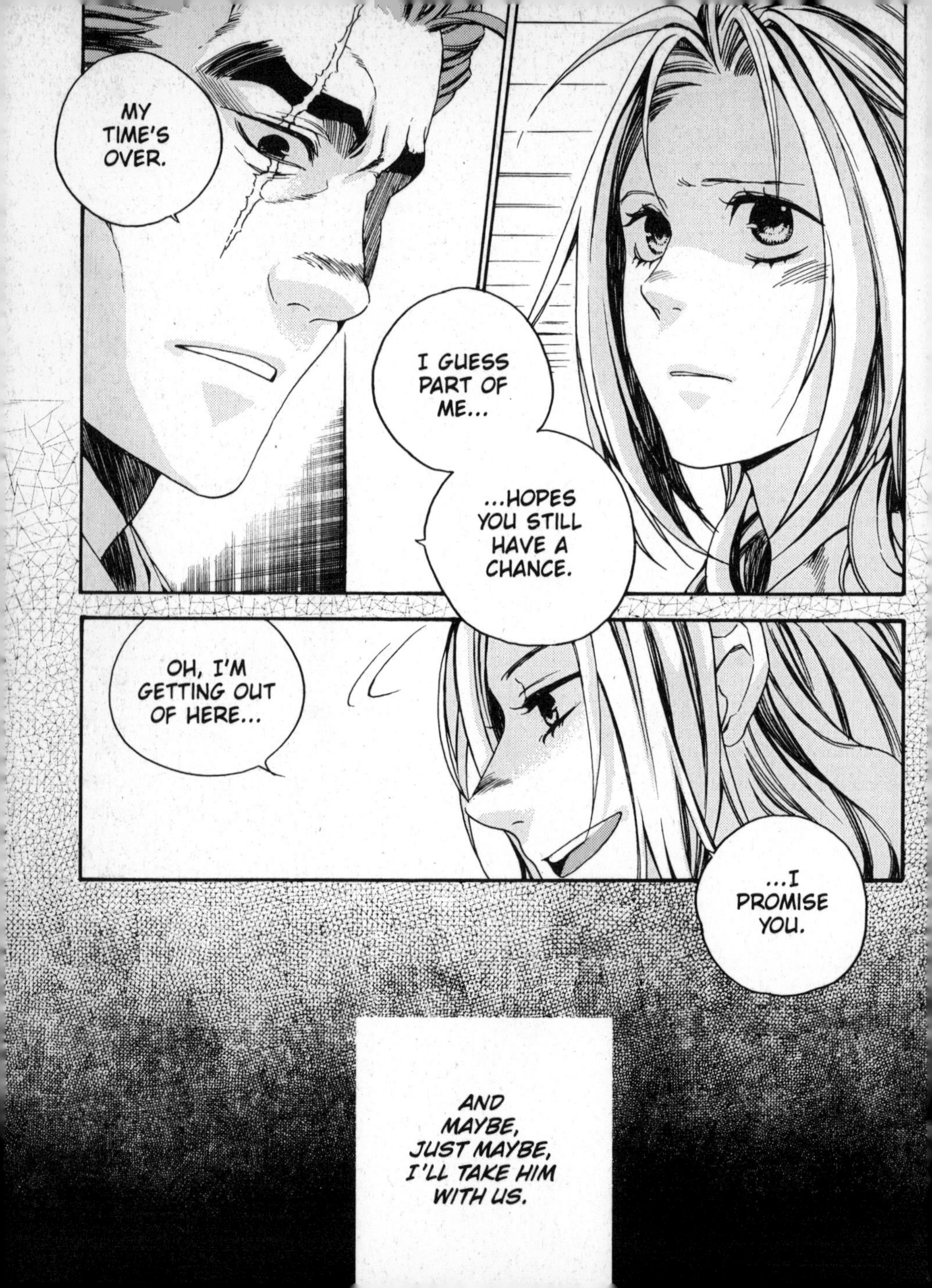
MY TIME'S OVER.
I GUESS PART OF ME...
...HOPES YOU STILL HAVE A CHANCE.
OH, I'M GETTING OUT OF HERE...
...I PROMISE YOU.
AND MAYBE, JUST MAYBE, I'LL TAKE HIM WITH US.

MAXIMUM
RIDE

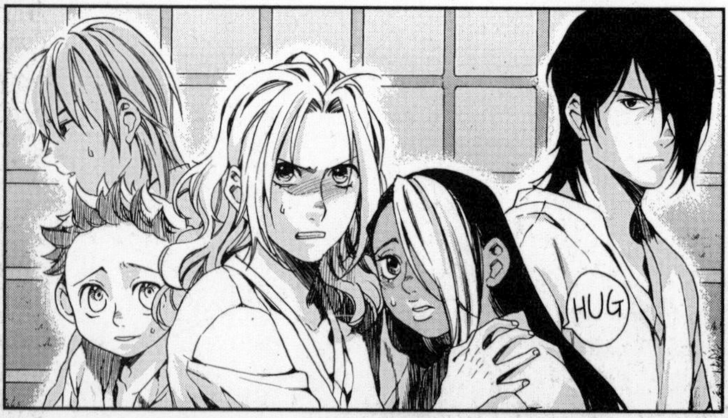
HUG

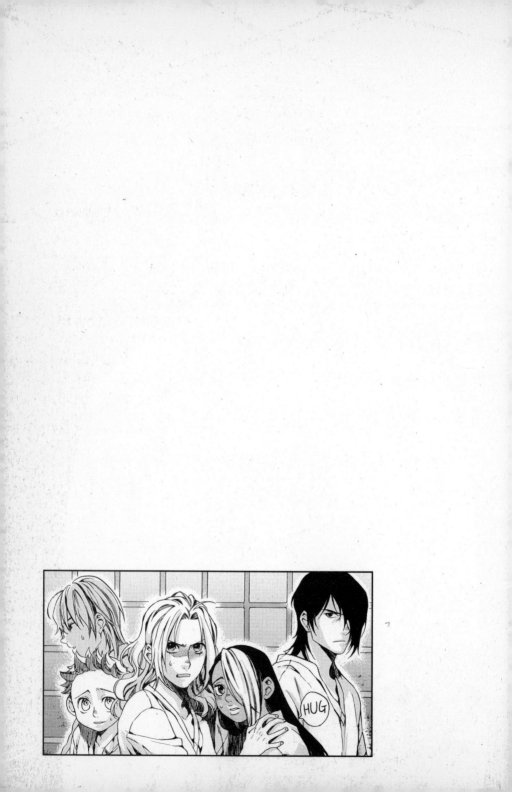

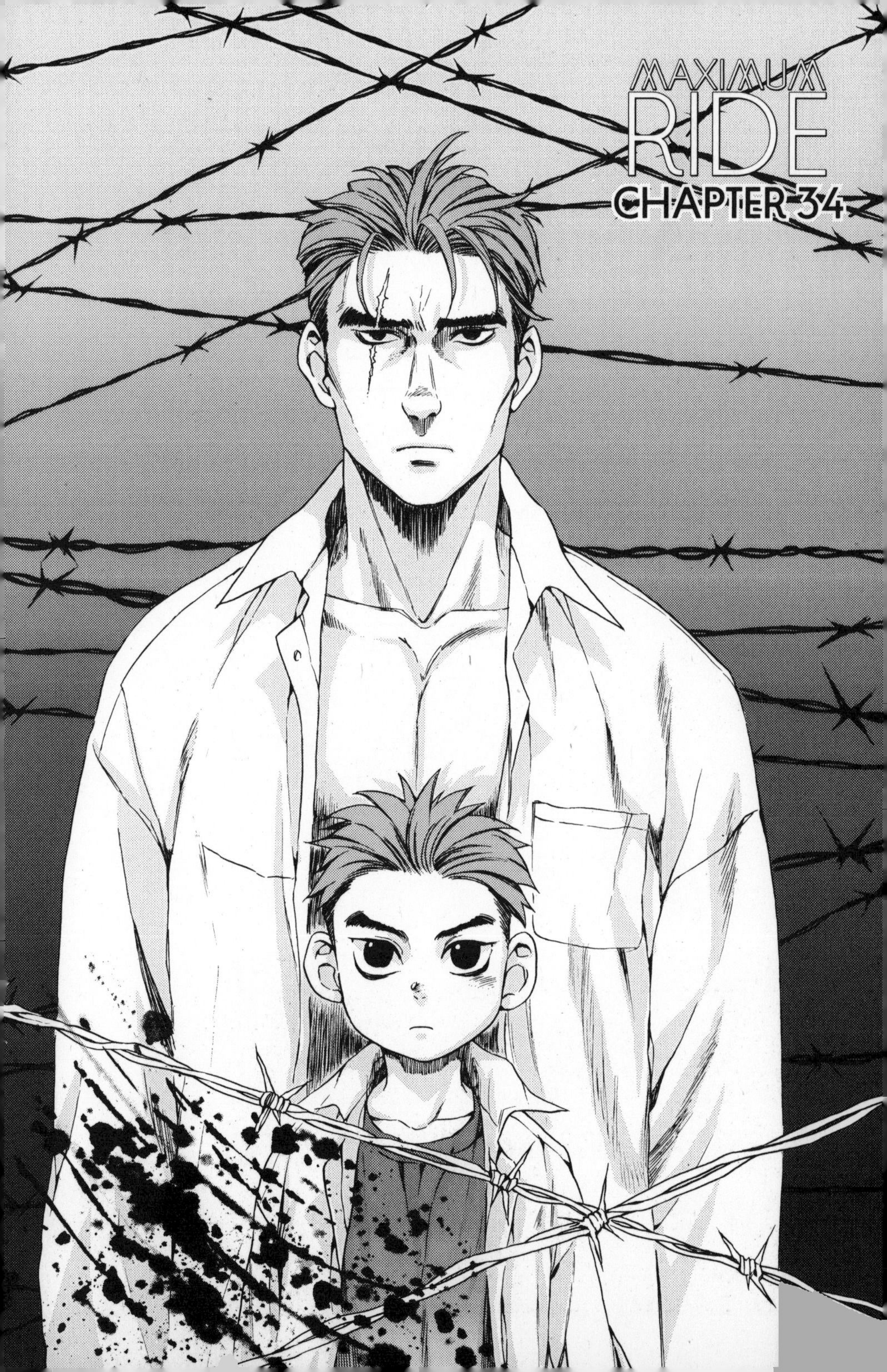
MAXIMUM
RIDE
CHAPTER 34

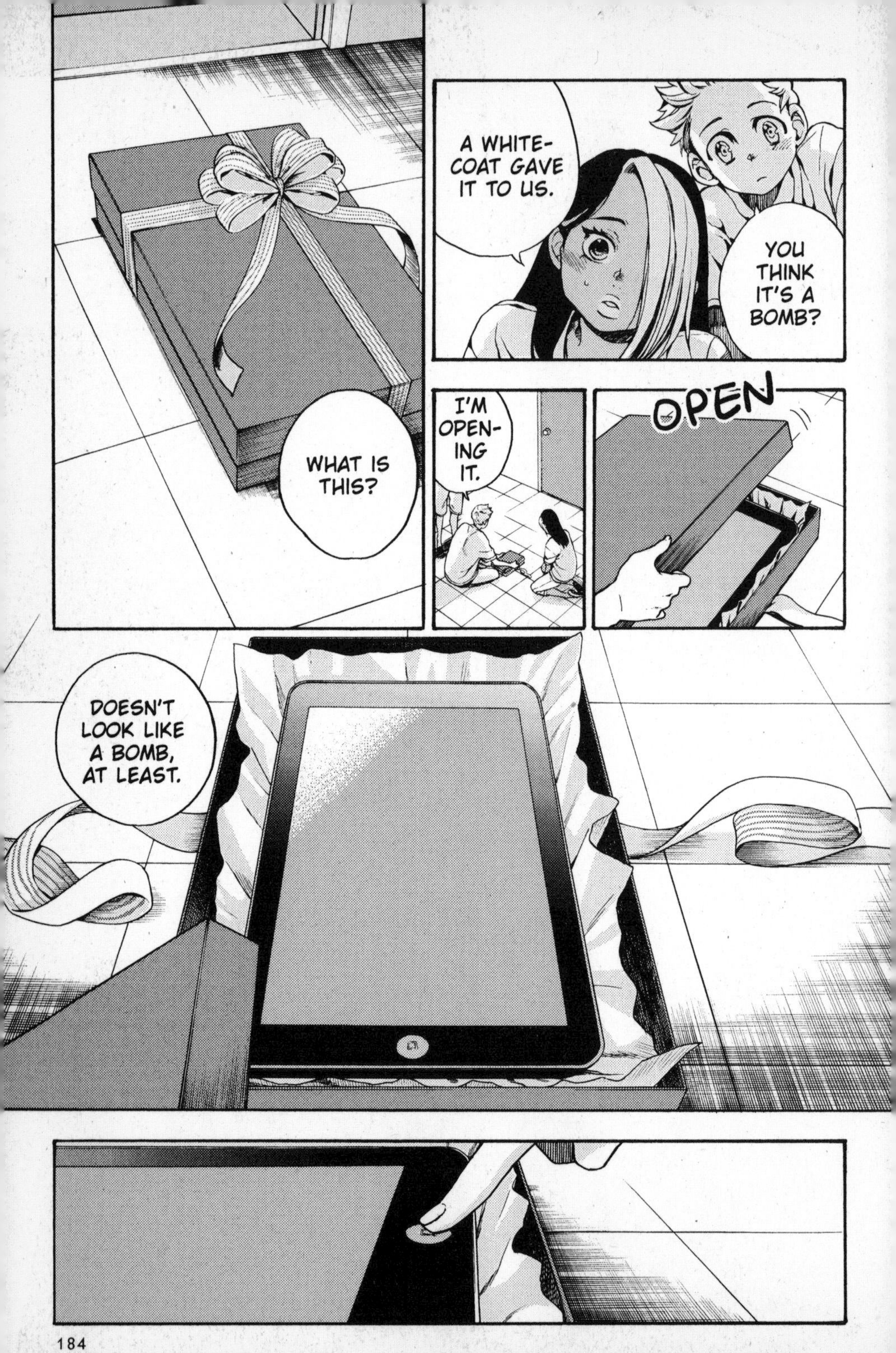
WHAT IS THIS?
A WHITE-COAT GAVE IT TO US.
YOU THINK IT'S A BOMB?
I'M OPEN-ING IT.
OPEN
DOESN'T LOOK LIKE A BOMB, AT LEAST.

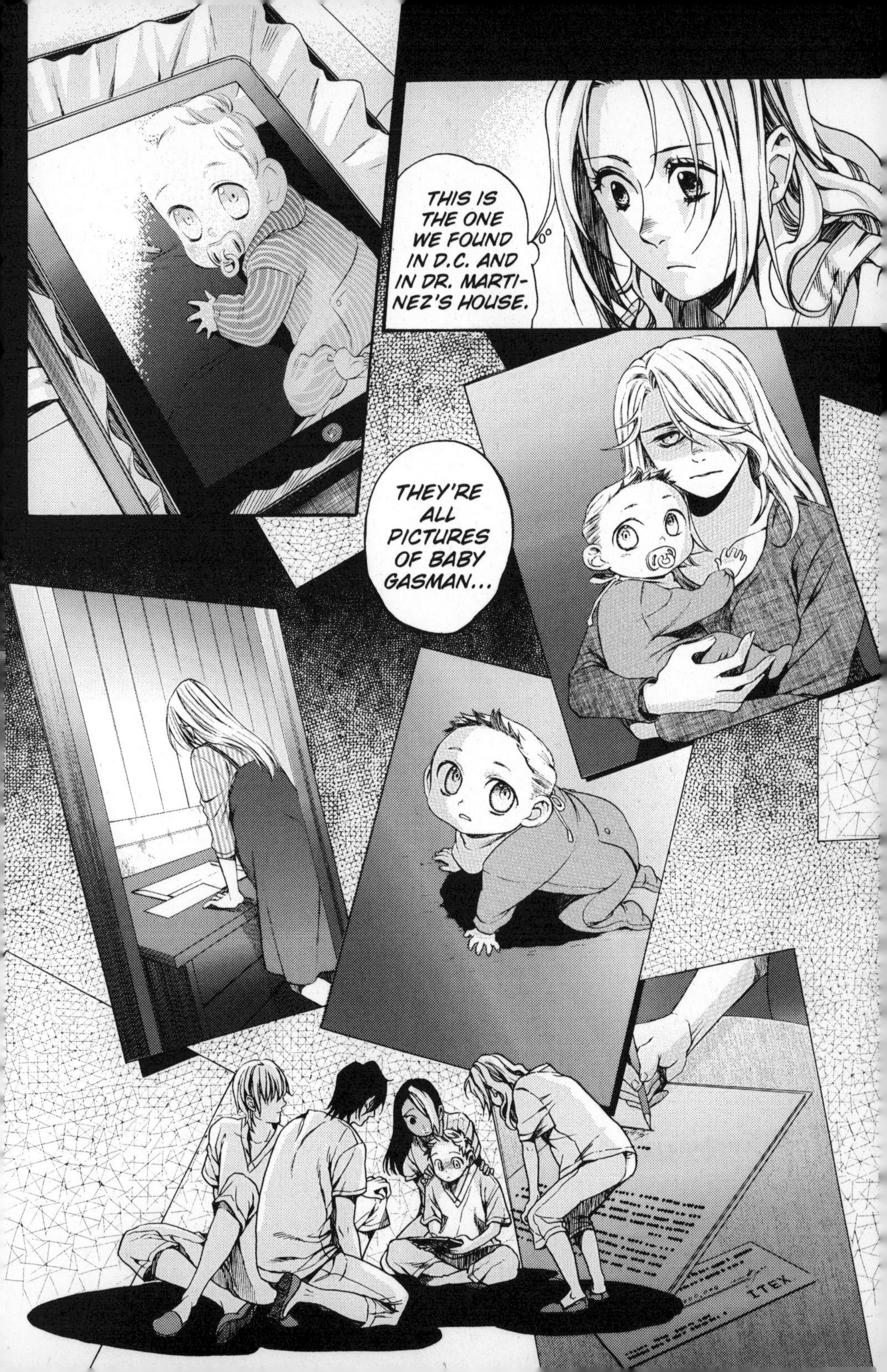
THIS IS THE ONE WE FOUND IN D.C. AND IN DR. MARTI-NEZ'S HOUSE.
THEY'RE ALL PICTURES OF BABY GASMAN...

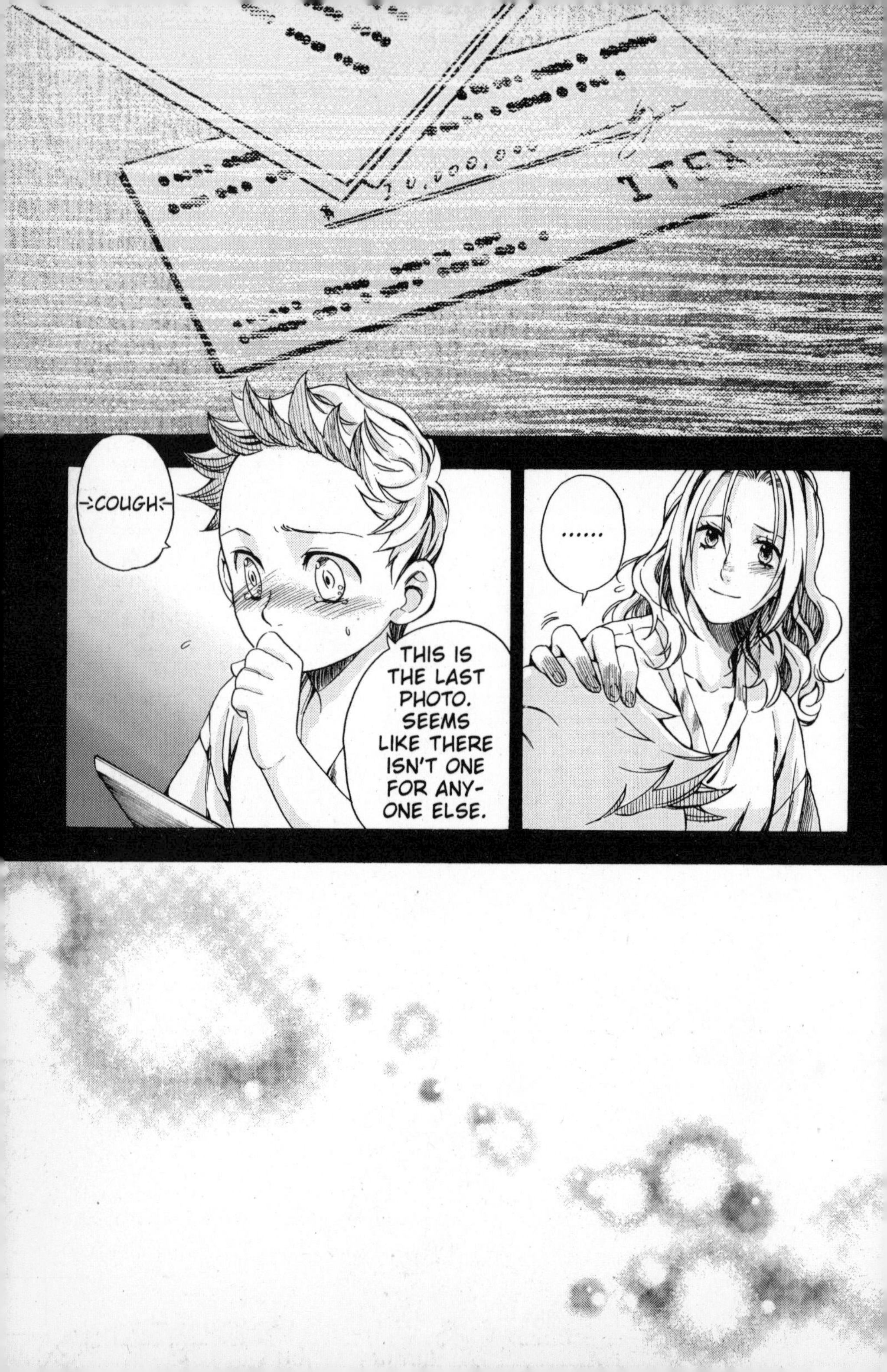
COUGH
THIS IS THE LAST PHOTO. SEEMS LIKE THERE ISN'T ONE FOR ANY-ONE ELSE.
......

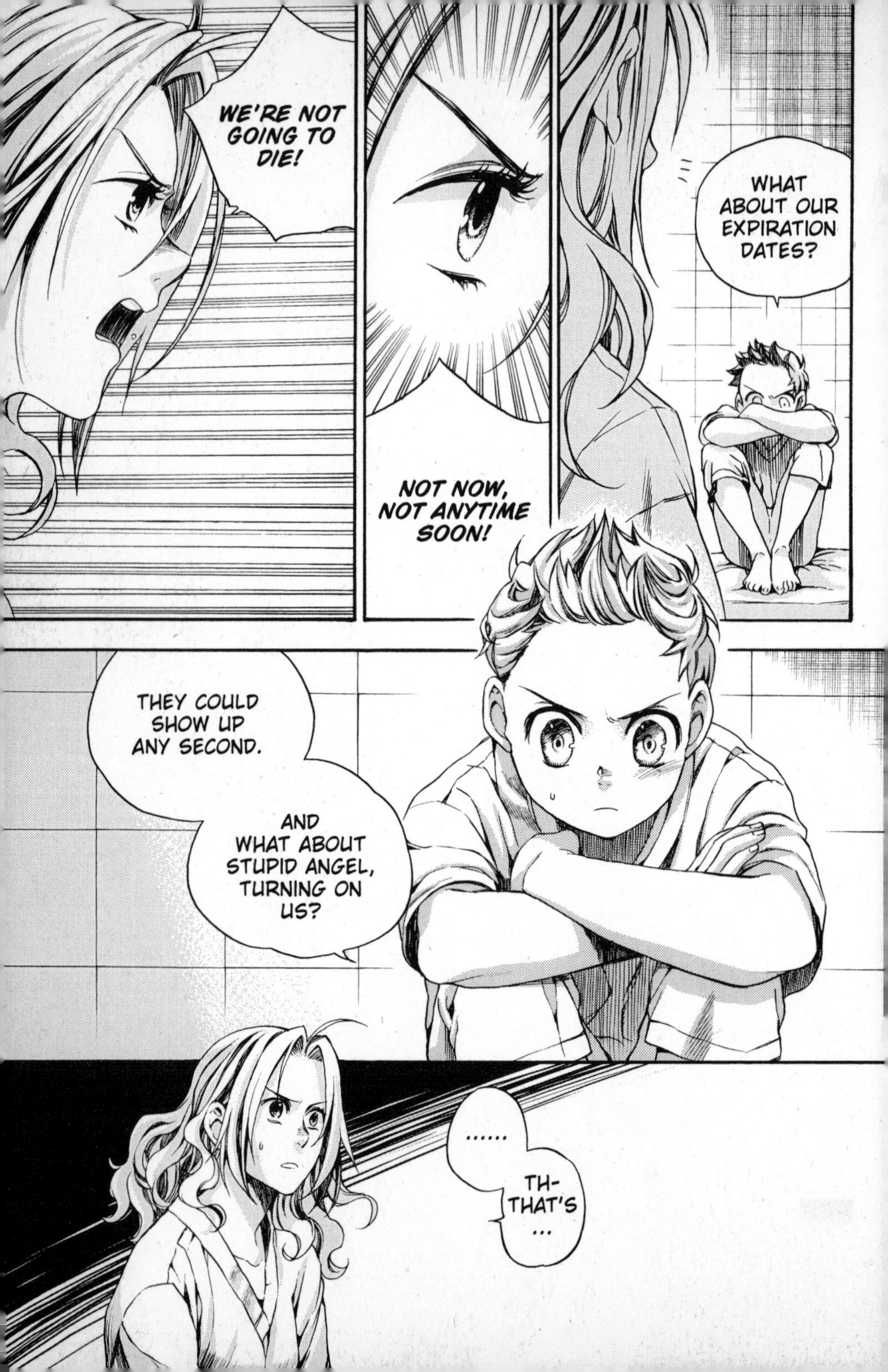

WE'RE NOT GOING TO DIE!
NOT NOW, NOT ANYTIME SOON!
WHAT ABOUT OUR EXPIRATION DATES?
THEY COULD SHOW UP ANY SECOND.
AND WHAT ABOUT STUPID ANGEL, TURNING ON US?
......
TH-THAT'S ...

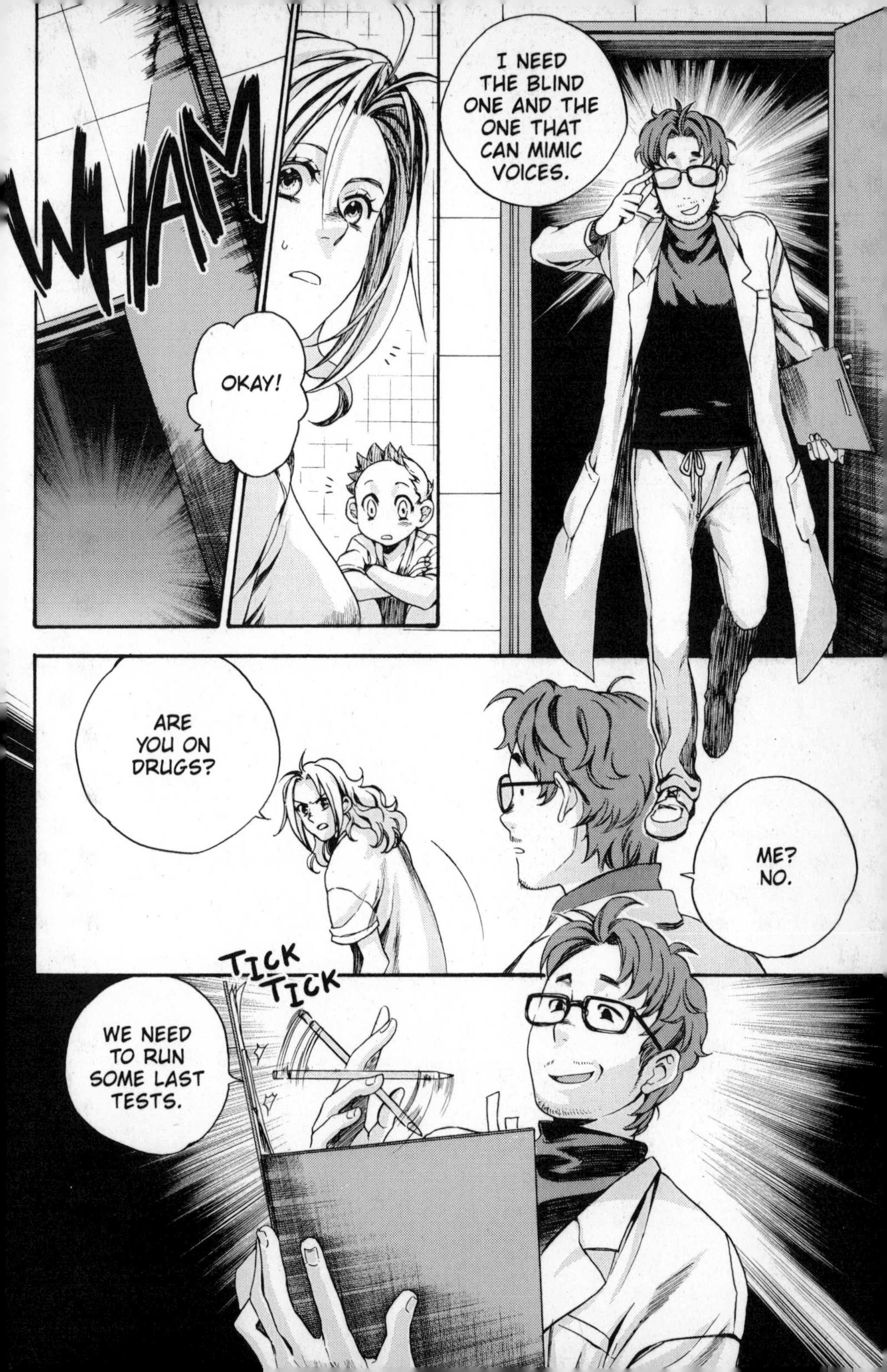
WHAM
OKAY!
I NEED THE BLIND ONE AND THE ONE THAT CAN MIMIC VOICES.
ARE YOU ON DRUGS?
ME? NO.
TICK TICK
WE NEED TO RUN SOME LAST TESTS.

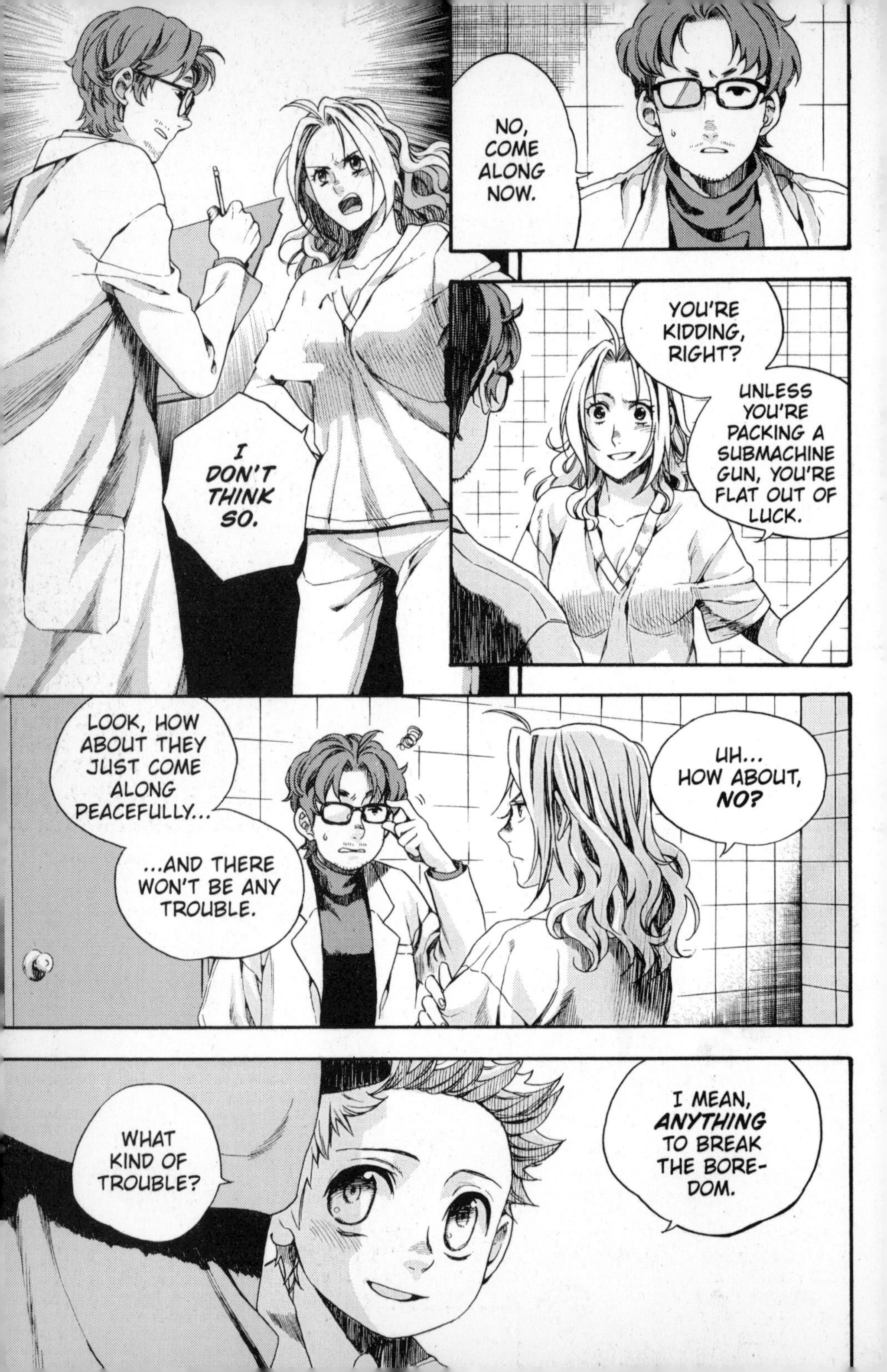
I DON'T THINK SO.
NO, COME ALONG NOW.
YOU'RE KIDDING, RIGHT?
UNLESS YOU'RE PACKING A SUBMACHINE GUN, YOU'RE FLAT OUT OF LUCK.
LOOK, HOW ABOUT THEY JUST COME ALONG PEACEFULLY...
...AND THERE WON'T BE ANY TROUBLE.
UH... HOW ABOUT, *NO?*
WHAT KIND OF TROUBLE?
I MEAN, *ANYTHING* TO BREAK THE BORE-DOM.

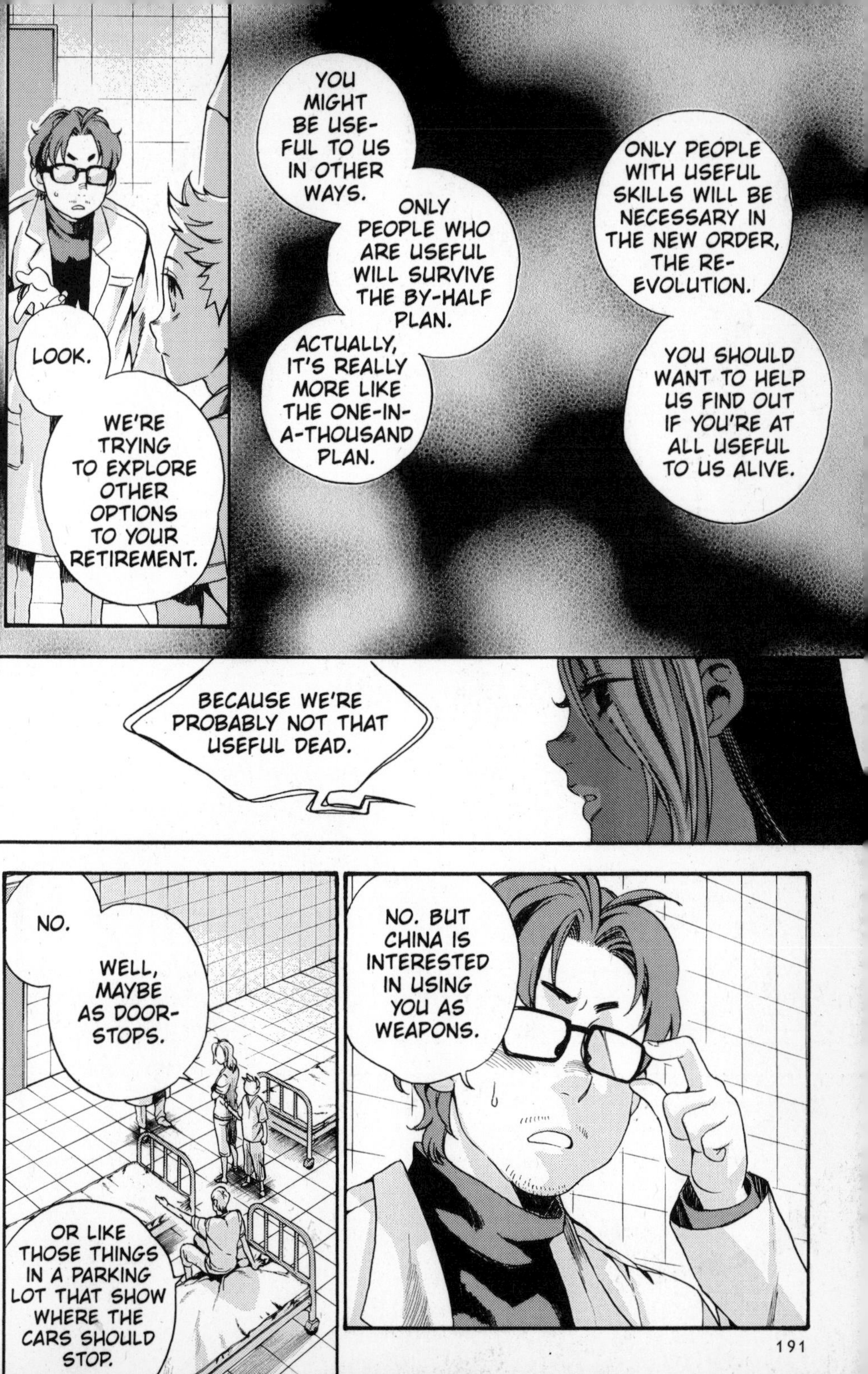
LOOK.
WE'RE TRYING TO EXPLORE OTHER OPTIONS TO YOUR RETIREMENT.
YOU MIGHT BE USE-FUL TO US IN OTHER WAYS.
ONLY PEOPLE WHO ARE USEFUL WILL SURVIVE THE BY-HALF PLAN.
ACTUALLY, IT'S REALLY MORE LIKE THE ONE-IN-A-THOUSAND PLAN.
ONLY PEOPLE WITH USEFUL SKILLS WILL BE NECESSARY IN THE NEW ORDER, THE RE-EVOLUTION.
YOU SHOULD WANT TO HELP US FIND OUT IF YOU'RE AT ALL USEFUL TO US ALIVE.
BECAUSE WE'RE PROBABLY NOT THAT USEFUL DEAD.
NO.
WELL, MAYBE AS DOOR-STOPS.
OR LIKE THOSE THINGS IN A PARKING LOT THAT SHOW WHERE THE CARS SHOULD STOP.
NO. BUT CHINA IS INTERESTED IN USING YOU AS WEAPONS.

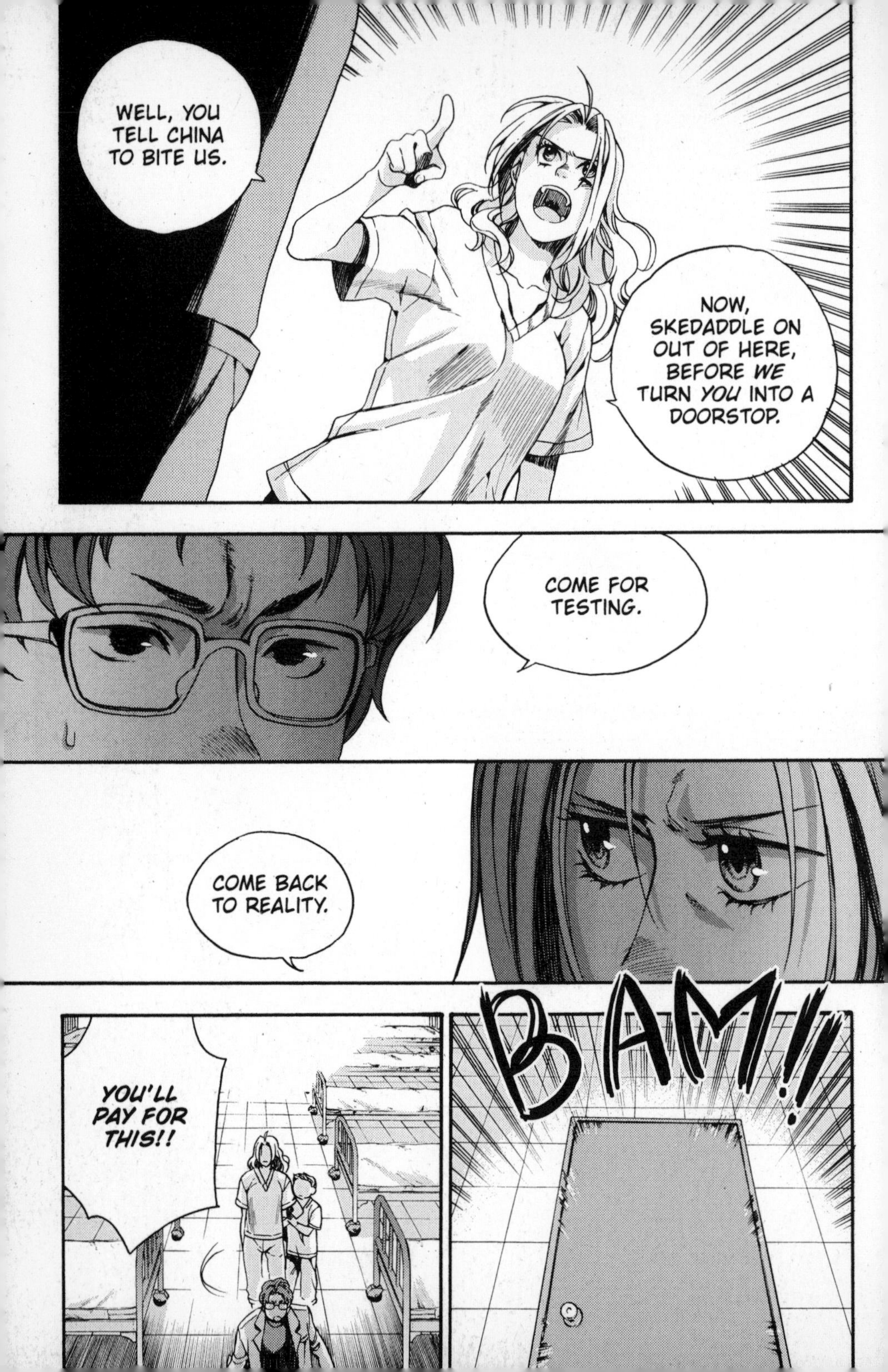
WELL, YOU TELL CHINA TO BITE US.
NOW, SKEDADDLE ON OUT OF HERE, BEFORE WE TURN YOU INTO A DOORSTOP.
COME FOR TESTING.
COME BACK TO REALITY.
YOU'LL PAY FOR THIS!!
BAM!!

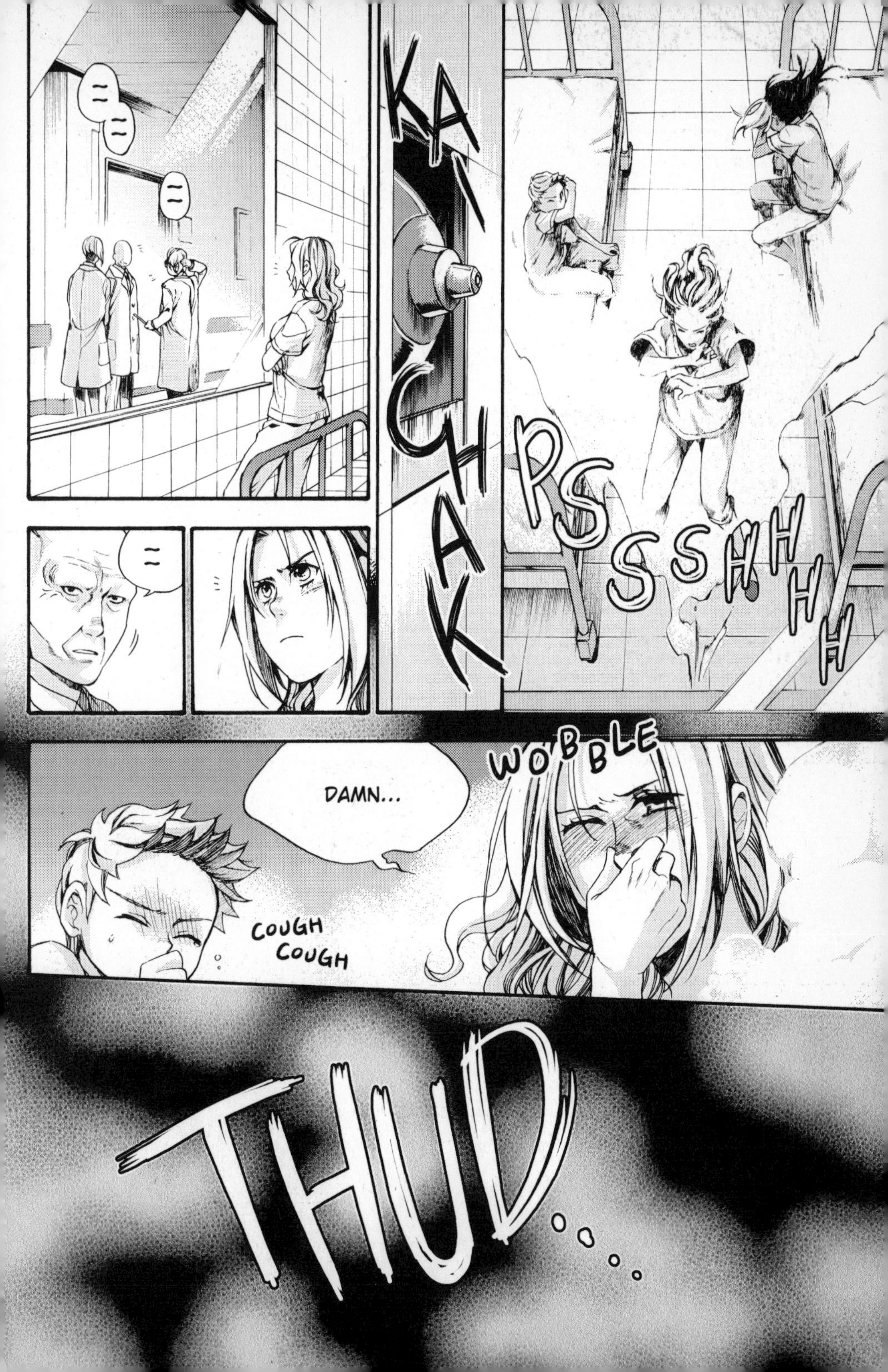

...
...
...
...
KA-CHAK
PSSSHHHH
DAMN...
COUGH COUGH
WOBBLE
THUD...

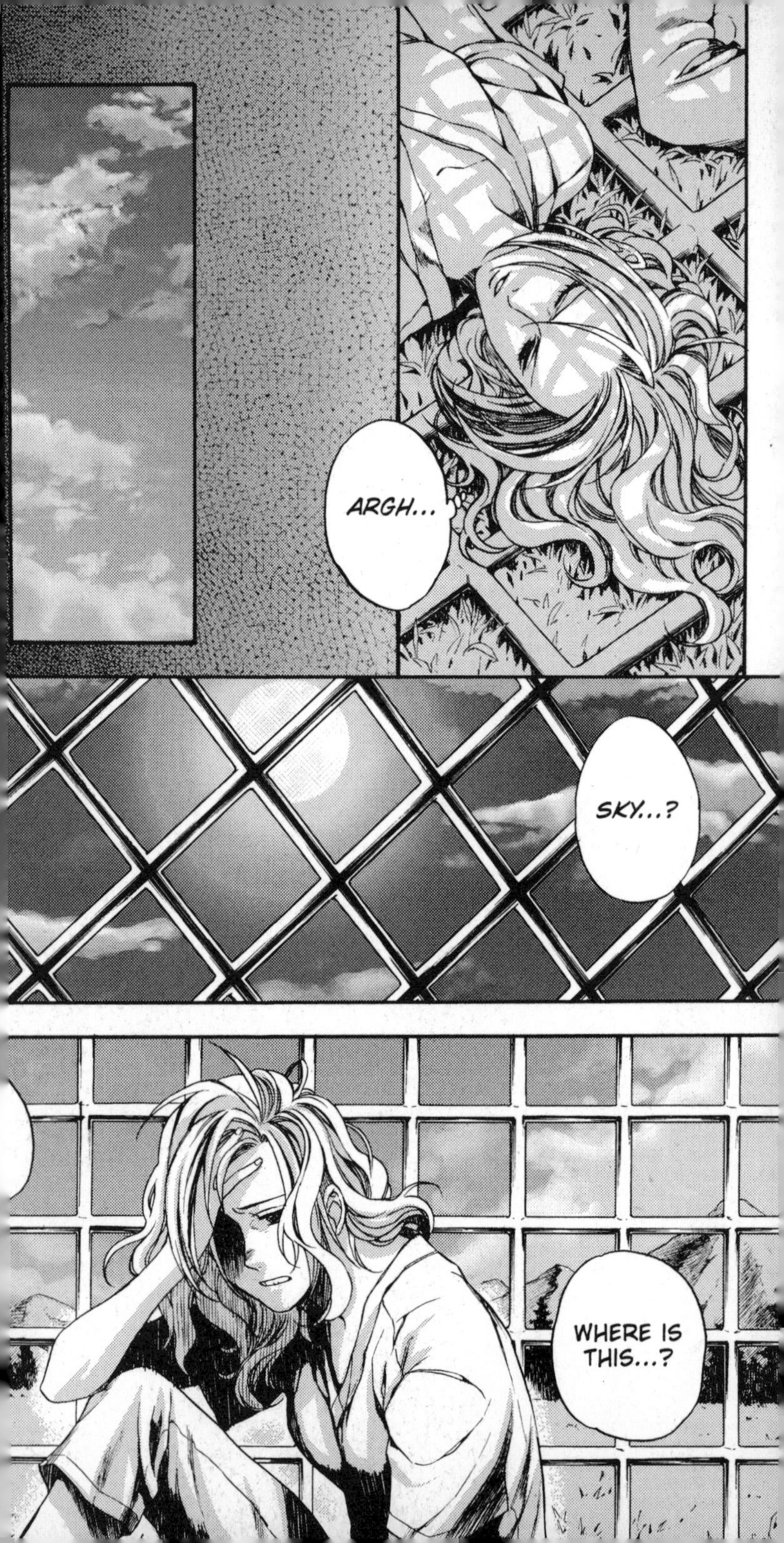
ARGH...
SKY...?
WHERE IS THIS...?

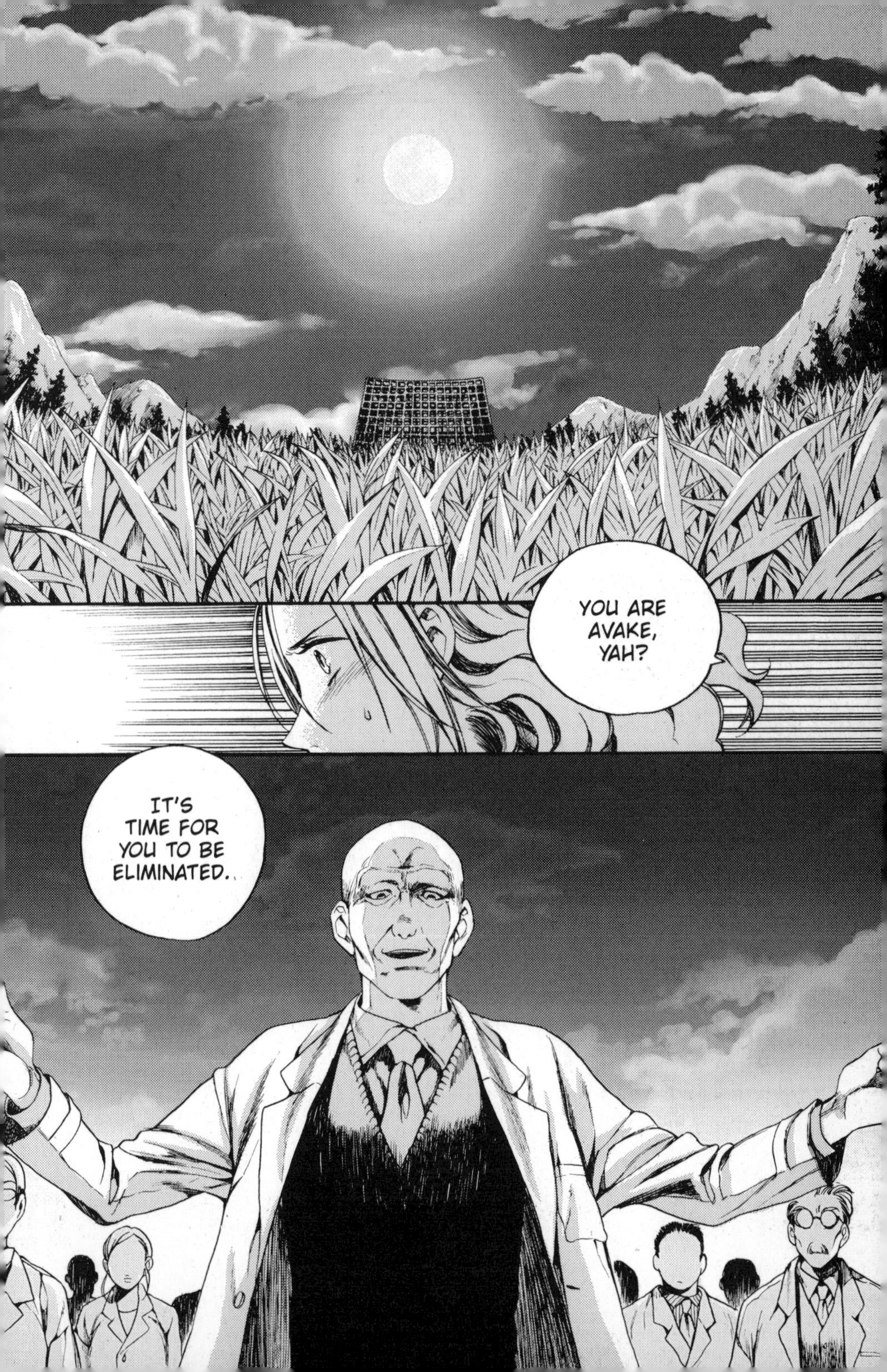
YOU ARE AVAKE, YAH?
IT'S TIME FOR YOU TO BE ELIMINATED.

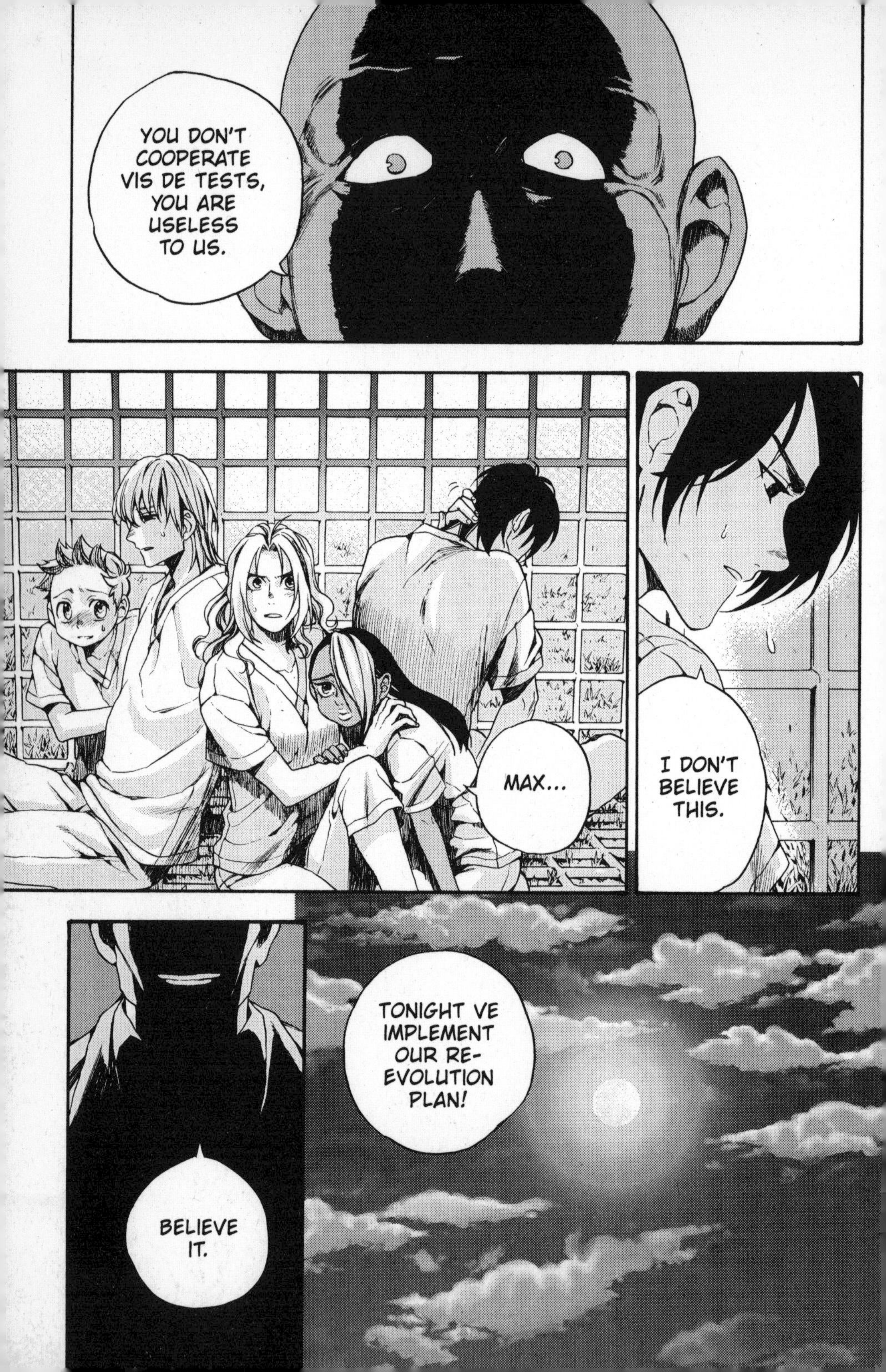
YOU DON'T COOPERATE VIS DE TESTS, YOU ARE USELESS TO US.
MAX...
I DON'T BELIEVE THIS.
BELIEVE IT.
TONIGHT VE IMPLEMENT OUR RE-EVOLUTION PLAN!

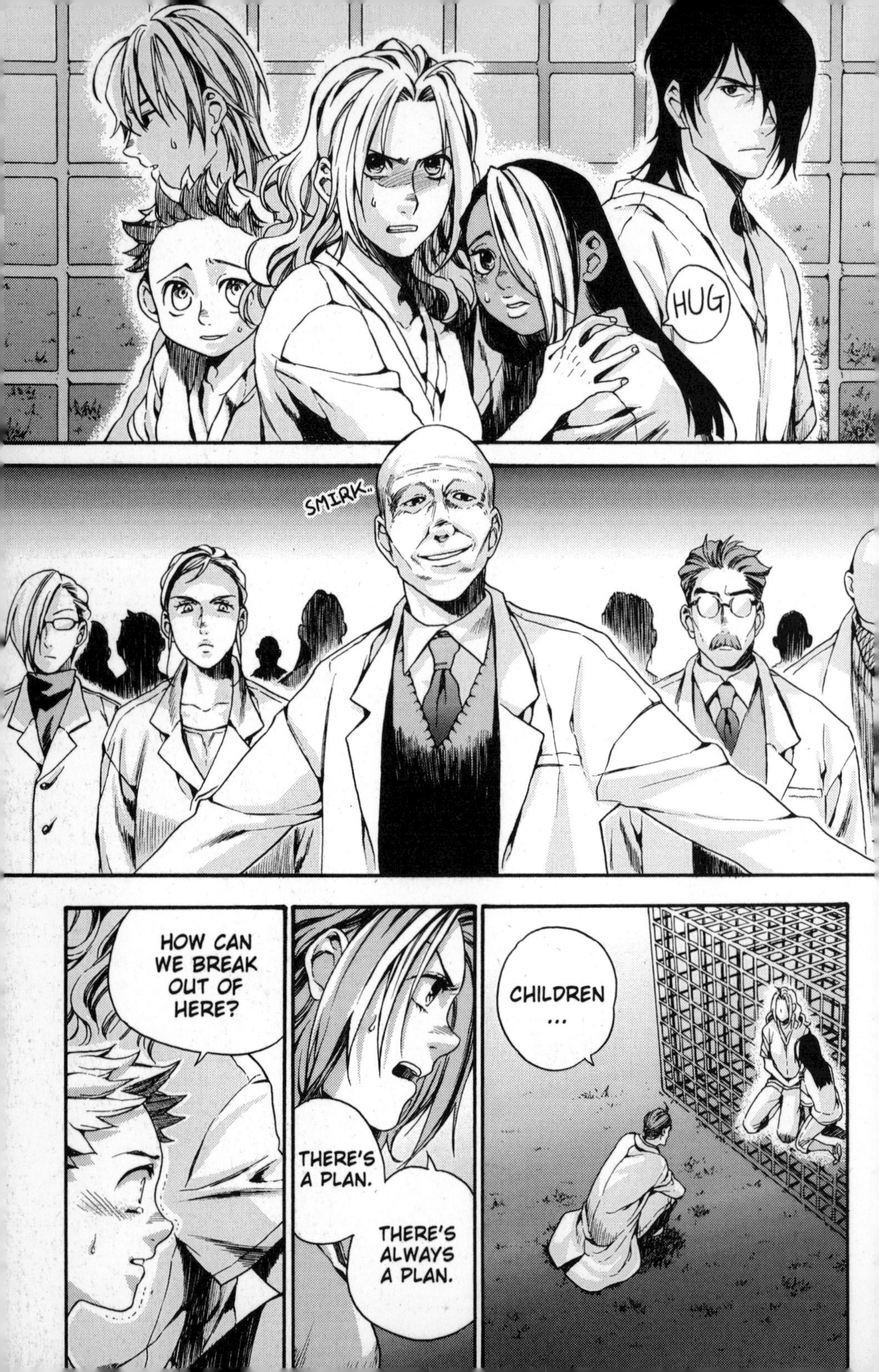
HUG
SMIRK..
HOW CAN WE BREAK OUT OF HERE?
THERE'S A PLAN.
THERE'S ALWAYS A PLAN.
CHILDREN ...

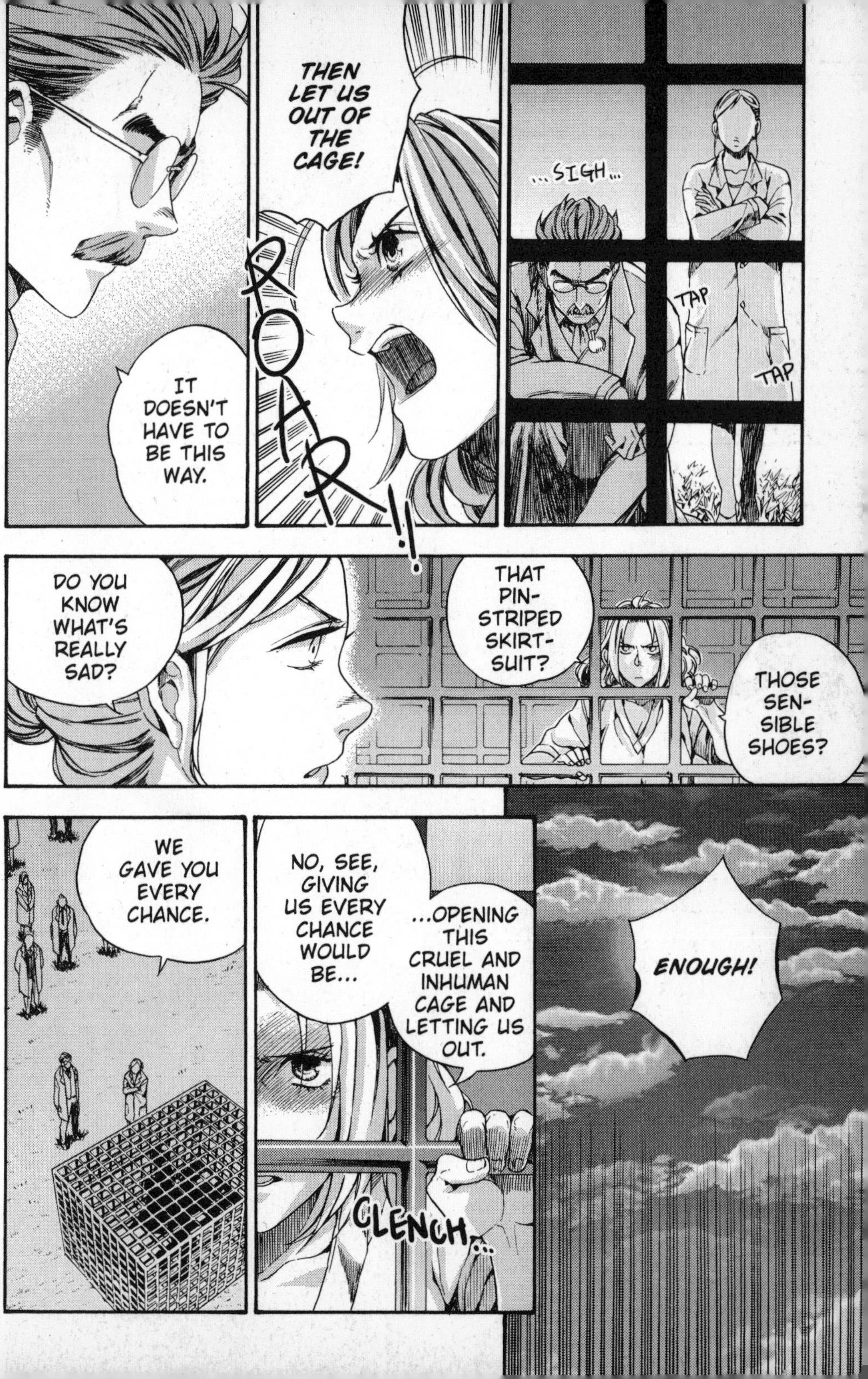
IT DOESN'T HAVE TO BE THIS WAY.
THEN LET US OUT OF THE CAGE!
ROAR!!
...SIGH...
TAP
TAP
DO YOU KNOW WHAT'S REALLY SAD?
THAT PIN-STRIPED SKIRT-SUIT?
THOSE SEN-SIBLE SHOES?
WE GAVE YOU EVERY CHANCE.
NO, SEE, GIVING US EVERY CHANCE WOULD BE...
...OPENING THIS CRUEL AND INHUMAN CAGE AND LETTING US OUT.
CLENCH...
ENOUGH!

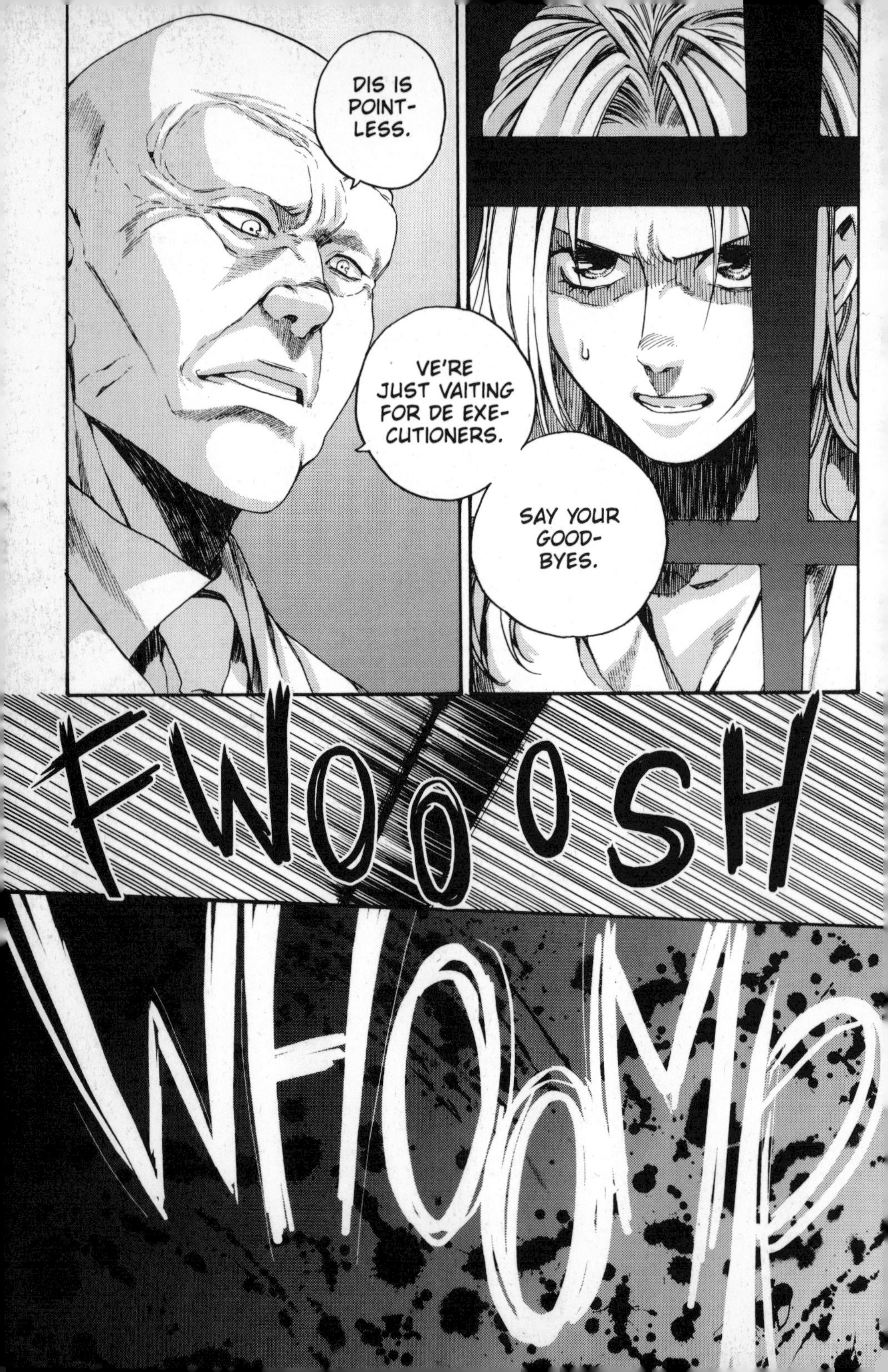
DIS IS POINT-LESS.
VE'RE JUST VAITING FOR DE EXE-CUTIONERS.
SAY YOUR GOOD-BYES.
FWOOOSH
WHOOOMP

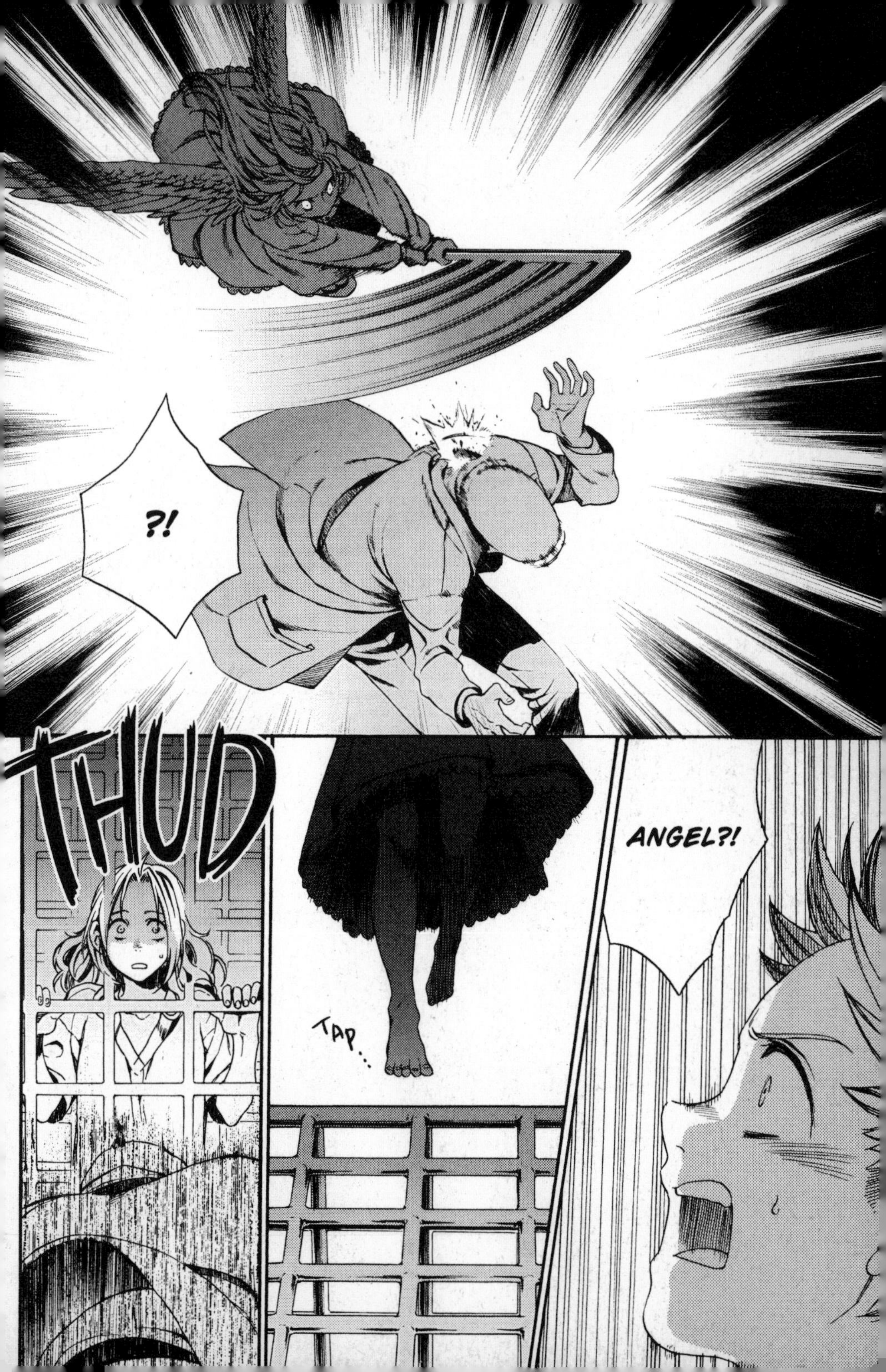
?!
THUD
TAP...
ANGEL?!

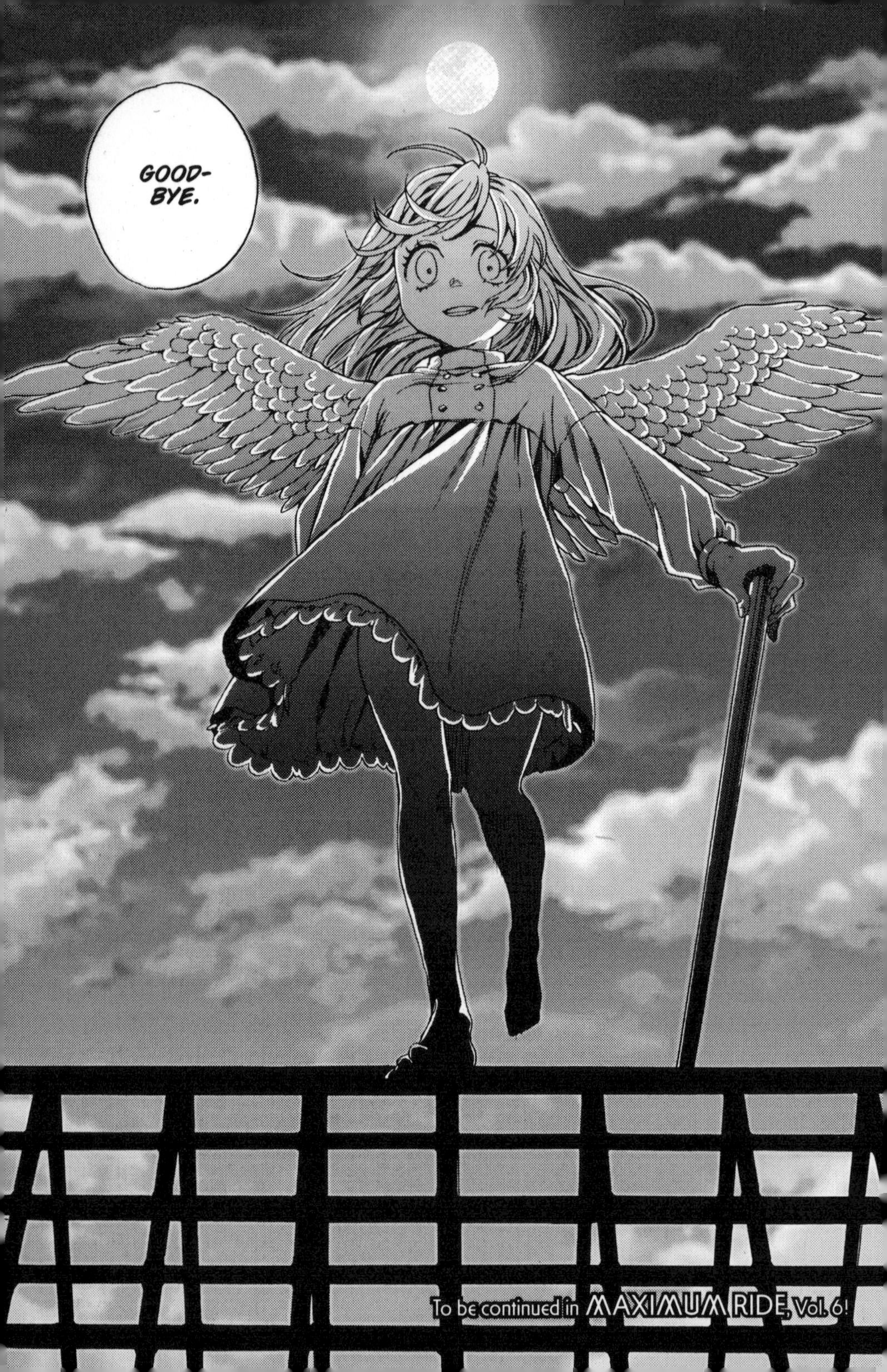
GOOD-BYE.
To be continued in MAXIMUM RIDE, Vol. 6!

MAXIMUM
RIDE

Read on to enjoy a bonus preview of

DANIEL X: THE MANGA, VOL. 2

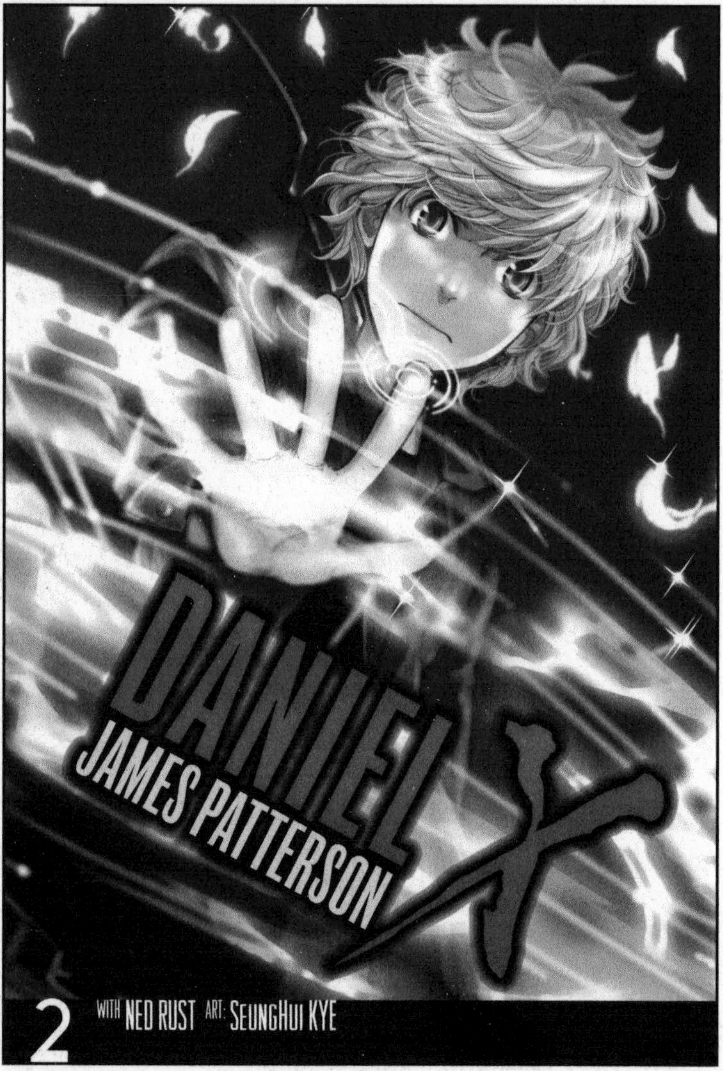
DANIEL X
JAMES PATTERSON
2
WITH NED RUST ART: SEUNGHUI KYE

IN STORES NOW!

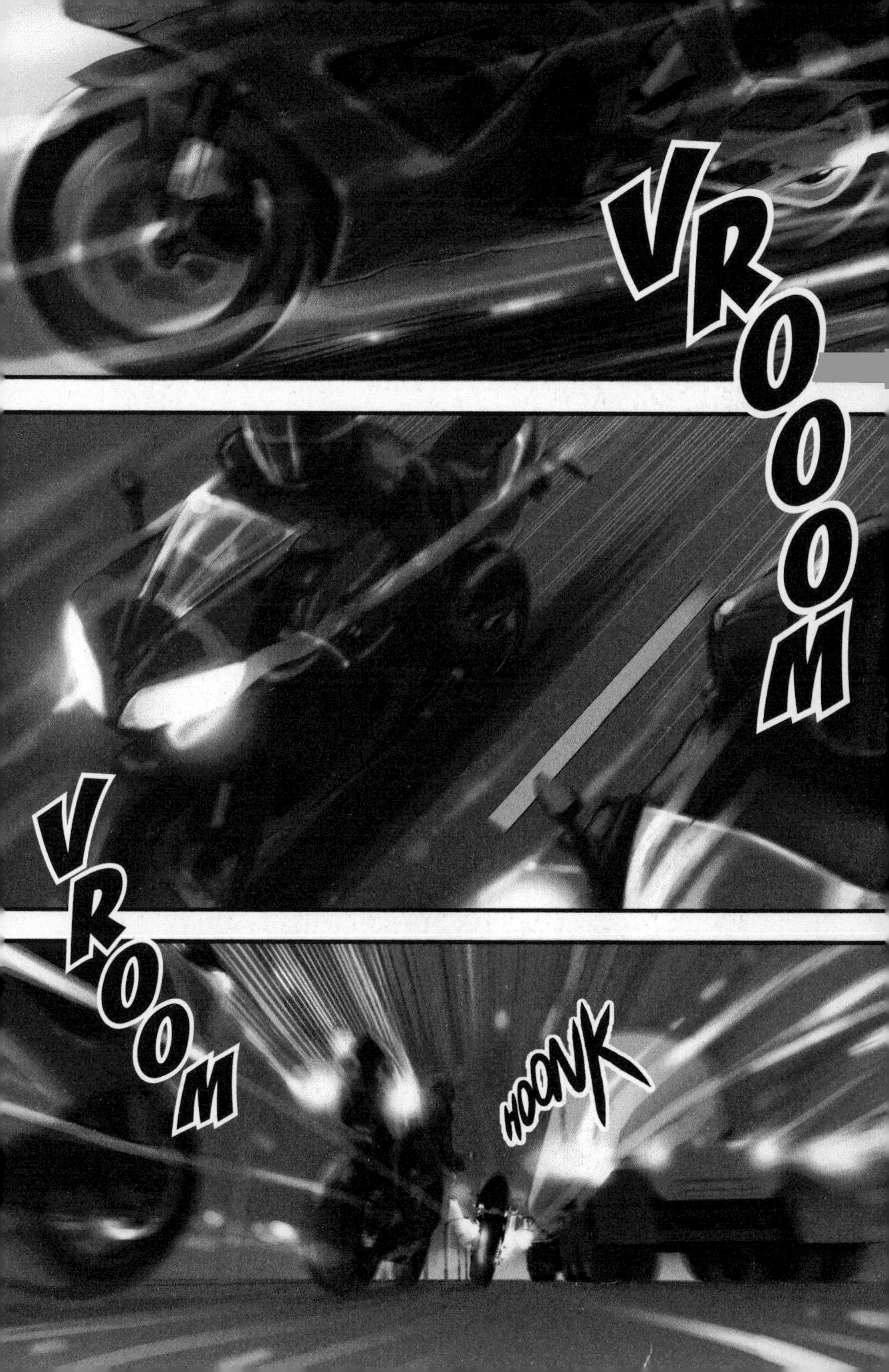
VROOOOM
VROOM
HOONK

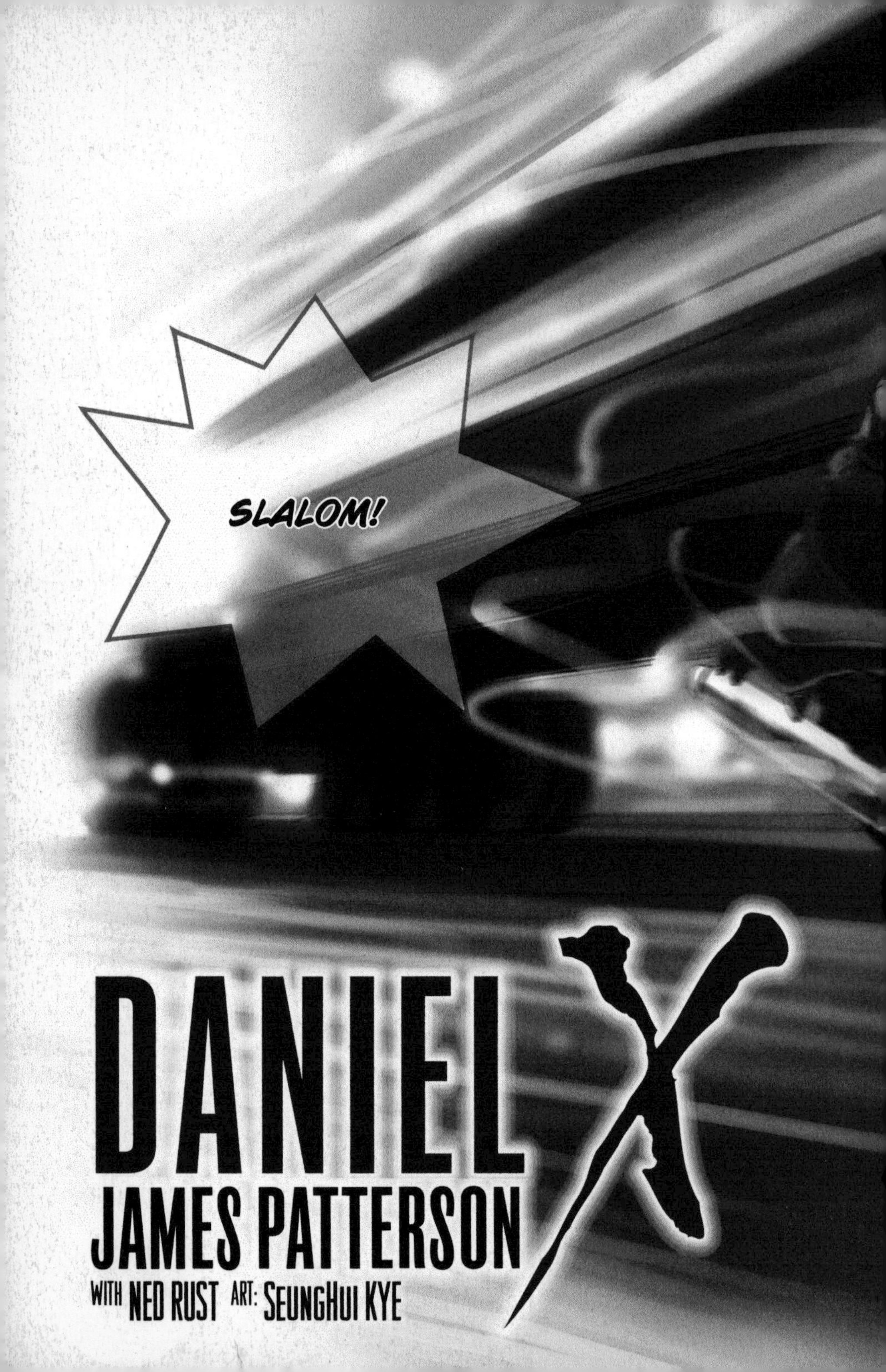
SLALOM!
DANIEL X
JAMES PATTERSON
WITH NED RUST ART: SEUNGHUI KYE

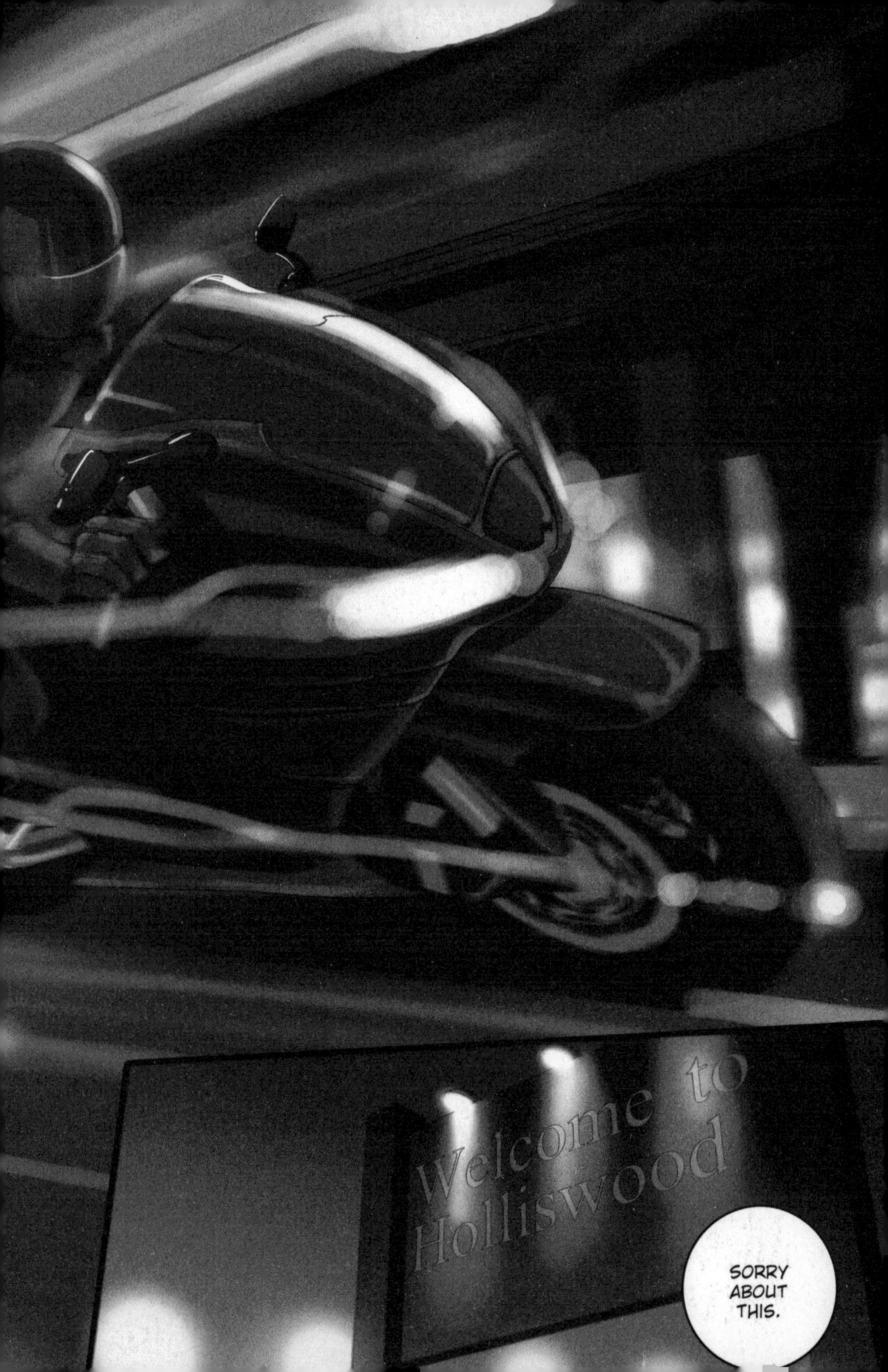
Welcome to Holliswood
SORRY ABOUT THIS.

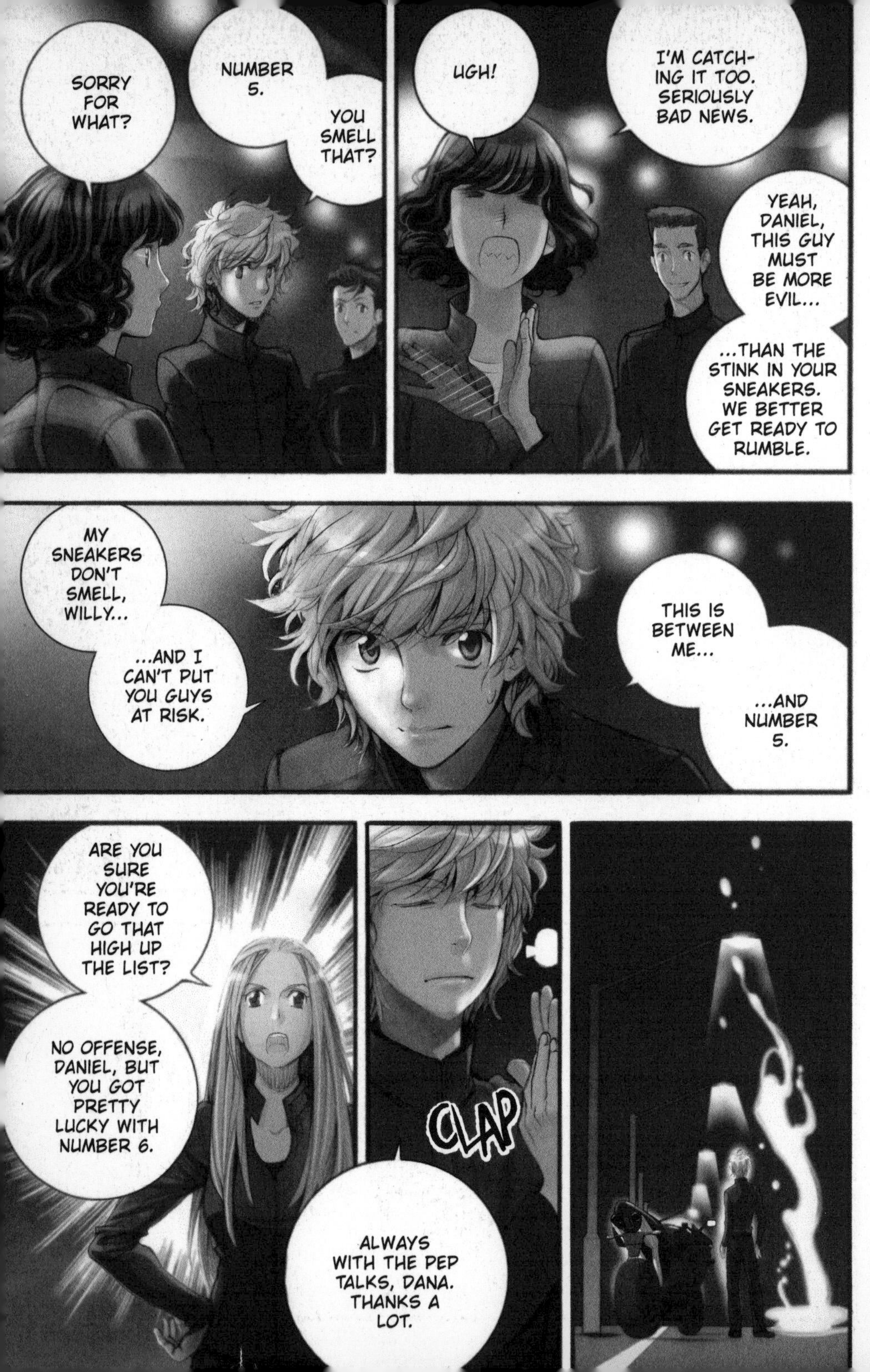
SORRY FOR WHAT?
NUMBER 5.
YOU SMELL THAT?
UGH!
I'M CATCH-ING IT TOO. SERIOUSLY BAD NEWS.
YEAH, DANIEL, THIS GUY MUST BE MORE EVIL...
...THAN THE STINK IN YOUR SNEAKERS. WE BETTER GET READY TO RUMBLE.
MY SNEAKERS DON'T SMELL, WILLY...
...AND I CAN'T PUT YOU GUYS AT RISK.
THIS IS BETWEEN ME...
...AND NUMBER 5.
ARE YOU SURE YOU'RE READY TO GO THAT HIGH UP THE LIST?
NO OFFENSE, DANIEL, BUT YOU GOT PRETTY LUCKY WITH NUMBER 6.
CLAP
ALWAYS WITH THE PEP TALKS, DANA. THANKS A LOT.

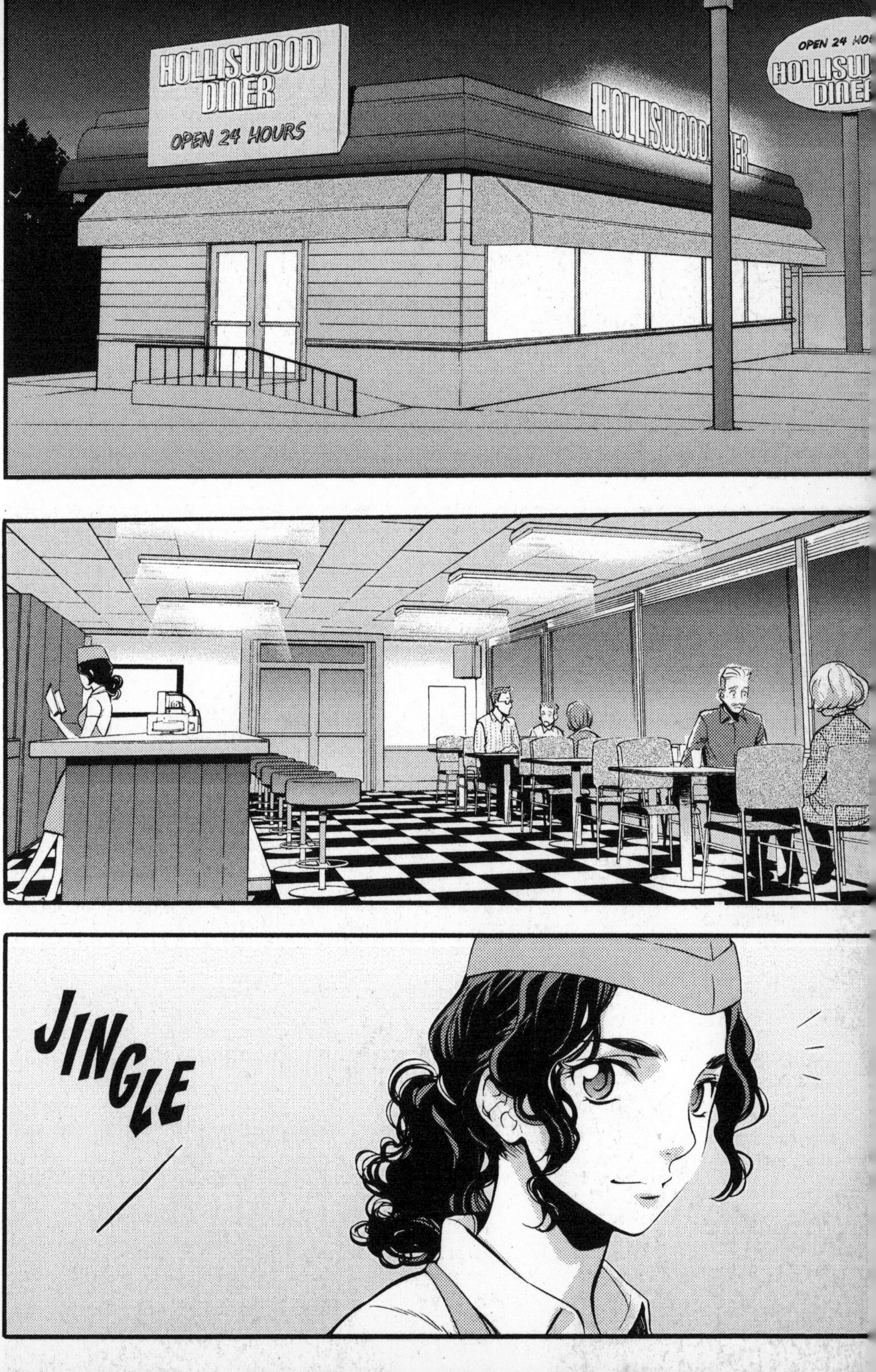
HOLLISWOOD
DINER
OPEN 24 HOURS
JINGLE

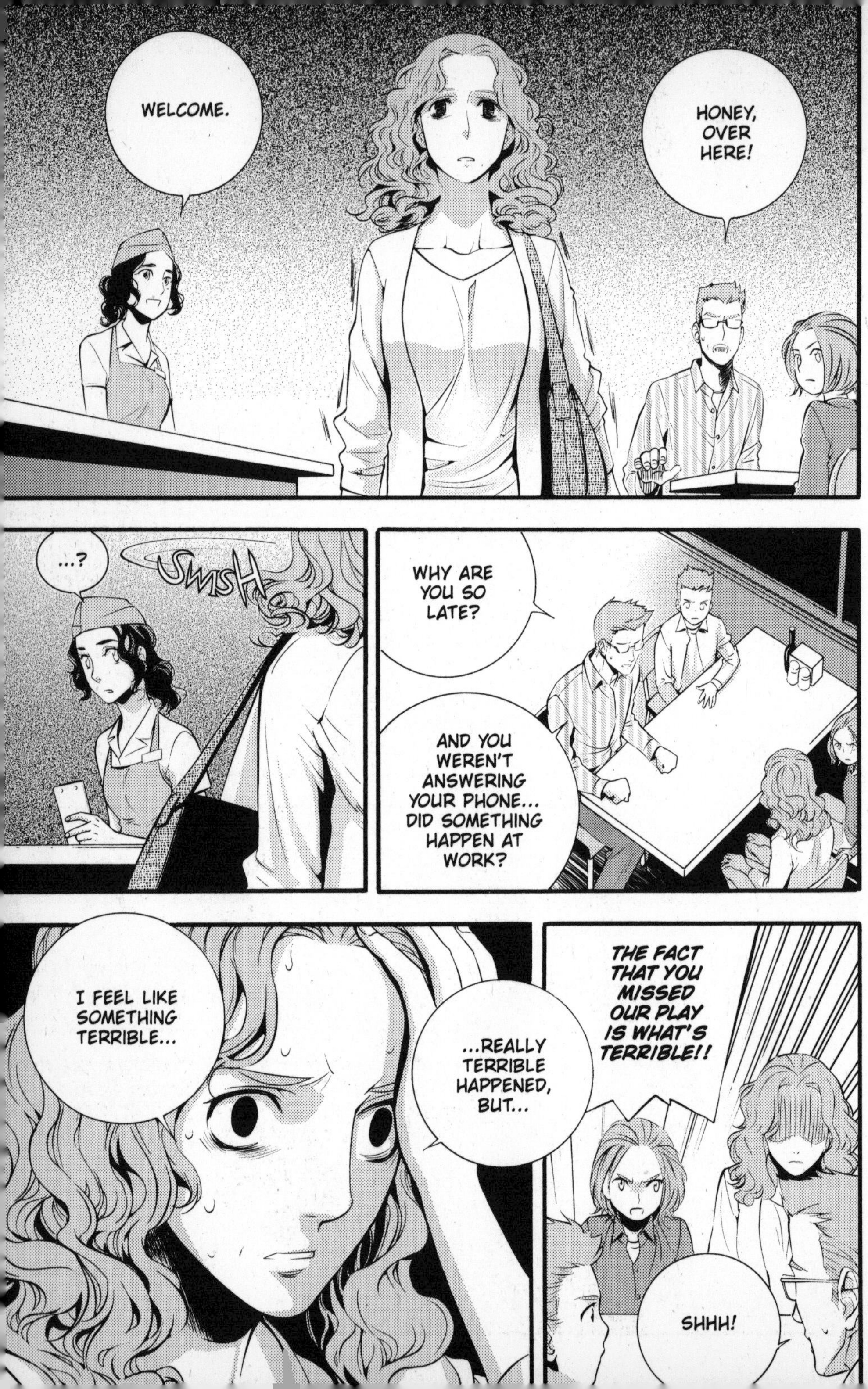
WELCOME.
HONEY, OVER HERE!
...?
SWISH
WHY ARE YOU SO LATE?
AND YOU WEREN'T ANSWERING YOUR PHONE... DID SOMETHING HAPPEN AT WORK?
I FEEL LIKE SOMETHING TERRIBLE...
...REALLY TERRIBLE HAPPENED, BUT...
THE FACT THAT YOU MISSED OUR PLAY IS WHAT'S TERRIBLE!!
SHHH!

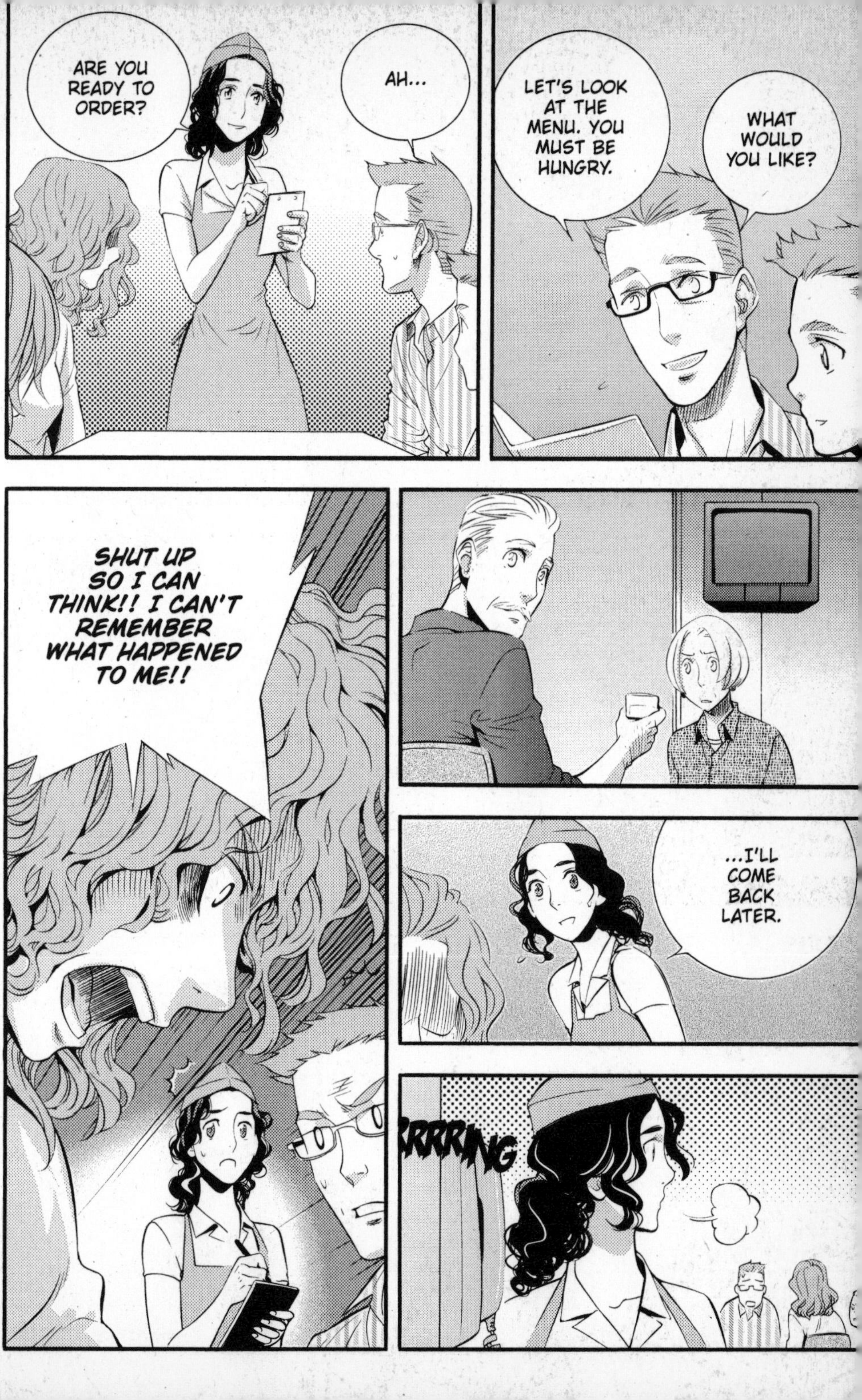
ARE YOU READY TO ORDER?
AH...
LET'S LOOK AT THE MENU. YOU MUST BE HUNGRY.
WHAT WOULD YOU LIKE?
SHUT UP SO I CAN THINK!! I CAN'T REMEMBER WHAT HAPPENED TO ME!!
...I'LL COME BACK LATER.
RRRRING

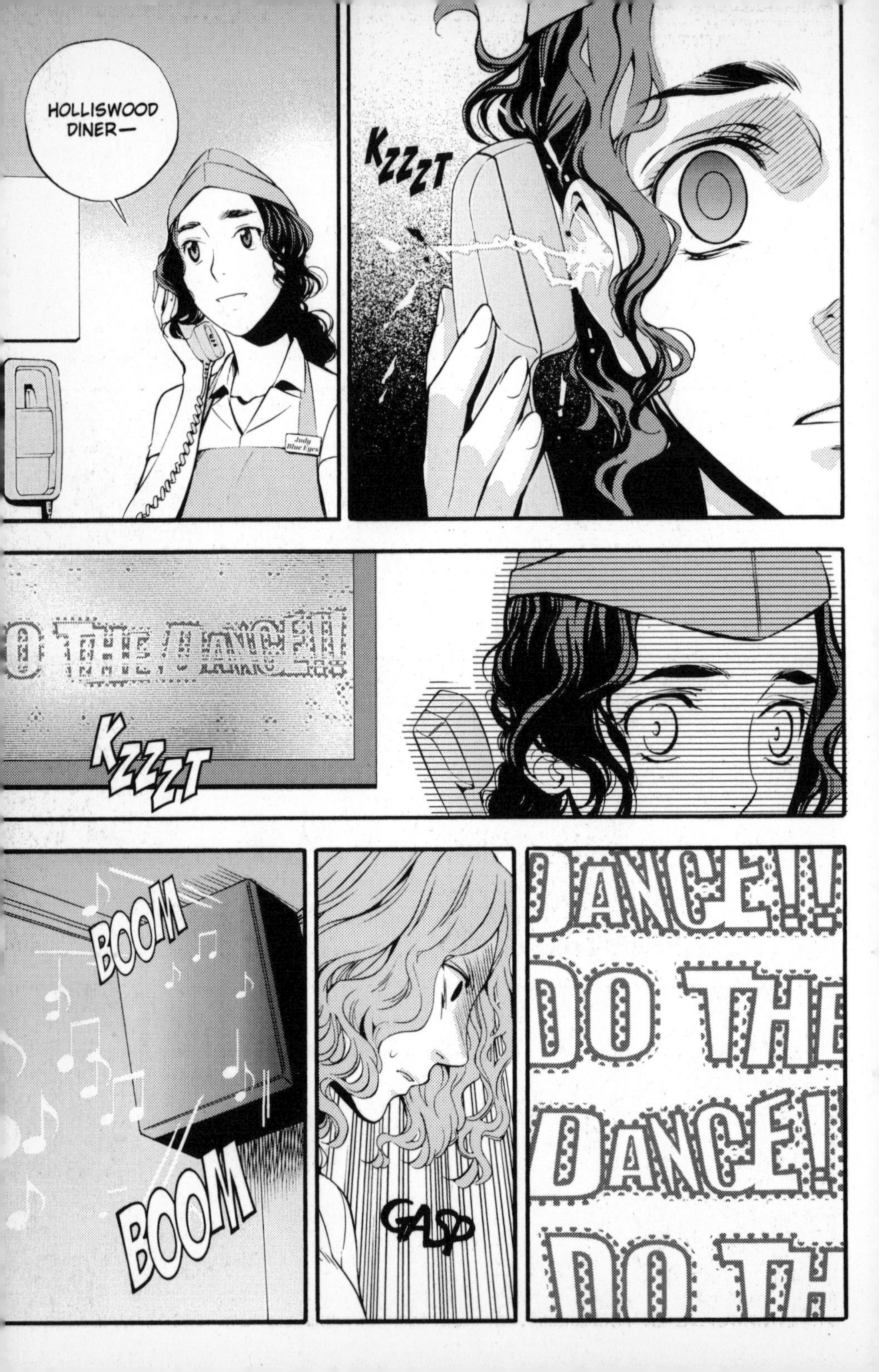
HOLLISWOOD DINER—
Judy Blue Eyes
KZZZT
O THE DANCE!!
KZZZT
BOOM
BOOM
GASP
DANCE!!
DO THE
DANCE!
DO TH

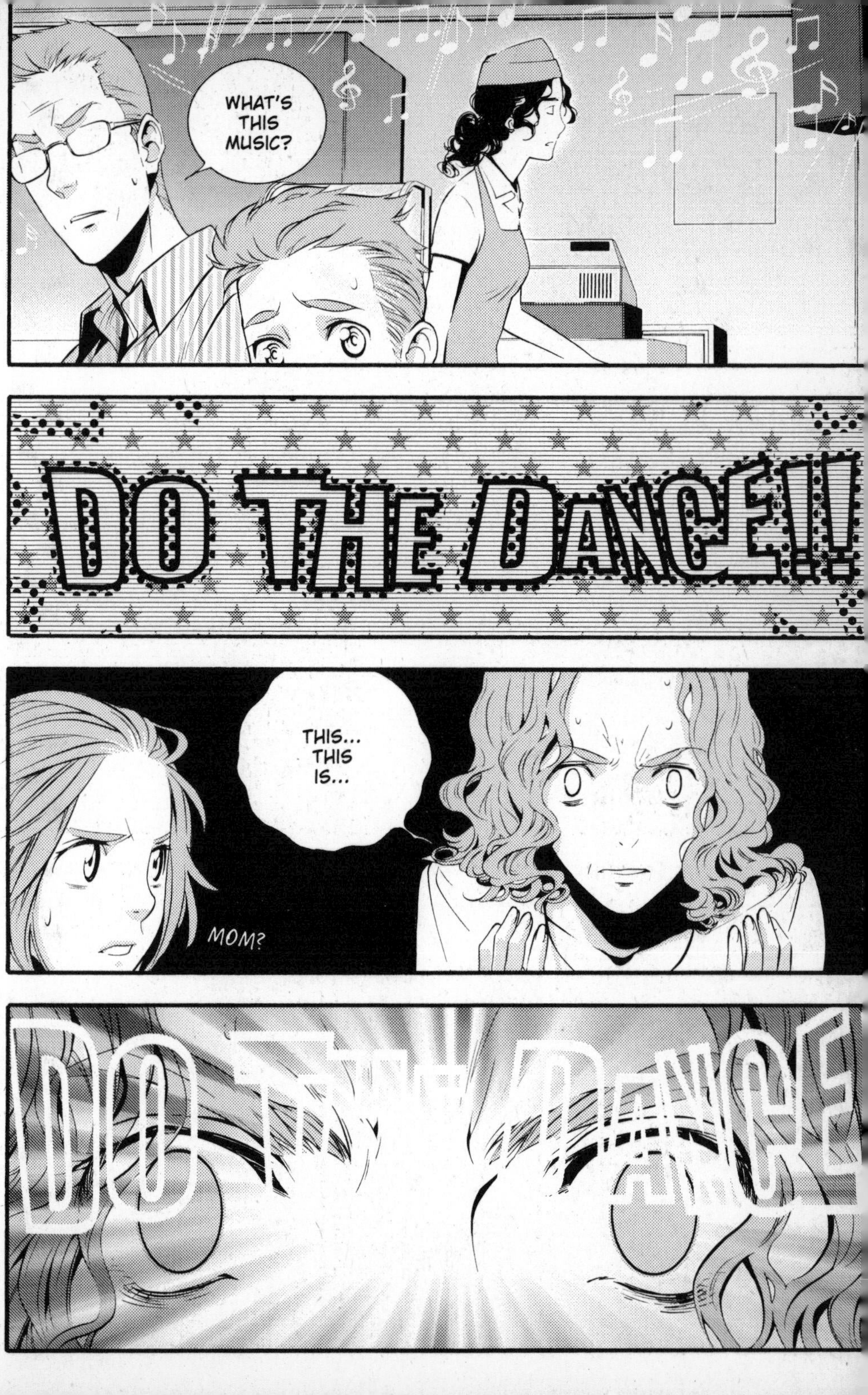
WHAT'S THIS MUSIC?
DO THE DANCE!!
THIS... THIS IS...
MOM?

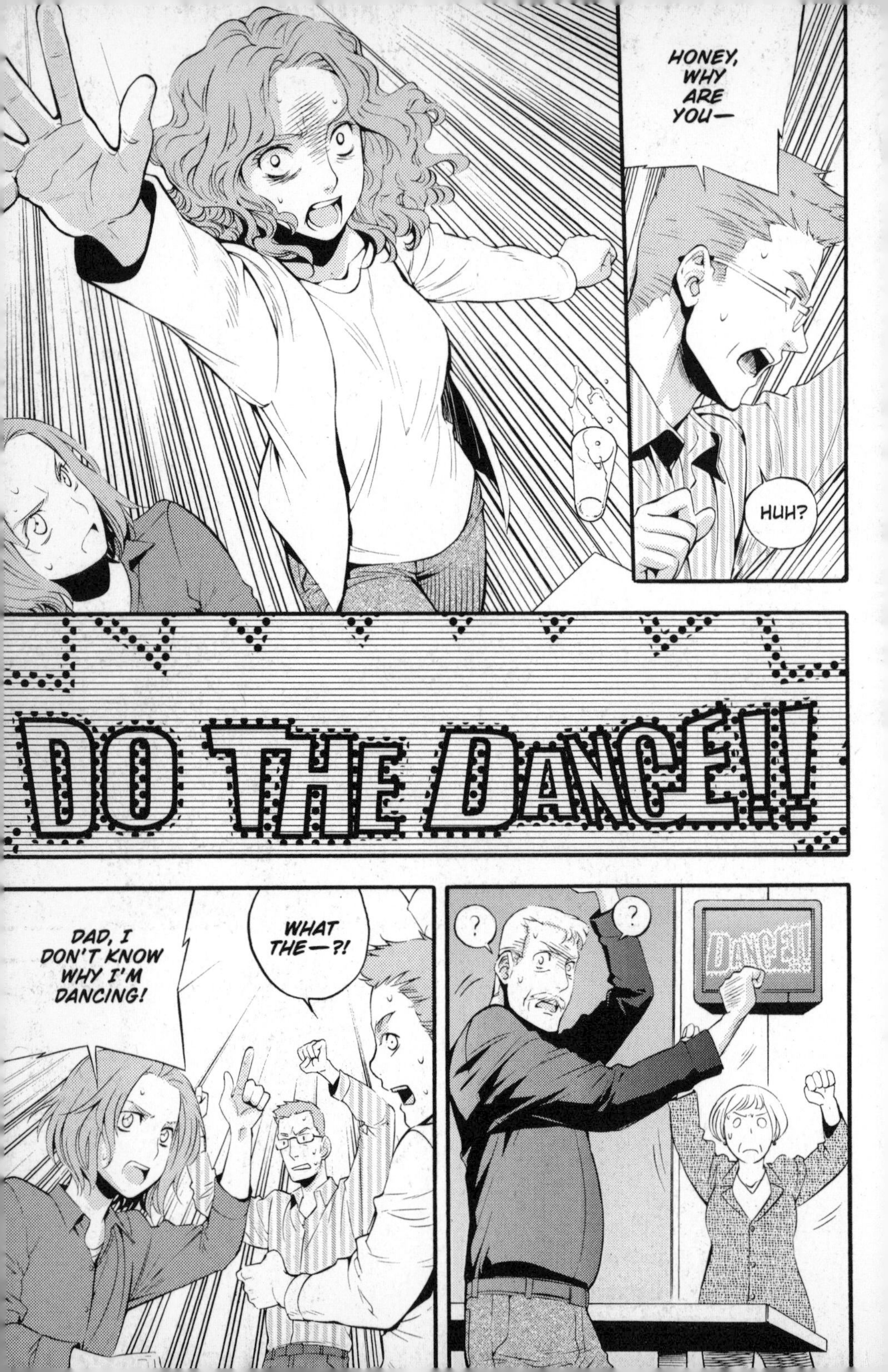
HONEY, WHY ARE YOU—
HUH?
DO THE DANCE!!
DAD, I DON'T KNOW WHY I'M DANCING!
WHAT THE—?!
?
?
DANCE!!

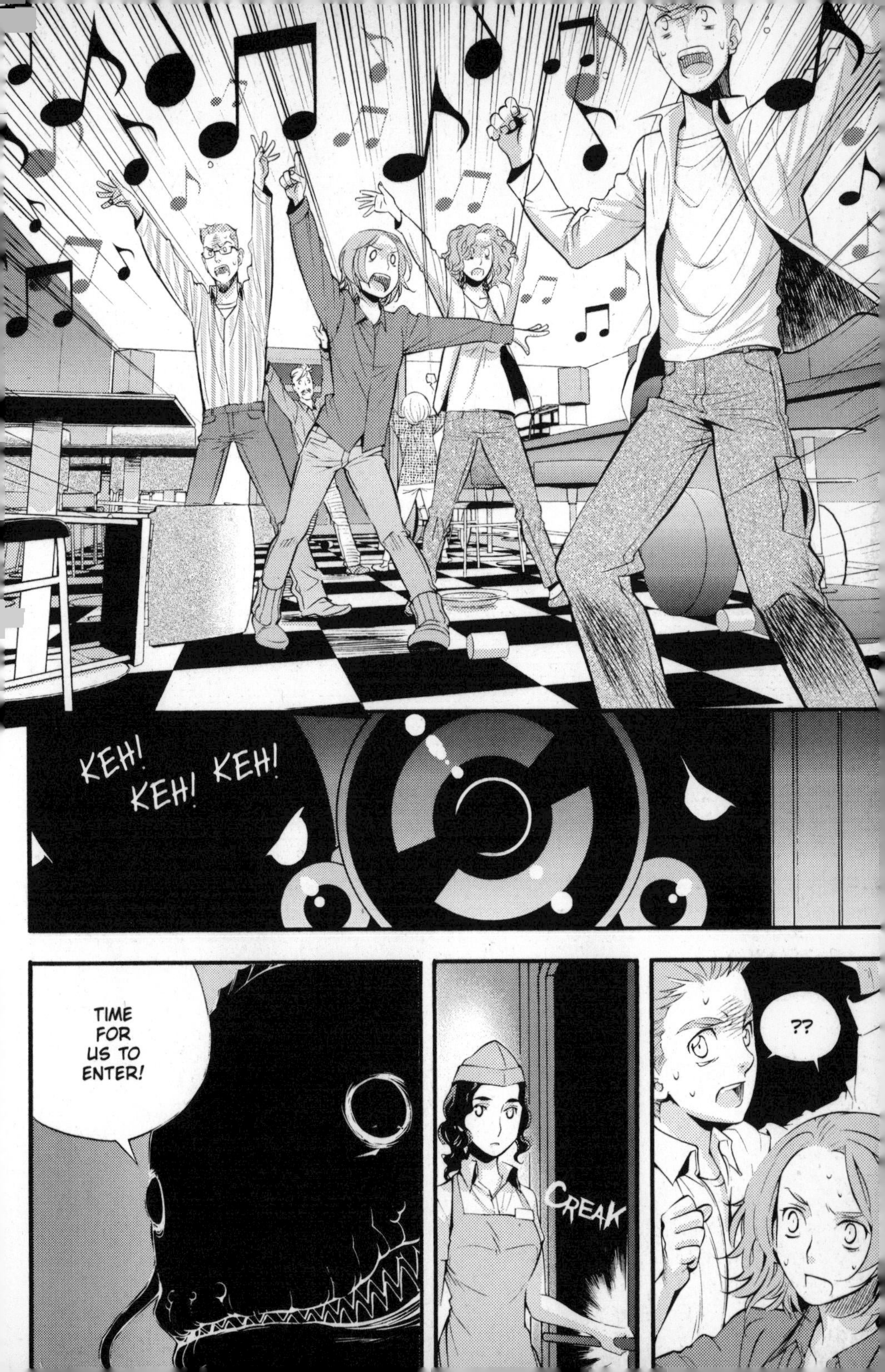
KEH! KEH! KEH!
TIME FOR US TO ENTER!
CREAK
??

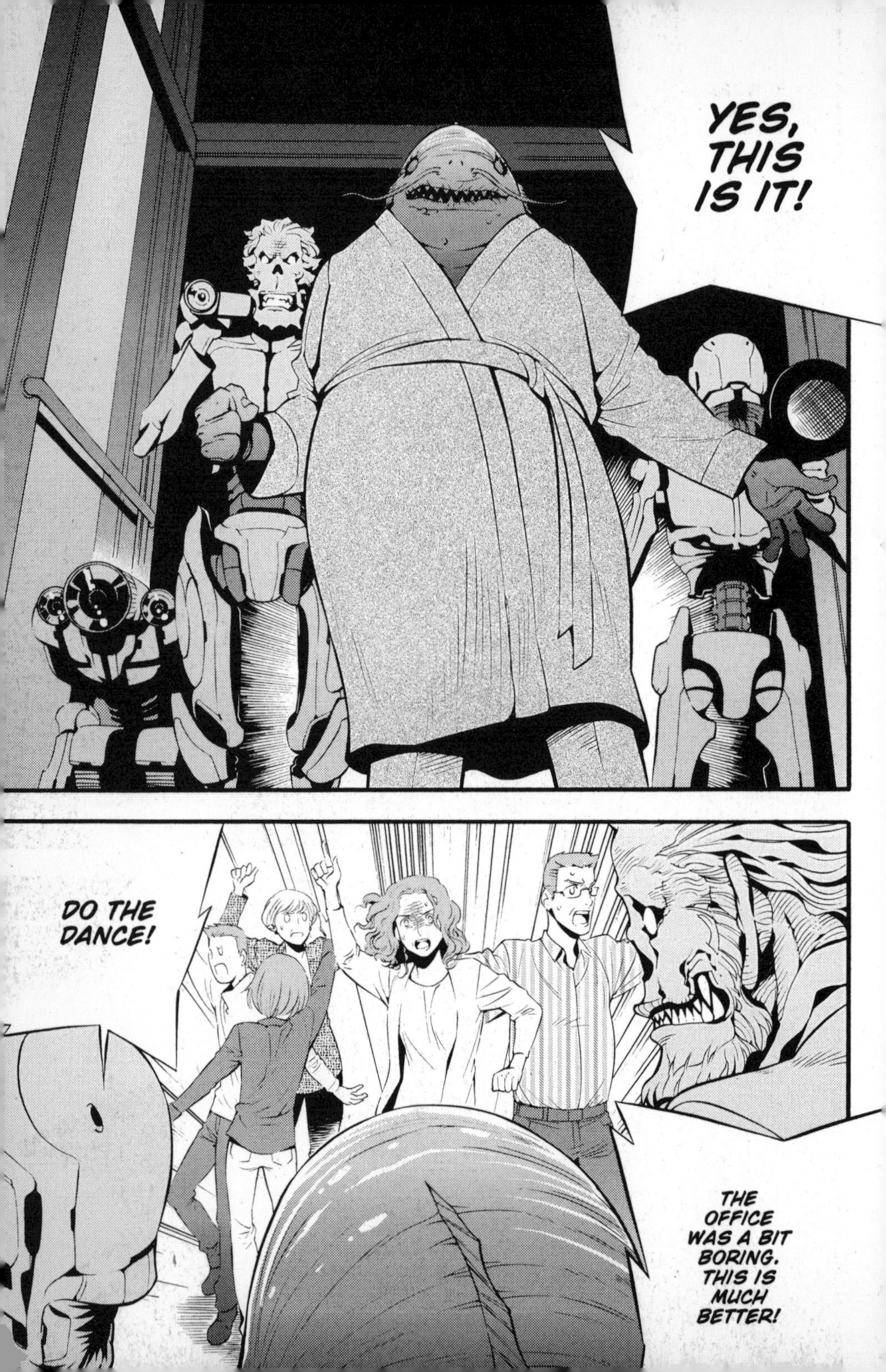
YES, THIS IS IT!
DO THE DANCE!
THE OFFICE WAS A BIT BORING. THIS IS MUCH BETTER!

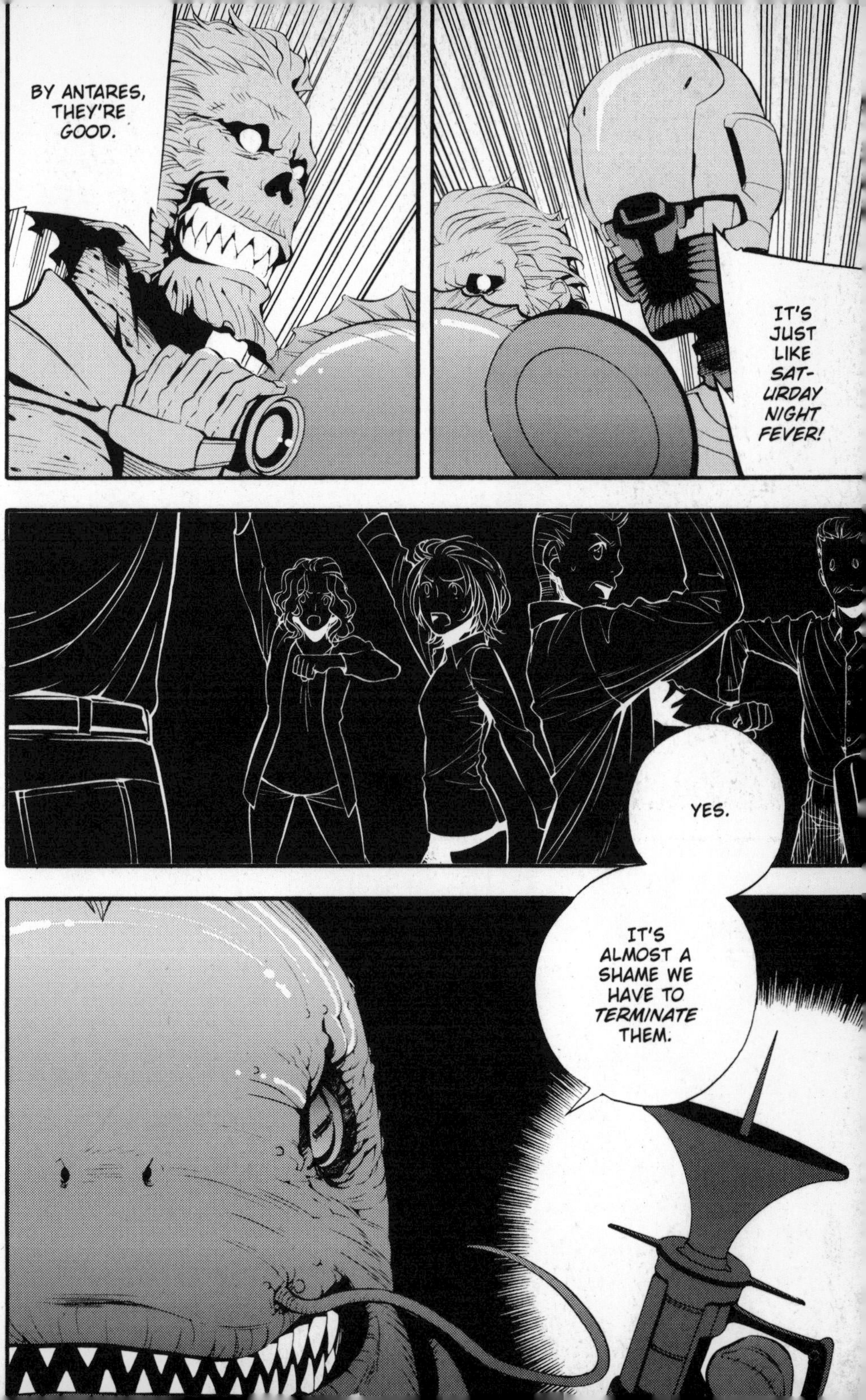
BY ANTARES, THEY'RE GOOD.
IT'S JUST LIKE SAT-URDAY NIGHT FEVER!
YES.
IT'S ALMOST A SHAME WE HAVE TO TERMINATE THEM.

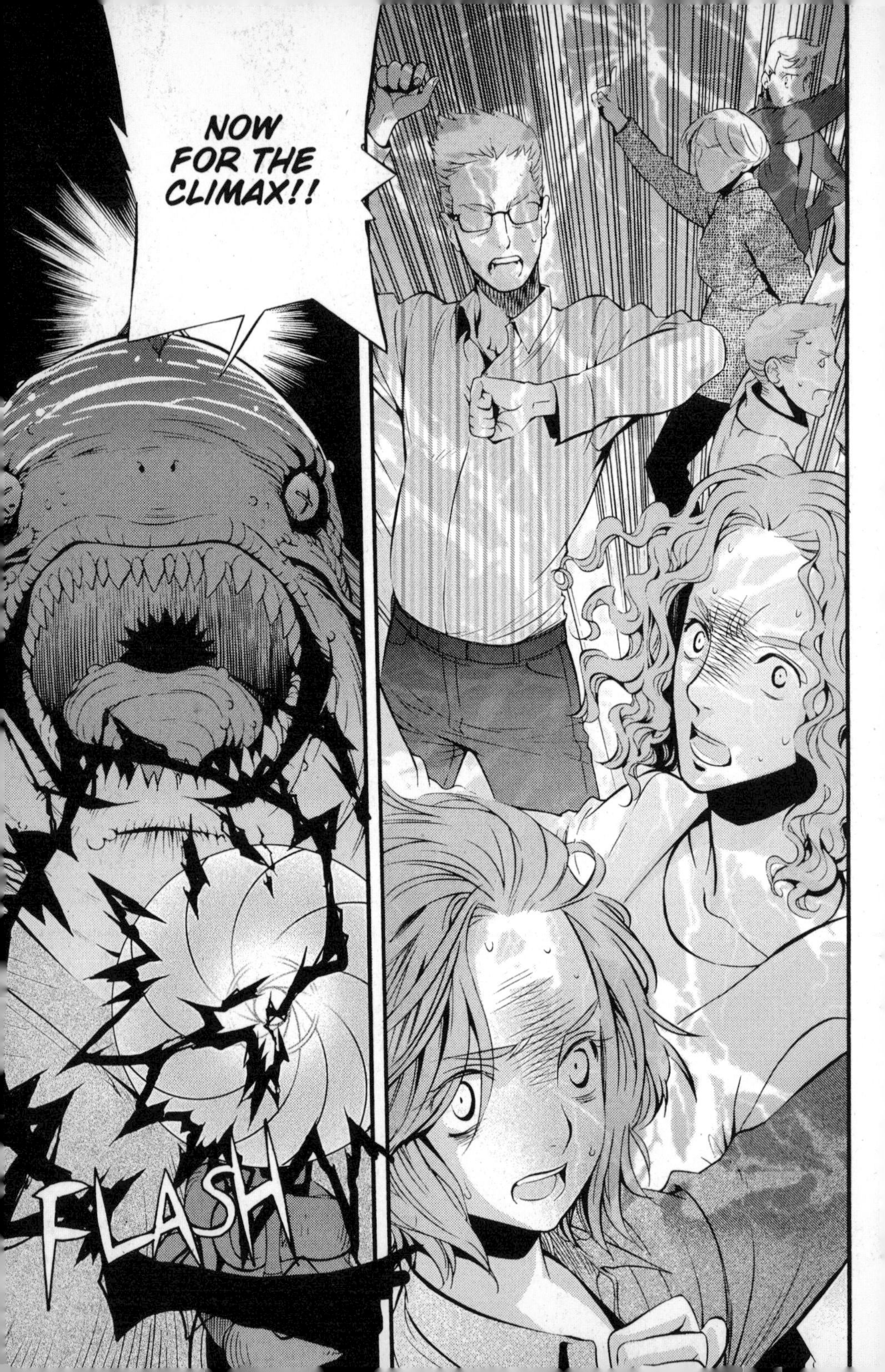
NOW FOR THE CLIMAX!!
FLASH

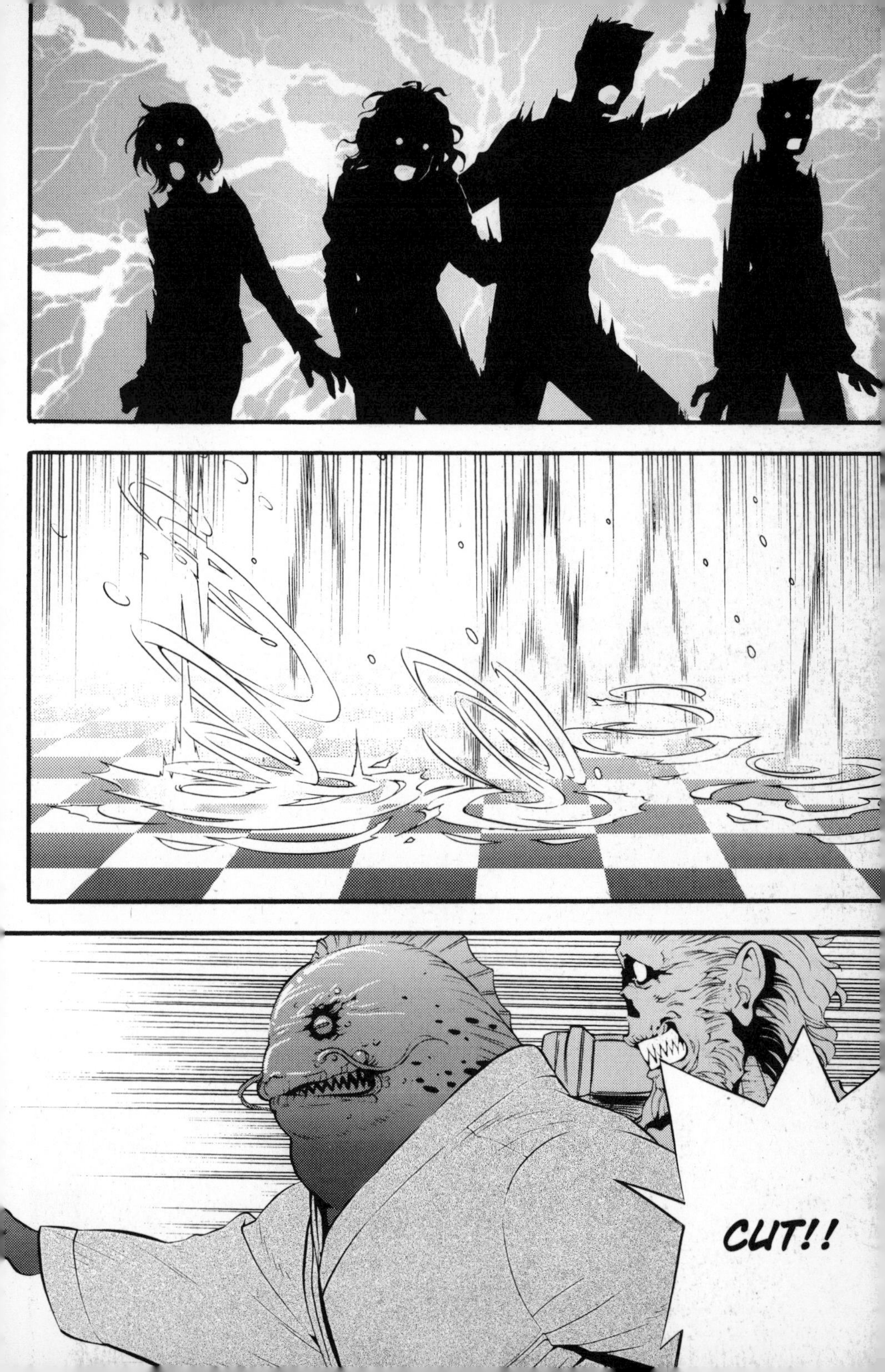
CUT!!

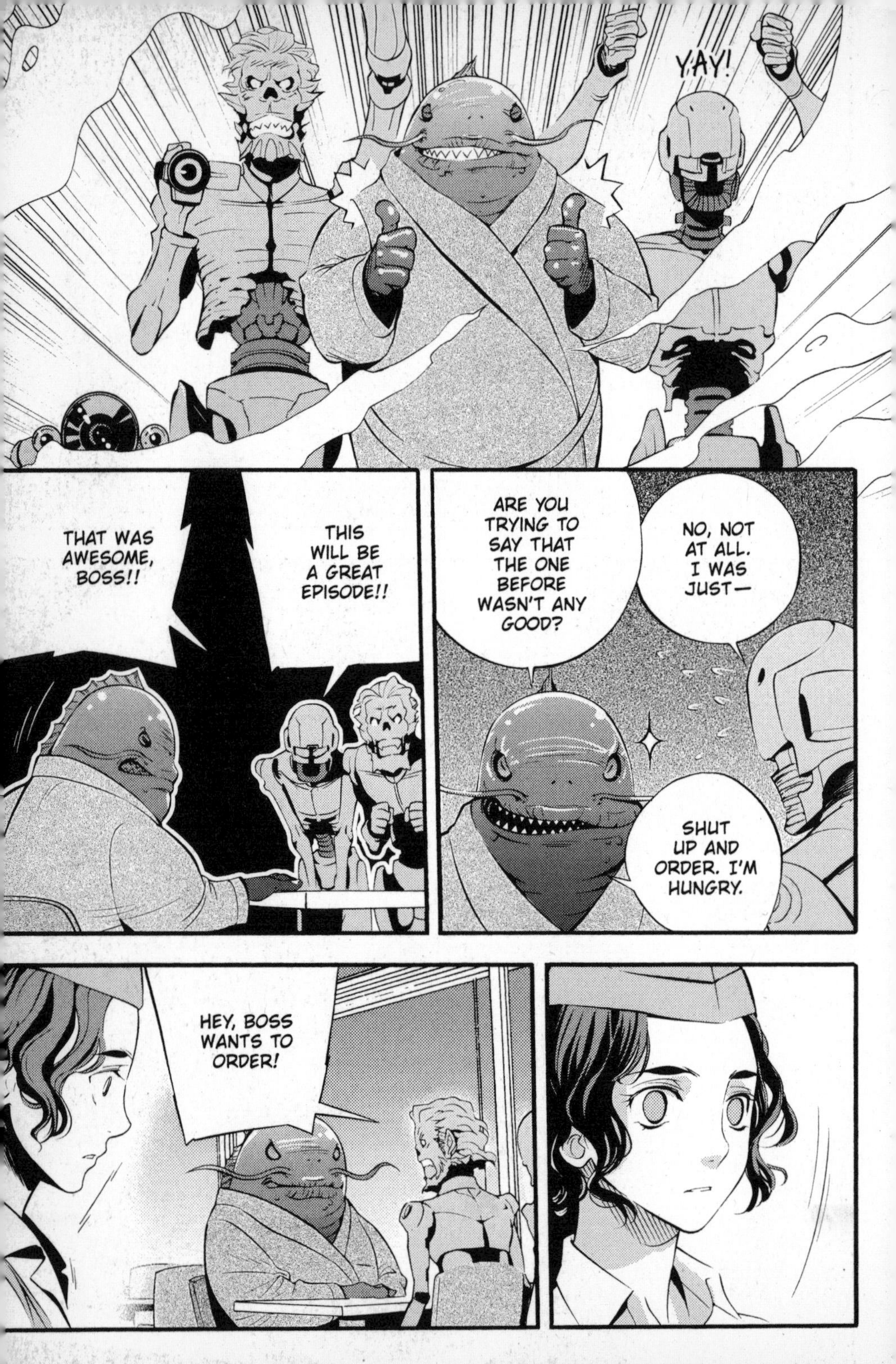
YAY!
THAT WAS AWESOME, BOSS!!
THIS WILL BE A GREAT EPISODE!!
ARE YOU TRYING TO SAY THAT THE ONE BEFORE WASN'T ANY GOOD?
NO, NOT AT ALL. I WAS JUST—
SHUT UP AND ORDER. I'M HUNGRY.
HEY, BOSS WANTS TO ORDER!

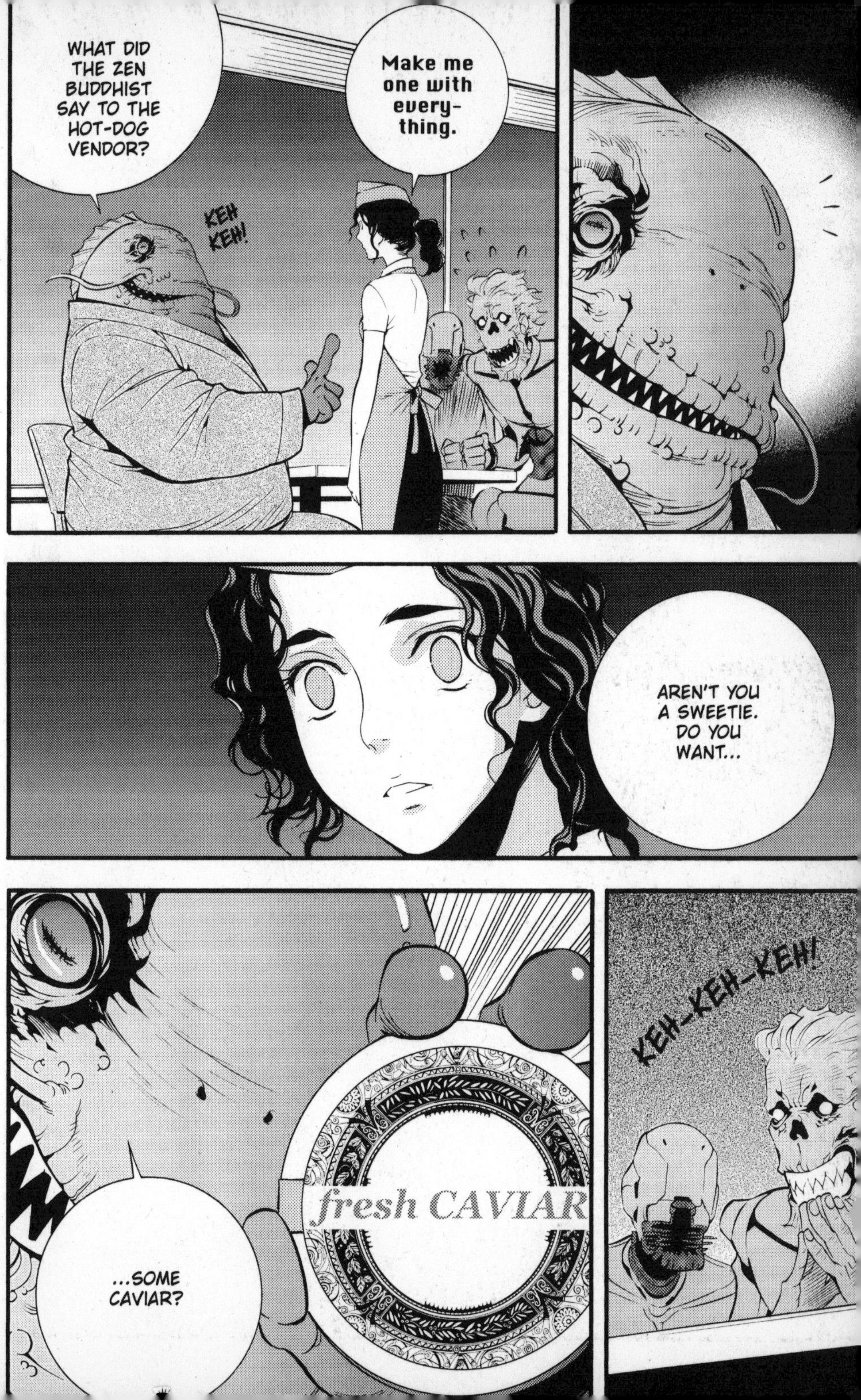
WHAT DID THE ZEN BUDDHIST SAY TO THE HOT-DOG VENDOR?
KEH KEH!
Make me one with every-thing.
AREN'T YOU A SWEETIE. DO YOU WANT...
...SOME CAVIAR?
fresh CAVIAR
KEH-KEH-KEH!

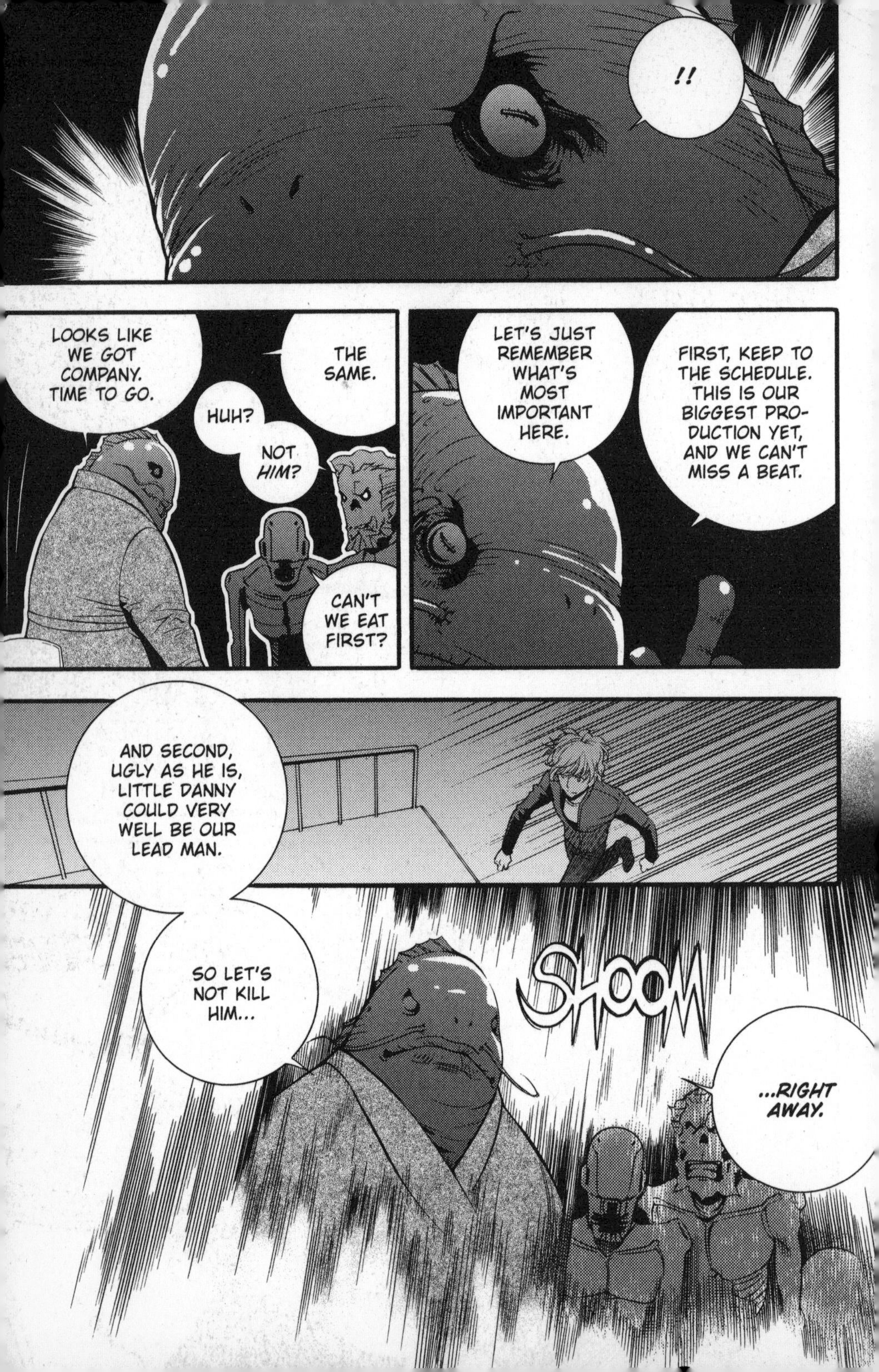
!!
LOOKS LIKE WE GOT COMPANY. TIME TO GO.
THE SAME.
HUH?
NOT HIM?
CAN'T WE EAT FIRST?
LET'S JUST REMEMBER WHAT'S MOST IMPORTANT HERE.
FIRST, KEEP TO THE SCHEDULE. THIS IS OUR BIGGEST PRO-DUCTION YET, AND WE CAN'T MISS A BEAT.
AND SECOND, UGLY AS HE IS, LITTLE DANNY COULD VERY WELL BE OUR LEAD MAN.
SO LET'S NOT KILL HIM...
SHOOM
...RIGHT AWAY.

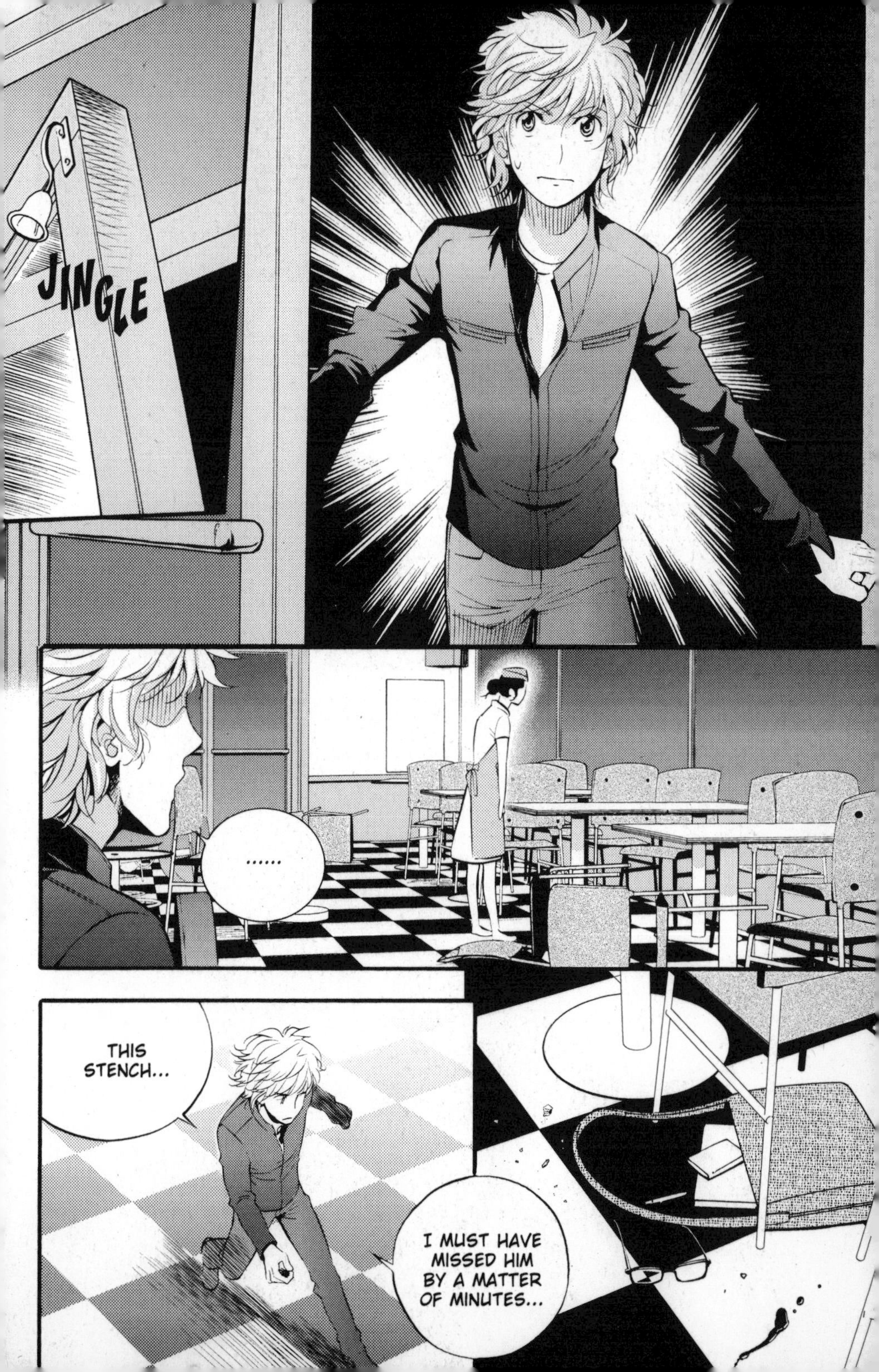
JINGLE
......
THIS STENCH...
I MUST HAVE MISSED HIM BY A MATTER OF MINUTES...

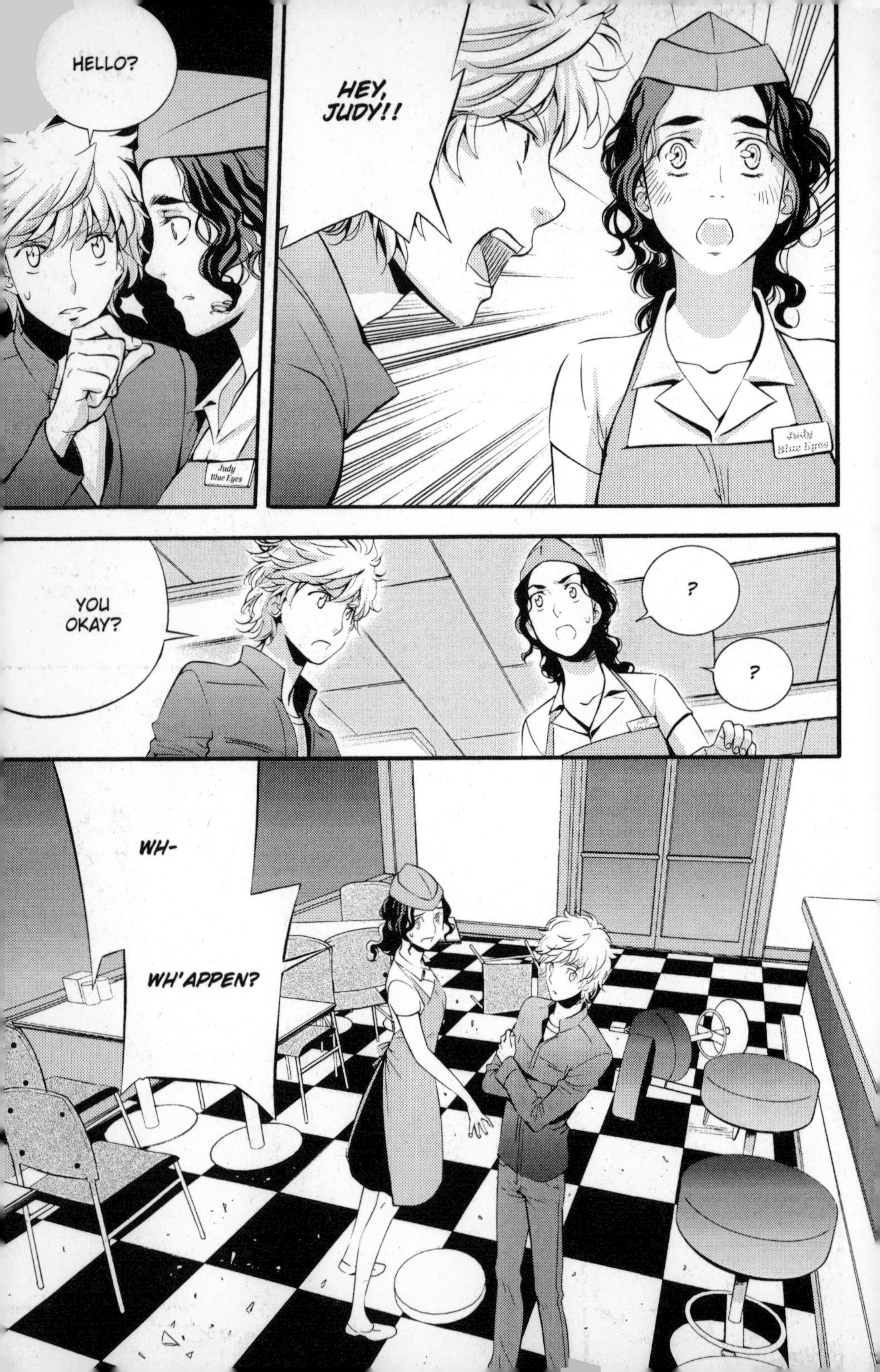
HELLO?
Judy Blue Eyes
HEY, JUDY!!
YOU OKAY?
?
?
WH-
WH'APPEN?

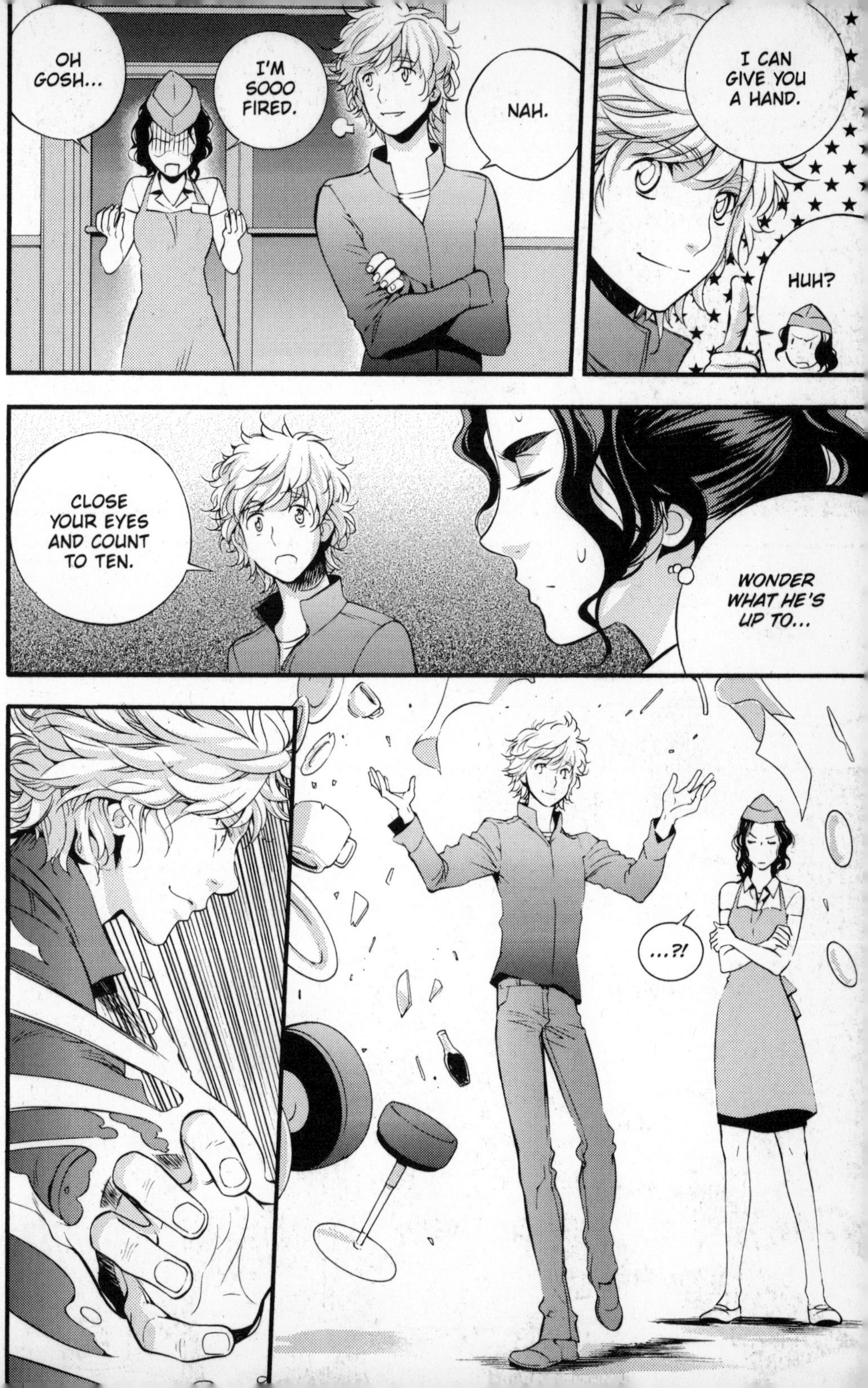
OH GOSH...
I'M SOOO FIRED.
NAH.
I CAN GIVE YOU A HAND.
HUH?
CLOSE YOUR EYES AND COUNT TO TEN.
WONDER WHAT HE'S UP TO...
...?!

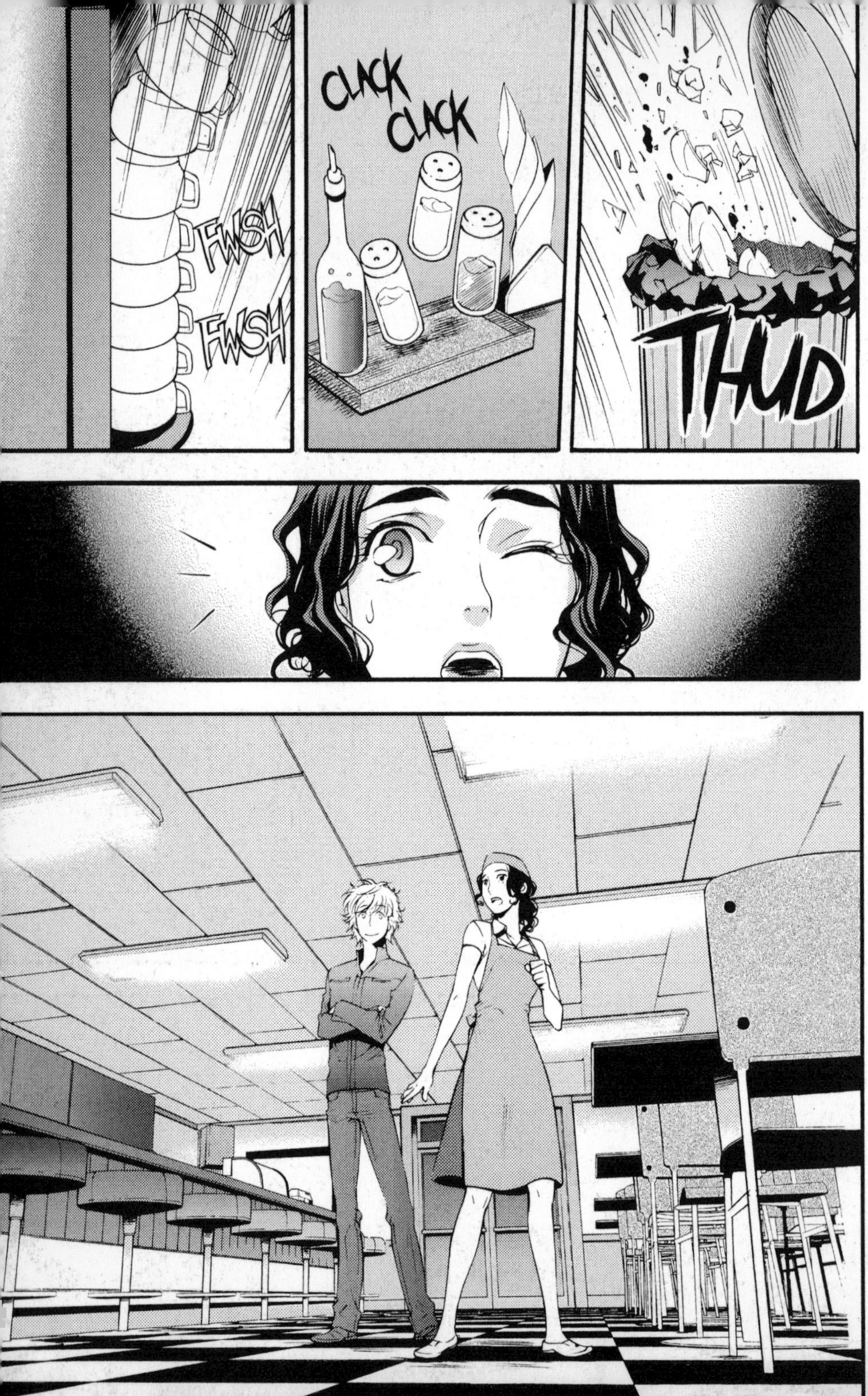
FWSH
FWSH
CLACK
CLACK
THUD

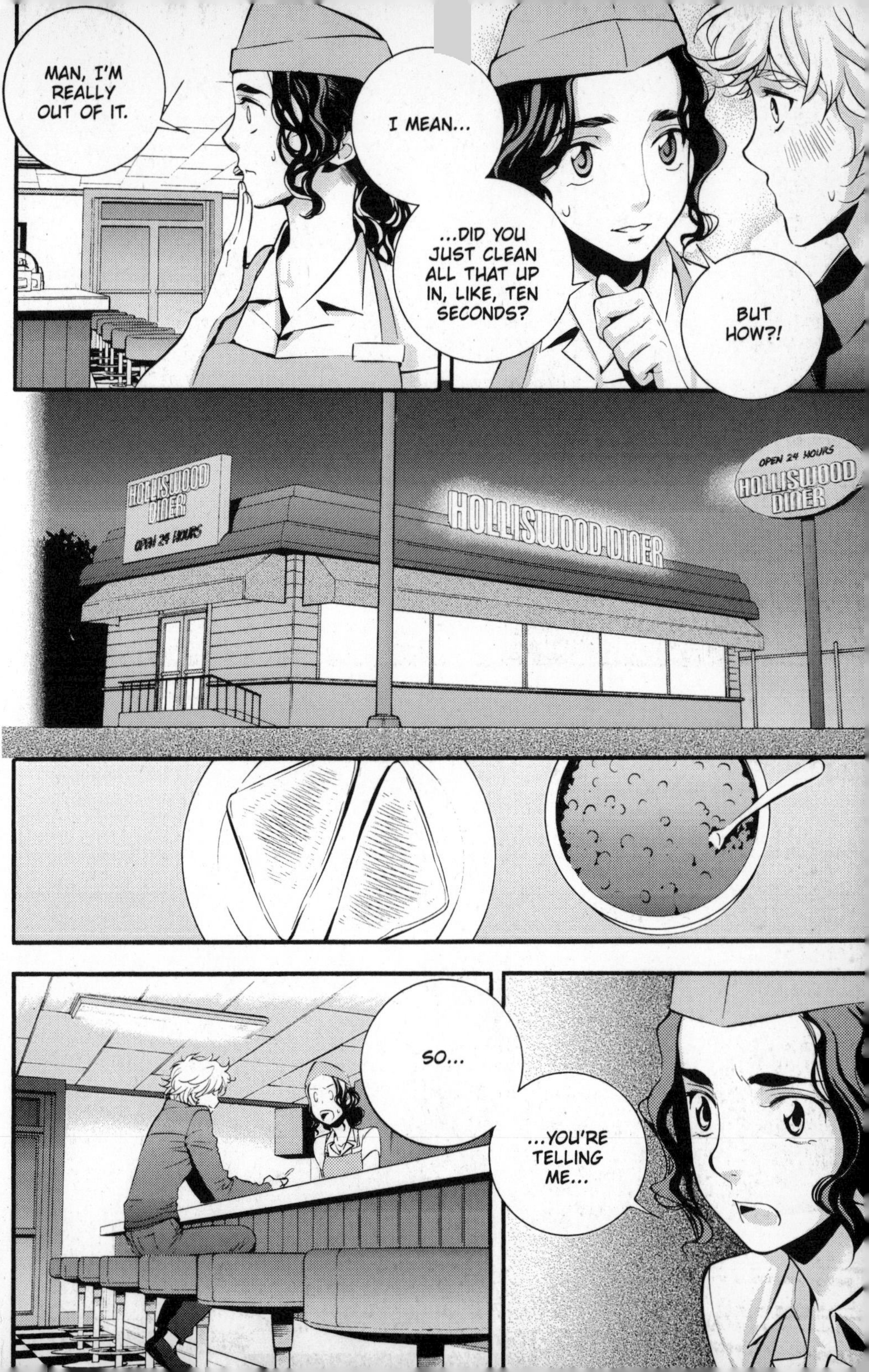
MAN, I'M REALLY OUT OF IT.
I MEAN...
...DID YOU JUST CLEAN ALL THAT UP IN, LIKE, TEN SECONDS?
BUT HOW?!
HOLLISWOOD DINER
OPEN 24 HOURS
HOLLISWOOD DINER
OPEN 24 HOURS
HOLLISWOOD DINER
SO...
...YOU'RE TELLING ME...

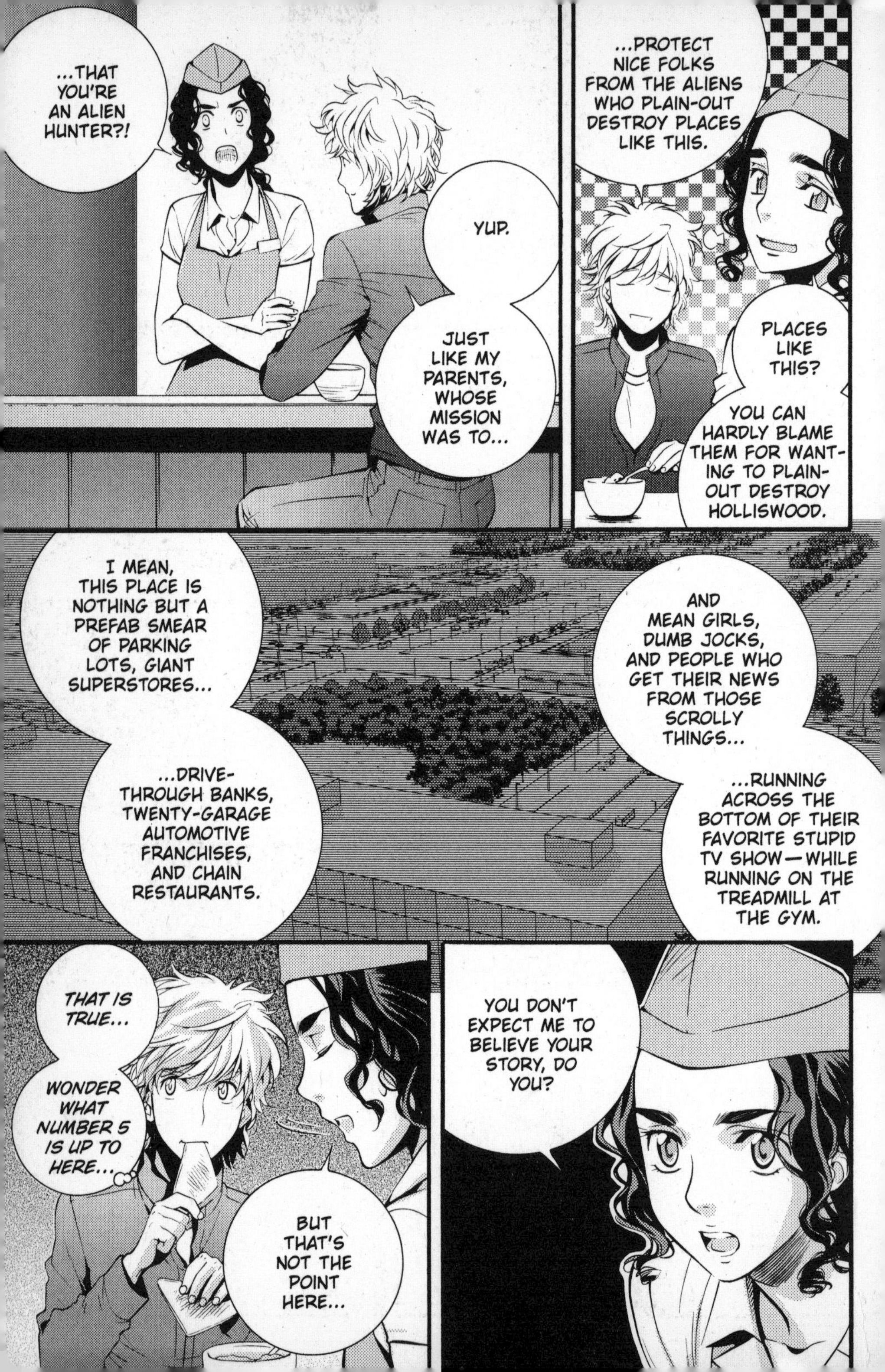
...THAT YOU'RE AN ALIEN HUNTER?!
YUP.
JUST LIKE MY PARENTS, WHOSE MISSION WAS TO...
...PROTECT NICE FOLKS FROM THE ALIENS WHO PLAIN-OUT DESTROY PLACES LIKE THIS.
PLACES LIKE THIS?
YOU CAN HARDLY BLAME THEM FOR WANTING TO PLAIN-OUT DESTROY HOLLISWOOD.
I MEAN, THIS PLACE IS NOTHING BUT A PREFAB SMEAR OF PARKING LOTS, GIANT SUPERSTORES...
...DRIVE-THROUGH BANKS, TWENTY-GARAGE AUTOMOTIVE FRANCHISES, AND CHAIN RESTAURANTS.
AND MEAN GIRLS, DUMB JOCKS, AND PEOPLE WHO GET THEIR NEWS FROM THOSE SCROLLY THINGS...
...RUNNING ACROSS THE BOTTOM OF THEIR FAVORITE STUPID TV SHOW—WHILE RUNNING ON THE TREADMILL AT THE GYM.
THAT IS TRUE...
WONDER WHAT NUMBER 5 IS UP TO HERE...
BUT THAT'S NOT THE POINT HERE...
YOU DON'T EXPECT ME TO BELIEVE YOUR STORY, DO YOU?

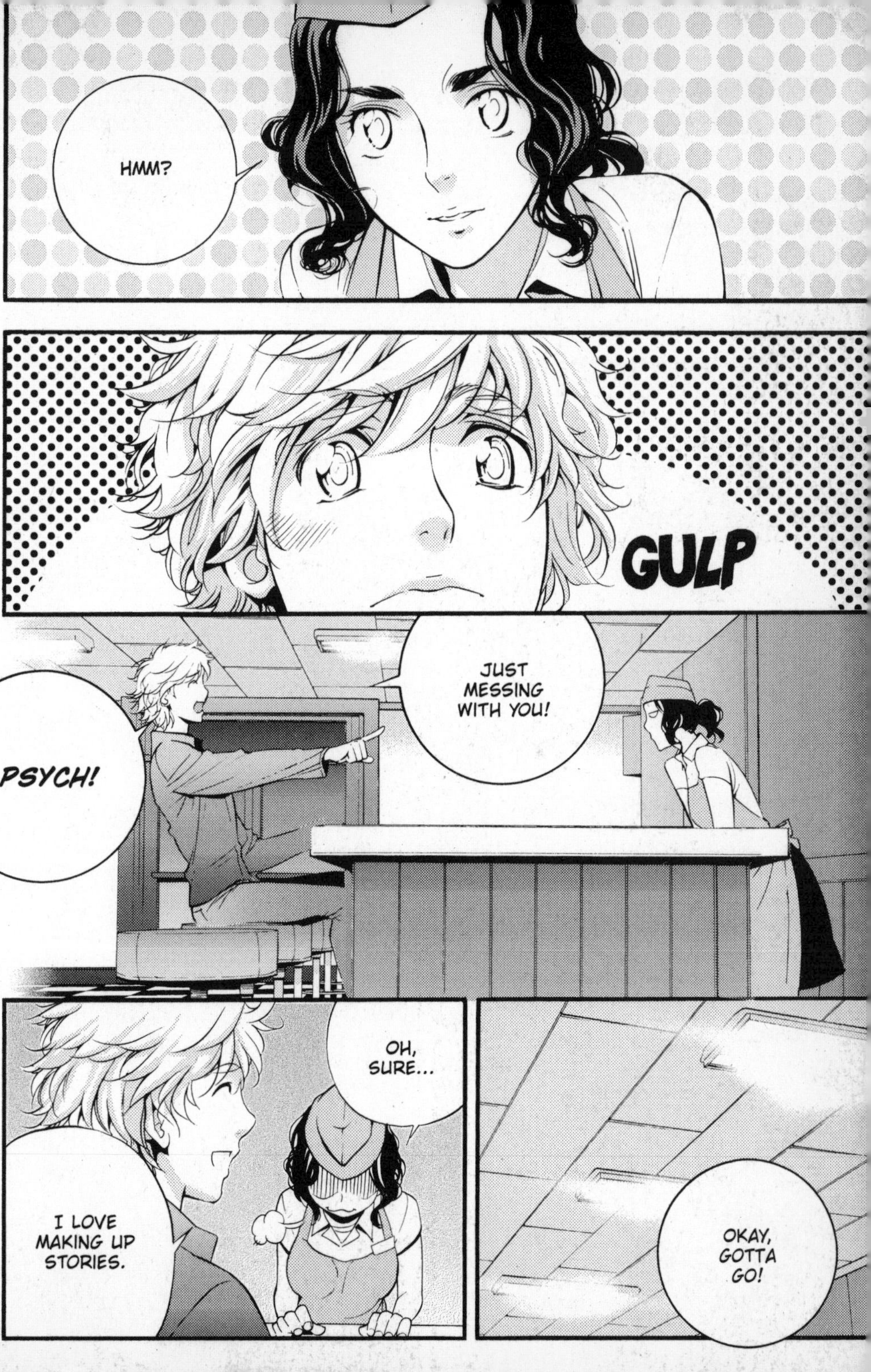
HMM?
GULP
PSYCH!
JUST MESSING WITH YOU!
OH, SURE...
I LOVE MAKING UP STORIES.
OKAY, GOTTA GO!

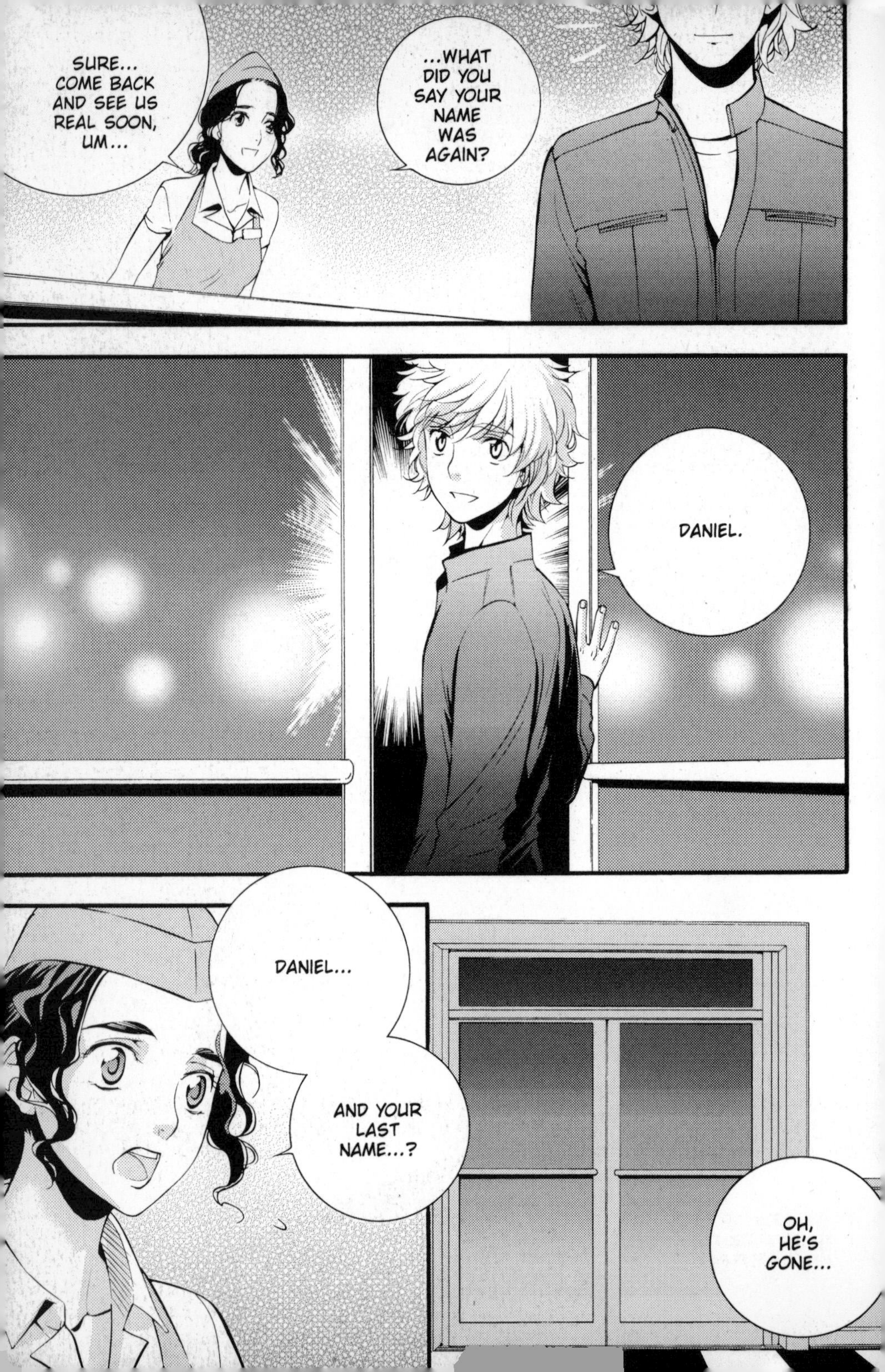
SURE... COME BACK AND SEE US REAL SOON, UM...
...WHAT DID YOU SAY YOUR NAME WAS AGAIN?
DANIEL.
DANIEL...
AND YOUR LAST NAME...?
OH, HE'S GONE...

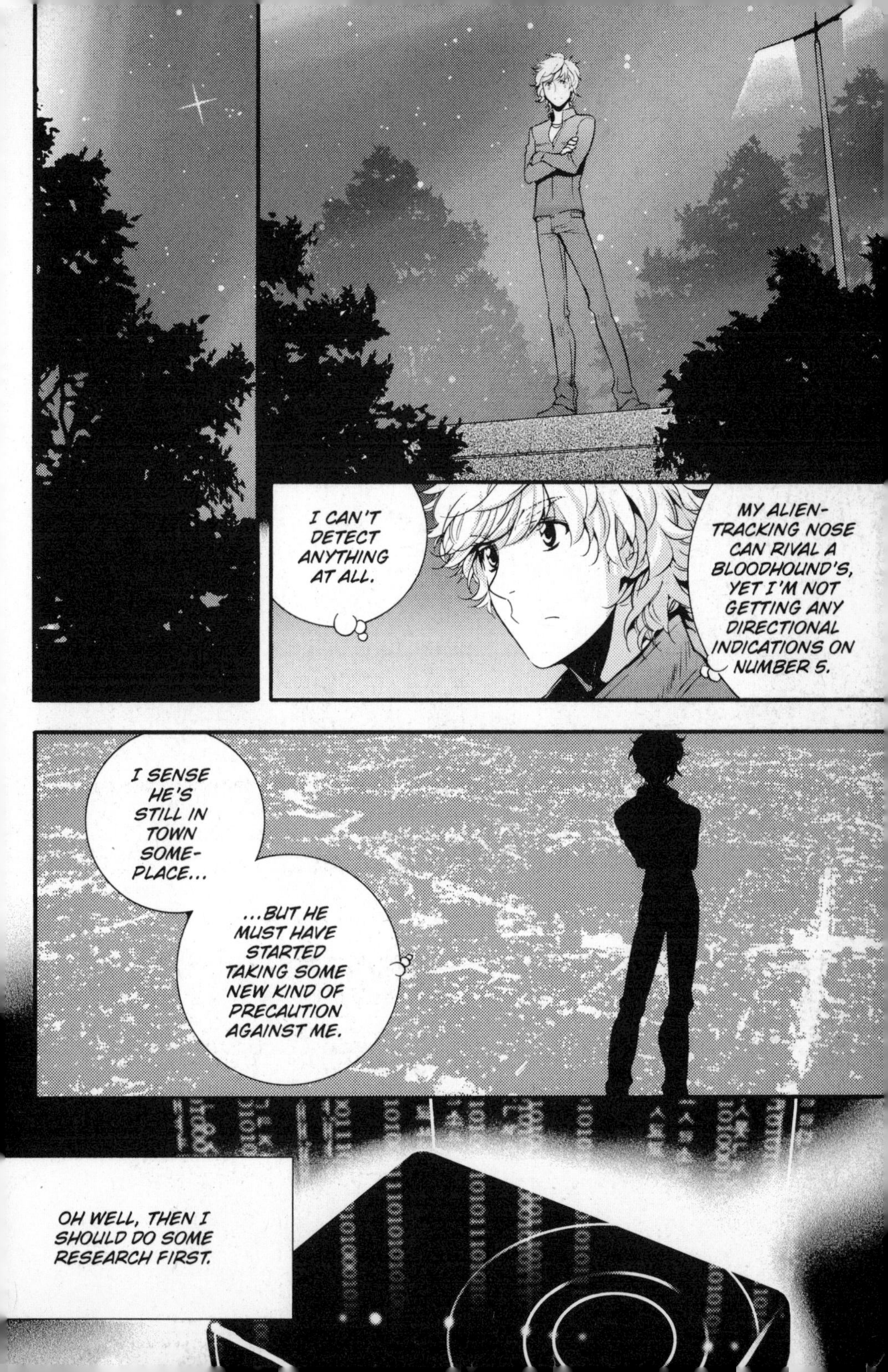
I CAN'T DETECT ANYTHING AT ALL.
MY ALIEN-TRACKING NOSE CAN RIVAL A BLOODHOUND'S, YET I'M NOT GETTING ANY DIRECTIONAL INDICATIONS ON NUMBER 5.
I SENSE HE'S STILL IN TOWN SOME-PLACE...
...BUT HE MUST HAVE STARTED TAKING SOME NEW KIND OF PRECAUTION AGAINST ME.
OH WELL, THEN I SHOULD DO SOME RESEARCH FIRST.

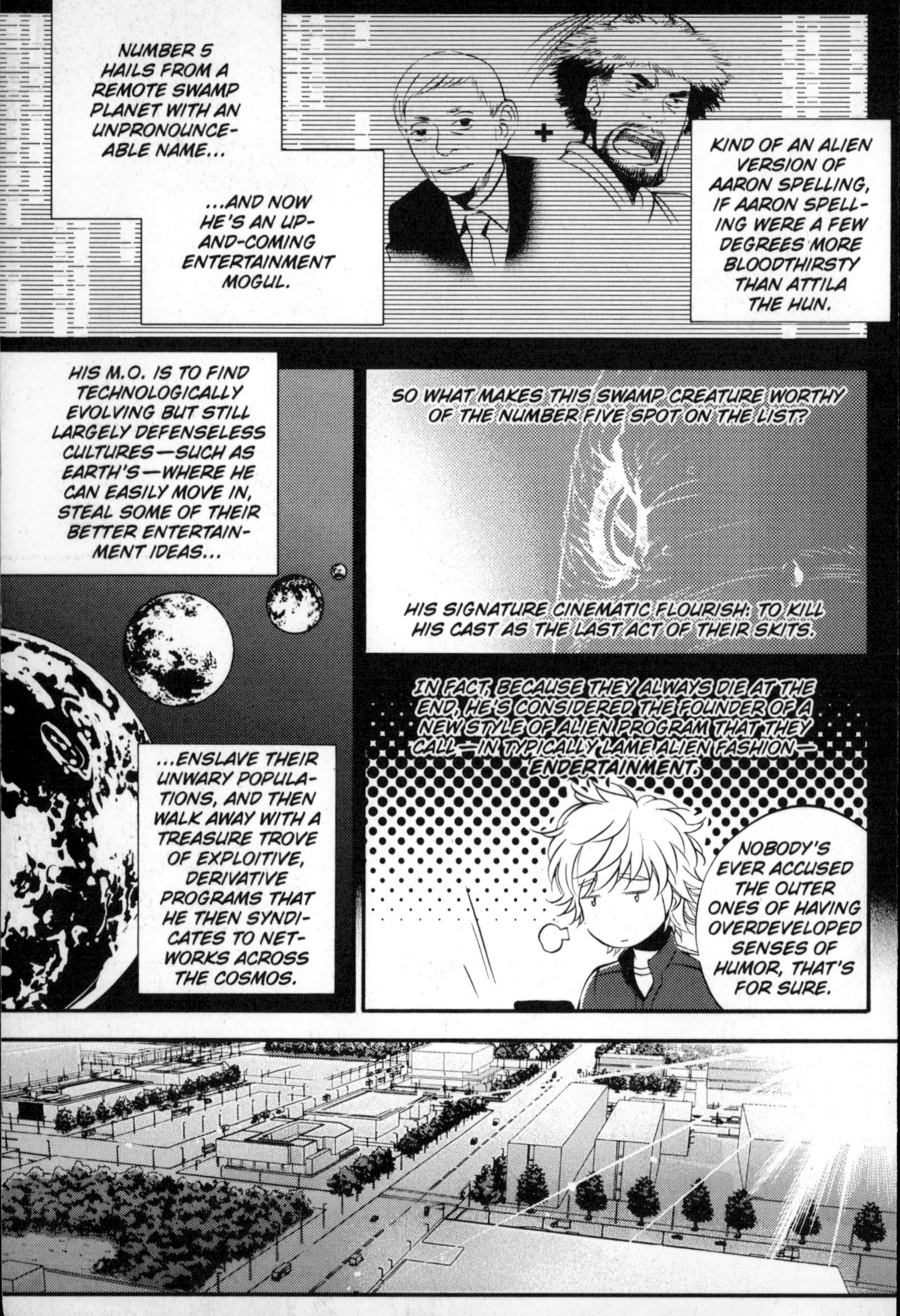
NUMBER 5 HAILS FROM A REMOTE SWAMP PLANET WITH AN UNPRONOUNCE-ABLE NAME...
...AND NOW HE'S AN UP-AND-COMING ENTERTAINMENT MOGUL.
KIND OF AN ALIEN VERSION OF AARON SPELLING, IF AARON SPELL-ING WERE A FEW DEGREES MORE BLOODTHIRSTY THAN ATTILA THE HUN.
HIS M.O. IS TO FIND TECHNOLOGICALLY EVOLVING BUT STILL LARGELY DEFENSELESS CULTURES—SUCH AS EARTH'S—WHERE HE CAN EASILY MOVE IN, STEAL SOME OF THEIR BETTER ENTERTAIN-MENT IDEAS...
...ENSLAVE THEIR UNWARY POPULA-TIONS, AND THEN WALK AWAY WITH A TREASURE TROVE OF EXPLOITIVE, DERIVATIVE PROGRAMS THAT HE THEN SYNDI-CATES TO NET-WORKS ACROSS THE COSMOS.
SO WHAT MAKES THIS SWAMP CREATURE WORTHY OF THE NUMBER FIVE SPOT ON THE LIST?
HIS SIGNATURE CINEMATIC FLOURISH: TO KILL HIS CAST AS THE LAST ACT OF THEIR SKITS.
IN FACT, BECAUSE THEY ALWAYS DIE AT THE END, HE'S CONSIDERED THE FOUNDER OF A NEW STYLE OF ALIEN PROGRAM THAT THEY CALL—IN TYPICALLY LAME ALIEN FASHION—ENDERTAINMENT.
NOBODY'S EVER ACCUSED THE OUTER ONES OF HAVING OVERDEVELOPED SENSES OF HUMOR, THAT'S FOR SURE.

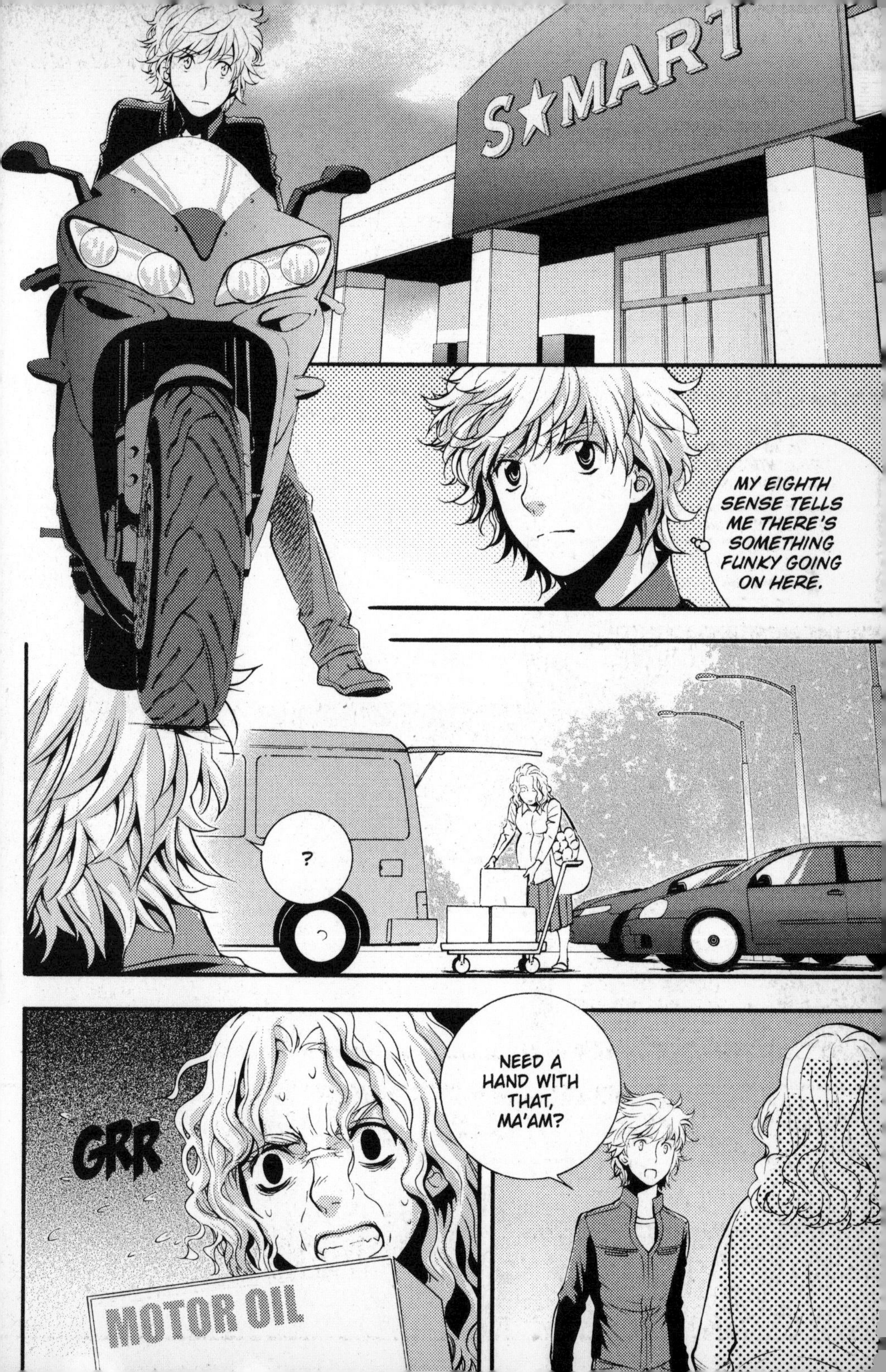
S★MART
MY EIGHTH SENSE TELLS ME THERE'S SOMETHING FUNKY GOING ON HERE.
?
GRR
MOTOR OIL
NEED A HAND WITH THAT, MA'AM?

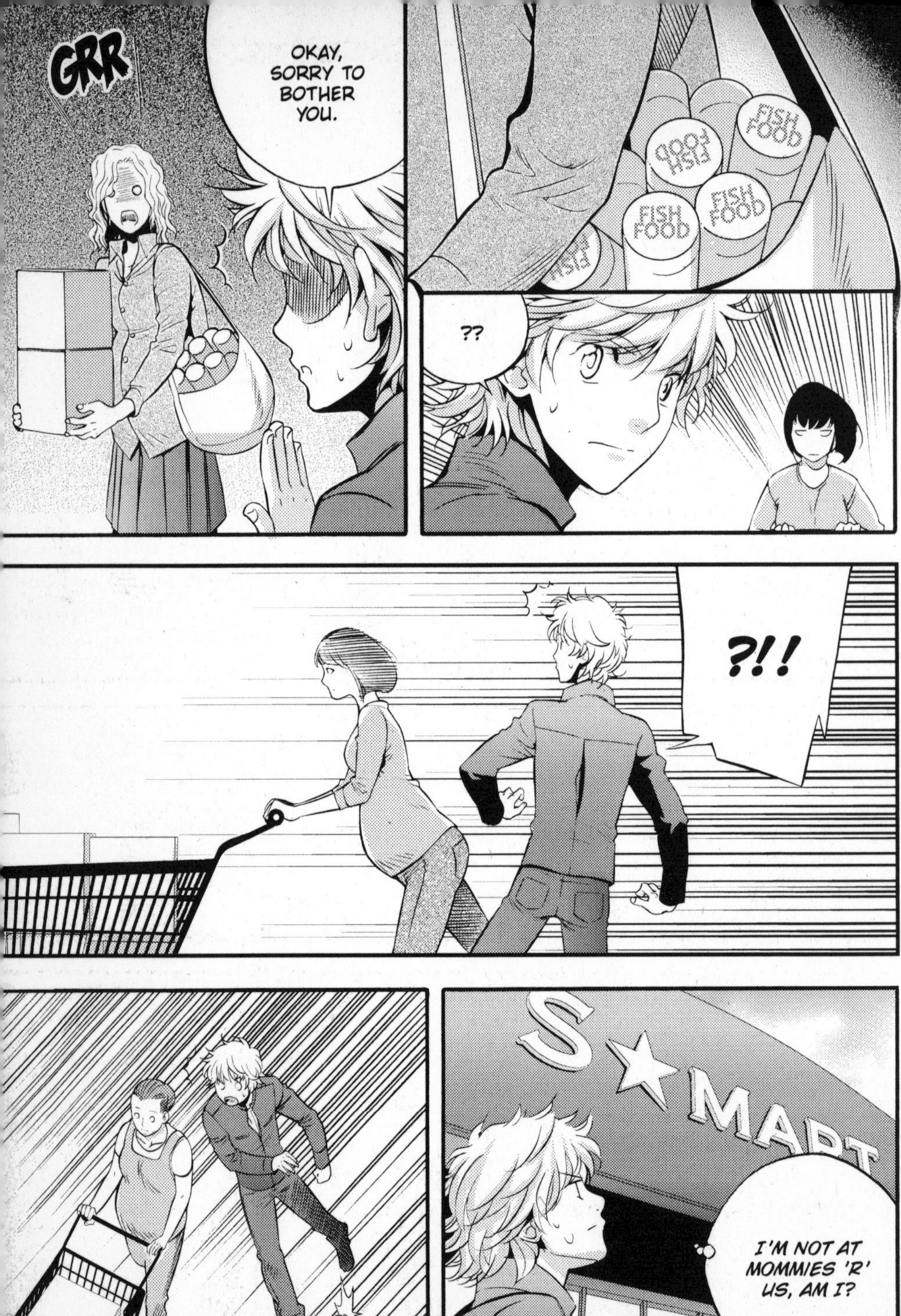
GRR
OKAY, SORRY TO BOTHER YOU.
FISH FOOD
FISH FOOD
FISH FOOD
FISH FOOD
??
?!!
S★MART
I'M NOT AT MOMMIES 'R' US, AM I?

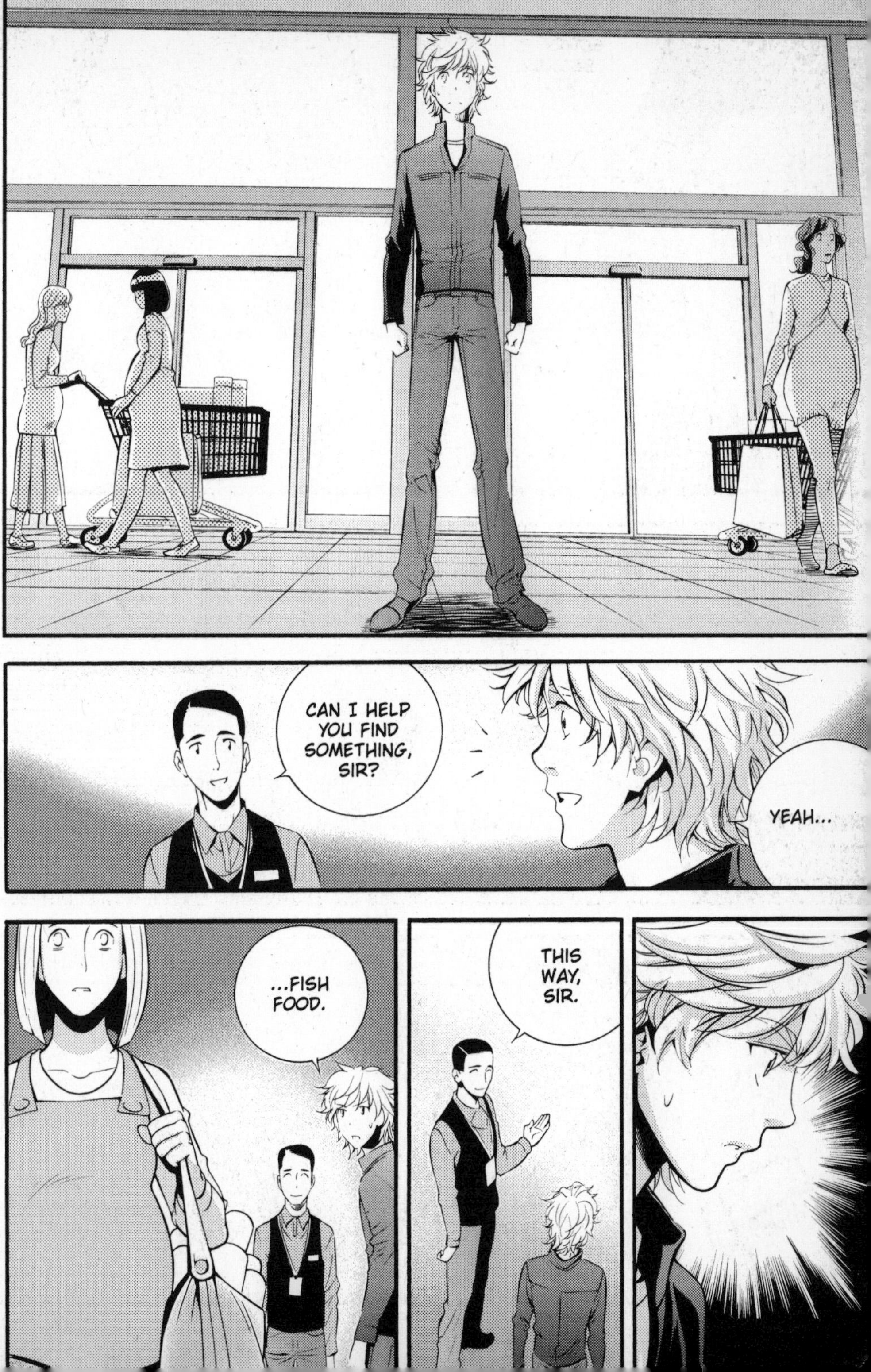
CAN I HELP YOU FIND SOMETHING, SIR?
YEAH...
...FISH FOOD.
THIS WAY, SIR.

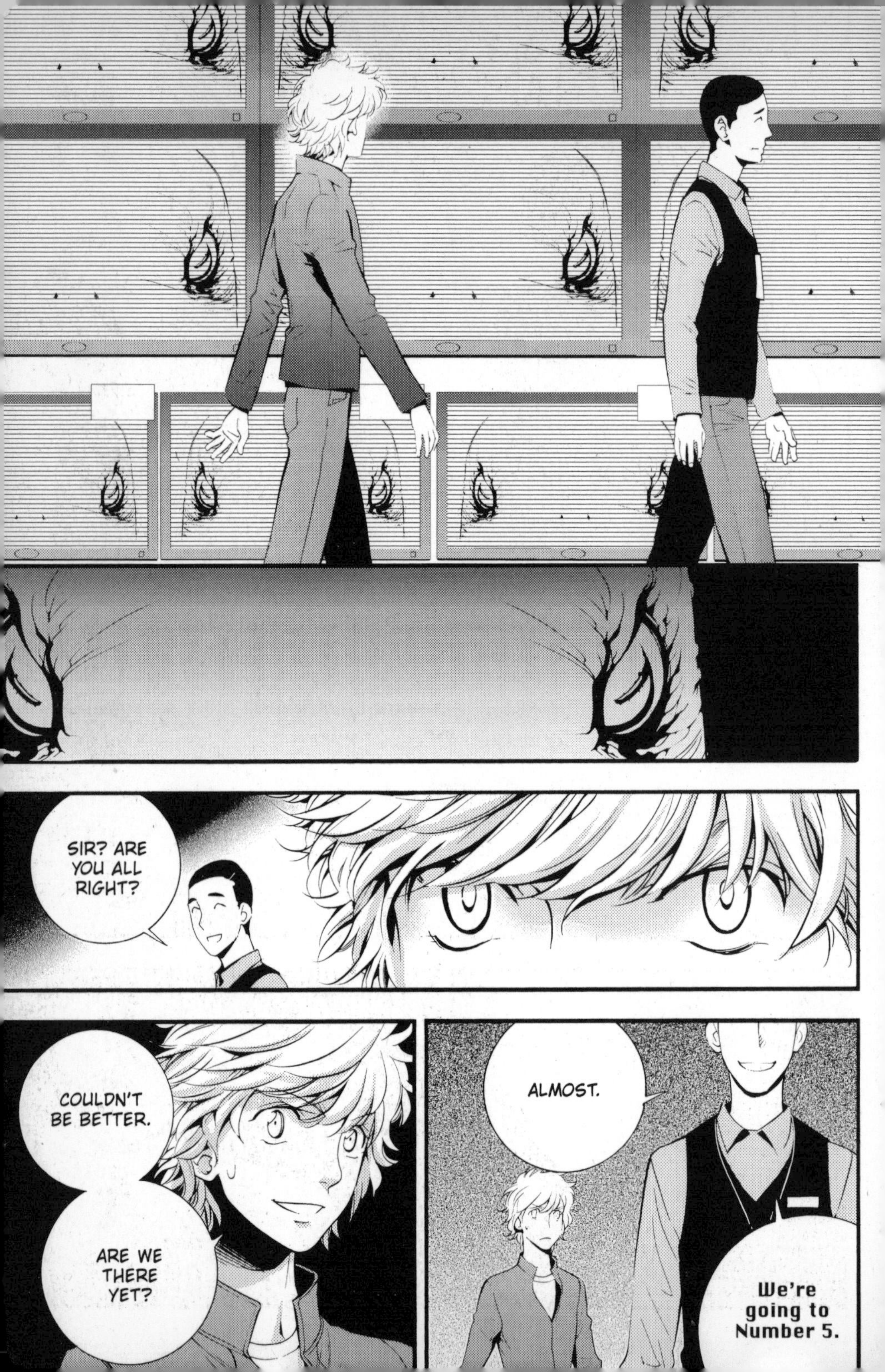
SIR? ARE YOU ALL RIGHT?
COULDN'T BE BETTER.
ARE WE THERE YET?
ALMOST.
We're going to Number 5.

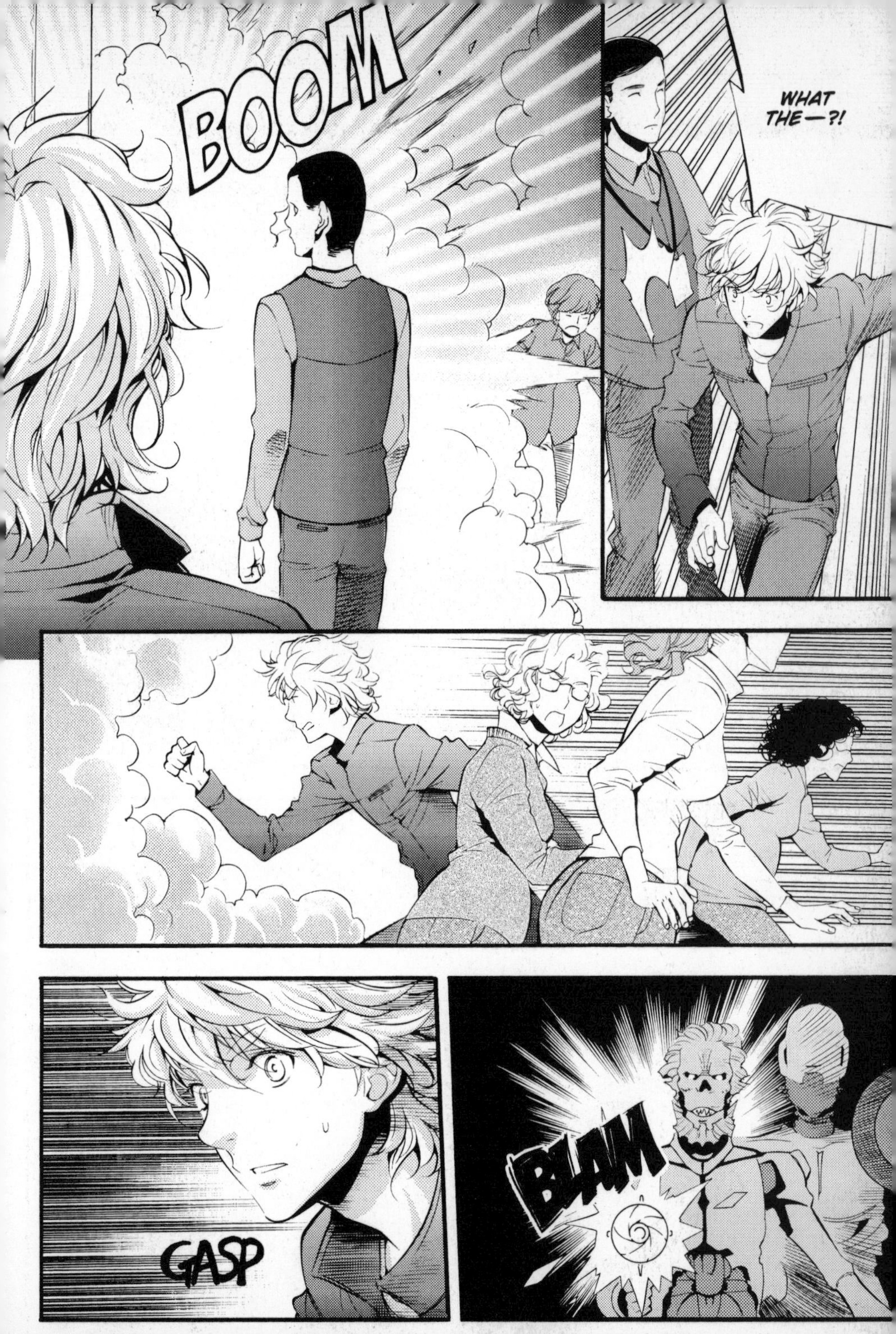
BOOM
WHAT THE—?!
GASP
BLAM

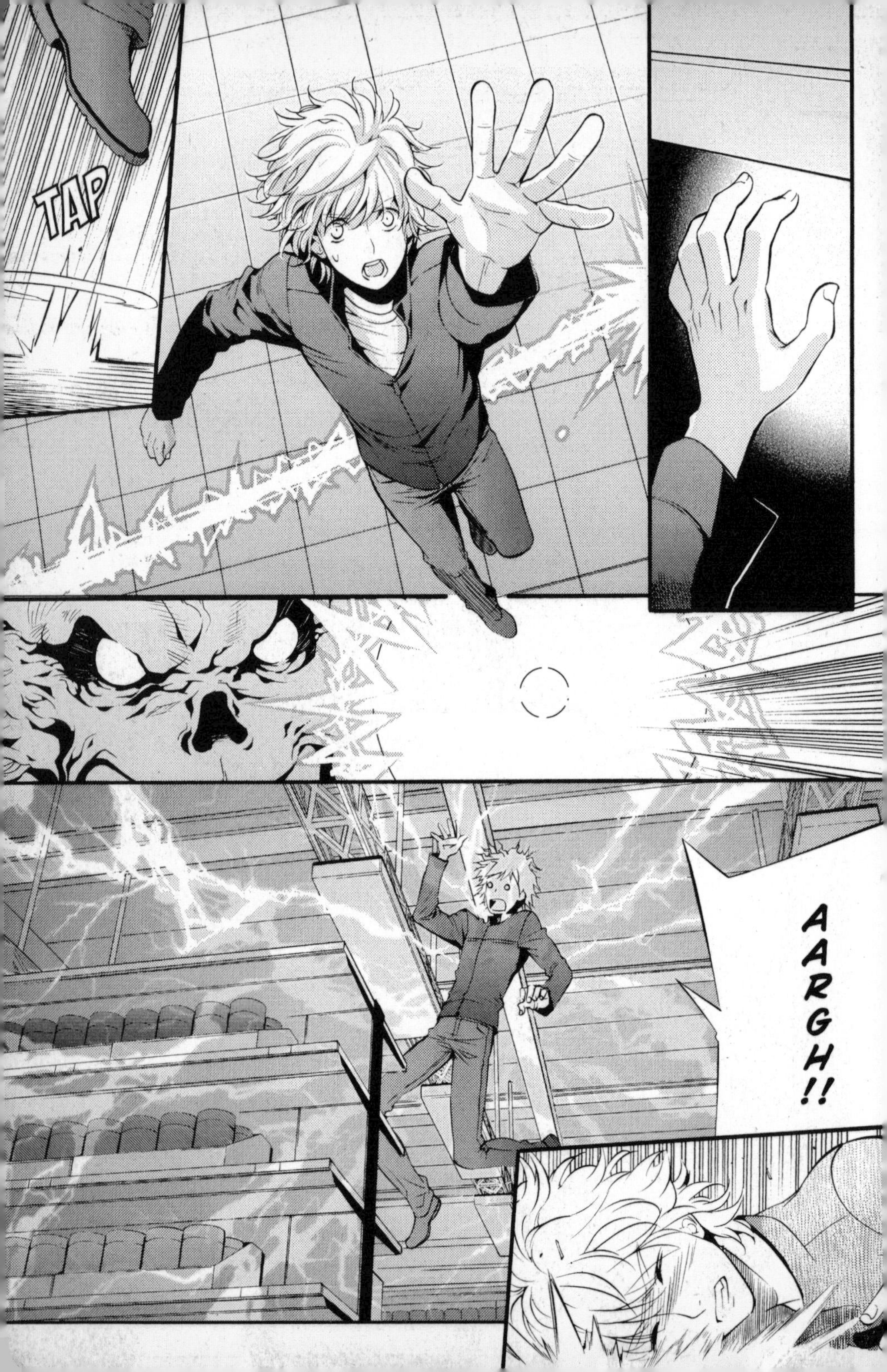
TAP
AARGH!!

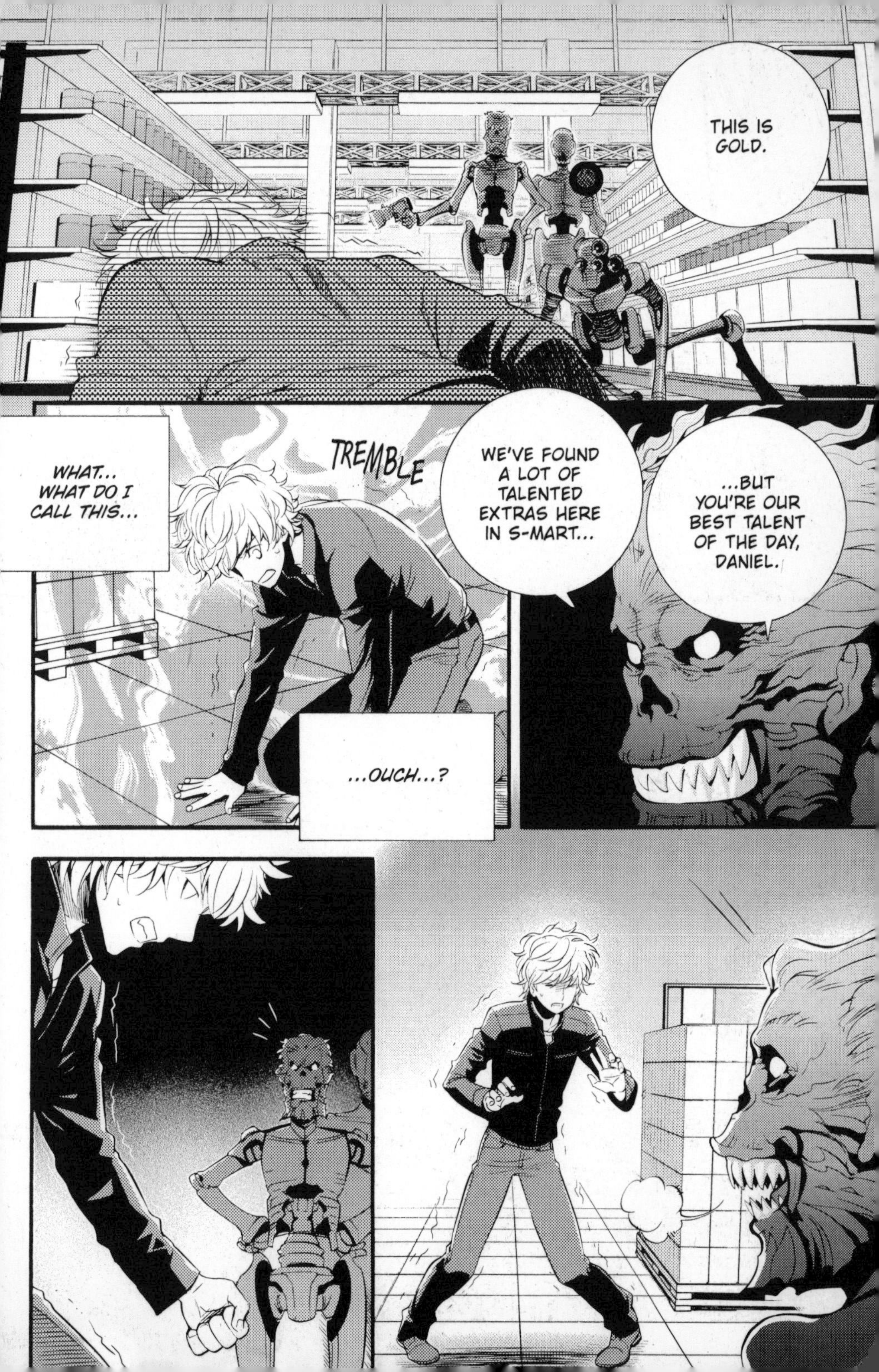
THIS IS GOLD.
WHAT... WHAT DO I CALL THIS...
TREMBLE
...OUCH...?
WE'VE FOUND A LOT OF TALENTED EXTRAS HERE IN S-MART...
...BUT YOU'RE OUR BEST TALENT OF THE DAY, DANIEL.

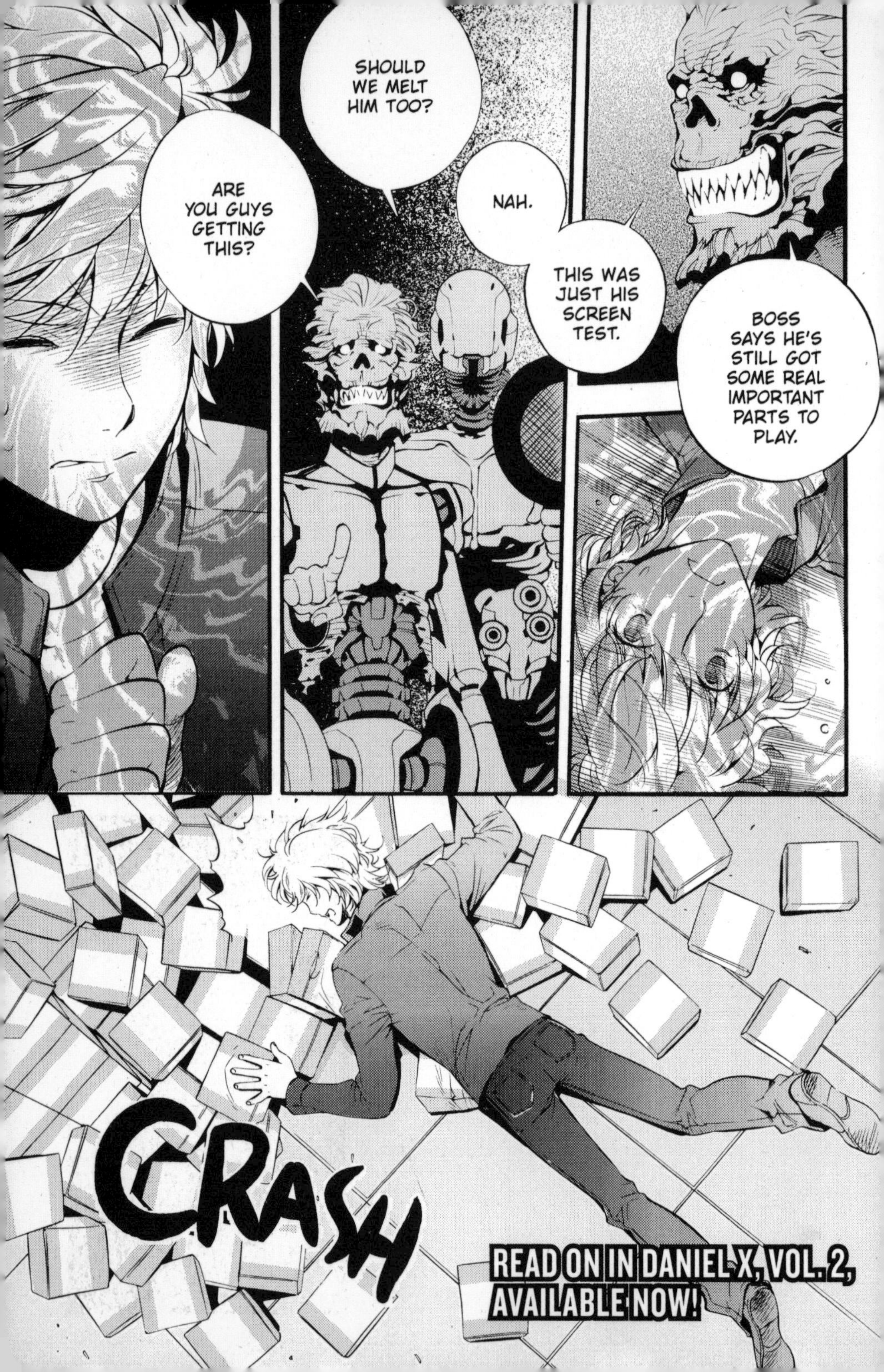
ARE YOU GUYS GETTING THIS?
SHOULD WE MELT HIM TOO?
NAH.
THIS WAS JUST HIS SCREEN TEST.
BOSS SAYS HE'S STILL GOT SOME REAL IMPORTANT PARTS TO PLAY.
CRASH
READ ON IN DANIEL X, VOL. 2, AVAILABLE NOW!

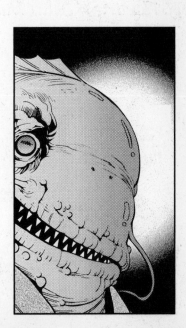

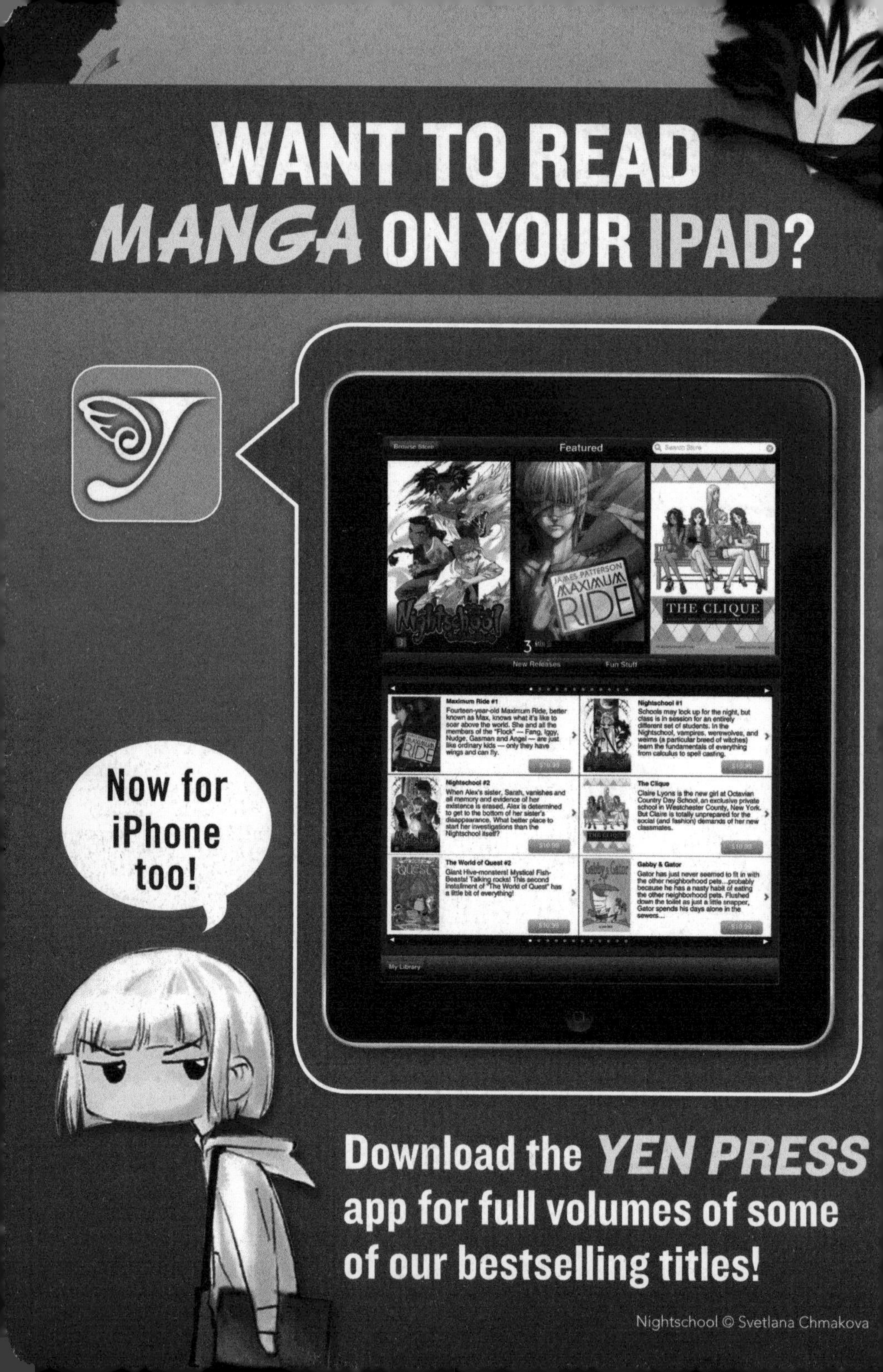

WANT TO READ
MANGA ON YOUR IPAD?
Browse Store
Featured
Search Store
JAMES PATTERSON
MAXIMUM RIDE
THE CLIQUE
New Releases
Fun Stuff
Maximum Ride #1
Fourteen-year-old Maximum Ride, better known as Max, knows what it's like to soar above the world. She and all the members of the "Flock" — Fang, Iggy, Nudge, Gasman and Angel — are just like ordinary kids — only they have wings and can fly.
Nightschool #1
Schools may lock up for the night, but class is in session for an entirely different set of students. In the Nightschool, vampires, werewolves, and weirns (a particular breed of witches) learn the fundamentals of everything from calculus to spell casting.
Nightschool #2
When Alex's sister, Sarah, vanishes and all memory and evidence of her existence is erased, Alex is determined to get to the bottom of her sister's disappearance. What better place to start her investigations than the Nightschool itself?
The Clique
Claire Lyons is the new girl at Octavian Country Day School, an exclusive private school in Westchester County, New York. But Claire is totally unprepared for the social (and fashion) demands of her new classmates.
The World of Quest #2
Giant Hive-monsters! Mystical Fish-Beasts! Talking rocks! This second installment of "The World of Quest" has a little bit of everything!
Gabby & Gator
Gator has just never seemed to fit in with the other neighborhood pets...probably because he has a nasty habit of eating the other neighborhood pets. Flushed down the toilet as just a little snapper, Gator spends his days alone in the sewers...
My Library
Now for iPhone too!
Download the YEN PRESS app for full volumes of some of our bestselling titles!
Nightschool © Svetlana Chmakova

Can't wait for the next volume? You don't have to!

Keep up with the latest chapters of some of your favorite manga every month online in the pages of YEN PLUS!

MAXIMUM RIDE

DANIEL X

SOULLESS

WITCH & WIZARD

ARON'S ABSURD ARMADA

Visit us at www.yenplus.com for details!

YEN+ Plus

MAXIMUM RIDE: THE MANGA ⑤

JAMES PATTERSON
& NARAE LEE

Adaptation and Illustration: NaRae Lee
Background assistant: MunJoo Cho

Lettering: JuYoun Lee

This book is a work of fiction. Names, characters, places, and incidents are the product of the author's imagination or are used fictitiously. Any resemblance to actual events, locales, or persons, living or dead, is coincidental.

Yen Press
Hachette Book Group
237 Park Avenue, New York, NY 10017

www.HachetteBookGroup.com
www.YenPress.com

Yen Press is an imprint of Hachette Book Group, Inc. The Yen Press name and logo are trademarks of Hachette Book Group, Inc.

First Yen Press Edition: December 2011

ISBN: 978-0-7595-2971-7

10 9 8 7 6 5 4

BVG

Printed in the United States of America